Family Law in Action

Law and Society Series
W. Wesley Pue, Founding Editor

We pay tribute to the late Wes Pue, under whose broad vision, extraordinary leadership, and unwavering commitment to socio-legal studies our Law and Society Series was established and rose to prominence.

The Law and Society Series explores law as a socially embedded phenomenon. It is premised on the understanding that the conventional division of law from society creates false dichotomies in thinking, scholarship, educational practice, and social life. Books in the series treat law and society as mutually constitutive and seek to bridge scholarship emerging from interdisciplinary engagement of law with disciplines such as politics, social theory, history, political economy, and gender studies.

Recent books in the series:

Derek Silva and Liam Kennedy, eds., *Power Played: A Critical Criminology of Sport* (2022)
Erez Aloni and Régine Tremblay, eds., *House Rules: Changing Families, Evolving Norms, and the Role of the Law* (2022)
Florence Ashley, *Banning Transgender Conversion Practices: A Legal and Policy Analysis* (2022)
Kim Stanton, *Reconciling Truths: Reimagining Public Inquiries in Canada* (2021)
Daniel Rück, *The Laws and the Land: The Settler Colonial Invasion of Kahnawà:ke in Nineteenth-Century Canada* (2021)
Suzanne Bouclin, *Women, Film, and Law: Cinematic Representations of Female Incarceration* (2021)
Amanda Nelund, *A Better Justice? Community Programs for Criminalized Women* (2020)
Trevor C.W. Farrow and Lesley A. Jacobs, eds., *The Justice Crisis: The Cost and Value of Accessing Law* (2020)
Jamie Baxter, *Inalienable Properties: The Political Economy of Indigenous Land Reform* (2020)
Jeremy Patrick, *Faith or Fraud: Fortune-Telling, Spirituality, and the Law* (2020)
Obiora Chinedu Okafor, *Refugee Law after 9/11: Sanctuary and Security in Canada and the United States* (2020)
Anna Jane Samis Lund, *Trustees at Work: Financial Pressures, Emotional Labour, and Canadian Bankruptcy Law* (2019)
Shauna Labman, *Crossing Law's Border: Canada's Refugee Resettlement Program* (2019)
Peter McCormick and Marc D. Zanoni, *By the Court: Anonymous Judgments at the Supreme Court of Canada* (2019)

For a complete list of the titles in the series, see the UBC Press website, *www.ubcpress.ca*.

Family Law in Action

Divorce and Inequality in Quebec and France

Emilie Biland

Translated by
Annelies Fryberger and Miranda Richmond Mouillot

UBCPress · Vancouver · Toronto

© UBC Press 2023

All rights reserved. No part of this publication may be reproduced, stored in a retrieval system, or transmitted, in any form or by any means, without prior written permission of the publisher, or, in Canada, in the case of photocopying or other reprographic copying, a licence from Access Copyright, www.accesscopyright.ca.

32 31 30 29 28 27 26 25 24 23   5 4 3 2 1

Printed in Canada on FSC-certified ancient-forest-free paper (100% post-consumer recycled) that is processed chlorine- and acid-free.

Library and Archives Canada Cataloguing in Publication

Title: Family law in action : divorce an inequality in Quebec and France / Emilie Biland ; translated by Annelies Fryberger and Miranda Richmond Mouillot.
Other titles: Gouverner la vie privée. English Names: Biland, Émilie, author. | Fryberger, Annelies, translator. | Richmond Mouillot, Miranda, translator.
Series: Law and society series (Vancouver, B.C.)
Description: Series statement: Law and society, ISSN (print) 1496-4953, ISSN (ebook) 1925-0215 | Translation of: Gouverner la vie privée. | Includes bibliographical references.
Identifiers: Canadiana (print) 2022039332X | Canadiana (ebook) 20220393346 | ISBN 9780774866392 (hardcover) | ISBN 9780774866491 (PDF) | ISBN 9780774866545 (EPUB)
Subjects: LCSH: Divorce – Québec (Province) | LCSH: Divorce – France. | LCSH: Sex discrimination – Québec (Province) | LCSH: Sex discrimination – France. | LCSH: Equality – Québec (Province) | LCSH: Equality – France. | LCSH: Privacy – Québec (Province) | LCSH: Privacy – France. | LCSH: Domestic relations – Québec (Province) | LCSH: Domestic relations – France.
Classification: LCC HQ820 .B5513 2023 | DDC 306.89 – dc23

Canadä

UBC Press gratefully acknowledges the financial support for our publishing program of the Government of Canada (through the Canada Book Fund), the Canada Council for the Arts, and the British Columbia Arts Council.

This book has been published with the help of a grant from the Canadian Federation for the Humanities and Social Sciences, through the Awards to Scholarly Publications Program, using funds provided by the Social Sciences and Humanities Research Council of Canada.

First published in French (c) ENS ÉDITIONS – École normale supérieure de Lyon
[Gouverner la vie privée: L'encadrement inégalitaires des séparations conjugales en France et au Québec]

Printed and bound in Canada by Friesens
Set in Myriad and Sabon by Artegraphica Design Co.
Copy editor: Stacy Belden
Proofreader: Dallas Harrison
Indexer: Noeline Bridge

UBC Press
The University of British Columbia
2029 West Mall
Vancouver, BC V6T 1Z2
www.ubcpress.ca

Contents

List of Illustrations / vi

Acknowledgments / vii

Introduction / 3

1 Why the Liberalization of Divorce Leads to Unequal Access to Justice / 23

2 How Gender and National Context Shape the Legal Profession / 62

3 The Legal Encounter as a Situated Nexus of Power / 107

4 How Family Justice Frames Unequal Parenthoods / 150

5 Family Law and the Welfare State: Intertwining Economic Inequalities / 194

Conclusion / 238

Notes / 250

References / 265

Index / 288

Illustrations

Textboxes

1 Three collective studies in two countries / 18
2 The gendering of poverty post-separation / 177

Tables

1 Studies, sources, and data sets / 20
2 A few indicators for comparing judges / 65
3 Seven styles of judicial practice / 87
4 The bar in France and Quebec: Indicators for comparison / 88
5 Types of physical custody awarded by judicial rulings / 153
6 The gender of post-separation deviance / 158
7 National variations in the norm of co-parenting / 192
8 National differences in child support policies / 236

Acknowledgments

More than a decade of work with several research collectives went into the writing of this book. While I alone am responsible for the analyses it presents and the conclusions it draws, I would never have been able to arrive at them without the participation of many colleagues and students, whose investigations and conversations in France and in Quebec nourished my writing. In particular, I would like to thank Céline Bessière, Joanie Bouchard, Sibylle Gollac, Muriel Mille, Gabrielle Schütz, Hélène Steinmetz, and Hélène Zimmermann for their hard work, steady support, and unceasing encouragement. I also wish to thank the people who helped to bring out my first book on this subject, published in French in 2019. Although many of them were held over the internet due to the pandemic, presentations of my work in Strasbourg, Paris, Saint Denis, Montpellier, Lyon, Quebec City, Montreal, Gatineau, and Geneva, all offered unique opportunities for discussion that nourished the process of adapting it into English.

The research for this book was conducted in French. Preparing it for publication in another language is a demanding process – and a collective one. I am grateful to Robert Leckey for helping me to navigate the Canadian publishing world and to Randy Schmidt and Megan Brand at UBC Press for their unwavering and kind-hearted support.

Special thanks also to this book's three reviewers for their encouragement, their thoughtful reading, and their valuable remarks. Above all, I would like to thank this book's translators, Annelies Fryberger and Miranda Richmond Mouillot, for their precise attention to my words and ideas and their care throughout the process of adapting them to the English language. I also wish to thank ENS-Editions for allowing UBC Press free use of the English-language rights to my work and to express my immense gratitude to the groups and organizations that provided the funding for this translation: the Institut Universitaire de France, the Centre de Sociologie de Organisations, the Cité du Genre (IdEx Université de Paris, ANR-18-IDEX-0001), the Programme d'enseignement et de recherche sur le genre de Sciences Po, and the research group Justice et Inégalités au prisme des Sciences Sociales.

Family Law in Action

Introduction

Since its outbreak in early 2020, the COVID-19 pandemic has revealed the powerful role played by family relations in responses to the challenges of lockdowns, restrictions, and the overall economic and social crisis. The pandemic forced around-the-clock togetherness on couples and their children and pushed responsibility for the bulk of household tasks even more firmly onto the shoulders of women (Giurge, Whillans, and Ayse Yemiscigil 2021). It has also exposed – and even intensified – tensions and violence within families (San Martin and Tillous 2021). By curtailing mobility and increasing inequalities, the pandemic also limited the opportunities available to lower- and middle-class people hoping to start a new life or establish a new household or, at the very least, pushed those possibilities further off into the future. It also highlighted a paradoxical feature of contemporary couplehood: the power to exit an unsatisfying relationship is a core individual freedom guaranteed by Western nations, but when a couple ends a relationship, more often than not their living standard drops. This is particularly true of women raising children on their own. Single-parent families have suffered more acutely in the COVID-19 crisis because they are more likely to live in overcrowded housing than other family formations (Bernard et al. 2020) and because they were among the hardest hit by its economic consequences (Enquête québécoise sur la santé de la population 2021).

The pandemic also highlighted the space the law occupies in everyday life. With each wave of health measures, people had questions for themselves about what they did and did not have the right to do in terms of mobility, work, and contact with family and friends. For many separated parents, it challenged the ways in which they had shared childcare, raising questions and uncertainties. Should children continue to be shuttled back and forth from one parent to another, despite the risk of contagion? Should child support paid by one parent (usually the father) to the other (usually the mother) be lower because the non-custodial parent had lost his or her job? Or, to the contrary, should it go up because the custodial parent had lost his or her own job while facing higher costs due to school and childcare facility closures? In their courtrooms and offices, legal professionals, whose work routines and professional lives had themselves been upended by the pandemic, faced new disputes caused by the crisis.

The research for this book began eleven years before the outbreak of COVID-19 and continued through the pandemic. The circumstances in which this work was completed in 2020 and 2021 added urgency to the questions it addresses about the role of the law and its institutions and professionals in the dynamics of family inequality. The phenomenon of widespread divorce and separation has had an impact on the housing and working conditions, as well as the educational child-rearing arrangements, of a significant proportion of the population. These highly personal life events, in other words, significantly affect society as a whole, in all kinds of ways. Notably, they contribute to social and even generational inequalities: the material lives of poorer families are often affected in drastic ways when a domestic partnership ends (Desmond 2016). Generally speaking, children of separated parents grow up in circumstances that are less favourable materially than children whose parents live together (Abbas and Garbinti 2019). It is true that the very right to divorce was a victory for women's rights, making it possible for them to escape oppressive domestic arrangements. However, making it legally possible to end domestic partnerships has not actually eliminated gender inequalities.[1] Male violence against women and/or children is the cause of numerous separations, but separation does not reliably end that violence (Brown et al. 2021). The average income of women living in domestic partnership is already lower than that of their male partners, and separation only serves to sharpen that economic inequality. Women end up much poorer than men once they separate (Vaus et al. 2017).

The diversification of family forms has altered the conditions of social reproduction and, in so doing, has also transformed relations between genders and among social classes. In an era when capitalism is dramatically increasing wealth inequalities (Piketty 2014), when family relationships remain profoundly unequal (Bessière and Gollac 2023), and after three decades of massive reconfigurations to welfare states, shifts in the scope of public policy have had significant impacts on the structuring of social relations. At one time, national laws forbid divorce; then they restricted it, and, over time, they have liberalized it. Today, the force of these legal norms has placed legal professionals front and centre in the divorce process, making separation one of the few times when individuals are called to consider questions relating to their own rights and have cause to interact with legal professionals and even the court system. Family law, and the legal professionals who incarnate it in the eyes of separating couples, help to construct citizens' relationship to the state. Are the aspirations of these individuals being listened to by those who have the power to influence their very lives after they separate? Are their rights guaranteed by both the "law in books" and the way it is practised? Family law in action is ultimately a problem of democracy. This book seeks to understand how judicial policies – that is, public policies based on the law, its professionals, and its institutions – contribute to the reproduction of inequalities in contemporary societies.

More specifically, it compares two contexts – France and Quebec – in an attempt to shed light on their similarities and differences in the way in which their court systems manage the process of divorce and separation and the inequalities that result from it. The overarching conclusions of the analysis are the same on both sides of the Atlantic: judicial policies do not have much success in reducing the inequalities that are amplified by rising divorce rates, either within or among families. On closer examination, though, some important distinctions emerge in how the institutional reproduction of inequality occurs in either place. These distinctions have to do with the way in which institutions and professionals perceive inequalities: whether or not they find them acceptable or unjust; whether or not they believe they can make a difference in their encounters with them. In turn, their perceptions and practices depend on social relations and political compromises that remain significantly different in the two national contexts.

I began this work with the hypothesis that, in either context, these judicial policies are underpinned by two tensions that reveal the liberal and neoliberal impulses behind state interventionism today. The first tension I identify is informed by French philosopher Michel Foucault (2009) in his understanding of governmentality, which he explored extensively in his work in the late 1970s. This tension arises when the state takes on the role of guarantor of our individual liberties and, in order to promote these liberties, casts off its traditional nineteenth-century role as a repressive force. In the case of separating couples, the old repressive state imposed divorce as a kind of sanction, a punitive measure undertaken when one spouse was at fault. As the state's role was liberalized, so too was separation, which became more socially acceptable. "The state has no place in the bedrooms of the nation," declared Pierre Elliott Trudeau, Canada's minister of justice, in 1967. He made this statement as the House of Commons was debating draft legislation (Bill C-150) that would decriminalize homosexuality and abortion, in addition to allowing couples to divorce in court, which, until then, had been impossible in Quebec (Corriveau 2011, 123). Today, people have the right to choose their life partner as well as the form that their partnership will take (marriage or not). They also have the right to choose when and how to end that partnership if they wish – with or without a judge, in two months or two years, and so on.

Such self-limitation on the part of the state is anchored in the values of individual autonomy and responsibility. Rather than resorting to overt and broad-reaching constraint, the state relies on its ability to transform people's expectations and, above all, to produce consent. Norms for human behaviour in the liberal state are thus established in more diffuse ways than they were in the past. At the same time, they are more targeted: they take aim at behaviours that do not respect these norms of autonomy and responsibility, which are seen as increasing the burden of risk to society as a whole. In order to counter that risk, state power becomes more individualized – in the sense that it targets specific situations and populations, which are held up as social problems. In the case of separation and divorce, as we shall see, this shift means poor mothers raising their children on their own, separated fathers who no longer see their children, and "children of divorce," for whose futures we fear.

The second tension is created by the neoliberal turn in contemporary society, according to which the state should not have a monopoly on the power to intervene in people's private lives and, indeed, should be restrained from intervening wherever such restraint is possible. More and more, state action that targets private life makes use of market mechanisms, relying on the hybridization of public and private interventions. This shift has enlarged the scope of intervention of private legal practitioners into people's lives. In addition, new professional groups have emerged, chief among them family mediators; other groups, such as psychologists and social workers, are spending an increasing amount of time working with separated parents and their children. In part, the goal of this shift has been to limit the impact of separation on government spending (in the court system or on family benefits, in particular). At the same time, this trend has been driven by the governmental goal of meeting families' "needs" better and more precisely by expanding the array of services available to them.

Heterosexual coupledom, relationships between parents and children, and expanded family solidarities have all been affected by these changes in law and public policy. Indeed, the dynamic of capitalism has pushed the state to transmit this paradigm of "choice" into intimate relationships. As French-Israeli sociologist Eva Illouz (2019) has observed, the logic of the market has penetrated even the most intimate of human relations, right down to the way in which couples come together and separate. Indeed, as British sociologist Anthony Giddens (1991) has written, intimacy has become the ultimate expression of individual liberty and the source of human fulfillment and, as such, has become a political goal. As this book will show, however, in treating domestic partnerships as "pure relationships" between partners who are presumed to be fully independent and equal, and by assuming that individual liberty makes it possible "to transcend and overcome class, age, or gender determinism," legal norms and the professionals who mobilize them actually help to perpetuate these inequalities (Illouz 2019, 33).

Beyond the "Private Ordering" of Separation and Divorce

In order to understand how mechanisms of inequality operate through law and public policy, more must be said about the legal and judicial treatment of separation. In 1979, two American legal scholars introduced the term "private ordering" to describe the public recognition of individuals' ability to make their own decisions about how their separations would be organized (Mnookin and Kornhauser 1979). They based their work on the legal procedures that were then in force in the United States and the United Kingdom, highlighting the advantages of recent changes to the law: "The financial cost of litigation, both private and public, is minimized. The pain of a formal adversary proceeding is avoided" (956). This evolution in the government's view of its role in private life can be seen in the rise of non-contested divorce: two such examples are divorce by mutual consent, which was introduced in 1975 in France, and divorce for living separate and apart, which was legalized in Canada in 1985. It is now rare to designate a former partner as being "at fault," further curtailing the state's power to intervene in private life. In 2006, the European Court of Human Rights actually ruled against the French courts for admitting health-related evidence introduced during a divorce proceeding in order to prove that a man was an alcoholic.[2] The right to privacy, recognized in Article 8 of the European Convention on Human Rights, is considered a constitutional value under French law, which is another limitation on state involvement in family arrangements.[3]

The focus on individual responsibility goes back several years to 2017, when a couple in Quebec who could not agree on whom they would choose as godparents for their baby requested that a judge decide for them. The judge refused and ordered them to make the decision "jointly, in a civilized manner, so that a peaceful ceremony can be held" (Teisceira-Lessard 2017). This transformation in the government of private life remains uneven though, as can be seen in the privatization of divorce, which places power in the hands of separating couples while, at the same time, reinforcing the power of private professionals. Since most separating couples work with lawyers, this means that private life is not so much self-managed as it is managed by proxy. Rather than representing a turn toward the private sphere, the privatization of divorce is often merely a partial displacement of public institutions (specifically, the courts) with a move toward the sphere of private professionals, whose work is overseen by the public sector (training, funding, accreditation, the application of norms, and so on). It may also be seen as redistributing power within public organizations, shifting it from courtrooms to administrative structures such as the French Caisses d'allocations familiales (Family Benefit Offices).

The liberalization of family law has in fact taken place alongside the development of new forms of family regulation. In the 1970s, single-parent families became the targets of public redistribution. Since the 2000s, parenting support programs have expanded considerably (Martin 2015). This renewed interventionism has been fuelled by the construction of the idea of "family risks," chief among them poverty among "single mothers" and the supposedly negative effects of separation on their children (Schultheis 1992). To be more specific, the government of domestic partnership has diminished, and parenting conditions are now the main object of the government of separation. French sociologist Irène Théry ([1993] 2001, 398) describes the state as having become a "shepherd for parenthood." This sea change has not been limited to the courts: it structures family policy across the board. Family law no longer expresses pure legality, detached from other normative registers – not that it ever did. Now, however, the increased recognition of individual rights has also pushed at the bounds of how legality is understood to include psychological and behavioural knowledge. These new ways of thinking are visible in the categories of "best interests of the child" and "co-parenting," which inform lawyers' representations as well as the *Civil Code* itself. In this sense, litigation is now intertwined with a psychological approach to family interventions. The increased emphasis on the value of subjectivity not only is perceptible in realms such as consumption or sexuality (Illouz 2019), but it now also permeates the politics of family rights.

Judicial Policies and Intersectional Inequalities

The goal of this book is to examine how the tensions underpinning the government of separations – between self-limitation and normalization, between state power and the privatization of public policy – inform social relationships as they are arranged in the contemporary world. Because most public policy programs are targeted by social class, research tends to focus either on state oversight of the lower classes or on the relationship between the dominant classes and the state. The former has shown that people from less privileged classes, and women in particular, "are more dependent on the welfare state than other classes" and, at the same time, that the growth of the prison state affects mostly lower-class and racialized men (Siblot et al. 2015, 221). Individuals from these class groups maintain an ambivalent relationship with the state: they regularly experience subordination but may attenuate it by personalizing their institutional relationships by withdrawing from them, by mocking them, or by contesting them. At the other end of the social ladder, economic and/or social capital, as well as the law's prominence in elite education (Israël and Vanneuville 2017), gives members of the upper classes easier access to better professionals (Spire and Weidenfeld 2011) and makes them more likely to become involved in the production of norms (Spire 2012). As a result, members of the upper classes are more able to play with the constraints of the law, including in ways that help to reinforce their dominant social position (Lascoumes and Nagels 2014).

In contrast to the work cited above, the regulation of separation also reveals how professionals treat people from different walks of life – from the wealthiest to those with the lowest incomes – and how institutions help to differentiate and even produce hierarchies, within families (between father and mother, between parents and children) as well as among them (depending on their social position and/or national background). In the mid-1970s, the French feminist sociologist Christine Delphy (2013, 122) noted that "certain aspects of the state of marriage ... are reproduced in the state of divorce" and that "differentiated obligations for husband and wife" continued even when their domestic partnership ended. In the 1980s, American feminist scholars considered that the decline in at-fault divorce could be linked with an "illusion of equality"

(Fineman 1991), given that the court's ability to reduce economic inequalities among men and women had actually declined (Weitzman 1985). In the late 2000s, the Quebecois legal scholar Louise Langevin (2009, 25) came to a similar conclusion, observing that the jurisprudence of the Supreme Court of Canada relating to prenuptial agreements and separations of unmarried couples was based on an "outdated understanding of contractual freedom inspired by laissez-faire economics," making the lives of separated women more financially precarious.[4] In the following decade, in what was known as the *"Eric v Lola* case," the Supreme Court of Canada ruled that the absence of financial obligations between spouses in de facto couples (as distinct from marriage) violated the right to equality guaranteed in the *Canadian Charter of Rights and Freedoms*.[5] The court also concluded, however, that the Quebec government had the authority to protect contractual freedom (the freedom not to marry) over this right to equal treatment. As this book was being completed in early 2022, women in France and Quebec who choose to leave a common law couple still have no access to the legal mechanisms in place to compensate for discrepancies in standard of living that are a direct result of the partnership. They are in this way at a legal disadvantage compared to formerly married women.

Feminist analyses such as the ones described here deserve to be examined alongside class-based analyses. Together, they are able to document the scope of the inequalities structuring family relationships and practices, both in terms of demographics and in terms of standard of living and approaches to child-rearing. "Family patterns ... have become more unequal by education and other measures of social class," observes one American book on the topic (Carlson and England 2011, 1). At the same time, scholars of the legal and justice systems point to the impact of economic and cultural inequalities on access to the law and to the court system, even though these are considered to be "a basic right of citizenship" (Farrow and Jacobs 2020, 3). As French sociologist Pierre Bourdieu (1987) has shown, law, despite its appearance of neutrality and universality, is a powerful vector for differentiation between the professionals who understand it and are authorized to act in its name and the laypeople who depend on those professionals to inform them of their rights and to help assert them.

This book will analyze how public policy that targets separated people helps to reproduce the social order – that is, helps to uphold a hierarchical system of social, interdependent, and co-constructed relations of class and gender. These two dimensions of social status are not sufficient to explain mechanisms for differentiation and domination in contemporary society in their totality (Bilge and Hill Collins 2016). This book also identifies race as a significant factor in analyzing the ways in which white, native-born parents are treated compared with foreign and/or racialized parents. In analyzing the inequality regimes that structure the management of separation, the social constructions that encode gender and class remain the most revealing. Examining these regimes together shows that the attenuation of public constraints on private lives varies greatly from one family to another (along class lines) and within families (along gender lines). Divorce by consent reflects this unevenness and has served to legitimate the unequal allocation of resources and roles post-separation.

This analysis builds on a project begun in the late 2000s with several colleagues and students in Paris. This earlier project examined French trial courts and resulted in a book titled *Au tribunal des couples (Couples in Court)*, which was authored by a collective of eleven researchers called the Collectif Onze (2013).[6] In it, we showed that the courts participated in the reproduction of social relations by enacting through law the inequalities in and among families that arise from separations. We attributed this finding to three main factors: the ambiguities of formal law with regard to gender inequalities; the fact that courts are short on time and resources; and the social positions of judges, who are highly educated civil servants. Finally, we highlighted the fact that judges' interventions, though only occasional, are decisive, given the contexts of family crisis in which they occur and the official status of their words.

The present book, written in the same sociological vein, was first published in French in 2019 (Biland 2019) and then updated, adapted, and translated into English with the help of Annelies Fryberger and Miranda Richmond Mouillot. It also takes a resolutely empirical approach, combining field studies with statistical analyses of court cases in order to analyze the individualization of power relations explored by Michel Foucault (2009). These can be observed in the course of direct encounters between professionals and laypeople, while the quantification of a much larger number of cases makes it possible to make objective observations of determining factors. The book was also written to share a set of critical ambitions, which are based in work on the institutionalization of family and family strategies as a vehicle for class reproduction (including Bourdieu 1993a; Lenoir 2003) as well as in feminist research that understands the family as a central institution in the structuring of social relations between men and women (including Delphy 2013) and that analyzes the relationship between welfare states and patriarchy (including Lewis 1992). The economic impact of separation receives a great deal of attention in this book in an attempt to help return materialism to the heart of the sociology of the family. Finally, it includes the process of racialization[7] in the construction of unequal social relations, based on the abundant North American and British literature on this topic (including Miles 1993).

Published after several more years of research and writing, this book seeks to expand the scope of the conclusions reached in *Au tribunal des couples* and to push past some of its limitations. This expansion is first of all empirical: the surveys mobilized in the present text go beyond the courtroom, examining separations by situating the work of judges and courts within a chain of professional and institutional interventions in the lives of separated parents. This approach is widespread in the sociology of criminal justice, which includes police work and prisons, and it deserves to be extended to the civil justice system. When private individuals, rather than public prosecutors, undertake proceedings, the issue of recourse to the court is raised in a different, but equally important, way (Sandefur 2008). As a result, our fieldwork included law offices, as well as research into the reforms to public and private family law, so that judicial procedures and social policy could be examined together. Thus, this book's theoretical work is more explicitly bound up in critical policy analysis and considers that the experiences of citizens within judicial and social institutions have an impact on their private lives. This approach aims to establish a more precise understanding of judicial policies and to offer an analysis of the part they play in social reproduction. My hope is that such an analysis can be helpfully applied to other subjects as well.

This analytical framework identifies three interdependent mechanisms that contribute to the legal remaking of families after divorce and separation – in particular, with regard to their class and gender status. Inequalities within and among families stand out in the first moments that they seek out the legal and court system (Chapter 1); they are shaped during encounters with legal professionals (Chapters 2 and 3); and the legal interventions they experience result in unequal standards of living and ways of life following separation (Chapters 4 and 5). As family law has liberalized, the ways in which separations could be dealt with have multiplied, meaning that separations could be oriented in several different directions, leading to a "segregative democratization" similar to what sociologist Pierre Merle (2000) observed among French secondary schools. Separation was democratized in the sense that the divorce rate rose and became relatively uniform from one socio-professional category to another (Bessière 2008); it has remained segregative in the sense that significant social segmentation can be observed in separation-related interventions (Chapter 1).

Unequal access leads to new types of inequalities when separating people encounter lawyers and judges. While these professionals occupy a variety of institutional positions and approach their work in different ways, all of them are of higher social status than the majority of separating couples (Chapter 2). Not only do legal professionals encounter different categories of laypeople depending on the procedure being undertaken, but they also do not have the same types of power over them. Furthermore, depending on their social status, they do not perceive or treat these laypeople in the same way (Chapter 3). Among the lower classes,[8] and, in particular, among lower-class women, court intervention reinforces the "surveillance of private life" exercised by social and family services (Roman 2014, 330). The retreat of public constraints on private life is much less complete at the bottom of the social ladder than at the top, as it bumps up against social policies oriented toward disciplining welfare recipients (Dubois 2019). It is a retreat more palpable to people who belong to the social majority – white, native-born citizens – since behaviours in the private sphere are so strongly mobilized in the process of racial, ethnic, or cultural othering. Among the middle classes, more unobtrusive procedures prevail, in particular, because of their low cost;

these mesh with the socio-economic groups' limited and often distant exposure (on paper or even online) to institutions. Finally, among the (male) upper classes, the support of numerous qualified and highly invested professionals is accompanied by a "relativist relationship to the rules" that has also been observed in interactions between this population and tax administrations (Spire 2012, 12).

Finally, we shall study the impact of these interventions on life post-separation. "Unmaking a family" through the law simultaneously "remakes a family" by redefining parents' legal, educational, and economic responsibilities, taking part in the long chain of interlinked educational, social, and tax interventions that define and renew family norms. Strongly promoted by legal professionals, the norm of "co-parenting" encourages both parents to remain involved in a child's life or children's lives following their separation. At the same time, however, not just one, but a great many, family arrangements can be envisaged based on this norm, which is, in fact, a kind of fuzzy government: by recognizing the wide variety of possible parental practices, it authorizes and even fosters social inequalities in the care of children. The value placed on personal choice at the time of separation is often still purely rhetorical, given how strongly family arrangements post-separation resemble those that existed during the domestic partnership, which were likewise the products of often implicit micro-decisions (Belleau 2015). This paradigm of personal choice has not led to the de-gendering of parental roles but, rather, to "redoing gender" based on whatever practices were put in place during the domestic partnership (Walzer 2008). Thus, while a lack of involvement on the part of the mother is rarely an acceptable option, including in the eyes of lawyers, the involvement of separated fathers remains highly variable, ranging from prolonged absences to daily care. This differentiated regime of obligation favours those (often middle- and upper-class) fathers who know how to find flexibilities in the law and who delegate a portion of the labour of childcare to other women, either those close to them or professionals (Chapter 4).

Overall, widespread separation and divorce, made possible by women's participation in the labour market, have continued to act as impediments to greater social equality and maintained and even renewed the image of the male breadwinner. They have made women raising children on their own the priority targets of social policy, at the risk of institutionalizing their heteronomy, either in relation to their (former and current) partners, who may be more or less inclined to participate in private financial transfers, or in relation to public solidarity, which is becoming ever more conditional. The "partial transformation of the private patriarchy into public patriarchy" has incontestably improved the financial circumstances of many women, but it has done little to chip away at the feminization of poverty or to end patriarchal violence (Lamoureux 2016, 229). In this way, it shows the limits of a right to divorce whose emancipative aims were largely conceived based on private relationships (Chapter 5).

A Cross-National Comparison of Inequality Regimes

The findings presented in this book are all the more powerful because they are based on two national contexts, France and Quebec. This comparative approach seeks to test a theoretical framework grounded in France, where I was trained as a social scientist and where this research began in the autumn of 2008. Among Western countries, France has some of the oldest and most developed family policies (Commaille, Strobel, and Villac 2002). Historically, familialism in France has been a powerful state ideology (Lenoir 2003), underpinning the "republican social contract" (Robcis 2013). The theory of state that inspired this analysis, rooted in the work of Pierre Bourdieu (2012) and Michel Foucault (2009), is strongly linked to the French context from which it emerged (Commaille 2015). As I worked, I became increasingly interested in whether it would remain a useful framework if applied to another society and another political system.

In 2010, a little less than two years after this research project began in France, I accepted a position as a professor at the Université Laval in Quebec City and took the opportunity to pull together another research team.[9] Building on the work of the French team, the Quebecois team began by conducting research in the Superior Court, then moved to other fields, such as law firms. This research, in turn, inspired the French team. Some team members travelled between France and Quebec, and the long-term nature of both projects made possible the in-depth comparison offered by this book. I returned to France in 2014, but research continued in Quebec. Certain members of the French team continued to work together, joined by others,[10] and turned their attention to other subjects (such as appeals courts and family law reforms). The latest data referred to in this work were collected in October 2021, during research travel undertaken as soon as the Canadian borders reopened, following their closure during the pandemic.

The result of this long-term and in-depth comparison of the two contexts stakes what I believe to be an original claim in the international literature on the liberalization of family law. One of the most recurrent themes in sociology, and, no doubt, the most accurate, understands the rise in separations as indicative of transformations in private life. This social fact is all the more interesting for sociologists who may be uncomfortable with "methodological nationalism" in that it transcends national borders (Beck 2007). The international literature on family justice has highlighted similarities among Western countries (Maclean, Eekelaar, and Bastard 2015), underlining the trend toward the liberalization both of domestic partnerships and of their institutional oversight.

France and Quebec, which share similar legal traditions (Normand 2011), are no exception to this trend. Indeed, they even seem to bear a particular resemblance to each other in comparison to other countries in North America and Western Europe. In both places, family law is a part of the *Civil Code*,[11] which uses similar terms to set out the rights and obligations of parents toward their children. The divorce rate, the rate of children born to unmarried couples, and the rates of children with separated or divorced parents are similar to and often higher than average for countries in the Organisation for Economic Co-operation and Development[12] (or the national average in Canada).[13] By contrast, variation in marital status among social classes is relatively low (Laplante and Fostik 2017), notably in comparison to the United States (Carlson and England 2011). In both places, six out of ten children are born to unmarried couples (Girard 2018; Papon 2018). On average, the courts pronounce one divorce for every two marriages celebrated (Milan 2013; Prioux and Barbieri 2012), and separations among unmarried couples are even more prevalent (Statistics Canada 2019). Finally, procedures for at-fault divorce make up less than 10 percent of all divorces, and non-divorce family procedures account for half of all family law cases (Belmokhtar 2012; Kelly 2012).[14]

These legal and socio-demographical similarities provide a solid foundation for comparison between the two cases, but they leave at least two questions unanswered. First, how can these resemblances be explained in two jurisdictions located several thousand kilometres apart, each with its own legal system and its own body of legal standards, in the absence of any kind of international institution organizing their congruence? Next, is it possible for us to conclude from this congruence that a resemblance exists between professional practices and lay experiences in the two places? Empirical studies conducted in both contexts show that transnational exchanges remain limited in family law, meaning that national context still matters a great deal in the government of private life (see Textbox 1). There are resemblances between the two jurisdictions in terms of racialization processes, but they do not intersect in the same way with class and gender inequalities. In Quebec, gender

TEXTBOX 1 Three collective studies in two countries

This work is based mainly in field research, conducted in court hearings and in meetings between lawyers and clients, as well as interviews with legal professionals and a qualitative analysis of the cases observed. These studies were carried out in five trial courts in France (in Carly and Belles, mid-sized cities in the greater Paris region; in Valin, a regional capital; and in Marjac and Besson, each of which has a population of about 150,000) and in three districts of the Superior Court of Quebec (Montreal, which has about two million inhabitants; Quebec City, 560,000 inhabitants; and Albanel, five thousand inhabitants). This book also occasionally refers to studies of two French courts of appeal (Paris and Besson). In 2020 and 2021, this fieldwork was expanded to include interviews with lawyers in France about the spring 2020 lockdown and with lawyers and judges in Quebec about their experiences with lesbian, gay, bisexual, transgender, and queer parents.[15] With the exception of Paris, Montreal, and Quebec City, which as major cities have unique identities that cannot be disguised, the names of all places and people in this work have been changed.

inequalities tend to be taken into account to a greater extent than they are in France, but differentiation by class is also stronger.

These differences stand out in the three mechanisms that shape post-break-up inequalities. There is a greater diversity of approaches to divorce in Quebec than in France, leading to more marked socio-economic selection in access to law and justice (Chapter 1). In interactions between legal professionals and laypeople, the higher social status and the lofty institutional role of judges in Quebec are more likely to create significant distance between judges and the citizens whom they encounter in their courtrooms than in France. This means that they are more likely to take a paternalistic approach (Chapter 2) but, at the same time, to be more sensitive to the condition of wealthy men's ex-wives (Chapter 3). From the perspective of standard of living and parental practices, the norm of co-parenting has been appropriated differently in the two places – more symbolically in France and in more practical terms in Quebec (Chapter 4). As a result, gender inequalities relating to childcare labour are less marked in Quebec than they are in France. The way in which private duty and public responsibility are connected in the two

The second series of investigations is based on courtroom data. In France, our research team created a database of about three thousand cases from seven trial courts whose final rulings were handed down in 2013 (Data set F-TC-2013). In Quebec, this kind of first-hand analysis was not possible; however, we did have access to several databases put together by the Quebec Ministère de la justice (Ministry of Justice): longitudinal data on court activity (Data set Q-SC-1981–2011); a data set of two thousand child support orders from 2008 across the province (Data set Q-CSO-2008); and the list of most cases scheduled in the three courts we studied between October and December 2013 (Data set Q-PHD-2013).

A final series of studies combining interviews, documentary research, and, in France, participatory observation made it possible to document the debates over, and reforms of, child support ongoing in both countries since the 1990s.

For clarity, when French and Quebecois sources are quoted together, French citations appear first and Quebecois citations below.

TABLE 1 Studies, sources, and data sets

	Field studies	Quantitative court data (unpublished)		Study of child support reforms	
		QUEBEC			
Locations	Three Superior Court districts: Montreal, Quebec City, and Albanel (semi-rural)	Q-SC-1981-2011	Data from the Ministère de la justice on the activity of the Superior Court relating to family law (management information system) (1981–2011)	Interviews: 33	12 lawyers and notaries 2 former Supreme Court judges 7 civil servants or equivalent positions 4 social workers and psychologists 5 (ex-)deputies 3 directors of non-profits
Observations	131 cases heard by 21 judges; 61 meetings between 10 lawyers and their clients	Q-PHD-2013	8,862 cases scheduled in the three districts (preliminary hearings) (October–December 2013), put together by our team	Written sources	8 parliamentary debates (1995–2012) Around 100 documents related to child support (1979–2013) from public structures, professional orders, and activist groups
Interviews	23 trial judges; 2 appeals court judges; 3 administrative personnel; 41 lawyers	Q-CSO-2008	2,000 child support orders handed down in 2008 throughout Quebec, Ministère de la justice database		

Cases	40: 36 observed in hearings; 4 with lawyers			

FRANCE				
Locations	5 trial courts: 2 in the Paris region; 1 in a regional capital; 2 in mid-sized cities 2 courts of appeal: Paris and Besson, a mid-sized city	F-TC-2013	2,983 cases with decisions handed down in 2013, in 7 trial courts, put together by our team	Interviews: 18	8 high-ranking civil servants or equivalent positions 1 family judge 1 magistrate at the Court of Cassation 3 academics 2 deputies 5 directors of non-profits
Observations	341 cases heard by 20 judges 48 meetings between 14 lawyers and their clients			Observations: 15	14 participant observations (participating as "experts") 1 debate session at the Assemblée nationale
Interviews	20 trial judges, 7 appeals court judges, 4 clerks, 53 lawyers			Written sources	Around 50 documents related to child support (1999–2015): official reports, academic and activist texts
Cases	100 cases observed in hearings				

places offers some insight here: while, on both sides of the Atlantic, governments have made single-parent families a priority for public re-distribution, Quebec's government has chosen to focus on private transfers rather than on social benefits, meaning that less privileged women face more precariousness there than they do in France (Chapter 5). Comparative sociolegal scholarship is a long process in which we should seek out neither ideal nor foil. As this transatlantic research project will show, studying what is said and done in other places can be a precious resource for imagining the conditions under which the goal of recognizing individual rights could truly be made congruent with the goal of reducing inequalities.

Why the Liberalization of Divorce Leads to Unequal Access to Justice

1

"Existing evidence reveals that civil justice experiences can be an important engine in reproducing inequality, suggesting that access to civil justice merits greater attention from inequality scholars," writes Rebecca Sandefur (2008, 340), an American sociologist who has devoted much of her research to this issue. The situation for people living in France and Quebec is quite different from those living in the United States: legal aid is more broadly available, meaning that low-income people going through separations have easier access to lawyers; family mediation is also publicly funded. Nevertheless, as pathways to separation have diversified, we must consider how these approaches are appropriated by professionals and by separating couples. Studies on both sides of the Atlantic show that the unprecedented range of options available for dealing with the legal consequences of separation has led to a segmentation of modes of intervention as well as of members of the public: socio-professional background and gender significantly affect the types of professionals available to help people through separation as well as the types of services that can be expected from them. Now that people have the right to separate, and the right to choose how they will go about it, differentiation in the ways in which procedures are appropriated and the varying availability of professionals represent the main forms of inequality faced by couples when they separate.

To analyze the social impact of the liberalization of divorce, we will begin by tracing the history of divorce reform in France and Canada. The legal requirements surrounding separation have loosened in most Western countries but in different ways depending on the nation and its legal system. In many European countries, certain types of divorce have taken place outside the court for years now: in Denmark, Estonia, Lithuania, Norway, Portugal, Russia, and Ukraine, uncontested divorces are purely administrative, pronounced by an authority outside the court (Sénat 2010, 10). Divorce without a judge has been possible since 2017 in France, although only if each party has a lawyer and they are able to come to an agreement over all aspects of their separation.[1] In Quebec, as well as elsewhere in Canada, divorces cannot be pronounced without a judge. At the same time, however, alternatives to courtroom hearings are both more numerous and have existed for longer than in France.

On either side of the Atlantic, these reforms testify to the liberal understanding of the relationship between individuals and the state that was discussed in the introduction: the ability to end a relationship without recourse to a third party has become an important feature of conjugal rights. However, this liberal view is partially counterbalanced by a more interventionist stance, which holds that the judicial system is needed to guarantee women's rights and the protection of children. At the same time, a managerial approach in public administration and the court system reinforces this liberal understanding as it seeks to reduce the number of separations and divorces pronounced by judges as a way of lightening court caseloads. These changes have transformed how the different aspects of separation are assigned to be managed by the public and private sectors. Historically, the courts have played a central role in the public dimension – a role that is now being called into question. Both financially and ideologically, the state now sees it as beneficial to outsource what was once the sole purview of the courts to the private sphere of divorce professionals such as lawyers, mediators, and so on.

Even more in Quebec than in France, the recognition of the right to divorce has given rise to new forms of class inequality and, to a lesser extent, gender inequality. Families often consent to being directed to one procedure or another – directions that are often justified in terms of their specific "needs." But, in the process, differences in the ways in which citizens relate to professionals and the state are accentuated, depending on the life history and current social status of the couple or the family in question. As a result, the increasing number of possibilities available to separating couples has become a major driver of inequality today.

The Same Justice for All or to Each According to Their Need?

France and Quebec, as described in the introduction, are similar in multiple ways, both in terms of marriage practices (with a divorce rate close to 50 percent)[2] and in terms of court procedures. In both places, family law distinguishes between married and unmarried couples. For the latter, family courts deal only with questions relating to children; for the former, the courts also deal with financial relationships between the ex-spouses – in particular, the division of their assets. Furthermore, the French and Canadian Divorce Acts maintain a distinction between fault divorces and the far more common forms of divorce in which the cause of separation is not examined.[3] Finally, in both places, trial courts are competent to rule in family law (Tribunaux Judiciaires in France and the Superior Court of Quebec), and judges hand down rulings on their own, *in camera*.

These commonalities show that family law is not an individual affair: in both jurisdictions, the court system processes huge numbers of cases each year – nearly thirty thousand new cases were filed in Quebec in 2011 and close to 400,000 in France in 2016.[4] As can be seen, the numbers are much higher in France (6 new cases per thousand inhabitants) than in Quebec (3.5 cases per thousand). This difference may be explained by the fact that Quebec has been promoting alternatives to courtroom proceedings for the settlement of separation-related issues for much longer. Moreover, France and Quebec have taken different approaches to lightening caseloads in their court systems.

Two Approaches to Reducing Caseloads

In Quebec, there has been a long downward trend in the number of family law-related cases and hearings. The number of cases has dropped by over 30 percent since 1995, while divorce trials, whose hearings are generally the longest, dropped by 72 percent between 1981 and 2011. This drop is a far sharper decrease than that of the number of divorces, which declined by 32 percent over the same period.[5] In France, by contrast, the number of new cases went up by more than 20 percent between 2004 and 2016. Since 2017, though, it has dropped since a portion of divorces was pronounced outside the court system. Rather than comparing divorce rates in the two places, which are similar, it is the institutional characteristics of divorce in the two places that should be examined to explain how family law differs from one context to the other – how it is determined who goes to court, why, and under what conditions.

In France, there are four forms of divorce[6] and two forms of non-divorce family procedure.[7] In divorce cases, both parties are heard separately and then together with their lawyers if they have legal representation. In non-divorce family procedures, the judge hears all of the parties at the same time, which has meant that, until 2017, anyone requesting that the court system intervene in their separation shared the same experience – that is, a single court hearing.[8] These hearings are very short: according to our observations, they range in length from three minutes to an hour and twenty minutes, with an average length of eighteen minutes (Collectif Onze 2013, 15).

Canadian divorce law recognizes that couples have grounds for divorce if there has been a breakdown of their marriage for one of three reasons;[9] additionally, married or unmarried parents may petition the courts to determine who has custody of their children. In contrast to France, there is no connection between motive and procedure: what happens depends mostly on the degree to which the two parties are able to come to an agreement. If they can agree, they do not need to be heard by a judge; only cases where couples disagree are brought before judges. As a result, many divorcing couples never enter a courtroom. The remaining minority, unable to come to an agreement, must take part in hearings that last anywhere from a few hours to several days. The length of these trials is due to procedural form, which is adversarial in Quebec: lawyers play a central role, examining and cross-examining the parties and any witnesses they may call. Additionally, some parties encounter judges in brief hearings at which only their lawyers speak. These hearings occur at the beginning of the divorce proceedings in cases where provisional agreements are needed or to prepare the outcome of a settlement or agreement.

Whereas, in France, each judge has her or his own docket (known as a *rôle*) and hears a wide variety of cases over the course of a half-day, the Quebec court system has two types of docket: one for simple or preliminary hearings (*rôle pratique*) and one for trials (*auditions sur le fond*). Preliminary hearings deal with urgent procedures (safeguard measures) or provisional and interim measures, all of which are limited in time (generally lasting between thirty days and a few months, depending on the time needed to move to the next step of the procedure). In such cases, the parties may agree, but they need to have a judge authorize their procedure (for example, in order for a simple divorce case to proceed with few formalities), or they may be unable to agree, in which case lawyers must submit arguments and parties must testify. In Quebec, trials take place only for cases where people cannot agree to the outcome of their divorce or separation. These cases have their own docket and are not presided over by the same judge.

The observations that follow paint a more vivid picture of the differences between family litigation in France and Quebec. In France, hearings must move quickly: time constraints place strict limits on interactions. Mathilde Tabarès, the judge described below, was in her late thirties and had been working as a family judge for eighteen months at the time of our observation. Before this time, she had worked as a deputy public prosecutor, a sentence enforcement judge (*juge d'application des peines*), and a juvenile court judge. The morning of our observation, she had fifteen divorce hearings on her docket. The first six were divorces by mutual consent, and all of them ended with a divorce pronouncement. The nine that followed were conciliation hearings. These hearings are to determine whether the two parties agree to the divorce and serve to set provisional measures, which will remain in place until the divorce is finalized.[10]

During the first hearing, the couple's lawyer said nothing beyond a goodbye to the judge at the end. At the second hearing, the judge praised the woman for the "nice harmony" between her and her ex-husband and explained to the man: "It's a simplified procedure and quick: we only see each other once." The third mutual consent hearing lasted a bit longer than the others (twelve minutes) and was more complicated. The woman, who was fifty-two years old, was receiving public legal aid (provided by the government to low-income users of the court system to cover some or all legal fees). The judge received her alone at the beginning of the hearing, and she broke down in tears. A few minutes later, when her ex-husband and their lawyer entered the hearing room, the woman expressed doubt over the divorce settlement. Nevertheless, she accepted it. The next hearing was over in half the time. "It's for tax reasons," the woman explained immediately, similar to the parties in the previous case. The judge qualified the next cases as "simple": "You have no children. You already have separate residences ... There isn't much. Both of you have taken your things. No debt. Neither of you pays income tax."

The judge then moved to the conciliation hearings. The first hearing was extremely brief – just four minutes long – because the woman was absent. The next hearing was hardly any longer: a man, married in Eastern Europe some forty years earlier, appeared without a lawyer. With no arguments, the proceedings were quick. The other hearings, in which both parties and their lawyers were present, took between twenty and forty minutes. The longest hearing was for a couple of sales representatives, both in their early forties, whose son attended a private elementary school. Both of them agreed to the divorce, and both agreed that the child would live mainly with the mother. But the questions of who would pay for his schooling, and who would reimburse the couple's consumer debts, were more contentious. Tabarès ended the hearing at 12:05 p.m., in strict accordance with the three hours allotted to them.[11]

Our observations in Quebec City a year later were quite different: the duration of each case varied greatly, and lawyers played a central role in the proceedings. At 9:15 a.m., Louise Lavoie, fifty-one years old, a former civil lawyer who had sat on the bench of the Superior Court for the past six years, entered the courtroom for preliminary hearings. She was greeted by some twenty lawyers and not a single party. Over the course of about ten minutes, the judge and the lawyers agreed that six uncontested petitions for safeguard orders would be heard first. Dealing with them took forty minutes: four cases in which child support payments did not follow state guidelines; a petition for an extension to an already existing safeguard order; and a request for the service of process by email. The judge departed for about ten minutes, then returned and began examining a half-dozen interim safeguard orders. Each of these took between six and thirty minutes. Only two parties were present: a woman appearing with her lawyer, who did not speak, and a man representing himself. All of the cases were about court dates, extensions of orders already in place, and agreements that the judge dictated to the court clerk for immediate entry into the court record.

After a fifteen-minute lunch break, the judge heard two contested cases. The first concerned an eight-year-old child who suffered from bipolar disorder and attention-deficit-hyperactivity disorder. His parents, a thirty-nine-year-old employee and a thirty-seven-year-old former nanny, could not come to an agreement over his custody or expenses related to his behavioural and mental health issues. Each parent was examined and cross-examined by their lawyers. The child's babysitter, unable to make it to the court date, testified by telephone. The judge had another hearing scheduled for 2:30 p.m., meaning that the lawyers did not have time to enter their concluding arguments; they agreed to return the next day. The following case involved a thirty-one-year-old soldier and a twenty-six-year-old hairdresser who could not agree on a custody arrangement for their two young children. Their work schedules and the choice of a childcare facility were both a problem. Moreover, the woman alleged that the man was violent toward the children, a charge the man denied. The hearing ended at 4:40 p.m., and then each lawyer gave a five-minute summation.[12]

These observations show the different approaches to lightening caseloads taken in the French and Quebecois court systems. In France, until 2017, divorce and separation litigation used a simplified format with a single, rapid, and relatively standardized hearing: in each case that she hears, Tabarès asks the parties approximately the same questions. In Quebec, there is a great deal more variation in the type of case and the type of court appearance, in terms of both the professional interactions and the involvement of the parties. These contrasts raise the question of why the courtroom continues to play such a significant role in French divorce proceedings when it no longer does in Quebec.

With a Judge or Without?

Two key processes feature in the Quebecois approach to divorce and separation: first, recourse to the court system without judicial intervention and, second, recourse to the law without court intervention. In 1997, a change was made to the *Code of Civil Procedure* establishing that judges were no longer the only people competent to rule in legal proceedings.[13] This act empowered civil servants working for the Quebec Ministère de la justice (Ministry of Justice), known as special clerks (who hold a law degree and are often lawyers), to finalize most agreements between divorcing or separating parties.[14] Judges still preside over litigation or agreements that require divorce to be granted by the court and/or that require certain legal exemptions, such as the non-standard child support payments in the case heard by Louise Lavoie recounted earlier. In 2008, special clerks handed down over half of child support orders.[15]

Since 2014, lawyers from the Service administratif de rajustement des pensions alimentaires pour enfants (Child Support Recalculation Service) of the Commission des services juridiques (Legal Aid Commission), Quebec's public legal aid agency,[16] can modify, under certain conditions, the amount of child support payments, while the commission's Service d'aide à l'homologation (Homologation Assistance Service) can approve most changes to child custody and access agreements, providing that both parents are in agreement.[17] Granting official approval to parental agreements thus no longer lies within the sole purview of judges: it now involves work from other civil servants in the courts (special clerks) and outside them (lawyers from the Commission des services juridiques). The public side of the legal system is far more diverse than it once was, further lowering the number of divorcing couples who appear before judges in the course of their separation.

If they wish to avoid the courtroom, though, couples must be capable of reaching an agreement together. Since the mid-1990s, a number of resources have been put in place to help keep divorces out of court. The most widely known of these is the public funding of family mediation. Parents filing petitions to the court are required to attend an information session on post-separation parenting, and they have access to five hours of free mediation, which are also available to parents who have not filed with the court. People wishing to modify their agreements are also eligible to two and a half hours of mediation. In 2018–19, a research team that I belonged to conducted an online survey of 1,550 recently separated parents. Our results showed that around half of them used family mediation services – more than the number who used the services of a lawyer, which was approximately one-third of the respondents.[18] In total, 84 percent of people using mediation services arrive at a partial or complete agreement (SOM 2017, 6). Currently, it is likely that a significant number of agreements submitted to the courts for homologation were arrived at through mediation. That being said, parties using mediation are not required to obtain court approval for their agreements, and more than half of them do not seek it (32). Mediation has thus been a key factor in reducing divorce litigation.

The fact that a divorce takes place outside the courtroom does not mean that the separating couples do not encounter the law or legal professionals. In 2012, three-quarters of family mediators were legal professionals, lawyers, or, more rarely, notaries (Ministère de la justice du Québec 2012). The introduction of family mediation was an opportunity for non-legal professionals, particularly psychologists and social workers, to receive public recognition for their expertise in the field of separation.[19] Over time, though, legal professionals noticed an opportunity to capture a part of this market and to diversify their work. Separating couples thus encounter professionals who are overseen and financed by the government and who, more often than not, rely on their legal expertise. Moreover, to encourage couples to come to an agreement with each other, the Ministère de la justice, the bar, and legal non-profits have developed a range of tools for professionals (such as the child support guidelines discussed in Chapters 4 and 5) as well as for ordinary citizens (brochures, online resources, information sessions). These tools have all contributed to the broad dissemination of family law outside the courtroom and even outside professional settings.

Overall, the situation in Quebec closely resembles the one described by Robert Mnookin and Lewis Kornhauser (1979) in the United States in the late 1970s. Courtrooms and judges are no longer central, while legal professionals in various positions have maintained a key role in the process of separation and divorce. "The shadow of the law," as Mnookin and Kornhauser called it, is made even longer by the prospect of having to appear in court, which, however unlikely, often remains a stressful thought for couples going through separation.

Contrasting Political and Legal Configurations

The diversification of the separation process was propelled by two main factors; first, material incentives and constraints (both temporal and financial) on separating couples and, second, political and legal opportunities and obstacles driving reform initiatives. Quebec has sought to shrink the jurisdictions of judges and to outsource a portion of separation procedures. This goal, and the change it has driven, may be imputed to limitations specific to Quebec's political and legal circumstances (overlapping state and federal competencies as well as the institutional obstacle of the trial itself). It also came about through the mobilization of non-legal actors, who lobbied for many years to make more resources available outside the courtroom. In France, there has been much more widespread opposition to outsourcing family justice. At the same time, the managerialization of court-related activities arrived much earlier there than it did in Quebec. This explains why there is much less diversity in French divorce and separation procedures and why the diversity that now exists was so long in coming.

In Quebec: Justice outside the Courtroom

Nearly three-quarters of Quebec's residents believe they do not have the financial means to pursue legal action in court (Justice pour tous 2018). At the same time, a committee chaired by the chief justice of Canada reported that "the civil and family justice system is too complex, too slow and too expensive" (Action Committee on Access to Justice in Civil and Family Matters 2013, 1). It is true that legal costs in Canada are high: a decision based on a mediation agreement costs each party an average of over two thousand dollars (Society of Mediators

2017, 7). The lawyers' fees for a trial lasting several days are colossal. Moreover, getting one's day in court can take a long time: in 2011, a lawyer working for the Superior Court estimated that obtaining a court date for a divorce would take about six months in Quebec City or Albanel and up to two years in Montreal.[20] Traditionally, each party is represented by his or her own lawyer, driving up costs even further. In preliminary hearings, barely 1 percent of cases involve no lawyer at all, while 59 percent of them involve just one lawyer. Non-representation is rare in contested divorces: just one party was not represented in the twenty-one hearings we observed that lasted for three hours or longer (in addition, two men representing themselves did not wish to be observed). By contrast, representation of both parties by a single lawyer was rare (9 cases out of the 130 cases observed).

This scenario makes family mediation an attractive alternative – all the more so when one considers that the income threshold for legal aid eligibility did not move at all from the 1980s to the mid-2000s, meaning that, over that period of time, fewer and fewer people in Quebec were eligible for free or reduced-cost legal services. As many political and legal actors are aware, the cost of litigation is a major factor driving socio-economic inequalities. A desire to expand access to the legal system is one of the main motivations behind reforms that seek to move divorces out of the courtroom. As promoters of these reforms often point out, if trials are costly, other ways to settle disputes should be available. The lawyer in charge of family law at the Ministère de la justice provides a concrete example: "The cost of the child support recalculation service [initially $280; lowered to fifty dollars in 2020] is lower than the cost of obtaining a new decision through the courts."[21] Simply put, financing out-of-court alternatives has allowed Quebec's government to avoid addressing the issue of the socio-economic selection exercised inside the court system: the government has succeeded in structuring the semi-public market of mediation, child support recalculation, and other minor amendments to divorce agreements without exercising any further oversight in the historic market of private legal counsel.

The financial argument has not been deployed on its own: it is backed by a normative critique of trials themselves. Because they are adversarial in nature, trials have been accused of fostering conflict between ex-partners rather than defusing it. By its very nature, dispute resolution can seem to be at odds with litigation, raising questions about the desirability of the latter and encouraging the invention of other ways to address disagreement. This discourse can be heard frequently among legal professionals and even more among non-legal ones practising a "psycho-social" approach to separations. In Quebec, the psycho-social outlook and its methods began to be developed in the early 1980s by social workers from the Quebec and Montreal court systems. These professionals, who were responsible for conducting investigations into high-conflict divorce cases, became interested in mediation as a possible option to settle disputes before litigation took place.[22]

This approach spread progressively to the private sector and was officially recognized at the 1992 Sommet de la Justice (Justice Summit), which was convened to discuss legal reforms to be implemented in the coming decade. The Summit report quotes the Liberal minister responsible for the status of women, Violette Trépanier, who describes mediation as a more just means of resolving conflict than trials: "The mediation experience will be particularly beneficial to children, as experience shows that amicable settlements arrived at through mediation are always more equitable when it comes to visitation and custody rights" and produce higher child support payments (Sommet de la Justice 1993). These words express a new definition of justice that places less emphasis on the institution and focuses more on the idea of a moral principle that can be achieved outside the court system. This positive view of "justice outside the courtroom" was promoted and spread widely, as is evident in a statement by the Québec Protecteur du Citoyen (Ombudsman) during a parliamentary debate on child support collection: "Experience shows that many hearings have been avoided in this way, to the satisfaction of all parties involved. As the saying goes, a bad settlement is better than a good trial" (Protecteur du Citoyen 1996).

One vehement objection to the move away from litigious divorce was expressed by feminist groups and, in particular, groups working to defend and promote the rights of victims of family violence. During debates on draft legislation on family mediation, representatives from two groups that help women victims of intimate partner violence argued that mediation was inappropriate for violent relationships. In the end, they succeeded in making it a voluntary procedure rather than a mandatory one (Regroupement provincial des maisons d'hébergement et de transition pour femmes victimes de violence conjugale and the Fédération de ressources d'hébergement pour femmes violentées et en difficulté du Québec 1997). However, this course of action remained the exception, and, overall, the goal of moving separations out of the courtroom remained a priority.

One explanation for this situation is that family law falls under federal and provincial jurisdictions. Concretely, divorce law is governed by federal law, which requires that divorces be pronounced in court.[23] At the same time, and by contrast, the provincial government handles the civil procedure itself, the rights of unmarried couples, and the obligations relating to children, which means that the provincial government must act within the limits defined by which jurisdiction has what competence. Provinces, in other words, cannot mandate "divorce without a judge," but they can provide an array of alternatives to trials. Indeed, since the 1980s, family law has become a field in which Quebec has affirmed a specific legal identity within the Canadian federal system (Revillard 2007b). Family law was also one of the first legal fields in which private conflict prevention and resolution processes were developed, an approach that was then extended to all legal procedures by the new *Code of Civil Procedure*, which went into effect in 2016.[24]

That said, seeking approaches to separation outside the court system is not unique to Quebec: it is just as widespread in the rest of Canada, at both the federal and the provincial levels, as well as in the United States. In 2000, Morris Rosenberg, the deputy minister of justice, gave the opening address at a symposium on the accessibility of the Canadian justice system in which he declared "justice is complex and multidimensional, and the justice process must provide more than formal, adversarial proceedings designed to find guilt or innocence, and winners and losers" (Department of Justice Canada 2001, i). In 2013, the Federal Action Committee on Access to Justice in Civil and Family Matters confirmed that access to the justice system cannot be reduced to the "formal justice system (courts, tribunals, lawyers and judges)" and argued for a "more expansive, user-centered vision of an accessible civil and family justice system" (2). Between 2000 and 2013, provincial governments invested a great deal in the development of alternatives to litigation for separating parents. Quebec's child support recalculation service, for example, was preceded by equivalent services in six other provinces (Protecteur du Citoyen 2012, 4).

Quebec, in other words, was participating in a broader trend in North America. Indeed, John M. Haynes (1981), an English-born American mediator who taught mediation throughout the English-speaking world, also trained several Quebecois who were pioneers in the field of family mediation in Quebec.[25] If there was a feature in the spread of mediation that was specific to Quebec, it was the high degree of public involvement in the process when compared to neighbouring jurisdictions through the government funding of family mediation, special clerks, and legal aid. If we are to understand why the somewhat maligned institution of courtroom proceedings is now mostly reserved for long trials in Quebec, we must recall that the right to "a fair and public hearing by an independent and impartial tribunal" is one of the basic rights guaranteed by the *Canadian Charter of Rights and Freedoms* since 1982.[26] Violation of this right is a prosecutable offence in all jurisdictions in Canada. While this right pertains to both criminal and penal matters, rather than to matters of civil law, the standard of equity as it is construed for criminal trials influences civil trials and helps to define the range of possibilities open to the federal and provincial governments. This is most manifest in the adversarial approach to proof, which is standard in civil trials and means that lawyers must examine and cross-examine parties and witnesses. In sum, their very structure makes Quebec trials lengthier than French hearings.

Significantly, the bar, whose Quebecois members are much more numerous than in France, has been the most influential civil society group in the crafting and implementation of these successive reforms. It has accepted a number of these reforms, while ensuring that none of them reduces their jurisdiction, as the lawyer in charge of family law for the Ministère de la justice from 1979 to 2015 pointed out to us. The idea of a child support recalculation service emerged in the mid-1990s but did not go into operation until 2012: "The Bar held things up. If I hadn't been there, it would have been dropped ... We wore the Bar down

... It's all about money for the Bar. As if we were taking business from them."

As the next chapter will show, these reforms had a major impact on the work of lawyers but less so on that of judges. Institutional tradition places judges in the role of arbiter, above the parties. It is ill-adapted to amicable dispute resolution, although the official definition of a judge's duties has evolved: according to Article 9 of the *Code of Civil Procedure*, the mission of trial and appeals courts includes "facilitating conciliation." However, this definition came into use several years after family law had begun to move away from courtroom litigation. Furthermore, the independent judiciary is a constitutional norm in Canada,[27] making it even less likely that there will be any change to the adversarial structure of trials and strictly limiting the kind of administrative intervention into judicial work that has taken place in France.

In January 2012, statisticians from the Ministère de la justice in Quebec informed me during an informal meeting that they were creating an indicator for the duration of case processing in the court system. One of them mentioned that the courts were "none too eager to give accounts, because they are rightfully invested in maintaining their independence." The ministry did in fact have access to a relatively large amount of data on court activities, but the data were neither used nor published. The ministry's limited involvement in the statistical analysis of court activity was more indicative of the distance that it maintains from the courts themselves – at least compared to France – than it was a matter of actual access. Article 324 of the *Code of Civil Procedure* caps the duration of judicial deliberations (two months for child upkeep or custody or for a non-contested case; six months for other contested cases) but not the length of time before a case reaches a judge. Significantly, the notion of "unreasonable delay," over which the Supreme Court of Canada handed down two major rulings in 2016 and 2017, is only applicable to those proceedings defined in Article 11 of the *Canadian Charter of Rights and Freedoms* as "criminal and penal matters."[28] All of this means that family trials have changed little over recent years; they are a residual part of the system in the sense that a wide and diverse range of alternatives to litigation is now available.[29]

France: From Quick Hearings to Out-of-Court Settlements?

At first glance, the situation in France would appear to be the direct opposite of the one in Quebec. There has been a less marked turn away from litigation in France, and procedural reforms there have long been limited to the courts themselves. Alternative forms of conflict resolution are less widespread and less financially accessible in France than they are in Quebec; proportional to its population, France has twelve times less the number of mediators than Quebec (Haut Conseil de la famille 2014, 37). According to our observations in 2009–10, only 4 percent of separation cases went through mediation. Moreover, the costs of mediation must be borne by the parties themselves unless they are eligible for legal aid. Since all civil court documents are issued free of charge, and lawyers' fees are much lower than in Quebec, mediation is less attractive as an alternative. Until 2017, one common way to reduce lawyers' fees was for parties divorcing by mutual consent to share a lawyer: 85 percent chose this option.[30] Furthermore, for unmarried couples, legal representation was not mandatory; only half of the cases involved even one lawyer.

The fact that, until the recent reform, separations in France involved two lawyers much more rarely than in Canada may also be explained by the fact that the French court system has far fewer procedural requirements. As shown in the description of Mathilde Tabarès's courtroom earlier in this chapter, French civil judges work in a different way from their Quebecois counterparts. The French legal system is inquisitorial rather than adversarial, meaning that judges interact more directly with parties (Jolowicz 2003). Whereas most of the people with whom Louise Lavoie spoke in her courtroom in Quebec were lawyers, Tabarès was exchanging directly with the parties themselves. Indeed, in low-conflict cases, the lawyers barely spoke at all. The proactive role played by judges in French hearings allows them to cut the cases shorter more easily than their counterparts in Quebec, and it is important for them to keep cases moving at a rapid pace, given their extremely high caseloads. Compared to Lavoie, Tabarès's manner of speaking was also more standardized, with a much tighter focus. Procedural obligations required her to confirm each party's identity, to confirm that they each consented to the divorce, and to go over the different measures provided for at that phase of the process. French family judges also must take care to identify any points of contention and question them accordingly, rapidly verifying whether both parties agree to divorce and whether they also agree to certain aspects of the outcome of their separation.

The French system is built on the idea of making litigation available for all, and it has sought to guarantee this by reducing the number and the length of hearings, making court personnel responsible for a kind of assembly line processing of court cases. In 2010, the twenty-eight family judges whom we studied working in Valin, Marjac, Carly, and Belles each heard 885 cases (Collectif Onze 2013, 23). By comparison, each judge in the Superior Court of Quebec handed down an average of 170 family law–related decisions per year.[31] Even when one considers that approximately half of the cases they heard pertain to other matters, this number is still far lower than it is for their French colleagues.

The political configuration that led to this situation can be explained in two ways. First, in the French context, where direct intervention by judges is still the norm and courts have limited means available to them, courtroom management has been a major priority in the reforms to the court system. This configuration has limited the latitude that trial judges have with regard to the presiding judges of their courts and even their independence from the French Ministère de la justice. Second, much more than in Quebec, political debate in France has centred on the role of judges. A long-standing reluctance to do without them has been overtaken recently by a kind of managerial logic to justify new ways of avoiding trials.

As a percentage of the gross domestic product, the budget for French courts is smaller than every other country in Western Europe, with the exception of the United Kingdom (European Commission for the Efficiency of Justice 2020, 25). To address this lack of funding, the French court system was included in France's agenda for managerial reform starting in the early 2000s (Vigour 2006). One of the key goals of these reforms was to accelerate the pace at which cases move through the courts, particularly in criminal proceedings, both by streamlining cooperation between the police and state prosecution (Bastard and Mouhanna 2007) as well as by increasing use of what is known as "immediate appearance" (*comparution immediate*) (Douillet et al. 2015). This may be attributed in part to the fact that the European Court of Human

Rights was quicker than the Supreme Court of Canada to recognize the problem of "unreasonable delay," which is also an issue in civil trials.[32]

Generally speaking, the French court system moves more quickly than the Quebec court system: on average, trials take ninety days less (274 days compared to 382 days) (Lamari, Noreau, and Leduc 2020, 54). Reducing processing times for divorce cases indeed became a "performance indicator" for civil courts in the early 2000s, with a certain measure of success: between 2004 and 2010, the average length of a divorce case dropped by over two months – from 13.3 months to 11.6 months. The delay for a divorce by mutual consent has decreased the most – from 8.8 months to 2.6 months (Belmokhtar 2012, 1). The burden of speeding up the divorce process was placed on trial court personnel, to the point that family judges have been described as "the Mr. and Mrs. Fix-its of divorce acceleration" (Bastard et al. 2014). These reforms have increased the power of presiding judges over their trial courts, intensifying the pressure on family judges and clerks.

In Carly, a trial court we studied in the greater Paris area, case flow was one of the presiding judge's main preoccupations. In a preparatory meeting with two of our researchers before this investigation began, he suggested a line of inquiry that fit with his concerns: "Is asking for numbers influencing work of judges and clerks?" he wondered, explaining that "everyone's got their eyes on the statistics." He added that he was obliged to tell his colleagues "I want you to hand down a certain number of decisions per year."[33] Three years later, members of the research team returned to Carly to present the project's initial findings. When it was mentioned that four or five cases on the docket were postponed each day, he expressed concern: "That means four or five delayed rulings a day."[34]

In contrast to Quebec, where the Ministère de la justice has only limited say in the work of judges, and chief judges have little latitude in what they can ask of their colleagues, the French Ministère de la justice has exerted increasing control over the work of judges, with district presiding judges as their intermediaries. In France, the court system has come to be seen as a type of "public service," which is subject to reform as in any other branch of French administration (Vigour 2018). This explains why the question of streamlining divorce and separation cases emerged at the heart of the court system (with judicial hearings) rather than at its periphery, as was the case in Quebec. Strong opposition to moving family cases out of court has also kept French divorce reform focused within the court system. In Quebec, changes to the litigation landscape are perceived as technical and have sparked little controversy within the Assemblée nationale (National Assembly). In France, by contrast, the prospect of shifting divorce by mutual consent out of the hands of judges mobilized academics, lawyers, activists, and members of Parliament. This breadth of concern was not because of practical considerations but, rather, because of the principles and values driving the change.

Among expert opinions produced on the topic, a report from the Commission sur la repartition du contentieux (Commission on the Distribution of Court Litigation) submitted to the minister of justice in 2008, under the direction of Serge Guinchard, a professor emeritus at Université Paris 2, shows the persistence of the conviction that family cases ought to be heard by judges. This conviction contrasts with Quebec, where the question of access to the justice system has been disconnected from the work of judges:

> The traditional function of a judge is to safeguard liberties, equality, and democratic values and to restore social peace by *"juris dictio."* The modernization of the institution of the courts must be to the benefit of this core function ... The number one founding principle of all democracies is to effectively guarantee the right to have access to a judge, at one point or another in the resolution of a conflict or the examination of a non-contentious matter. This right to access a judge may be in pursuit of a claim; it may be exercised after a certain lapse of time, but it remains a right guaranteed by the Constitutional Council and by Article 6 § 1 of the European Convention on Human Rights. (Guinchard 2008, 40)

This normative stance, however, is tempered by the recognition of the contractual freedom of spouses, who are free both to marry and to dissolve their marriage. From this perspective, moving away from litigation could help them to exercise these freedoms more easily.

In addition to these two conflicting norms, a third norm has influenced the French approach to the litigation of family matters – namely, the protection of vulnerable, victimized, or less powerful people in domestic partnerships, who are generally women and children. Ensuring that they are protected has been an argument in favour of judicial intervention. In a previous report, Françoise Dekeuwer-Défossez (1999, 96), a professor of law, argued that "[i]t's an issue of recognizing their freedom and their autonomy, in line with a general trend in family law, as well as of preserving the possibility of peaceful future relations, which is particularly precious when children are involved," although she did acknowledge that "the heart of the debate remains the actual freedom of divorcing spouses from pressure and even violence, which is what makes amicable divorce possible" (101).

The contradictory nature of these different goals (access to justice, contractual freedom, protecting the vulnerable) has created rifts in intellectual, professional, and political groups. In 2016, as divorce by mutual consent was about to become an out-of-court procedure, members of the bar were divided (Portmann 2016); the right wing of the Senate wanted no part in it (Bas and Retailleau 2016), the left-wing Front de gauche deputies were opposed to it,[35] and the Défenseur des Droits (France's ombudsman, created in 2011), along with the Syndicat de la magistrature (a left-wing union of magistrates), demanded that the procedure be reserved for couples without children. In addition, women's groups were nearly unanimous in their opposition to it.[36] This widespread opposition explains why the reform took so long to go into effect and why it was only forced through by a Socialist majority in an Assemblée nationale loyal to the president's aims.

The triumph of this legislation marks much more of a victory for the managerialization of the court system than it does for the rise of a "left-wing" view of family transitions. The move away from litigation was taken up as a cause by the Conseil de modernisation des politiques publiques (French Council for the Modernization of Public Policies) and became part of the French state's reform agenda (Conseil de modernisation des politiques publiques 2008). From the managerial point of view, lower courtroom caseloads and savings for the state budget are the prime goals in the effort to rein in the use of litigation. Given the high rate of separation and divorce, this perspective deems the specialization of judges in "more complex cases" desirable for the sake of efficiency (3).

In 2016, as he took over as minister of justice, Jean-Jacques Urvoas (2016) inveighed against the lack of resources available to the court system and appeared to have taken up the idea that reducing judges' scope of action had become the right solution to pursue. Internal streamlining was thus followed by a series of attempts to do the same externally. Two lower-profile policy reforms confirmed that the policy goal and ideal of "judges for all" were being called into question. The first wave of reforms went into effect in 2017 and allowed family judges to homologate agreements between unmarried or formerly married parents into the court record without hearing them in court. The scope of the reform was significant since non-divorce family procedures made up around half of the cases in family courts. At the same time, a three-year experiment was undertaken in eleven trial courts, in which mediation was required for all non-violent family disputes over changes to child-related decisions. Mandatory mediation was seen as another way to lower the number of cases going to trial and to help judges refocus on their "core vocation" (Boussard, Mato, and Kim 2022).

The second policy reform went into effect in 2020; similar to the reform of divorce by mutual consent, it decreased the number of decisions to be handed down by family judges – in this case, for those relating to child support.[37] As long as the two parents agree to the child support payment specified in the national guidelines, the French Caisses d'allocations familiales (CAF) (Family Benefit Offices) are now empowered to officialize their child support agreements. Until the change, petitions to the family court related to requests from the CAF represented a significant number of non-divorce family cases, meaning that the main administrative channel feeding into the family court system should refer significantly fewer cases to it in the future (Collectif Onze 2013, 28).

Together, these three reforms appear to be moving France toward a system that resembles the one in Quebec: the prerogatives of the private wing of the legal world have been reinforced, as have those of administrative bodies such as the CAF. Nevertheless, significant differences remain. First, in Quebec, the move away from the courtroom was designed as a way of reducing costs for users of the justice system. In France, to the contrary, the mutual consent reform made divorce more expensive for users since it requires each party to have his or her own lawyer. Before the reform, individuals were able to share representation, and they often did. A 2018 survey of French lawyers revealed that this extra cost was the main hurdle to divorce brought up by their clients (Honnorat 2018, 9). Moreover, as we know, Quebecois judges' specialization in more "complex" cases – a category that deserves further analysis – has led them to devote longer and more in-depth work to a smaller number of cases, whose trials last several days and whose rulings may be dozens of pages long. In France, the strict oversight of civil procedures and a chronic lack of resources in the courts prevent judges from devoting this kind of time and attention to their cases. Finally, the role of the law and of lawyers outside the courtroom is more diffuse: lawyers and notaries have much less of a presence in the field of family mediation in France, and resources for public information are far less extensive there. In sum, national context still matters in the ways in which professions and organizations are involved in separations.

Unequal Access to Justice

The paths that these reforms have taken have led to differences among separated people, both in terms of procedures and in terms of the professionals whom they encounter. The more numerous possibilities for divorce in Quebec mean that socio-economic inequalities are more marked there. Nevertheless, the mechanisms for inequality are similar on both sides of the Atlantic, as is the fact that more privileged people have access to a broader range of professionals, both public and private. By contrast, those from less privileged backgrounds, especially people in financially precarious situations, have far less latitude in deciding whom they can seek out in the course of their separations. They are constrained both by their lack of resources and by the demands of public administrative bodies. In most cases, they have access only to public resources or to publicly funded private resources. Compounding these class inequalities are gender inequalities, which are starker among the lower classes, where women are the primary targets of public services. Men tend to slip through the cracks and regularly confront these procedures alone.

Three Institutional Paths in Quebec

In Quebec, separations occur in three ways, depending, broadly speaking, on whether the parties are members of the lower, middle, or upper class. For the less privileged, the path to separation and divorce generally begins in a legal aid office. These offices employ lawyers who work exclusively for people eligible for legal aid. They are involved in more than one-third (38 percent) of family court litigation.[38] This number is completely out of proportion with the number of lawyers practising in Quebec since legal aid lawyers represent just 2 percent of members of the bar (Barreau du Québec/Centre interuniversitaire de recherche en analyse des organisations 2009, 20). Legal aid lawyers, who are younger and more likely to be women than bar members as a whole,[39] therefore face a considerable caseload: up to fifty-seven cases in the Montreal offices that we studied, compared with ten or twenty in most private offices, over the three months examined.[40] As a result, legal aid lawyers meet with many clients a day, and initial appointments tend to last less than half an hour, compared to an hour in a private law office. Because of this high caseload, the functioning of legal aid offices can be considerably thrown off when they are down one or more team members. "We are 'high-volume' lawyers," an attorney working in a small country office explained. During the COVID-19 pandemic, one lawyer on her team was ill and two were so overwhelmed with work that they had to take time off for exhaustion, which forced the office to limit the number and the kind of cases it took on.[41]

Clients seeking legal aid begin with an examination of their eligibility. Several conditions are taken into consideration, including income, property, financial assets, number of children, and marital status. These conditions explain why recent immigrants, particularly in Montreal, represented a significant portion of legal aid recipients in the meetings we observed (23 percent) and were hardly present in our observation of meetings in private firms. After being frozen for decades, the threshold for eligibility was raised in 2016, but it still does not include most of the more stable members of the working class. Essentially, anyone whose income is higher than the minimum wage and/or who possesses some assets is disqualified. Legal aid beneficiaries tend to belong to the most precarious segments of the lower classes: the working poor (part-time workers earning minimum wage), stay-at-home mothers, and people moving between "odd jobs" and periods of unemployment or under-employment due to health problems. Although they ostensibly came to appointments to discuss their separations, in the meetings we observed, debt problems or problems with housing authorities often came up (Biland and Mille 2016).

According to the Commission des services juridiques (2018, 89), seven out of ten legal aid clients are women. The predominance of women among legal aid recipients can be explained by persistent inequalities between men and women in the job market, by income, and by employment rate (Institut de la Statistique du Québec 2021). Moreover, among the poorest mothers, three-quarters have sole custody of their child or children.[42] This means that they are more likely to be eligible for financial aid and to request child support. One-quarter of the legal aid recipients we encountered also received last-resort financial assistance. To be eligible for this money, they are required to request child support from the other parent and seek out legal aid in order to do so. Thus, two-thirds of women with an annual income of less than fifteen thousand dollars, but fewer than half of men with the same revenue, sought assistance from a legal aid office.[43] Finally, women are more likely to initiate legal proceedings than men are, and so they are usually the first to seek legal counsel. Since divorcing or separating couples cannot be represented by the same legal aid office, men must often turn to private sector lawyers who accept legal aid payments. Applying for these may be a complex process, and because legal aid payments are rather low, private sector lawyers who accept them are becoming rarer (Jeune Barreau de Montréal 2016, 9). As a result, when a claimant is represented by a legal aid office, his or her ex-partner is likely to appear in court without a lawyer.[44]

These conditions for eligibility can come as a surprise. In one meeting that we observed with Marion Alfano, a twenty-seven-year-old lawyer in a legal aid office in a working-class neighbourhood of Montreal, a client, originally from Pakistan, discovered these conditions for eligibility on arriving at an initial consultation. Looking as if he had just arrived from a day of heavy work, he explained in somewhat uncertain English that he wished to contest the child support payment that his ex-wife was requesting for their children. Alfano checked her computer and informed him she could not provide him with legal counsel, as his ex-wife had already received aid from this office. Three times, speaking slowly, she explained the procedure for obtaining a legal aid voucher: call the Montreal bar, ask for a private sector lawyer who accepts legal aid cases, make sure they verify his eligibility. After she had gone over what he should say over the phone, she asked several times whether he understood. The man's reply of "ok, ok" seemed to express his bewilderment at all the steps that were needed more than it did his understanding of them.[45]

The fact that a separate form of legal aid is available through private law firms, the specific rules that it must follow, and the difficult working conditions of the lawyers who provide it serve to create differences in the way women and men are treated and ensure that the most precarious members of the working class are treated differently from members of other social classes. Women are more likely to receive legal counsel than men but at the price of exposing their private lives, an issue to which we will return later in this book. And the time they are granted by lawyers is much shorter than the time granted to members of other groups: "With 350 or 400 cases [in family law each year], we can't spend fifteen hours on a case," Charles Lavoie, a lawyer with the legal aid office in Albanel, explained to us.[46] Men often end up confronting complex legal procedures alone – procedures that can be downright opaque in cases where their cultural capital, including their mastery of English or French, is limited. Indeed, they may be dissuaded from making any kind of claim at all.

The absence of a lawyer for one of the parties in the most common dispute – child support – discourages any kind of in-depth litigation. Child support–related issues are considered to be minor and are structured by precise calculation rules: for lawyers, coming to an agreement is distinctly preferable to going to trial. Legal aid recipients, while overrepresented in court dockets for preliminary hearings, are few and far between on trial dockets, as this Montreal judge admitted in an interview: "There are people who, even if they have complex questions for the judge, don't have the means to go to court. So there are cases we'll never hear, because there are people who give up because they don't have the resources to go to court, and we're very aware of that."[47] Only three of the twenty-one cases (or 14 percent compared with 38 percent of the preliminary hearings) that we observed in hearings lasting over an hour involved a legal aid lawyer: a courier and a cook, both earning minimum wage; a part-time doorman and a financial aid student who had been living "on the margins" for a long time; and a woman welfare recipient whose ex-partner was an information technology consultant. Two of these three couples came from outside Canada: from North Africa and the Caribbean respectively. Indeed, compared to other social groups, lower-class couples who end up in court face multiple types of difficulty, including health issues, addictive behaviours, intimate partner violence, and/or child abuse. The normally quick and simplified treatment provided for the separations of the less privileged is not designed to address the complex configurations of these cases. One judge described the lower-income couples who end up in her courtroom as being "in rough shape." She added that "each of them could do with a good few months of therapy."[48] Her words reveal the social distance between her and these parties, but they also reflect the conditions that bring such couples to court: unless their problems are unusually complicated, their separations take place outside courtrooms.

When such cases do end up in court, they are always linked to custody or visitation rights, which are highly sensitive issues because they affect the "best interests of the child." Nearly all of them involve allegations of parental deviance, such as violence or the consumption of alcohol or drugs (Biland and Schütz 2014). This type of deviance justifies judicial intervention as well as the involvement, either through affidavits or testimonies, of other public sector professionals, such as social workers in child and youth protection centres (*centres jeunesse*) or doctors and medical workers from community health centres (*centres locaux de services communautaires*).[49] Court hearings are one of the many forms of oversight practised on the lives of impoverished families – oversight that involves multiple institutions and multiple professional groups from the public sector.

At the other end of the social spectrum, institutional encounters for the wealthy involve a different set of professionals and mobilize considerably more resources (Biland and Mille 2017). In Quebec, membership in the upper class is most often defined based on individual annual income, and "big money people" are generally defined as those earning more than $100,000 per year (Baril 2013). Most members of this group – men as well as women – are represented by a lawyer (85 percent). Since, as a rule, men earn significantly more than their ex-wives,[50] this lack of differentiation between the genders is made possible by a "provision for costs," which stipulates that the receiver of support (usually the woman) can have her ex-partner advance part of their lawyers' fees under certain conditions.[51] The lawyers of these wealthy clients practise in the private sector; their hourly rates are high (up to $660 for one of the lawyers we interviewed), and they offer their clients a wide variety of services.

In early 2021, we interviewed a lawyer in his late thirties who had worked for one of Quebec's most prestigious family law firms for the past two years. He explained how much his practice had changed since joining the firm. After his bar internship in a legal aid office and some work in unspecialized law offices, the change was stark: his hourly rate was considerably higher (he now billed more than even the most experienced lawyers in the city where he used to practise), and he had become familiar with a range of practices reserved for the wealthiest clients. "Sometimes we coach our clients through mediation, from the shadows," he reported, adding that his firm called in retired judges to preside over private mediation sessions, at a cost of around ten thousand dollars per day. He was particularly pleased to be able to work with junior lawyers and an experienced paralegal who prepared impeccable case files for him.[52]

A few years earlier, a member of our research team spent the day with Marie-Josée Besnard, a lawyer in her forties working in a large business law firm in Montreal.[53] She described spending seven and a half hours with a thirty-seven-year-old man, a graduate of Hautes études commerciales Montréal, who worked as a financial executive in a large firm. He and his wife, who were in the midst of a divorce, were disputing the custody of their children, aged five and eight. During the course of this lengthy appointment, which included lunch, paid for by the client, she and the ex-husband wrote several documents for the court proceedings. The man was working with a number of other professionals, in addition to Besnard, with whom he emailed and texted frequently, including a "separation coach," and he had undertaken a day of private mediation (at a cost of fourteen thousand dollars) and a day-long settlement conference with a judge.[54]

As this encounter shows, the more privileged the couple, the more likely they are to seek out many types of professionals, from both the private and the public sectors, over the course of their separation. These professionals include lawyers as well as psychologists or personal development specialists. Mechanically, the wealthy take up the majority of judges' work time: three-quarters of their child custody orders are handed down by judges, compared to half of the separating population as a whole.[55] This is a structural phenomenon: in a country where divorces must be pronounced by a judge, wealthy couples are more likely to be married (83 percent compared with 49 percent for the population as a whole). More surprisingly, and despite the fact that they are no more likely to be involved in contested cases, wealthy couples are over-represented in long trials (making up one-third of the twelve trials we observed that lasted a day or longer).

There are two reasons that the separation of wealthier couples "merit" more attention from judges. First, the financial stakes in their divorces are considerable, requiring more in the way of legal and financial expertise from professionals. Second, men in these couples frequently request shared physical custody, despite little prior involvement in the labour of parenting over the course of their married lives. More often than not, this leads to conflict with their ex-wives, who did devote their time to caring for the children. Generally speaking, significant inequalities between spouses tend to lead to diverging interests when they separate. Given their financial resources, this makes them more likely to litigate or seek arbitration. The near-total absence in our ethnographic studies of wealthy couples in which both parents worked may indicate that fewer unequal situations are more likely to be settled outside the courtroom.

Canadian law professor Martine Valois (2012, 218) has noted that, "[f]rom their position at the front lines, judges are the first to have noted their courtrooms' desertion by middle-class parties, and the increasing occupation of the Court's time by wealthier litigants." Our research in the courts confirmed this observation: people who were neither eligible for legal aid nor endowed with significant financial wealth were rarely seen. So what happens to all the people who inhabit the vast space in between, ranging from the stable working class to middle-class couples with significant cultural capital? This entire segment of the public would appear to be conscious of the high cost of legal proceedings and receptive to the idea of mediation as a satisfactory alternative.

More specifically, as the following observation shows, lawyers tend to encourage people with limited incomes to fall in with this line of reasoning in the name of financial reality – litigation is a cost they can ill afford, as this hearing before Gabriel Forest, a judge and former criminal lawyer in his fifties, illustrates. A forty-two-year-old truck driver and a thirty-seven-year-old waitress, both earning minimum wage (around twenty thousand dollars), have three daughters, aged eleven, seventeen, and nineteen, and have been separated for seven years. Their hearing, which lasted for three and a half hours, was mostly taken up by financial issues relating to the seventeen year old: contact lenses, a computer, intensive English classes, horseback riding. Both parents seemed tired, and, during his cross-examination, the father began to look uncomfortable. At one point, he groans, which irks the judge, who exclaims:

> It's normal, the parties aren't capable of speaking to each other! ... I'm not criticizing. You're going to have to try and talk to each other to avoid ending up here again. With your annual incomes, you can't afford to appear in court. I find it deplorable. Luckily you both have competent, honest lawyers. There are several things you could have worked out between you, with a bare minimum of effort. Put your pride to one side and talk it out, otherwise you're going to pile up court cases and lawyers' bills.[56]

The low cost of mediation, along with its focus on amicable solutions, makes it all the more attractive by comparison. These incentives for clients are congruent with those of lawyers: publicly funded mediation is most lucrative for lawyers whose clients are higher-income members of the working class and the middle class. Mediation guarantees lawyers income from the government at approximately the same hourly rate that they bill in their private practices (around $110). Moreover, it allows them to avoid overly frequent court appearances and aligns with their own goals of promoting amicable conflict resolution during separations – a subject to which we will return. Seeking out mediation is not merely a financial consideration, however. It is also linked to cultural capital (Noreau and Amor 2004). Among the 1,550 recently separated parents whom we surveyed in 2018–19, half chose to participate in family mediation. There would seem to be a link between this choice and the fact that their income and education levels were higher than the average person in Quebec (their average yearly income was fifty-eight thousand dollars, and nearly two-thirds of them had a college degree or higher). Indeed, regression analysis of this sample shows that, controlling for other variables, income and education levels are positively correlated to family mediation (Poitras et al. 2022). Are relatively well-off and educated parents such as the ones we surveyed more likely than other groups to espouse the "democratic" ideals expressed in mediation (Commaille 2015)? Or are they more comfortable expressing themselves verbally, something that this approach of "government through speech" requires (Memmi 2003)? Chapter 3 will explore interactions between legal professionals and laypeople to shed light on possible answers to these questions.

A Multi-Track Justice System in France

Let us now turn to the question of how people who decide to end their domestic partnerships in France are oriented down the path of separation or divorce. The first thing we observed in our study was that differences among the social classes are not as stark as in Quebec. This comes as no surprise since, at the time this research was conducted, all couples were required to appear before a judge. Nevertheless, we did find that the type of proceeding, case duration, and legal representation were all factors leading to different experiences and outcomes for different separating people.

At the beginning of the 1970s, statistics on the justice system pointed to a variation in the divorce rate depending on social background. The divorce rate ranged from less than 1 percent to more than 9 percent depending on whether the spouse was a farmer or a manager, and the profession of the wife was the stronger determining factor (Boigeol and Commaille 1974, 5). Thirty years later, the differences among occupational categories were less marked: the percentage of men (excluding farmers) who had separated from their first partners had risen to 15 percent among workers and 18 percent among managers (Bessière 2008). Growing divorce rates across all social and occupational categories raise the question of how each segment of society approaches separation. By 1977, two years after the introduction of divorce by mutual consent, half of managers were already using this procedure, compared to one-quarter of skilled workers (Baillon et al. 1981). Forty years later, divorce by mutual consent has become the most popular proceeding by far for couples in which both partners work (91 percent of such cases). By contrast, among lower-income groups, it is far rarer: just 12 percent of women and 6 percent of men who undertake this procedure receive full legal aid.[57]

Marital status is also unevenly distributed across social groups: non-divorce family procedures are far more common among groups with lower occupational status than they are among the middle and upper classes: 58 percent of cases in which the father is a skilled worker are non-divorce family cases, compared with 38 percent involving fathers with managerial occupations. The differences in marital status (marriage or common law) among social groups are not the only reason for this gap.[58] Petitions filed at the request of an administrative body must also be taken into account, such as the CAF or the prefectoral authorities for requirements regarding foreigners.[59] Lower-class parents are more exposed to these injunctions than the rest of the population.

As I showed in an article published with several colleagues, the impact of socio-economic status on legal proceedings can also be felt in the length of time taken by different types of cases (Biland et al. 2020). Of all types of separation procedure, divorce by mutual consent has been targeted by policy efforts intended to reduce delays. The wait time for this type of divorce is thus far shorter than for contested divorces and shorter again for non-divorce family cases (averaging 104, 168, and 198 days respectively between the filing and the first ruling).[60] Our observations showed that judges and clerks were making efforts to reduce the duration of cases of divorce by mutual consent: before the hearing described earlier in this chapter, Tabarès explained to us that she "slides" these cases up to the beginning of her morning sessions, knowing that the hearings are quick and that the parties nearly always show up. In the small district of Marjac, Étienne Paletot also offered what he called an "agreement incentive" to lawyers who untangled particularly contentious cases, putting them first on the docket.[61]

Giving priority to mutual consent cases, as these judges described, creates class inequalities. Since members of the middle and upper classes are more likely to undertake this type of divorce proceeding, they are the primary beneficiaries of this acceleration in the court system. Within a single type of procedure, class differences are still significant. For non-divorce family cases where both ex-partners work in managerial occupations, for example, the wait time is an average of eighty-four days shorter than it is for couples in which one ex-partner is a skilled worker or employee and one is not actively employed. This difference may be explained in large part by the presence of lawyers: cases in which there is at least one lawyer take forty fewer days to process than cases with no legal representation. Inversely, legal aid cases involving unmarried parents last an average of thirty-five days longer.

Moreover, the length of procedures varies significantly from one court to another due to the unequal distribution of resources among jurisdictions. Particularly in the region of Paris, the districts with the fewest resources are also the ones hearing the highest proportion of cases with parties who are members of the lower classes and immigrants. Between December 2015 and February 2016, professionals working in the trial court of a poor *département* on the outskirts of Paris spoke out against the court's lack of resources. They estimated that parties in family cases had to wait about a year before their first hearing. Court data confirm their observation: these parties are at a significant disadvantage compared to their neighbours in the city of Paris.[62] The average wait for a court decision in a family case rises from 135 to 210 days (nearly three months more) depending on whether the case goes to court in Paris, where the parties are more likely to be wealthy than in other regions, or in this poorer suburb.

A third factor explains why judges tend to give less attention to cases involving less privileged parties, which is that these parties rely much less on lawyers than the rest of the population. In four out of five cases involving two parties with high-level or intermediate occupations (or one party in a high-level occupation and the other with an intermediate occupation), each person was represented by a lawyer. This number dropped to barely half of the cases involving workers, employees, or those without an occupation. As we have seen, cases in which at least one lawyer is involved are heard an average of forty days faster than those in which there are none. And, as also mentioned above, unmarried legal aid recipients, whose eligibility must be evaluated by a dedicated office at the trial court, must wait an average of thirty-five days longer.[63] Moreover, legal representation has an impact on trial length: of the 189 non-divorce family hearings that we observed, those with no lawyer lasted an average of thirteen minutes, those with one lawyer an average of seventeen minutes, and those with two lawyers an average of twenty-seven minutes. In other words, middle- and upper-class couples, although they are in the minority when it comes to this type of proceeding, get more time with judges than their less privileged counterparts.

Additionally, legal representation is affected by gender. Excluding divorce by mutual consent (for which both spouses must now be represented by a different lawyer), men are less likely to have legal representation than women (58 percent compared to 77 percent).[64] The reasons for the lack of legal representation among men in France are similar to those in Quebec: men are less likely to initiate divorce proceedings, they tend to earn higher incomes than women, and they are less likely to have the children in their care. All of these reasons mean that they are less likely to be eligible for legal aid, and amicable divorce requires both parties to have a lawyer. These factors also help to explain why members of lower-income groups are less likely to undertake these types of procedures.

Gender differentiation and class are in fact tightly linked: representation gaps are much narrower among middle- and upper-class parties than among lower-class ones. Among the upper classes, men's greater financial solvency, their more frequent willingness to share custody, and their common wish to reduce the child support they pay push them to be involved in their divorce or separation proceedings, which thus serve to motivate professionals to follow their cases carefully. Overall, we observed that French lawyers are slower to attend to parties from less privileged backgrounds, and, once they do, they usually spend less time with them. This unequal attention may also be explained by the way in which legal professionals prioritize different types of family-related conflict. As in Quebec, child support is at the bottom of the list and tends to be dealt with in a rapid and routine way, and this contrasts with disagreements related to physical custody or assets, which, for different reasons (the "best interests of the child" or legal complexity), demand lawyers' attention and engagement. Pierre Terreau, a judge in his fifties, spent many years as an investigating judge before taking over as the head of the family chamber in the Marjac trial court. In an interview, he expressed the limits of the attention he was willing to devote to financial disagreements between lower-class parties. He gave the example of a hearing for the divorce of a thirty-one-year-old health aide and a thirty-nine-year-old woodworker:

> I think there was agreement over pretty much everything except the amount of the child support for the two children, and it was a matter of twenty-five euros [€150 requested by the woman and €125 agreed to by the man]. So it was really a small case. When there's really such a small discrepancy between the proposed amount and what's being offered, we'll do a kind of overall analysis of the situation of the two parties, I'd say, in terms of income and expenses, but we aren't going to get into the kind of detailed accounting that would be done, I'd say, when someone is asking to pay four hundred euros, and the request is for seven hundred or eight hundred euros, if you see what I'm saying.[65]

These inequalities in access to law and justice increase when one takes into account professional interactions outside the courtroom. Over the course of our observations, the time that lawyers spent with separating couples varied just as much in meetings with clients as it did in the courtroom. In the Besson district, for example, where law firms often serve a socially diverse set of clients, we noted that lawyers consistently devoted less time to clients of lower socio-economic standing: "Of the forty meetings in which the profession of the client was known, those in which the client's occupation signaled lower class status ($n = 16$) lasted for an average of forty-one minutes, compared with fifty-five minutes for middle-class clients ($n = 11$) and sixty-one minutes for upper-class ones ($n = 13$)" (Bessière, Mille, and Schütz 2020).

Other professional interventions reveal just how finely grained targeting by social class really is: it is unusual to call on experts for a family case, but, when it does occur, the differences are striking. When home visits by social workers are requested, it is nearly always for parents of lower-class status, whereas accounting expertise is sought out almost exclusively in cases involving married couples with significant financial capital. Outside mutual consent cases, home visits are requested in 10–15 percent of cases involving couples who are working-class or self-employed workers. By contrast, a financial expert is involved in 5 percent of cases involving parents in upper management occupations and in no cases in which one of the parties is a worker or employee and the other not employed outside the home (Biland et al. 2020).[66]

To understand why the majority of home visits occur in cases involving lower-class families, a little more must be said about the goals of social worker investigations and the conditions under which they take place. These investigations take the form of home visits by a court-appointed psychologist or social worker. This professional examines the family's living conditions and questions the parents and the children in order to evaluate "the family's material and moral circumstances," "the conditions in which the children are being raised," and "the extent to which there are grounds for measures to be taken in their best interests."[67] A member of our team examined fifty-five home visit reports (Minoc 2017). Her research revealed that the social distance between judges and parents from less privileged situations gave rise to a sense of strangeness or foreignness with regard to their family situations (particularly with regard to families with other countries of origin). From this perspective, home visits may be perceived as helping judges to better understand families living at a significant remove from their own experiences of the social world.

At the same time, however, they constitute a much greater intrusion into the private lives of these families than a brief court hearing, confirming the extent to which the judicial system and the social system intertwine in many separations involving poorer families. Investigations involving upper-class parties are significantly different: they relate mostly to financial matters and economic status and thus scrutinize a couple's professional activities more than their intimate lives. Just as important, they are requested by the parties themselves rather than being ordered by judges, which means that more privileged parties are able to choose the experts they call into their cases and, thus, to exert greater influence over investigations than is possible for families for whom a judge has ordered a home visit.

Finally, wealthier separating couples have access to collaborative law, an alternative form of conflict resolution in which clients and their lawyers meet together for group negotiations. This practice is entirely private in the sense that there are no state accreditations or regulations regarding the fees of these professionals.[68] The time required for these negotiations means that their cost is necessarily high. The practice is thus reserved for people of significant means, generally those seeking to negotiate the financial outcome of their separation without involving the state – in particular, the tax authorities (Bessière and Gollac 2022, 3).

Grace Dupont-Bernard, a lawyer in her fifties, has been the Besson Bar Association's most active promoter of collaborative law. In early 2014, she gave a presentation titled "Settling Conflicts without Judges" at a large public conference in Paris. A few weeks later, she presented this practice to two members of our research team: these "four-person meetings," she explained, tend to last about two and a half hours, and only people with a certain "level of culture" are able to "concentrate enough" and "know how to make the effort."[69] The recent growth of this practice is evidence of the significant role of the private sector in divorce and separation among the upper classes. Whereas, in Quebec, the loosening of divorce law has targeted middle-class couples, in France, this trend is seen, for the most part, as a means of serving the dovetailing interests of the upper classes and the country's more expensive lawyers.

**

The ways in which separations are governed today shed light on the problematic relationship between individual rights and social inequalities. France and Quebec have responded to rising rates of divorce and separation in different ways. Both jurisdictions share a goal of fostering amicable and self-regulated forms of separation, but contrasting policies in their justice systems have created different outcomes. In France, the principle of a "judge for all" has long been held up as an ideal, but, despite its universalist aspirations, it has never translated into the same experience for everyone. In Quebec, the principle of "to each according to their need" has become "to each according to their means." Beyond differences in the two systems themselves, the liberalization of divorce is experienced differently by individuals depending on their social status, their gender, and even their national background. The challenges they face in separating are constructed for the most part by the institutions that end up governing their family lives, which depend on legal professionals' representations of different types of family conflict and different publics.

The first form of inequality that separating couples face, as we have begun to see, arises from their access to institutions and professionals. Despite the legal aid system, members of the lower classes have limited access to lawyers; they are less likely to be represented by lawyers; and, when they are, they are able to spend less time with them. In Quebec, they are less likely to appear before a judge, and, in France, their time in the courtroom is more limited. These socially inflected experiences of the justice system are also inextricably linked to gender: among the lower classes, the justice system comes together with social services to monitor mothers and leave fathers to fend for themselves. Among the middle and upper classes, gender differences are less stark. The wealthy are more able to choose who is involved in their family cases in both the public sector and the private sector. Depending on the balance of power between the two parties, they are also more able to decide between settling their disputes out of court (which tends to mean negotiation away from the gaze of the state) and investing significant time and financial resources in long court cases.

The COVID-19 pandemic, particularly during the lockdowns imposed in France and in Quebec in the spring of 2020, revealed the scale of inequalities in access to family justice as well as the varying ability of court systems to deal with this crisis. Limited and difficult access to the courts in France and in Canada in 2020 caused a drop in the number of divorces in both countries.[70] At the same time, this public health and economic crisis created greater demand in the justice system: lockdowns made life unbearable for some couples and intensified family violence; lockdown rules and contamination risk made custody sharing between parents more complicated; and lost revenue or higher living expenses made adjustments to child support payments an urgent issue.

In France, the situation was particularly difficult for families awaiting a court decision (Bessière, Biland, and Oehmichen 2020). Family courts essentially halted in-person hearings between mid-March and early June 2020, narrowing their activity to urgent cases such as international kidnappings and protection order requests involving family violence. It became apparent that courtroom personnel often lacked the technology to exchange information with judges and lawyers, meaning that even cases that did not require a hearing were unable to move forward; when judges did rule, the parties could not be notified. In May, the chief judge of the Court of Cassation warned that France's courts were facing a "digital emergency" (Arens 2020).

These failures in the court system have encouraged those who could to avoid court or to reduce court involvement to a minimum, further weakening this public service. French lawyers who work in alternative conflict resolution – particularly in collaborative law – quickly noted the importance of expanding the services they could offer remotely. "There's no choice," observed a family lawyer in Northern France with whom I spoke by telephone in April 2020. "Otherwise, we can't provide responses to people's problems." As she continued, "that creates enormous inequalities between people who are able to opt for alternative approaches and people who have to depend on judges."

In Quebec, too, the crisis had a major impact on the work of legal professionals. The associate in the prestigious family law firm with whom we spoke in January 2021 noted that, as wait times for court settlement conferences had grown longer, his firm had expanded its private mediation practice, which is so costly that only the wealthiest parties can afford it. At the other end of the legal and social spectrum, a legal aid lawyer whose office serves a vast geographic region that includes an Indigenous community explained that phone meetings had actually made access easier for clients who lacked the resources to come all the way to his office. Initial meetings were much more likely to be attended during the lockdown because they took place over the phone. However, the lawyer also noted that the process often came to a halt after the initial meeting as so many clients were unable to submit the documentation required as proof of income over the internet.[71] Even more during the pandemic than before, access to the law and justice depends on access to technology: the inequalities structuring the latter affect the former.

It must be said, however, that the pandemic had less of an impact on family justice in Quebec than it did in France. The Court of Appeal was already holding some hearings by video-conference (notably, in order to better serve remote regions), and the Superior Court was able to effectively expand this practice. The pandemic augmented the court's power to set behavioural standards well beyond the courtroom. Court decisions relating to parental duties received wide media attention as early as April 2020 when it was recognized that lockdowns (and, thus, the impossibility of travelling to the home of another) should not be an obstacle to the pursuit of shared custody and visitation rights, which should continue for all families (Marin 2020).[72]

These observations regarding the work of judges and lawyers during the pandemic, in addition to their role in society as a whole, are yet another reason to study these legal professionals' career paths, their working conditions, and their institutional roles, which is the subject of the next chapter.

How Gender and National Context Shape the Legal Profession

2

The previous chapter showed that the type of professional encountered by separated people varies depending on their social class and gender. This chapter will examine how the social traits of these different professionals interact with their working conditions to affect their evolving relations with families. Accounting for their professional trajectories and their daily work practices is a necessary step toward analyzing their contribution to inequalities in the wake of separation and divorce. Trial judges and family lawyers are the two main types of legal professional in the public and private sectors with whom separating couples interact. The way in which these professions are structured has deep historical roots, but traditional professional roles have been affected by changes in the way separations are handled by the law. How do the members of these two professions position themselves when encouraging conciliation and non-litigious divorce? How do they go about ruling when dealing with heavy caseloads? I will answer these questions with a threefold comparison: between the professional contexts in the two countries, between the professions of judge and lawyer, and between men and women representatives of these professions.

This next step in the comparative study of France and Quebec uses a comparative sociology of professions, with findings from the sociology of work as a foundation. Many comparative studies of the legal profession exist. *Lawyers in Society*, a three-volume work published in the late 1980s by Richard Abel and Philip Lewis, may be considered the founding work in this field. Its third volume, *Comparative Theories*, takes a genuinely comparative approach, using thematic entries (training, feminization, neo-corporatism, and so on) to explore different contexts (Abel and Lewis 1989). In their preface, Abel and Lewis encourage researchers to study "what exactly lawyers do for their clients, and how this varies across societies" (xii). Despite this exhortation, the approach they call for is largely missing from most of the book's chapters, which spend much more time on theoretical examinations than on empirical sources. While this comparative perspective has gained ground in recent years, most comparative work has mobilized more quantitative data than qualitative sources (Maclean and Eekelaar 2013; Schultz and Shaw 2013).

It is striking to observe the gap between studies conducted in single nations, which make much of observing professional practices (for example, Eekelaar and Maclean 2013; Eekelaar, Maclean, and Beinart 2000; Mather, McEwan, and Maiman 2001; Sarat and Felstiner 1995), and comparative studies, which make little reference to them. Such a gap is due to the one-off nature of most international research collaborations, the high legitimacy of quantitative data in comparative studies, and the desire to compare a large number of countries. This chapter, by contrast, offers a comparative ethnography based on multi-year studies in two different countries. It uses quantitative data to draw the contours of the groups studied and analyzes professional trajectories through both interviews and observations of professional practice in the workplace. It is particularly attentive to the role of gender in the bar and the judiciary, but while quantitative approaches focus on career paths and sentencing in an absolute sense, this chapter will instead show how these elements are tightly linked to professional practices and professional identities. The latter depend on gender, all the while helping to construct it.

The two-jurisdiction comparison will deepen our understanding of the gendered mechanisms at work in legal professions and how they impact other factors that structure these groups. First, the differences between France and Quebec vary significantly depending on the group under consideration. These judiciaries are dissimilar in terms of social status and gender patterns as well as in terms of institutional regulation and roles. Working conditions in the two countries also differ considerably. These factors mean that judges relate differently to their three roles: they may act as arbiters, conciliators, and managers. By contrast, the practice of family law seems to be rather similar in the two jurisdictions: in both places, it is a field with little prestige and low pay, largely female dominated, with a few women in top positions. Because the trend toward out-of-court dispute resolution is older in Quebec, national differences are most notable in terms of daily practice: family courts play a much more significant role in day-to-day legal work in France.

An Ocean of Difference: Judges in the Two Jurisdictions

You will recall that, in France, divorce included a mandatory court appearance for much longer than it did in Quebec. This institutional difference is linked to the roles of judges in the two jurisdictions. As I showed in an article published with Hélène Steinmetz, trial judges in France occupy a front-line position in divorce proceedings (Biland and Steinmetz 2017). As a result, their work resembles that of street-level bureaucrats, and they indeed do hold a status similar to that of a civil servant, both practically and in terms of professional ranking. This status translates to significantly lower prestige and pay than that of their Canadian counterparts. By contrast, a series of socio-economic and procedural filters exists in Quebec that limits the number of cases that end up going to trial, which means judges are called on only as a last resort. Their position at the pinnacle of the court system parallels their elite social status.

These differences between judges in France and Quebec may be mapped onto the broader, long-standing differences between countries with legal traditions based in civil law and those based in common law (Ehrmann 1976). The last-resort position of the judiciary is a feature of countries whose legal systems are based in common law. Conversely, in the continental legal tradition, a position in the judiciary has a career path of its own, and adjudication by the court of divorce cases has tended to remain the default (Maclean, Eekelaar, and Bastard 2015).

Legal Elites or Civil Servants?

A quantitative overview of the profession in the two countries offers a striking illustration of the national differences in both career paths and working conditions (Table 2). As is the case elsewhere in North America, judges in Quebec are the elite of the legal profession because of both their professional experience and their social background. Judges of

TABLE 2 A few indicators for comparing judges

	France	Quebec
Number	3,382 (or 0.05%) per 1,000 inhabitants	194 (or 0.024%) per 1,000 inhabitants
Sex ratio	68% 20 out of 28 survey subjects (71%) were women	32% 11 out of 23 survey subjects (48%) were women
Age	Mean: 48 years Range among survey subjects: 27–55 years	Mean: 60 years Range among survey subjects: 48–73 years
Training	Law school or Institute of Political Studies; École Nationale de la Magistrature (National School of Magistrates)	Law school, bar certification, and legal experience; on-the-job training
Family law cases	Make up the core of the judges' practice over the course of several years	Tried alongside other types of cases throughout career
Annual gross salary	In 2022: €36,000 to €87,800[a] (between 1.5 and 3.7 times the national mean)[b]	$346,600[c] (7.8 times the provincial mean)[d]

Sources:

a École Nationale de la Magistrature, "Traitement des magistrats au 1er janvier 2020," https://www.enm.justice.fr/sites/default/files/grille_des_traitements_01-01-2020.pdf.

b *Insee,* Tableaux de l'économie française, 2020, https://www.insee.fr/fr/statistiques/4277700?sommaire=4318291.

c Judicial Compensation and Benefits Commission 2016, 16.

d ISQ, Main indicators for Quebec and its regions, 2021, https://statistique.quebec.ca/en/vitrine/region.

the Superior Court of Quebec are former lawyers with an average of twenty-three years of experience at the bar behind them. Nearly all of them have worked in legal firms and nearly half in commercial law (tax, trade, or corporate law), which is known for being the highest-paid sector in the profession (Barreau du Québec/Centre interuniversitaire de recherché en analyse des organisations 2009). As lawyers, most of them have played significant roles in a regional bar section or in the Barreau du Québec – a fifth of them have been bar president – as well as being members of community or business groups such as the Chamber of Commerce. In this context, a judicial nomination crowns an already successful law career. The social backgrounds of these judges match their elite social status. Nearly all were born in Quebec and trained at one of the province's law schools.[1] Among the half of judges who reported their parents' professional backgrounds, their fathers were likely to have occupied upper-class positions: 82 percent had a father who was a business leader or a qualified professional, and just 9 percent had a father who was a manual labourer or a low-level employee. Half had another close family member (in their own or their parents' generation or a spouse or child) who was a lawyer or a judge.

The political aspect of judicial appointments is additional evidence of the elite status of judges in Quebec: the federal minister of justice appoints judges to the Superior Court. A quarter of judges receiving federal appointments in Quebec between 1989 and 2003 had some degree of connection to the political parties in government (Hausegger et al. 2010, 643). The appointment of judges in this way – late in their career and based on a significant amount of social capital – is common practice in countries with a common law legal tradition and does not foster gender parity in the field. Barely one-third of judges are women, a proportion similar to that of Canada as a whole as well as the United States (Schultz and Shaw 2013, 9).

Superior Court judges are better paid than the premier of Quebec and the prime minister of Canada, which reflects and contributes to their high social status. These high salaries, along with their lifetime appointments, are intended to help guarantee the impartiality required of them once they are appointed. Moreover, the constitutional norm of judicial independence requires them to keep a greater distance from public debate than members of the bar as well as from the Ministère de la justice, whose high-level civil servants are also lawyers. Professional ethics in the Canadian judiciary require public discretion with regard to private convictions and an appearance of impartiality (Morton 2002). In an interview, Marc Lachance, a fifty-year-old judge from a family of rural legal professionals who has sat on the Superior Court for five years, reflected on the nature of a judge's role:

> The private life of a judge should be private. So we don't sign petitions. One time, I went to a restaurant and they wanted me to sign some petitions: we don't sign petitions. We don't take a stance in public on any political issues. It's our normal professional duty – discretion. Because if I take a stance on a political issue, who can say whether or not I'll end up having to hand down a ruling about it?[2]

For all the reasons outlined above, members of the Superior Court are a fairly cohesive and homogeneous group: there are relatively few of them (under two hundred), they all earn approximately the same salary, and they are all of a similar age (80 percent are between fifty and seventy years old). They have known each other for some years (average seniority is ten years), and unless they are appointed to the Court of Appeal or the Supreme Court, they will remain with the Superior Court for the rest of their careers. They all learned to be judges on the job, with the help of their fellow judges: in interviews, several mentioned their gratitude for the support of more experienced colleagues. This observation is particularly true in family law. Only one in five judges worked in that field during their time as lawyers, but nearly all of them must master it as judges, given the proportion of family law cases that end up in court.

Finally, judges in Quebec work with a wider variety of other professionals than their counterparts in France, such as law clerks (who manage cases), legal secretaries, clerks of court (who take notes during hearings), and court ushers (who greet parties and witnesses and provide other material assistance to judges). Judges may also work with other legal professionals, such as lawyers working in the court's research department or special clerks (discussed in Chapter 1). Courts in Quebec hew closely to the North American legal system, in which a "proliferation of sub-judges" helps judges to maintain their elite status by allowing them to concentrate on the tasks that are seen as the most prestigious and highly specialized (Fiss 1983, 1463–64). Judges in Canada actually have greater power than judges in France: as is the case in the United States, constitutional review occurs starting in the first instance, and judges are authorized to rule in constitutional matters – indeed, this is recognized as their official and legitimate contribution to public policy.

French family court judges differ from their Canadian counterparts in several ways – they are younger, more likely to be women, and make less money. The proportion of women judges in the French judiciary is higher than average among other members of the Organisation for Economic Co-operation and Development.[3] Among family judges, who preside in the lower courts and work in a field that is socially constructed as feminine (family law), women are even more strongly represented; the same is true of judges in juvenile court (Paillet and Serre 2014). Judgeships in family courts tend to be early-career positions, which offer another explanation for the lower civil service rankings of family court judges (they tend to hold the ranking of second grade, which requires seven years of professional experience or of being vice-president in a trial court). French judges are recruited through competitive examinations and train at the École nationale de la magistrature (French National School of Magistrates). The youngest among them are twenty years younger than the youngest members of the Quebec Superior Court. This method of recruitment has encouraged women to enter the judiciary and diversified the social backgrounds of its membership. Although less data are available, French judges tend to come from more middle-class backgrounds rather than from the upper echelons of the professional world (Mouhanna 2012).

Their understanding of legal impartiality differs from that of their counterparts in Quebec (Roussel 2003). In our interview with Dominique Bazot, a former civil servant and a family judge with twenty-two years of experience in the field who is a member of the Syndicat de la magistrature (the left-wing union of judges), the contrast between her view on the independence of the judiciary and that of Marc Lachance was immediately clear:

> Our impartiality is statutory ... I have opinions about politics and unions and things, but that doesn't mean that these opinions are in charge. You can't be a hypocrite, though – they do influence me to a certain degree, I don't believe in pragmatism, right – you can't sell me that rotten baloney. We're not above civil society, we're citizens for better or for worse, often disastrous policies are imposed on us.[4]

Of course, not all French judges are active in unions as Bazot is and few are so open about holding political opinions. But this kind of language, spoken in the context of an interview, would be unthinkable in Quebec. Bazot's words convey an immanent idea of justice in which judges do not hold themselves above social issues but, rather, are immersed in them. As mentioned, this outlook comes in part from the fact that French judges are similar to other public servants in several ways, beginning with their pay scale, which is based closely on that of Category A civil servants (the highest rank, requiring at least three years of post-secondary education). They are promoted based on "merit," which is evaluated by a hierarchical superior, giving presiding judges in French courts significantly greater power than a chief judge in Quebec. In other words, the line between judiciary and public administration is less clear in France than in Quebec: in Paris, the majority of top-ranking civil servants in the Ministère de la justice are judges, who return to the courtroom after their service at the ministry. This porosity is one key explanation for the force of management reforms analyzed in Chapter 1. Finally, French trial judges are a more heterogeneous and less stable group than their Canadian counterparts in the Superior Court: the career paths that they follow mean that they rarely hold their positions for more than five years.

In summary, judges in Quebec form an elite and largely self-regulating group, whereas French judges occupy a far less dominant position and are far more subject to their hierarchy.

Arbitrate, Conciliate, or Manage?

How do these differences play out in the concrete work of judges? In both contexts, the institutional role of family judges comprises three different dimensions: that of an arbiter, when they must decide between the disputed claims of ex-spouses; that of a conciliator, when they work to settle disputes; and that of a manager, when they handle the flow of cases or work through backlogs. These three dimensions combine in different ways depending on the types of litigation and the social positions that characterize the two contexts.

In theory, according to French law, a judge's primary role is as conciliator. In practice, because of time pressures and heavy caseloads, this aspect of their work is minimal. In most cases of divorce by mutual consent, judges merely take the time to ensure that both spouses consent to the divorce agreement. These cases are almost universally approved: only 18 of the 857 divorce agreements analyzed (2 percent) were not.[5] In contested divorces, conciliation generally consists of the judge encouraging both parties to sign the *procès-verbal d'acceptation* (an official acceptance of the divorce proceedings), in which they agree to abandon any further judicial inquiry into the reasons for their separation, even though this may mean limiting their expression of grounds for the divorce or leaving them in a state of distress or confusion.

In Marjac, we sat in on conciliation hearings led by Pierre Terreau, a judge who was recently put in charge of the family chamber. During one of the hearings, a woman in her sixties, who was a farmer, had filed for divorce. Taking a piece of paper covered in tight handwriting from where she had been holding it under the table, she began: "I prepared this to explain the separation to you." The judge interrupted: "Today I am not looking at motive; it's not the place." The woman tucked the paper into her canvas bag, saying "I understand." When interviewed, Terreau justified his refusal by explaining what is most at stake in conciliation hearings:

> It's almost a formality to ask them if they do or do not agree with the divorce ... That means that, if they agree in principle to the divorce, we won't go with a contested divorce, and presto that gives you a quicker, simpler procedure in which grounds don't have to be

specified. But that's their only advantage ... A hearing that lasts just a few minutes isn't there to help people work things out. An interim divorce order is like an off-the-rack shirt from China – it comes in two sizes: either both parties agree to divorce without looking at the grounds for divorce, or one of them refuses.[6]

As Terreau pointed out, heavy caseloads and inadequate resources for investigation mean that family judges limit the amount of work they put into most cases and make it a priority to bring parties into agreement, even when these agreements are fragile or reproduce power imbalances between ex-spouses (Collectif Onze 2013, 51–56). Moreover, they seek to curb the expression of family conflict, particularly when demands do not fall within strict procedural bounds.

Not only do judges have little time, they also have little experience in family court, meaning that many of them do not feel particularly at ease in cases where they must decide between two conflicting claims. When it comes to child support payments, for example, judges often choose a figure halfway between the figures proposed by the two parties; for custody, more often than not, arrangements made before the hearing are simply approved by the judge. Michael Lipsky (1980, 129) calls this a "rubber stamping attitude": judges either approve whatever is already in place or try to find an arrangement that is as close as possible to the demands of the two parties.

Generally speaking, family trial judges do not have great confidence in themselves as arbiters: in France, their discretionary power has often been seen as rather summary. The codification process that structures the civil law tradition tends to reduce the scope of their jurisdiction to merely applying the law (Troper 2007). In practice, they do have a certain latitude since they are empowered to make case-by-case decisions (Lipsky 1980). But family judges in lower courts do not seek to give prominence to this aspect of their work and even express unease in matters where their latitude is the greatest. This relationship to the law is not the only thing judicial work in France has in common with other administrative jobs. Access to the courts and working conditions are two other key elements. First, there are far fewer intermediaries between judges and parties in their jurisdictions in France than there are in Quebec. Because of a shortage of employees and a certain disregard for the Code de l'organisation judiciaire (*Code of Judicial Organization*), hearings are often held without a clerk of court.[7] Moreover, the more frequent absence of lawyers, particularly in non-divorce proceedings, means that judges end up socializing litigants into appropriate court conduct as well as dealing with behaviour that is sometimes aggressive.

The following passage describes events that took place during the morning of observation with Sophie Batement, a forty-year-old judge. At the time, Batement had worked in the Valin family court for the past five years, after working as a juvenile court judge. It was the sixth hearing of the morning. It began, as all the others did, with the clerk going into the hallway to call the parties. From Batement's chambers, we hear her irritated voice saying "be polite!" On her return, in reply to Batement's query, the clerk observes "Mr. T. is not happy," and, indeed, he is behaving aggressively. First, he complains that the judge is running late. "I got a summons for 9 a.m., and I get called at 10:30!" He is representing himself, while his ex-wife is accompanied by a lawyer; the issue is child support for their fourteen-year-old daughter. As a temporary worker in the building industry, he has until now been exempted from paying any. Now, his ex-wife is requesting two hundred euros. Calmly, the judge apologizes for running late: "Sir, despite the fact that we're running an hour late, which I'm very sorry about, let's try and go ahead with the hearing." The lawyer's reply – "we also had to put up with Mr. T's irritation" – sparks the ex-husband's ire again. "You think it's fun to get shit like that at your house [to be served with papers]? You think I enjoy that?" His tone becomes menacing, and he makes threatening gestures, shifting in his chair, and even rises and makes a move toward the judge. The clerk looks furious. "I'm going to go get the police if you keep that up!" The man retorts "I'm going to get it up the ass." A little later, the lawyer accuses the man of not seeing his daughter regularly enough. He cuts her off: "Me? I'm not getting anywhere. I'm going backwards." Fairly gently, the judge tries to get him back on topic by saying "I think I understand you don't agree with these demands, but I'm the one you should be speaking to." The man grows angrier: he refuses to pay the child support, refuses the change in summer holidays, and denies earning what the lawyer says he does. The ex-wife tries to speak up, but the judge cuts her off. The man asserts: "When I have my kid, I make her happy, that's all, just like anyone else." The woman manages to interject: "It is always about you – I have problems, too!" The man becomes aggressive again. The judge calls him to order: "I'd like to tell you something; you shouldn't make your ex-wife pay for whatever you want her to pay for through your daughter." She brings the hearing to a close and shows everyone out.[8]

As this scene shows, the working conditions of employees of French courts, including the judges, resemble those of bureaucrats to a far greater degree than in Quebec. Naturally, a court appearance is not quite as simple as a trip to the emergency room or a meeting with a social worker: there are security checkpoints, and one is likely to encounter police officers and handcuffed suspects. Courts nevertheless remain relatively accessible. People can walk past the offices of the judges and the clerks, whose doors are often left open. Judges do not always wear robes during hearings, which they hold in their offices rather than in hearing rooms.

These similarities between the court and other public services weaken judges' self-assurance with regard to their ability to make discretionary decisions and discourages them from straying too far from managerial norms. The mandate to conciliate might lead one to believe that the role of a judge is somewhat similar to that of a social worker, and many judges object to this conflation. While some of their objections come from a desire to defend the skills and knowledge specific to their profession, they may also be attributed to a lack of time and resources that weighs on their capacity to lend a patient and attentive ear during conciliation hearings.

Working in the Superior Court of Quebec is a wholly different experience. The first contrast that stands out is the far greater degree of decorum in Canadian courts, highlighting the special status of the judge. Neither lawyers nor the public have access to certain parts of the building, which are open only to court personnel – judges even enter the courtrooms through different doors. They also decide when hearings begin and when they end and call recesses if needed. Everyone rises when the judge enters or leaves the courtroom, and litigants and witnesses offer evidence standing, facing the judge, after taking an oath. They are required to look at the judge while speaking. Court ushers maintain decorum in the courtroom: they work in the service of the judges, bringing them water and paperwork, open the door for them when they come into and go out of the courtroom and, during one hearing, even reminded one of the researchers to dispose of her chewing gum.

This spatial organization finds its origins in the English courtroom architecture of the fifteenth century and reifies the distinction between the judiciary – judges, clerks, ushers – and the rest of society – lawyers, litigants, and witnesses (Mulcahy 2011). Even their seats, which are elevated above the courtroom floor, help to make the pre-eminent position of the judges into a concrete reality. They do not even eat in the courthouse cafeteria: they break for lunch in a special dining room in a restaurant in the city, further underscoring their position outside the rest of society and, thereby, their impartiality. In our interview with him, Marc Lachance applied this understanding of judicial impartiality to many aspects of his daily life:

> Some newly appointed judges find it a little sad, because sometimes they get invited to dinner with lawyers they know. But you have to make choices ... When a judge is appointed, there's really that independence there. They set up everything to ensure our independence. But it's also up to judges to internalize it and not put ourselves in situations.[9]

These material and relational aspects are important for understanding why judges in Quebec take on the role of arbiter with far more confidence than their French counterparts. They have much more time to hear contested cases, often have more professional experience, and enjoy a higher social rank. Beyond that, they work in conditions designed to remind the world that they are able, legitimate, and neutral arbiters. Judicial practice in Quebec is a far cry from Pierre Terreau's "off-the-rack" justice; rather, it is "bespoke," in the words of Andrée Pinard-Garon, a former civil lawyer, who is the daughter of an accountant and married to a lawyer:

> I like to call my family law "bespoke" law, because it's made to measure to meet the needs of every family in their own reality. It might be a dad or a mom – but usually a dad – who's a trucker. Truckers work in a way that's very different from you and me. Often they'll leave on a Sunday afternoon, especially if they're long-distance truckers. And they'll get home at noon on Friday. So it's up to me to set up my child hand-overs so they suit, so it fits with that ... I'm telling you, I do "bespoke" law – it's "tailor-made."[10]

These words illustrate these judges' "illusio," which is rooted in their belief in their own ability to make a difference through informed, carefully thought through, and even innovative decisions.[11] By the end of a typical hearing, the amount of information on the circumstances of each party they have collected and the time they have spent listening to their requests and claims mean that they can work in a much less standardized way than their French counterparts.

At the same time, a judge's work entails more than just the rigorous examination of a few carefully selected cases. When I asked her what had changed since she was first appointed in the 1990s, Pinard-Garon replied without hesitation: "In addition to making decisions, judges work as conciliators and managers."[12] Despite the hushed atmosphere of the Quebec courthouse, judges now spend a significant amount of time on management tasks. This stood out in our observations of Louise Lavoie described in Chapter 1. The morning we spent with her included more than a dozen different cases, including derogatory agreements, extending the duration of provisional agreements, or authorizing unusual procedures. It should also be noted that many judges are in charge of a court chamber, or even responsible for a rural courthouse, in which no judge seats permanently. In these functions, they work closely with the court clerk's office and with lawyers to reserve courtrooms, to ensure cases are ready, and to check that their colleagues are available for hearings. Finally, in order to process cases more quickly, they now work in new ways: they hold telephone conferences with lawyers; they hand down rulings "from the bench" (that is, in front of both parties at the end of the hearing); or they even read their rulings to parties over the phone in the days following a hearing.

Despite this, the caseload remains high, meaning that judges in common law countries must still carry out less noble tasks in addition to deliberating (Eekelaar and Maclean 2013; Mack and Roach Anleu 2007; Resnik 1982). In interviews, the use of terms like "high-volume courtroom," "managing the court," and even "poutine" (a nickname for hearing rolls, where the scheduled cases are extremely varied) pointed to the expanding presence of these activities. They nevertheless occurred less frequently than their equivalents in France (where terms such as "mass," "flow," and "stock" were employed). Even the connotations of the words used by the Quebec judges were more neutral, evoking a sense of successful judicial rationalization that allowed them to focus on the most important cases. From such observations, we may conclude that management activities do not take place at the same scale, nor do they have the same meaning in the two jurisdictions.

The same was true of conciliation: judges in Quebec spoke of it more frequently than their French colleagues, as if it might potentially constitute the future of their professional practice. In our interview with Gabriel Forest, a forty-eight-year-old judge married to a lawyer, who had been appointed two years previously, he placed great emphasis on this role:

> The judge's approach in family law – and it is laid out in the *Code of Civil Procedure* – is about facilitation and conciliation. The judge isn't just there to hand down a ruling, but to facilitate cooperation and try to bring the parties together to talk things over ... And by the end, sometimes, we get to a situation that's been negotiated, where the two parties are relatively happy. And much more likely to sell the settlement to the children involved. I think that scenario is preferable to one where a decision is imposed by a court saying "that's black and that's white. You have to deal with it, because that's my decision."[13]

As these words show, critiques of the court adjudication of separations (which has been accused of entrenching conflict) have filtered into judges' discourse, encouraging them to modify their practice. "Justice is a hammer, and a hammer leaves marks," one judge told me, shortly after deferring a hearing so that the parties and their lawyers could attempt to come to an agreement over visitation rights.[14] These principled reasons for preferring conciliation are bolstered by practical concerns. During one of the hearings described in Chapter 1, Gabriel Forest was observed discouraging parents to appeal to the court, given their lack of financial resources. Boiled down, justifying conciliation in these terms follows questionable socio-economic reasoning; essentially, Forest was saying that the parents could not afford to bicker. This passive stance takes a personal toll on judges as well: several of them mentioned feeling bored sometimes during hearings, and lawyers noted that certain judges even nodded off.

Concretely, taking on the role of conciliator happens in two key ways. First, since the early 2000s, judges who wish to can preside over settlement conferences where, instead of issuing a ruling, they act as facilitators as the parties and their lawyers negotiate a settlement, which becomes binding only if they both agree to it and the judge signs it. Gisèle Fontaine, a sixty-six-year-old former civil lawyer married to a lawyer, had been on the bench for fourteen years when we interviewed her. Of the judges we spoke to, she was the most enthusiastic about settlement conferences. She explained that, when parties appeared in court, she liked to tell them

> you know, there is another way to do what you are in the process of doing. I think that you are aware that the Superior Court offers a service that is called a settlement conference, where you can sit down with your lawyer and a judge [*laughs*] who won't do what I'd do today, which is decide for you – they'll help you to see if you can't figure out a solution. I want you to know that this possibility exists so that you can be in charge of the final outcome of all of this litigation. It will also make it possible for you to avoid the agony of a trial.[15]

Conferences, another tool designed to help keep cases from going to trial, nevertheless remain optional for both judges and parties. Acting as a conciliator in a hearing is far more complicated than it is in a settlement conference, as Albert Savard explained to us. The sixty-five-year-old son of a small business owner and a teacher, who was from a rural background, had at the time of our interview been on the bench for twelve years. He was quick to acknowledge that the most difficult part of his first years as a judge had been "to wait, not to speak up, to keep quiet." He felt that it was necessary not to step in too soon: "The judge often comes into the courtroom with the beginnings of an opinion, and you have to resist wanting to validate that opinion. If you don't, you end up squarely on the side of the party pleading in favour of that opinion."[16]

For judges with whom we spoke in Quebec, the path to realizing their aspirations to conciliation is narrow because of the adversarial system, which sets fairly strict limitations on what they can and cannot do. Indeed, lawyers can file disciplinary cases against judges who appear to have been lacking in impartiality. Generally, the judges we observed spoke little during their interrogations of the parties: they might have asked for a small detail or for clarification on a point they did not fully understand, but they did not let their opinions show. In Quebec courts, furthermore, audio recordings of hearings – which are non-existent in France – function as concrete incentives to judges to moderate their speech.

Judges were, by contrast, happy to open up about their perspective at the close of a hearing. In our observations, concluding remarks were not so much an occasion for concrete attempts to reconcile the two litigants as they were an opportunity to remind them that they were not abiding by the norm of the amicable settlement of disputes. Conciliation thus became a kind of moral gesture, seeking to impose the judicial norm of negotiated divorce – as Pinard-Garon's language reveals in her attempt to call two working-class parents into line at the close of a short hearing. The case involved a man and a woman, both employees of a convenience store, aged twenty-four and thirty-five, respectively. They were appearing in court for safeguard orders for their two young daughters. Officially, neither one of them contested the orders, but, during the hearing, it became apparent that the two parents were not really in agreement over shared custody. They ended up coming to a provisional agreement. Before leaving the courtroom, the judge looked both parents in the eye:

What I would like to say to you, Monsieur and Madame, is that you will always be the parents of M and A [their two daughters]. [Spoken to the woman] Monsieur will always be M and A's dad. [Spoken to the man] Madame will always be M and A's mom. No one can replace a dad, no one can replace a mom. I ask that both of you show respect to each other, especially when the children are there. They are little, but it goes by very fast ... Out of love for your children, respect each other. And you'll be avoiding a lot of trouble in eight or nine years and particularly when they're teenagers. Adolescence goes much more smoothly when they learn good values young, believe me. That is my hope for you. Have a good day.

In an interview, she clarified her words: "I try to get a little bit of good sense into the parents' heads."[17]

In complete contrast to French judges, the historical role of judges in the Superior Court is based on their power to make discretionary decisions. Their effectiveness is guaranteed by their dominant social position and by working conditions that give them the time and the resources to deepen their involvement with cases. This model is not set in stone: increasing caseloads and the standards for settling divorces amicably have encouraged new practices to emerge, for both management and conciliation. Nevertheless, the constraints of management in Quebec are a far cry from those in France, and conciliation practices are developing at the margins of regular adjudication. In France, judges have no choice but to act as managers; in Quebec, they still spend most of their work time on ruling-related activities.

Internal Styles of Judicial Practice

These major differences between the judiciaries in the two countries do not mean that professional practice within each judiciary is homogeneous. There are also significant internal variations – in France, because of the heterogeneous nature of the judiciary; in Quebec, because judges' individuality is prized. A comparison of these variations begins with our observation that, in both countries, judges engaged in two opposing ways. Some judges remained distant from the parties, interacting with them as little as possible and appearing as emotionally impassive as they could. Some took an interventionist, proactive stance, speaking with the litigants more than required and seeking to learn more about them. Our main hypothesis for this comparison was based on gender: women judges appeared to be more invested in family law. In France, they tended to remain in family law longer; in Quebec, half of them were former family lawyers. Did this mean that they were more likely than their male counterparts to adopt an interventionist stance, and, if so, did this stance give rise to the same practices on either side of the ocean?

In France, Céline Bessière and Muriel Mille (2014) have shown that many women family judges do adopt this interventionist stance. When speaking of their work, judges reported that they appreciated the opportunity to listen to the parties' points of view and sought to teach about the law during hearings. In this sense, the judges' practice resembled social work: they tried to follow up with cases and find concrete solutions using what little latitude they had (such as ordering psycho-social evaluations in order to investigate child welfare). Such an interventionist stance may result in moralizing with the litigants. It is grounded in psycho-pedagogical principles, such as the importance of a paternal presence, which judges learn in continuing education cycles organized by the National School of Magistrates and, above all, in their experiences as judges in juvenile court. We conclude from this information that it is because so many more women magistrates used to work as juvenile judges that they take this stance: in France, gendered practice is tightly linked to career paths.

Aurélie Vermeer, a twenty-seven-year-old judge, was one example we observed. She sat in a juvenile court before becoming a family judge in Carly and enjoyed the work immensely. In our interview, she mentioned it several times as justification for leaving her "neutral position" to conciliate parties in order to "get to an agreement." In this vein, she recalled a case in which the father, whose ex-wife had left him for a woman, refused to allow her to see their children. According to Vermeer, the mother had become detached from the case; in particular, she had refused to allow a psycho-social evaluation:

> I stayed with this case a long time, even though the lawyers were super angry, they were complaining outside because they were waiting ...

So here I stepped outside my role as purely a family judge, and I felt I had to explain to Madame that there were a certain number of things she needed to understand. And so they got said. It was a pretty painful hearing, but I explained to the mother that she had to understand that for her children it was difficult to accept her sexual orientation, that it raised a lot of questions, and that she had to be patient, and not push too much responsibility onto the father, because even if there had been some influencing of the children, she had to give it time. And, well, you know, I got a mediation agreement for the mother and the children, and simple visitation rights, which the mother hadn't accepted before ... The dad, whether he liked it or not, agreed, since he had been asking that there be no visitation or overnights ... I didn't want the mother to feel that the court had completely left her by the wayside, but she also had to understand that she had some responsibility in the situation, and also that the father understood that you couldn't just sweep the mother out of the way, whatever her life choices were. But that takes time, you see. And I spent an hour on that hearing, even though I schedule hearings every fifteen minutes, but I couldn't get that all squared away in a quarter hour.[18]

In her account, the judge was expressing a heteronormative moral stance. She showed a nascent acceptance of a minority sexual orientation (she prevented this lesbian or bisexual woman from being completely disqualified in her role as a mother) while justifying restricting her rights (mothers who are not allowed to have their children for overnight stays are rare indeed, as we will see further on). As we observed no other similar cases, we cannot draw any conclusions about the attitude of judges toward non-heterosexual parents. In the early 2000s, a study of rulings by the Court of Appeal showed that stereotypes about gay and lesbian parents were an obstacle to their parental rights (Gouron-Mazel 2002). Another such study would be welcome, given recent advances in lesbian, gay, bisexual, transgender, and queer (LGBTQ) parental rights. We have included Vermeer's account here to show that certain judges, who tend to be women and former juvenile court judges, take an interventionist stance with parties and that this stance is underpinned by explicit norms about the family in the name of the importance of conciliation.

Other judges whom we observed – in this case, generally men – also tended to show a certain loquaciousness with parties. In contrast to Vermeer, they did not justify this to us by deploying the norm of conciliation; instead, their words were provocative, bearing witness to the difficulty that these judges have in taking on the role of family judge. Étienne Paletot, who transferred to family court after his local court closed, was the most striking example of this finding. In our interview, he showed a marked aversion to his new function and to being exposed to the litigants' private lives. To a newly separated couple, he declared "it's surprising to have children and then separate a few months later," and he added "you're getting separated four months after you bought a house together. You couldn't be any more inconsistent than that!" (Collectif Onze 2013, 143).[19]

More often, however, we observed negative internal perceptions of the role of family judge manifested in an attitude that was particularly distanced from their work. This stance may be described as bureaucratic in that it declines to personalize the judicial relationship. Terreau, another judge in Marjac, rejected the idea of moralizing with parties, for example. He described this type of distant stance as "sanitized."[20] Highlighting his impartiality and his self-control, he tried to learn as little as possible about family stories, as we saw in the hearing where the woman farmer tried to read the written statement she had prepared. He was careful to comply with the minimal procedural requirements, both in order to hew to managerial norms and to avoid being "invaded" by the private lives of the parties. This bureaucratic distance suggests that the decreasing litigiousness of divorce cases – particularly the tendency not to examine grounds – is not merely a way of protecting the "personal boundaries" of the litigants. It is also a way for judges – particularly those who are not invested in family law – to limit their exposure to private misfortunes.

This distance takes a different form in Quebec: Canadian judges "have the duty to act in a reserved manner,"[21] and, according to the Ethical Principles for Judges of the Canadian Judicial Council, they "must be and should appear to be impartial with respect to their decisions and decision making."[22] It would therefore be unthinkable for a judge in Quebec to speak to parties as sharply as certain French judges do, and the kind of remove described in Terreau's case is thus more common and expected in this context. But, while Terreau's attitude of applying rules impersonally resembled Max Weber's (1978, 975) portrait of a bureaucrat "without anger and passion," judges in Quebec have a judicial model that is specific to countries working in the common law tradition: that of a sphinx looking down from on high. In Quebec, judges remain impartial – and appear impartial – throughout hearings so that they can make the best decisions, arrived at privately and independently, during their deliberations. Here, the remoteness we observed was not a show of submission to the set rules; to the contrary, it was seen as a show of impartiality, one condition for making creative decisions that could become case law. Judges' shows of detachment during interactions with parties could be correlated to their role as independent arbiters.

Although it was broadly accepted in the 1970s, the image of the judge as sphinx is now seen as outdated in terms of doctrine and jurisprudence, and it has been explicitly rejected by the chief justice of Canada himself.[23] It is a vision of judges that is poorly adapted to their work as managers and conciliators. Unsurprisingly, it was mobilized among older male judges: they fit the profile, in terms of age and gender, of what was long the dominant model in the court. This attitude could also be observed among more recently appointed judges – perhaps because they lacked the self-assurance of their more experienced colleagues. In addition to age and experience, social background may also explain this detachment. Albert Savard, a judge from a less privileged and more rural background than many of his fellow judges, could be seen earlier in this chapter emphasizing the importance of impartiality during hearings. He confided to us "there were no lawyers in my family, and we weren't very wealthy."[24] He was one of the few judges to have worked full-time before entering law school, and he subsequently worked as a lawyer in a small town. His practice hewed to the most literal definition of the role, which seemed to us to be linked to the fact that his resources were more institutional than social.

This hypothesis is borne out by comparison with judges who took a more interventionist stance during hearings. For the most part, this group was made up of men of at least sixty years of age and some women of the same generation. Their common trait was that they did not practise family law during their time as lawyers. They could be distinguished from the preceding group by their elite social backgrounds and, in particular, by the presence of older family members working in the legal profession. Their interventionist stance was rooted in personal and often inherited resources, which raised their confidence in dealing with cases.

Philippe Nadeau was one such judge whom we interviewed. At sixty-five, he had sat on the bench of the Superior Court for twenty years, and his father was a judge before him. During our conversation, he underlined his lack of formal training in family law, emphasizing the personal resources he had had to mobilize in order to formulate rulings. He recalled that, when he presided for the first time before a well-known family lawyer, he said to her, "you know, the only experience I have in matrimonial law is with my own divorce." He did not regard this lack of experience as detrimental, however. In his view, family law was not a highly technical field, requiring mostly that one "show a lot of good sense." To him, this personalization, rendered legitimate by his social background, justified his interactions with parties in divorce cases:

> It often happens that at the end, independent of my ruling, I give them advice. "If I were you, I would do this, this, or this ... Yesterday midmorning ... I took the opportunity because I felt things were going really badly, in terms of the children, so I always give my usual sermon. I told them, "I feel like I'm changing out of my robes to put on my clerical collar and give you a sermon" ... but you never know. When it comes from someone who has authority and who is objective, I always hope that it will have some effect and that maybe their relationship will improve after that. [25]

This judge, with his background and experience, jokingly evoked the image of a priest as possible inspiration for his practice. The analogy made sense to him, having grown up in an era when the Catholic Church still played a central role as a community authority (Dumont 1993). To borrow a category from political sociology, his stance may be compared to that of the *honoratioren* (notables): protected by his extensive capital, often inherited, and by genuine social prestige, he felt invested with the capability and the legitimacy to act on behalf of the common good (Weber 1978).

Pinard-Garon's earlier words to the young parents in Albanel are another example of this moralistic interventionist stance, based on personal character traits and on social authority conferred by her function. The "paternal" – even paternalistic – figure identified in the 1970s in countries with legal systems rooted in the common law tradition remains strong as it is perceived to be compatible both with the standard of impartiality and with the mission of conciliator (Ehrmann 1976, 91). However, it still differs from the kind of interventionism that we observed among French judges, in that the Quebecois judges described here speak little to parties during hearings, reserving their moralizing words for the end.

Avoidance of family, the judge as sphinx, and paternalist interventionism were all traits we noted in the majority of judges. Other judges, mostly women, did engage in other types of interventionist behaviour, which differed both from the paternalism of their colleagues in Quebec and from the psycho-social attitudes of their French counterparts. These judges approached their function as experts. They were highly invested in their work and often undertook coordinating roles within the family courts or participated in training new judges and in updating the lengthy unpublished handbook to which judges refer for comments on legislation and jurisprudence (it comes in at over five hundred pages). Some also sat on the Pan-Canadian Family Law Committee, which brings together representatives of courts from across the Canadian provinces and territories. Finally, they were often responsible for what were seen as the most complex family cases, particularly those that raised relatively new questions in the field of family law.

Unlike non-specialists who, like Nadeau, felt that family law was a matter of "basic good sense," these judges emphasized advances in jurisprudence – to which they referred extensively in their long rulings – as well as the financial skills that must be mobilized to deal with such cases and to come to rulings that are likely to contribute to case law. Madeleine Lagacé was one such judge, and the week-long divorce trial of a millionaire ex-banker we observed provides an example of this type of case. After two days spent hearing evidence from real estate and financial court appraisers, she expected her decision to be long and complex. Before she could make it, she had to assess the couple's net worth and update it based on their official separation date, using the appraisers' conflicting evidence. Ultimately, she handed down a long ruling (sixty-six pages) that would upend the parties' lives, enjoining the family, who had been living in a European capital for several years, to return to Quebec in order to adjust their lifestyle to the father's reduced income.[26]

The interventionist stance of these judges was most perceptible in their writing. Psycho-social framing was present in the way they dealt with cases, and it even played a central role when it came to child custody. But it was expressed more in written rulings than in oral hearings, during which technical questions and procedural points were much more common. More than anything, the economic barriers to access to the courts meant that these expert judges spent much more time dealing with complex financial questions than their counterparts in France. The fact that these judges with family law expertise are mostly women can be explained by two connected factors. For some, specializing in family law in the Superior Court was an extension of their prior professional experience in the law, as they had already specialized in that branch. Because of the gendered differentiation of specialization in the practice of law, as I will discuss in the following section, two-thirds of these former family law attorneys are women. Nevertheless, not all judges who work primarily in family law cases specialized in them during their careers practising law. Some of them worked in administrative law or in various other fields related to civil law. One judge, who was appointed about a decade ago, firmly believed that gender stereotypes, and even gender assignment, played a major role in women's over-representation in family law:

> I didn't sign up for the family chamber. It wasn't in my professional background, before I was on the bench. And once you're there, little by little, no rush, you cordon us off into fields where it is mostly women ... [describing what a colleague says about women judges] "You're so perceptive, you're so human ... You're so diplomatic, you are so careful ... These are such important rights for society, we have

TABLE 3 Seven styles of judicial practice

		Intervention		Distance	
France	Social	Majority women, former juvenile court judges	Bureaucratic	Majority men	
	Provocative	Men			
Quebec	Paternalistic	Majority non-specialist, wealthy, older men	Avoidance of family law	Former criminal lawyers (men and women)	
	Expert	Majority women specialists	Sphinx	Majority non-specialist, non-upper-class men	

to put our best qualities into them because we're changing people's lives, and you have the emotional intelligence, the approach, the tact."[27]

Table 3 shows how institutional roles in different countries shape internal variations within the judiciary. Where they fall on the spectrum of practice between detachment and intervention affects judges' attitudes during hearings and what they invest in their writing. In France, as in Quebec, contrasts remain between the practices of men and women judges. These cannot be explained with some illusory statement of essential femininity or masculinity but, rather, by the gendered differentiation of career paths and the gendered scripts that characterize discourse surrounding family law, a field that remains markedly feminine and relatively undervalued.

Diverse Bars, Diversifying Practice

These gendered mechanisms are also at play in the work of lawyers. Before discussing them, let me note that the morphological differences between the two jurisdictions are less significant than they are in their judiciaries. Of course, because lawyers occupy most public, private, and non-profit functions relating to the law in Quebec, they are more numerous on the North American side. However, as Table 4 shows, qualification for entry into the two groups (law school and then bar admittance), average age (around forty), and sex ratios (male-female parity), as well as pay and seniority disparities that leave women in second place, are all similar in the two countries. Within the field of

TABLE 4 The bar in France and Quebec: Indicators for comparison

	France[a]	*Quebec*[b]
Number	69,900 (1 per 1,000 inhabitants)	28,500 (3 per 1,000 inhabitants)
Percentage of women	56% Among survey subjects: 36 out of 48 (75%)	55% Among survey subjects: 16 out of 25 (64%)
Mean age	45 years	45 years
Training	Bachelor of laws, examinations, bar admission course, bar certification	Bachelor of laws, examinations, bar admission course, bar exam
Annual salary	Women: €51,100 (mean) Men: €100,700 (mean)	Women: $90,000–$110,000 (median) Men: $110,000–$130,000 (median)
Style of practice	36% individual practice 33% employees 30% partners	Private practice: 32% individual practice 37% employees 31% partners
Specialization in family law	25% (personal and family law; multiple choices possible)	9% (personal and family law; one choice possible)

Sources:

a Défenseur des droits, 2018, https://www.cnb.avocat.fr/fr/les-chiffres-cles-de-la-profession-davocat (the annual report of the French constitutional authority in charge of legal that ensures respect for rights and freedoms).

b Barreau du Québec 2015, 2022.

family law, heterogeneity was another commonality between the two jurisdictions. Since the 1970s, the increasing incidence of divorce has driven up demand for legal services and led to greater segmentation of the market for legal counsel in the United States as well as in France and Quebec (Heinz and Laumann 1982).

This diversity is immediately perceptible among the field's limited ranks: the number of lawyers advertising as family law specialists is quite low in proportion to the number of family law cases heard by the courts. Because the field is perceived as being reasonably non-technical, and because many cases are resolved relatively quickly (particularly in comparison to criminal cases), many lawyers in Quebec practise family law alongside other types of law that fall under the broader category of civil law in Quebec. In France, they take on other cases concerning social welfare, juvenile rights, or legal guardianship. Lawyers end up working on family cases for a wide variety of reasons, sometimes because there is a high demand or sometimes because a client in a criminal case or a business deal has asked for help with a divorce – accounting for all of them is beyond the scope of this chapter.

My interest here was in understanding how certain members of the bar ended up practising family law for all or most of the time. I analyzed the impact of this degree of specialization on professional practice, with regard to what is expected of bar lawyers in the era of no-fault divorce. To what extent do they engage in emerging practices of out-of-court dispute resolution? How much time do they continue to spend in the courtroom? Here, a spectrum of practice emerged, stretching from negotiation to trial. Where a lawyer fell on this spectrum depended on the lawyer and, in particular, on her or his gender, bearing in mind that women make up the majority of the "family bar." In England and Australia, the discourse of political decision makers (Thornton 2007) and of professional associations (Webley 2011) often associates mediation with a "fictive feminine" – assigning it qualities that are commonly attributed to women – and litigation with an "imagined masculine" – assigning it traits commonly attributed to men. We will explore what can be learned about the gendered nature of career building and professional practice from the work of lawyers in France and Quebec.

A Feminized Specialty

Family law is one of the least prestigious fields of the law and pays much less than other fields do. In Quebec, family lawyers earned an average annual income of sixty-three thousand dollars in 2007 (Barreau du Québec/Centre interuniversitaire de recherché en analyse des organisations 2009, 48). The same year, criminal lawyers and lawyers working in the broader field of civil law earned a little over eighty thousand dollars, while labour lawyers and trade lawyers earned upwards of one hundred thousand dollars annually. The average hourly rate of a family lawyer is $156, compared with $233 for a corporate lawyer. France differs from Quebec in that family lawyers generally charge a flat fee instead of an hourly rate. The widespread use of legal aid payment mandates limits the earning potential of lawyers working in the field. Only immigration law is less lucrative (Défenseur des droits 2018, 36).

Low pay and the predominance of small firms both help to explain why family law came in second to last when one thousand members of the Quebec bar association were asked to rank sixteen legal specializations in order of prestige (Kay 2009, 919). This may also be due to the fact that family lawyers work for private individuals, and their practice remains oriented toward the courtroom. By contrast, more prestigious specializations such as corporate law tend to be used by companies to provide counsel rather than for litigation (Karpik 2003). As is true in other professions, the low prestige of family law corresponds to a high presence of women in this field (Cacouault-Bitaud 2001). Why do more women than men specialize in it? Below, our interviews with Claire Robin, a French lawyer in her early forties, and Denise Morneau, a lawyer practising in Quebec who is twenty-five years her senior, shed light on the gendered mechanisms at work in the legal profession:

> For nine years, I worked in a general practice firm, and because of the person I was working with, Maître[28] Dupont-Bernard, I pretty rapidly began working in family law. Even though, in the beginning, it was criminal law I had training in ... *So your intention was to practise criminal law?* I admit I like it. My intention was to do that, but since I ended up in a general practice firm, working with someone who did only family law, or practically only that ... I had more cases for

her. And then I moved to the firm I'm with now. My partners wanted a woman to take over family law. So that they could keep advancing in their fields. So that clients would know who to go to. Now they know that they come to me for family law, and to T. for construction law, or contract law. We complement each other.[29]

— Claire Robin, lawyer in Besson, in practice since 2006

My practice is essentially – maybe 98 percent – family law ... I also really like the human side. Columns of numbers, corporate law, that didn't really speak to me, bankruptcy and things like that, and I did a bit of criminal law too. It wasn't necessarily a conscious process, it was a bit unintentional, over time. I realized that I really liked family law, and then it was as if I kind of neglected the other fields ... Sometimes, a gentleman would have an appointment with Mr. L., who was the senior lawyer in the office ... There were just three of us back then: Mr. L., Mr. C., and me. I was the youngest, and Mr. L. would say to the guy, "well, now, Ms. Morneau will be taking care of your case because I don't do that, or she's the specialist with that sort of thing."[30]

— Denise Morneau, lawyer in Albanel, in practice since 1977

At a generation's remove from each other, the two women entered the profession in fairly different ways. Morneau, who was older, came from a small town. She had been working in a nearby firm ever since graduating from law school and passing the bar. Robin, who was younger, grew up in a much larger city, studied law for many years in three different cities, and held a juris doctor degree in criminal law.

The first point that their career paths had in common was that both returned home to practise in small, general practice firms. Morneau was hired by a firm run by men and, at the encouragement of her "mentors," progressively began to specialize in family law. Robin worked with a well-known family lawyer in Besson who was the local pioneer in the practice of collaborative law profiled in Chapter 1. A year before our interview, she had come on as a partner in a firm with two male partners of the same age, another general law practice located on the outskirts of Besson, and, at the time we spoke to her, she had become "the specialist" in family law there.

Some of our women interview subjects highlighted their interest since childhood in "helping others," implying a significant degree of gendered socialization in their early years. For Morneau and Robin, this socialization occurred later on: their specialization in family law was the result of a gradual adaptation to the professional possibilities that opened up to them as they moved through their careers. Encouragement from older colleagues, while in neither case a strong constraining factor, was nevertheless determinant for both women: "No one said, 'Denise, you're the only woman in the office; there are four of us, three men and a woman. You go do the family law.' No, it happened kind of naturally, because I liked it," Morneau explained to us. As Robin recalled, "I was the first woman to join the firm, and family law got handed to me naturally."[31] Both women used the same word: "naturally."

Put another way, the feminization of family law reifies the gender stereotypes that women are better qualified to deal with "emotional" and "affective" issues (these adjectives were used in interviews in both France and Quebec). These gender scripts are not simply imposed from the outside: in both cases, they were mobilized by the women lawyers themselves. Both Morneau and Robin underlined the satisfaction that their practice brought to them and emphasized their ability to listen to their clients, which they perceived as necessary to alleviate conflict and achieve satisfactory outcomes. Both women also reported feeling satisfied with their specialty. While it might have given them lower professional status than some of their male counterparts, their status nevertheless remained higher than their women counterparts working in general practice or as associate lawyers. Robin acquired her professional expertise working alongside an experienced professional and was able to use this experience to achieve the senior status of partner,[32] which Morneau had also achieved.

How do professional "success stories" such as these two women share compare with those of the smaller number of men practising family law? The average annual earnings of women lawyers in family and personal law in France are lower than those of their male counterparts (Défenseur des droits 2018, 36). By contrast, women family lawyers in Quebec tend to charge a higher hourly rate than their male counterparts (averaging $159 per hour compared with $148 per hour for men), according to the Barreau du Québec/Centre interuniversitaire de recherché en analyse des organisations (2009, 62). When we spoke to her, Morneau described family law as a "pink ghetto," suggesting that women family lawyers might be isolated from the rest of the profession but that they could make a comfortable place for themselves within that space. Can we infer from this that the glass ceiling is somewhat thinner in family law than in other specialties?

You will recall that, in France, some women lawyers, by promoting collaborative law, have carved out a niche in alternative forms of conflict resolution in order to reach wealthier clients while, at the same time, deploying a form of professional expertise as an alternative to adjudication by the court. These lawyers are one force behind upmarket segmentation of family legal counsel: by promoting these forms of expertise, they are able to advance their cause as well as their careers. We spoke with Cécile Martin-Dubois, a forty-year-old lawyer in Paris who was one of the most active members in the field of collaborative law in France and a frequent presenter at workshops and conferences for non-profit and professional groups. The daughter of a doctor and an academic, married to a corporate lawyer, she began her career working in criminal law with a future president of the bar. She stopped working for a time after the birth of her first child and, two years later, founded her own firm, specializing in family law, while training in collaborative law.

At the time of our interview, her firm, which is located in one of the most elegant neighbourhoods in Paris, billed €250 per hour (by comparison, at the same age, Robin charged an hourly fee of €180). Martin-Dubois acknowledged that she did not follow the "model" of collaborative law down to the letter but that she did spend a great deal of time networking, both in political circles and in the inner circles of the legal profession, to advocate for this form of practice.[33] It is too early to draw any firm or definitive conclusions about how successful this feminine enterprise really is. If these women lawyers have achieved enviable positions in the field of family law, are they recognized and known outside their specialty?

In Quebec, women clearly have the "upper end of the bar" when it comes to family law, in terms of both prestige and remuneration, and they hold positions of responsibility outside their field. When we spoke with Marie-Line Gittelman, one of Montreal's best-known women lawyers, she noted that, after she was admitted to the bar in the early 1980s, she was not hired by the tax law firm that she had hoped to work for – she believed they passed her over because she was pregnant. The daughter of two lawyers, she quickly made the choice to found her own firm, specializing in family law. She practised solo for a decade or so, then took on a younger woman lawyer as a partner. By the time of our interview, her firm had grown to be one of the biggest family law firms in Montreal (with about a dozen lawyers). In the 2000s, her firm was heavily involved in constitutional cases that sought to make family law less discriminatory toward gay and lesbian couples. This shift, along with her firm's involvement in a high-profile divorce case, brought Gittelman a certain degree of notoriety: she began hosting a television show and published a much-publicized autobiography. Gittelman was brought up in English-speaking circles in Montreal, but, after her work, she began receiving widespread attention and found a place for herself among the French-speaking elite, inviting influential law professors to her dinner parties and representing a former politician as one of her clients. She reported billing $660 per hour and maintaining a pro bono practice,[34] but, like Martin-Dubois, she did not take legal aid cases.[35]

Gittelman was one of approximately ten legal "stars" in Quebec who were nearly all from Montreal and had three traits in common: first, legal expertise, attested to by their involvement in cases in the court of appeals or the Supreme Court that helped contribute to case law or to change jurisprudence; second, public advocacy in support of social movements (women or disadvantaged groups especially), usually by lending their voices as experts to public authorities; and, third, public renown and media attention, thanks to public rankings (such as the online publication *Best Lawyers in Canada*) and television coverage. For them, the "pink ghetto" can be a lucrative place: from 2015 to 2017, the president of the Barreau du Québec was a family lawyer, a partner in a specialized law firm in Quebec City. Moreover, as we have seen, a significant proportion of women judges in Quebec are former family lawyers.

There were major differences between these Quebec women lawyers and their French counterparts. First, there could be no comparison between the notoriety of the former and the latter: the women lawyers in Quebec had public profiles, whereas the women lawyers in France, above all, were active in professional circles. Family law practice in Quebec is far more politicized: the women described in this group saw the law as a vector for social change, engaging in cause lawyering that is common practice in North America (Sarat and Scheingold 1998). The impact of the North American context, in which women lawyers have mobilized strongly in favour of women's rights and have politicized the issue of gender in their professional roles, can be felt all the way to Montreal (Menkel-Meadow 1985). French lawyers have also taken on an advocacy role, but mostly for LGBTQ issues and/or issues of violence against women, and we did not encounter any of these women in our study on "ordinary" separations.

On both sides of the Atlantic, these lawyers did have two points in common. First, their careers were "feminine" in the sense that motherhood played a role in their choice of specialty – not in terms of its content but, rather, in terms of the working conditions that it made possible, such as in smaller organizations where peer pressure was lower than in big law firms (Bessy 2016, 212). Second, as is true in the United States, they achieved professional success by seeking out a wealthy clientele, which contrasts with the diversity of clients present in most family law firms (Mather, McEwen, and Maiman 2001). In both places, the prestige and the solvency of both lawyer and client fed into one another.

To Plead or to Negotiate?

As for judges, the question of what impact these social and professional characteristics have on work practice deserves to be raised. In both contexts of our study, the reputations of practising lawyers – that is, the ways in which they speak about each other – were a polarized phenomenon. On one end of the spectrum, we found those who enjoy courtroom battles; on the other, we found those who prefer negotiating outside court. But, while French lawyers must bring all of their cases before a judge, this is not true in Quebec. We could therefore expect that national context would frame the spectrum of legal practice.

In France, until 2017, hearings were an unavoidable part of divorce, meaning that lawyers' activities were necessarily shaped by them: their schedules were defined by court dates. In our observations, family courts nearly inevitably ran late, either because judges were held up in hearings that lasted longer than they were supposed to or because lawyers working on the case could not appear at the same time (due to hearings scheduled at conflicting times, for example). That said, these hearings were brief, led by judges, and relatively informal. As a result, lawyers spent little time preparing their clients, instead seeking to clarify their situations to give additional weight to their closing remarks and statements. A day-long observation of two women lawyers as they shuttled between their offices and the courthouse illustrates the proportion of time taken up by hearings in their caseloads. The morning was spent with Caroline Sourice, a forty-year-old lawyer working full time in a small firm specializing in family law in Besson, in an appointment with a long-standing client, a doctor in his sixties. He was concerned about his ex-wife challenging the shared custody of their twelve-year-old daughter. "It's eating me up, you have no idea," he remarked to Sourice, as she reviewed the rulings in his file. She questioned him at length about his daughter's school and extracurricular activities and his medical practice. As she wrapped up their appointment an hour and a half later, Sourice let him know that a hearing had been scheduled for March 8, two weeks hence. "Should I dress up for it?" the doctor inquired. "As usual," she replied. As he prepared to depart, she quickly went over the upcoming hearing: "First we're going to plead. Then, if you want to say something, you can. But we'll need to talk it over before the hearing. You shouldn't say anything that can be held against you."

That afternoon, I met her associate, Béatrice Arnou, also a lawyer in her forties, at the courthouse.[36] She was appearing with a client she had never met but whose case Sourice had reviewed with her that morning. In the courthouse lobby, on Sourice's suggestion, Arnou suggested family mediation to the client, but neither he nor his new wife, who was accompanying him that day, seemed enthusiastic about the prospect. A few minutes later, a family judge, who was barely thirty years old, received them along with the opposing party. Arnou, since her client was the claimant, delivered the opening plea, explaining that the younger son, who was fourteen years old, had previously wanted to leave his father's home but now wished to return. Arnou then presented the father's claims: he shared physical custody of the younger son and had full physical custody of the older son, who had requested it during his hearing. She indicated that the child welfare worker appointed to the case had recommended mediation and noted that the mother was not contributing to school costs. She concluded by saying "I would like to petition for family mediation. We are requesting to extend the current provision until the mediation has been concluded. To open the lines of dialogue."

The respondent's lawyer gave a much briefer statement. She opened by expressing her annoyance that Arnou had not submitted her remarks and contested the claim that shared custody had resumed, requesting that her client be rewarded sole custody of the younger son. Arnou's client spoke up when the judge and the ex-wife's lawyer turned to the question of his and his partner's income, insisting that he had not earned the two thousand euros that they alleged was his monthly income. The judge then questioned the parents for five minutes to ascertain whether shared custody had resumed and whether the mother agreed to award full physical custody of the older child to the father. As soon as it was clear that the mother agreed, the judge brought the trial to a close, just twenty minutes after it had begun.[37]

What can we take away from this day of observation? First, judges are not alone in having to "manage the load" in France. Many lawyers must also deal with myriad cases at once, often discontinuously, which requires them to rapidly recall key details of each case, check whether anything about them has changed, and sometimes pass them on to their colleagues. Unavoidable time spent at court is not limited to hearings. A great deal happens outside hearings as well: conversations may reveal that someone is absent or running late; extra people may show up expecting to participate in the hearing (such as the new wife in the scenario described above); demands change; agreements are challenged;

litigation is resolved at the last minute. According to a process well known in the sociology of professions, lawyers must face uncertainty in their relations with colleagues and clients (Evetts 2003). Second, hearings in family courtrooms do not have the ritualized, performative features of trials in places such as Quebec. Litigants may show up uninvited or address each other. They interact rather informally, although this does not mean that the process is not governed by certain norms. Although parties are expected to remain calm, to keep quiet when asked, and to offer clarification when it is requested, lawyers rarely spell out these norms to their clients: Arnou offered no advice to her client before they entered the courtroom; Source was vague with her client.

Rhetorical or physical flourishes of speech were rare in the hearings we observed: judicial ritual in France is not showy. Statements were brief and generally consisted of a factual overview of the case, highlighting the points that were most important from a procedural standpoint rather than offering an elaborate history of a family's case. Legal references were unusual, and jurisprudence was mobilized only rarely. Concision and clarity, as well as the ability to respond to the opposing party or the judge's questions in real time, were the main skills that lawyers had to demonstrate. Finally, our observations shed some light on the perception of alternative dispute resolution as a pathway to separation: given her client's reluctance, it was unlikely that he would follow up on Arnou's petition for referral to mediation, even if the judge were to grant it. The day after these observations, in an interview, Source described a meeting with a client who had come for a collaborative law session: "You saw he wasn't very talkative. And he doesn't really want to do it. He doesn't say much. Really, he isn't ready ... He says his ex-wife asked for the collaborative law session. He's waiting to see what happens."[38] In her opinion, collaborative law could only be practised with people "who do not seem to have any mental health issues, who are able to reason, who demonstrate understanding." She added that the cost of the collaborative law process came to twenty-five hundred euros before tax, compared with twelve hundred euros for a classic divorce by mutual consent.[39]

To enhance their professional networks, bypass frequent court appearances, and avoid sometimes acrimonious conflicts between ex-spouses, more and more lawyers are attempting to expand their roles beyond court litigation. But as Source pointed out to us, mediation and collaborative law require clients who are capable of speaking before others, with a basic mastery of the legitimate language, both of which are contingent on gender and social position (Bourdieu 1993b). Alternative dispute resolution is, in other words, a new way for lawyers to practise social selection among clients. However, these approaches have not yet gained wide popularity in France. Among those people we interviewed, it appeared that this could be attributed to the fact that few lawyers specializing in family law have taken an interest in them as well as to the fact that the judiciary has remained the central figure in the imaginations of certain respondents.

Collaborative law is also a relatively elite practice in Quebec, although it was established earlier there: many French lawyers we spoke to mentioned that it was in fact "the Canadians," as they call the Quebecois, who had helped to train them. At the same time, another alternative to divorce hearings has already been institutionalized in Canada alongside this relatively "niche" market: family mediation. This alternative was presented by those we interviewed as universally accessible, in that it is state financed and supported by the bar association. Hélène Meadows, a Montreal lawyer who has practised mediation since the 1980s and collaborative law since the 2000s, explained the socio-economic differentiation at work in the two approaches to us in this way: "When both members of a couple make thirty thousand dollars a year and they have two children, I don't propose collaborative law; I immediately advise them to go for mediation."[40] To what extent has the institutionalization of family mediation changed the professional practices of lawyers, and what impact does this have on hearings, which are not only more unusual than in France but also more demanding?

Morneau, who has been practising family mediation since 2003, estimated that it made up one-quarter of her practice. She thought that it represented a positive change since she was admitted to the bar in 1977:

> A lot fewer [cases] go to trial now; we work out a lot more of them. Mediation helps with that, too. When people come to mediation, that's frequently something that gets mentioned: they don't want to be involved in a contested divorce and go fight it out in court, because

so often that leaves scars, huh? Difficult court cases, no matter the ruling that comes out of it, I think it leaves a bad taste in our clients' mouths, and they don't necessarily want to go through that two or three more times. That's what makes mediation an interesting option, too. People are aware of that, deep down, that if they both just take things with a little grain of salt, they might be able to reach an agreement more easily, and that will be easier to live with or accept than if it's handed down by the judge, who, however competent they may be, are still a third party. Plus, people know they get free hours of mediation.[41]

Morneau's words echoed the American family lawyers interviewed in the 1990s by Austin Sarat and William Felstiner (1995, 148), who also thought that an out-of-court settlement made possible by mediation was preferable to going to court. In both contexts, lawyers deemed it more flexible, more predictable, and less costly, as well as ensuring that this major life decision stays in the hands of the separating couple and not a third party. Morneau mentioned it as an advantage for herself too, in that it meant fewer trips to court and allowed her to limit her encounters with another Albanel lawyer who handled a large portion of family law cases in town and whose practices she found aggressive.

The appropriation of mediation by many lawyers specializing in family law was, for many, a way of distancing themselves from the image of the belligerent counsel. At the same time, it kept legal professionals central to the separation and divorce process, even outside the courtroom and even as the number of cases going to trial diminishes. Several lawyers argued for a legalized version of mediation, making a clear distinction between mediation practised by legal professionals and mediation practised by professionals trained in the field of psychology or social work. They reasoned that mediation with lawyers was "safer" for ex-spouses since it was more likely to ensure that their rights would be respected and that their agreements would be homologated by judges or special clerks, thereby ensuring the possibility of legal recourse later on if need be. They also recommended having agreements reviewed by legal professionals, whom they saw as better trained with regard to financial considerations.

In our interview with Pierre Côté, a sixty-year-old notary who had been an accredited mediator since 1992, he expressed regret at how few notaries had entered the field of mediation, meaning that the market had been left almost entirely to lawyers. He thought that notaries, with their specialization in property law, were more competent than lawyers to deal with the financial side of divorce. He spoke of this aspect in much greater detail than the lawyers in our study: "In mediation, you can take the opportunity to help people with planning how to maximize their revenue; we look at health insurance, life insurance, college savings, child life insurance."[42] As the words of this experienced notary show, the institutionalization of mediation has helped to expand the jurisdiction of legal professionals. By taking on this role, both lawyers and notaries are adding to the range of services they offer clients. Indeed, among small firms specializing in family law, mediation has helped to transform the profession overall, moving it away from costly and uncertain court proceedings and toward negotiation, a phenomenon that has been well documented in the case of corporate law (Dezalay 1990). Rather than hybridizing professions and practices, mediation was a complementary activity for the professionals with whom we spoke and, in some cases, even contributed to the compartmentalization of their approaches. Over the course of two mediation sessions that we observed with Morneau, she remained firmly in her role as a lawyer: although she offered legal counsel rather than court arguments, her approach to separation was hardly a psychological one.[43]

By contrast, what happens when lawyers appear in court? Let us recall that the two ends of our spectrum of practice – out-of-court settlements versus divorce trials – are linked by a continuum that includes everything from agreements signed without a hearing to short, uncontested hearings where judges and lawyers discuss cases among themselves. All along the spectrum and throughout the adjudication process, professionals remain in the dominant position, while non-professionals are held at a distance. In contrast to France, public and private legal professionals in Quebec frequently encounter each other without the parties. The preliminary hearing rolls are reserved for lawyers, which is a problem for people who choose to appear without representation. Parties are allowed to attend uncontested hearings but rarely do. "Spontaneous" speech of the kind observed in Besson is unthinkable: they may express themselves only if invited to by a judge or a lawyer. As we have seen, judicial ritual in Quebec is far more formal than it is in France and far more demanding in terms of language and behaviour. In this context, lawyers must assure that non-professionals adhere to these strict codes of interaction. It is up to them, not the judges, to "teach the client role" (Lipsky 1980, 61) and to call them to order if they do not adhere to behavioural norms, as can be seen in the following hearing. The parties in this day-long hearing regarding the custody of their four children are a craftsman in his forties and his wife, who worked with him. Once the judge, Jean Dumoulin, has arrived, the clerk calls the case by number and says "let us proceed," inviting the lawyers to identify themselves, which they stand to do. As she is raising her right hand "to swear to tell the whole truth," the woman bends down slightly. Her lawyer immediately cuts her off to remind her to straighten up: "You will answer directly to His Honour the Judge."

As the morning wears on, the man becomes more and more agitated. He shifts in his chair, passes notes to his lawyer. When the woman testifies that their accountant advised her to set aside the disability allowance she receives for their children "to keep it safe," he sighs noisily. The judge intervenes: "Please remain calm." The man immediately apologizes, and the lawyer adds "I'll explain to him," gesturing at him to calm down. The judge, who is sixty and has been on the bench for sixteen years, is directing his remark as much to the lawyer as he is to the man – she should do a better job keeping her client in line. Jean Dumoulin says little to the parties but takes a sententious tone when addressing the lawyers. He chides the man's lawyer several times during the cross-examination: "Madame is having a terrible time concentrating. We are not here to torture her." Confronted with photographs of the family kitchen she would like to enter as evidence, the judge asks ironically whether parental competence "is measured based on the ability to clean the counter? If I had to award custody because the other party didn't do the dishes ... "

In the middle of the afternoon, the woman's lawyer presents her case briefly and factually, arguing that her client is "the dominant parental figure, the centre, the heart of this family." The man's lawyer opens his argument with facts ("Monsieur put bread on the table") but goes on to present the case law for shared custody. The judge becomes irritated by the first decision of the Court of Appeal: "Everyone knows it but not everyone interprets it in the same way." Shortly thereafter, the lawyer cites one of Jean Dumoulin's own decisions: "I draw your attention to paragraph 37, which is a small gem." Half amused, half annoyed, the judge retorts: "Well, you can say that again ... Did you read paragraph 38 while you were at it? The parties had agreed to shared custody [unlike the parties in this case]." The lawyer does not push things any further, and the hearing is rapidly brought to a close.[44]

This account illustrates the wide-ranging role of lawyers in Quebec: in addition to ensuring that institutional norms are followed, they must pose the proper questions to their clients as well as to the opposing parties and any witnesses that may be called (in this case, a bank officer, a school principal, a neighbour, and a friend). Each hearing ends with a closing argument from each side. These are often much longer than those in France and require lawyers to mobilize any applicable jurisprudence. All of this takes place under the judge's gaze and, as we saw, may be subject to the judge's sometimes dry remarks. In the above quotation, the paternalistic stance described earlier in this chapter extended not only to the laypeople but also to the members of the bar.

Put briefly, relations between judges and lawyers in Quebec are far more asymmetrical than they are in France. In France, any criticism that judges may level at lawyers carries far less weight, due to their lower social status and their institutional role. In Quebec, going to court not only means dealing with the uncertainty of how the judge will rule, but it also means confronting the legal hierarchy. "We're jacks, not kings, you know. It's not that judges are necessarily more intelligent than us folks, but you have to respect them," observed François Charland, a lawyer with nearly forty years of experience, who had dealt with a large portion of family cases in Albanel.[45] In the course of our observations, it was easy to see that out-of-court dispute resolution felt more comfortable both to the clients and to the lawyers themselves. Judges may often call younger and/or less experienced lawyers into line when they think these lawyers are asking "leading" questions of their witnesses, for example, which may diminish their authority in the eyes of their clients.

A minority of lawyers nevertheless described the value they continued to place on the role of litigation in separation and divorce. Charland was one of them: "I argue, I argue, I argue – much more than the others, I think," he said. With time, he told us, he had learned to "adjust to the judge," forging a reputation as a fighter, which had won him many clients. This attitude reflected several things: his age (he entered the bar before mediation became widespread); his gender (this was evident in his style, expressed in jokes with clients about cars, which one might describe as virile); and the local market. In his small town, where few people had a great deal of cultural capital, his type of court presence was in high demand.

In Montreal, "star" lawyers advocating for the rights of women or disadvantaged groups were another group who called attention to the value of the courtroom, albeit for different reasons. In contrast to the opinions of most lawyers with whom we spoke, they criticized the compromises that resulted from out-of-court settlements. In bowing to the norm of non-contested divorce, they argued, women may accept arrangements to their disadvantage, whereas court proceedings offer a range of far more powerful tools (court appraisers, witnesses, and so on) that force men to reveal their assets. Taking a case to court has its financial cost, as these lawyers did not hesitate to remind their clients, but it may well be in their interests. Elisabeth Buckley is one such lawyer. An advocate for feminist legal reform in Quebec since the 1980s, she works in a small and specialized Montreal firm that bills four hundred dollars per hour. For the most part, the firm defends older women who have spent a great deal of time and effort supporting the careers of their husbands. Buckley was strongly in favour of court adjudication:

> Everyone is happy to avoid conflict, but when there's no conflict, it is to the detriment of spousal support. [*Frowns.*] It's not necessarily the best thing. I've seen judges say to women, "you know, if you don't settle, you're going to spend two years in court, it's going to be emotionally difficult." It's all to encourage them not to seek spousal support ... I think that if you did a comparative study with

> mediation agreements, you'd see that child and spousal support are lower, much lower than what the court awards.[46]

In the face of stereotyped representations of feminine practice oriented toward conciliation and care, and male practice focused on competition and refusing to compromise, our study offers a more nuanced perspective. It was able to confirm that there are gender differences in practice while highlighting the unequal ways in which careers are built and the different styles of professional practice. In Quebec, in cases where the client had the resources and the lawyer had the political convictions, lawyers had an almost gladiatorial attitude toward their practice of the law: Marie-Line Gittelman described herself as "a soldier heading to war" when pleading a family-related constitutional case.

***

In France and in Quebec, public policy as it relates to marital dissolutions rests largely on the shoulders of legal professionals, who enjoy elevated social standing and strong (if variable) links with public authorities. The agenda of non-litigated divorce has helped to evolve their roles and, to a certain extent, has increased the number of women in the profession, although this trend is still limited among judges of the Superior Court, which is the most elite of these groups. From one country to another, from one group to another, and within each of these groups, legal professionals appropriate the mandate to conciliate in different ways, depending not only on national oversight of professional jurisdictions but also on career paths and local work configurations.

One thing that all of these legal professionals have in common is that they work on and in the private lives of separated and divorced people. These professionals give legal form to family stories as they use the law to organize the outcomes of separations. In face-to-face interactions and in the writing of their casework, these professionals have many opportunities to comment on, or even judge, the lifestyles of laypeople. Some of their practice is rooted in a pedagogical approach to the law, which can foster a better understanding of norms and procedures, but their practices may also include social norms that go far beyond what the law requires. Public policy on individuals has a "dual dimension of order and benevolence, of coercion and integration" (Fassin 2015, 2). In the following chapter, we will see how these two dimensions interact as professionals encounter the public.

The Legal Encounter as a Situated Nexus of Power

3

One afternoon in February 2016, I joined lawyer Claire Robin in the lower court in Besson to sit in on her hearings: her first client of the day was filing for divorce by mutual consent. Although both lawyer and client were in their early forties, he appeared older than her, and his relaxed style of dress contrasted with her black lawyer's robes and professional attire. Right away, he informed Robin that his ex-wife had moved some twenty kilometres from their family home. This had ended their shared custody of their daughters: the eldest was staying with him to prepare for her high school baccalaureate exams, while the youngest, who was in middle school, was living with her mother. Because of this arrangement, the parents had reduced the father's child support payments from one hundred euros to fifty euros. "You should have told me so I could fit that in," the lawyer tells him. "There's a good faith clause." She explains that their divorce settlement cannot be approved by the court if it does not line up with the family's actual living circumstances. Her client replies that he is certain that Grace Dupont-Bernard, his ex-wife's lawyer, was supposed to inform Robin. Dupont-Bernard, arriving a few minutes later, reacts even more severely: although her client says that she telephoned the lawyer's offices three times without reaching her, she exclaims "Mrs. L.! In that case, you should leave a message!"

The lawyers advise them to modify their agreement immediately if they want any chance of the divorce going through that day. Dupont-Bernard dictates the changes to her colleague: each child's residence, parental visitation rights, tax residency, who pays for supplemental health insurance. Dupont-Bernard asks her client if she would like the child support payment to be maintained at one hundred euros, given that the mother, who works as a nanny, is out of work and currently receiving a monthly unemployment benefit of one thousand euros, whereas her former husband, a mechanic, makes €2,250 per month. "It's fine," the ex-wife assures her; the lawyer does not press her. Dupont-Bernard then adds that each parent will have only one child in his or her care in the eyes of the Caisse d'allocations familiales (the French family benefit office). But she does not point out that this means that her client will be losing the family benefit she is currently receiving, as it is reserved for parents with at least two child dependants. Nor does she mention that the father will no longer be able to claim any tax deductions for his children.

The two lawyers, who have worked in the same offices for the past nine years, leave the clients to go photocopy the modified agreement. Immediately, they stop calling each other by the formal "*vous*" and vent their frustration: "It's been two months – if they'd let us know." Shortly thereafter, when the hearing begins, the judge expresses her displeasure over the draft agreement. "It's a real mess," she observes to the clerk. She hears the wife's testimony first and also notes that "it would have been preferable to let [the] lawyers know." The wife repeats what she has said earlier: "That's what I tried to do, but I never got an appointment." The judge reminds both parties that the child support is "symbolic," points out that neither parent will be receiving family benefits, and approves the agreement.

With this episode in mind, let us return to the analysis of professional power undertaken in the previous chapter. There, I focused on the social backgrounds, institutional roles, and work environments of the professionals involved in the divorce process. Here, in the tense exchanges observed between these lawyers and their clients, we see that professional power also relies on the traits of the laypeople involved: it is relational, built on the interactions between professionals and laypeople. In the

Weberian tradition, authority is related to the degree to which a person can expect to be able to give an order and have it executed: "[A] willingness to submit to an order imposed by one man or a small group always in some sense implies a belief in the legitimate authority (*Herrshafsgewalt*) of the source imposing it" (Weber 1978, 37).

However, there were no explicit orders given in the situation described above. On the surface, it would seem that the judge did nothing more than approve a divorce settlement and that the lawyers were merely making sure that the divorcing couple's practical arrangements lined up with the law. In this scenario, though, the power structuring these institutional relations is not located in anyone's ability to issue commands or make decisions – instead, it lies in the ability to foster and produce consent. The power in this scene lies in the production of expectations and in the ability to orient certain people toward certain solutions, including encouraging them not to act or to change their reasons for action. "We give them direction, we advise them, but we can't impose anything on them," was Robin's explanation for why the child support did not end up being set at a higher amount.

As more and more value is placed on encouraging divorcing couples to negotiate and settle out of court, the power of professionals has become diffuse and, above all, highly variable. In the many observations of hearings and lawyer-client interactions that form the basis of this chapter, we see over and over the degree to which this power regime combines flexibility with normative pressures to varying degrees depending on the professionals and the public involved. As we shall see, asymmetries between professionals and laypeople at the social, cognitive, and institutional levels are the main condition of this power.

In the late 1960s, the sociologist Luc Boltanski (1969) observed that doctors' elite social backgrounds were a key factor in their role as producers and disseminators of childcare norms. Starting in the 2000s, French sociologists sought to define the relationship between class and gender in their analyses of professional self-perception and the ways in which professionals interacted with the public. Delphine Serre (2017), for example, studied the impact of the middle-class social position of female-dominated intermediary professions in the health and social sectors on the moral codes that they communicated to the families with which they worked. Research into bureaucratic encounters has tended to focus more on the impact of race, but it has also highlighted, in the words of Celeste Watkins-Hayes (2009, 11), that "professional identities are informed by both organizational cues and social group memberships."

As we can see, professional authority is not built on social background alone; it also comes from the cognitive asymmetry that exists between legal professionals and divorcing couples, in which the former enjoy the upper hand. The authority of highly qualified service professionals such as doctors and lawyers (known as *professions libérales* in France) is based on the fact that they have broadly recognized knowledge and expertise, in contrast to the public they serve, whose members generally do not possess this knowledge (Freidson 1970). This chapter began with a divorce hearing in which the judge and the lawyers did little to thoroughly and clearly explain to the divorcing couple what was at stake in a relatively complex set of legal questions relating to tax law, welfare benefits law, and family law. At the end of another hearing that we observed, the lawyers, judge, and clerk conceded that "the parties were a bit out of their depth" but that "the ex-wife's rights were respected."[1] Here, the laypeople were expected to trust their representatives, to whom, in the name of these representatives' legal competencies, they had delegated the task of ensuring the proper consideration of their rights. It should be noted that lawyers in these situations possess more than theoretical and technical knowledge: they also have acquired a practical understanding of the institutions involved in these situations. This knowledge stands in sharp contrast to that of most of their clients, who have little to no experience with the court systems; for most divorcing couples, the divorce hearing is the first time they have ever appeared in court. The institutional role of lawyers also functions as a last resort, authorizing them to decide in their clients' stead. While they do not systematically make use of this capability – far from it – it does carry significant weight in their work as counsel.

According to the American socio-legal scholars Austin Sarat and William L.F. Felstiner (1995, 142), "[t]he ability to manipulate symbols in legally efficacious ways, to identify and interpret institutional signals, to understand the legal meaning of divorce" is the very definition of legal professionalism. This professionalism functions by progressively deconstructing family stories into "portions that have tactical significance" (144). It also relies on being able to impose judicial temporality on family arrangements whose actual histories do not necessarily line up neatly (Noreau 1998). The power of lawyers may thus be said to lie in their ability to limit the expectations of divorcing couples by calling them to reality and reason, which may run against the grain of their initial emotional states (Sarat and Felstiner 1995, 147–48).

This chapter will discuss the analyses put forward in Sarat and Felstiner's classic work with two goals in mind. The first is to broaden the scope of their conclusions, which were drawn from observations of lawyers in the United States, by testing their validity against observations of lawyers and judges in their interactions with litigants in France and Quebec. The second is to explore the conditions of possibility of lawyers' and judges' power by situating it with regard to the respective stances of legal professionals and laypeople. In other words, this chapter will study how professional power varies from one end to the other of the social ladder and between genders.

To this end, we will explore two contrasting configurations, those of the lower class and those of the upper class. This contrast arises in part from the inequalities of access to law and justice in the two jurisdictions that we explored in the first chapter: the middle class, as we saw, largely choose more amicable forms of divorce. This distinction means that there is much less opportunity to observe how lawyers and judges work with middle-class clients over the long term. However, members of the middle class can generally be grouped with the lower or the upper class, depending on how their capital – be it cultural or economic – is structured.

The contrasts highlighted in this chapter are meant to shed light on the variability of power relations by focusing on their most salient differences. Rather than falling into a caricaturized view of class relations, it seeks to carefully and systematically explore the internal stratifications of each social group, depending on the structure and volume of their capital, as well as their gender, their background, and even their age. As we shall see, in many interactions we observed between legal professionals and laypeople from lower-class backgrounds, extreme asymmetries in resources and norms often led to more marked displays of professional power. The ways in which ex-spouses attenuated, avoided, or took advantage of this power tended to be polarized along gender lines: women, for the most part, invested more energy in relationships with professionals, allowing them to acquire a practical institutional sense, while men displayed more of a tendency toward retreat or avoidance.

The professionals whom we studied made less effort to moderate or lower expectations when working with members of the elite; instead, what often stood out as they related to one another was complicity and even benevolence. Nevertheless, social proximity offers no absolute guarantee that clients will live up to professionals' expectations. In rare cases, lawyers and judges were even more stringent in their expectations that members of their own or similar social groups live up to what they perceived as their shared norms. We will see that overconfident men who contest the exclusive professional authority of lawyers and stay-at-home spouses who deviate from the norm of professional activity break with these logics of affinity and risk becoming objects of disapprobation or even normative imposition.

To sum up, this interactional order was mainly structured by social stratification, linked to the gendering of social roles and assignments based on origin and appearance. It was, by contrast, largely unaffected by national configurations: there were few differences between France and Quebec in this regard compared with other aspects contributing to the unequal treatment of separation and divorce in France and Quebec. Such an observation obviously does not mean that social structures are identical in the two contexts, but it does testify to the renewed force of social inequality in contemporary liberal societies.

Institutional Proximity and Social Remove

As we saw in the divorce by mutual consent that had to be modified at the last minute in the Besson trial court, people with less privileged class status are often encouraged to lower their expectations in two ways: first, in terms of the services that they may expect from professionals (who were unreachable in this case) and, second, in terms of what they may ask of their former partners (unequal arrangements go unquestioned). As the sociologist Javier Auyero (2012) has shown in his ethnographic research on the waiting areas of social and administrative services in Buenos Aires, time is the first mechanism through which the expectations of less privileged people are lowered. As we saw in Chapter 1, these people wait longer for interventions by professionals; furthermore, as I will show here, professionals accord them less of their time. In addition to the mechanism of time, professionals' representations of family conflict among lower-class populations, as well as the resources that they are (or are not) able to mobilize in the course of their work, limit their commitment to these social groups.

Limiting Expectations

We saw earlier how, in Quebec, legal professionals sought to lower the expectations of lower-class groups by discouraging them from undertaking longer proceedings. Efforts to deter this public from using the court system were evident from the moment clients began discussing their choices for proceedings with their lawyers. François Charland, a family lawyer with a strong professional presence in Albanel, reported "testing" his clients to gauge their capacity to cope with adversarial proceedings, and this behaviour can be seen in our observation of his appointment with a factory worker seeking his counsel because she did not want to share custody of her young children with her ex-partner anymore. The client arrives accompanied by her mother and appears reserved, speaking in a timid voice with bowed head. Charland decides to run through a practice interrogation with her. Evidently, he is dissatisfied with the results: she has not grasped important information (the childcare schedule) and does not answer clearly enough. He exclaims that,

> right now, you're having huge difficulties explaining your viewpoint ... The other lawyer will be respectful, but she's going to go after you. She'll ask for sole custody for the father!" At the end of the exercise, he discourages the client from demanding sole custody. "I'm worried. You're going to need to be able to talk the judge into it, because it's the judge who decides on your children's future ... With all due respect, I don't feel you're strong enough to have sole custody."[2]

As this episode shows, the obstacles to justice encountered by less privileged populations are not merely economic; they are also social and cultural in nature. Proficient speaking is crucial in this context: questioning can be long and sometimes contorted in ways that bring social inequalities related to language skills to the fore. When such people do nevertheless make it into the courtroom, their modest resources tend to limit the procedural guarantees that are extended to them. For example, when the Quebec City courtroom's audio recording system stopped working during a divorce trial that we were observing between a health aide and a labourer over the father's visitation rights, Judge Albert Savard called for a recess so that the clerk could see to resolving the problem. When the malfunction was confirmed, however, Savard asked the lawyers whether they agreed to go ahead anyway. Both replied in the affirmative, estimating that their clients did not have "the means to go to appeals."[3]

Access to the law becomes even more problematic for parties representing themselves. Procedural requirements can be staggering for non-professionals: the non-represented party must question the ex-partner and directly confront the lawyer for the other party. In such cases, lawyers are quick to use procedural tricks of the trade or find other ways in which to underscore unrepresented parties' lack of competence. During another hearing in Quebec, we observed a man in his thirties appearing alone before Judge Louise Lavoie to request that his daughter live with him rather than with her mother. The mother's lawyer had filed a motion for an interim/safeguard order to change the location of the handover every second weekend when the father exercised his visitation rights. Her motion, being urgent, was given priority, while the man's procedure was postponed, which meant that the mother's lawyer was called to speak first, setting the main theme of the discussion: the father had forgotten to file an "Appendix 1," the form used for calculating child support. The man appeared lost. "I don't have a copy of it, I'm sorry. I had already filed it, with all my accounts, in November, for the last ruling. I wasn't expecting you to ask for the numbers again." Hearing this, the lawyer admonished him: "No, don't go telling me stories! You were supposed to bring it today!" Giving precedence to the mother's request, the judge enjoined the man to produce his tax records for the following

Monday, then scheduled the hearing to examine the father's request based on the lawyer's availability, a month later.[4]

This hearing illustrates the marked ambivalence shown by legal professionals toward parties without representation, the majority of whom are low-income men. Savard explained that, as a judge, he "has to be a bit pedagogical, he has to tell them how it works ... But at the same time, the judge must make sure he doesn't become their lawyer."[5] In the hearing with the father who had forgotten his "Appendix 1," Lavoie adopted a neutral, pedagogical tone, clarifying technical terms and laying out the different phases of the proceedings. But she also showed strict respect for procedural priority, which the mother's lawyer knew how to use to his client's advantage. Legal aid lawyers often described cases such as this one to us, complaining that judges paid more attention to non-represented parties. Here, however, the absence of a colleague was an advantage for the lawyer since he could be more directive with the father than he would have allowed himself to be with another lawyer. Access to a lawyer entails certain evaluations of one's demands and capabilities, but when the time comes to stand before a judge, going without legal representation may lead to rather violent symbolic calls to order. Deeming insufficient the verbal and procedural abilities of laypeople and discouraging them from undertaking demanding procedures, which are also the procedures that offer the most guarantees, are the first two facets of the power exercised by lawyers in Quebec over people in lower social classes.

In France, where hearings are brief and intended for all divorcing couples, the evaluation of financial and cultural capital is not as central. Still, depending on their resources, divorcing couples cannot all expect the same services. Lawyers who charge low hourly rates or are paid by legal aid often have heavy caseloads and can devote only a limited amount of time to each one. Lawyers with a socially diverse clientele often charge a flat fee, knowing that clients of lesser means will not be able to pay for extra hours. They let these clients know that their support will be limited, both in terms of time and in terms of intensity. Consider the appointment we observed with Caroline Source, a lawyer in a small firm in Besson specializing in family law, whom we met in the last chapter. On the day we were observing her, she was meeting with a fifty-year-old woman whom she had been advising for several months. Before the appointment began, she explained to us that it was a "very difficult, very complicated" situation: the couple adopted two children from overseas and then had a messy divorce, which took them not only to family court but also to juvenile court and all the way to criminal court. The conflict recently flared up again, when the eldest daughter, aged thirteen, told her psychologist that she would commit suicide if she had to stay with her father, a police officer, whom the lawyer described as a "sociopath."

The client has come in for a meeting because she must attend penal mediation, which was ordered by the public prosecutor for failure to deliver the children to their father during school vacation. During their half-hour interview, the lawyer listens to her client with empathy, punctuating her words with "all right" and "good" in a calm voice. She tries to reassure the mother when the latter describes her daughter's self-scarification and refusal to eat. But she also makes her understand that she will not be able to provide any concrete help with the penal mediation and limits herself to explaining what happens during the session and reminding her not to worry. Once the client has departed, the lawyer expresses her powerlessness to us: "What can I do?" But she is confident that her client will abandon her legal proceedings after penal mediation: "She'll do what's necessary, she's afraid of the law."[6]

In this case, Sourice's attitude toward her client could be explained solely by the latter's social position – the case left her with little latitude. The emergency petition that the lawyer had filed for the children not to see their father anymore had been rejected, and there was a negative psychological evaluation in the mother's file. However, it remains the case that lawyers can accompany their clients to penal mediation, which is something that did not happen here: the ex-wife, caught up in lengthy and complicated legal proceedings, could not afford it. Moreover, although it concerned children who were in danger according to the lawyer's own assessment, the appointment was three times shorter than her meeting with a doctor the previous day, even though the stakes there were much lower. The lawyer was less proactive, did not read the file, and abandoned the idea of filing a petition to have the father's visitation rights changed.

These smaller-scale legal services lead people with modest resources to limit their demands on the legal system. In line with Sarat and Felstiner's (1995) observations, most of the lawyers we met with described how they would make certain that their clients' "far-fetched" demands evolved toward more "reasonable" – that is, more "modest" – expectations. In Quebec, this meant accepting joint physical custody of children; in France, it meant agreeing to lower child support, as in the examples given here. Their goals were similar: to avoid stalemates with the opposing lawyer and to maintain respectability in the judge's eyes. But this pressure to lower expectations was never so marked as in cases where the separating couples had few resources to devote to the process.

Mastery of the law as well as dominant social norms are major vectors of legitimation for lawyerly power, and these vectors are particularly visible in the fairly rare cases in which women demanded full guardianship or refused to accept visitation rights or overnight stays for their ex-spouses. In Quebec City, we observed Séverine Pineault, a lawyer in a legal aid office, lowering the expectations of her client, a forty-five-year-old woman who worked a few hours per week in a school cafeteria. The mother wished to refuse overnight stays to her ex-husband, a taxi driver, on the grounds that he did not take care of their children, who were two and six, when they lived together. The lawyer's words echoed those heard often in the media as well as from other lawyers and judges: "It's often like that. Mothers do more childcare. He'll be forced to look after them; he'll change his schedule ... They [the children] will get used to it. All children are shaken up after a separation, but they adapt." She reinforced this idea by mobilizing her knowledge of judges' opinions and practices: "He'll definitely get them overnight ... The courts really insist on the fact that fathers are capable of getting more involved after the separation."[7]

Here, the legitimation of legal counsel came with an argument based on professional authority – "the courts insist" – grounded in a monopoly of legal and procedural knowledge and social authority – "it's often like that" – that was tightly linked to the lawyer's own social position. Such arguments were even less likely to be contested by clients in legal aid offices, most of whom were greatly removed from the world of law and litigation. In this case, for example, the client had immigrated from

North Africa just a few years before. She had nothing to say in reply when the lawyer, whose French Canadian name, skin colour, and accent all identified her as someone born in Quebec to Quebecois parents, told her that this was "the way things are in Quebec." Several factors come together in the type of advice lawyers give as well as in the chances that this advice will be heeded by their clients, and, throughout, socio-professional status was interlinked with national background and gender.

Generally speaking, women were more likely than men to be led to limit their demands. They were more often the ones to take legal action since they tended to be the ones responsible for the bulk of the everyday care of their children. They were also more often the ones to express their demands in a context in which public and professional discourses favour paternal involvement. As two members of our research team have shown, legal aid lawyers in Quebec tell women to "'deal with it' when fathers wish to exercise their rights," which, in the case described earlier, meant accepting the father's request for overnight stays (Mille and Zimmermann 2017, 54). When women clients seek more involvement from their ex-partners, they also can be discouraged from trying: as Mille and Zimmermann put it, lawyers "underline the few legal resources available to them" and say they want to "spare them useless undertakings" (54).

Intrusion and Moralizing

Although lawyers' meetings with low-income parents tended to be briefer than for other social classes, they nevertheless took the time to moralize with them. Indeed, we were able to infer from our observations that their social remove may actually encourage legal professionals to pay particular kinds of attention to these clients. We observed this in lawyers' use of specific procedures as well as in the ways in which lawyers interpreted and deployed their family histories. Social differentiation of legal interventions is partially institutionalized under the law. People who are dependent on welfare benefits are subject to certain obligations, which justify institutional surveillance of their private lives. Family courts, family benefit offices, and lawyers (in Quebec) must prove that parents who owe child support are unable to pay it and verify their incomes to do so. Moreover, as our study showed, the rules organizing access to legal aid have led French court clerks and Quebecois lawyers to scrutinize the resources of low-income persons more carefully than they do for the rest of the population. These financial checks led professionals to be aware of, and even to evaluate, the lifestyles of their clients in order to draw distinctions between people who deserved public support and those at risk of abusing it.

This finding was evident in our observation of a meeting between Pineault and a Quebecoise woman of about thirty-five who was consulting her about her oldest daughter, age seven, whose father was a welfare recipient. The woman arrived with her younger daughters, ages two and three. All three of them were wearing more or less the same style of clothing: simple but soberly elegant and feminine. ("A very middle-class look," I jotted down in my field notes.) The woman lives with another partner, who is the father of her two younger daughters, who are in her full-time care. The couple recently bought a house but appear to be heavily in debt. Immediately, the lawyer doubts that the woman would be eligible for legal aid. They had already met a few months earlier, and she had already been declared ineligible because she had thirty thousand dollars in funds in her bank accounts. She explains that she has gone to see a "private" lawyer, who charges five hundred dollars for a motion. However, she asserts, "my financial situation has changed. I don't have the money to keep paying her." The lawyer is suspicious. "What did you do with the thirty thousand dollars?" The woman explains that the couple spent eighteen months living with her partner's grandmother, which had allowed her to save up to redo the kitchen of their new house, which had cost twenty-five thousand dollars. At the same time, her partner makes forty-two thousand dollars a year, which is well above the ceiling for legal aid. The lawyer indicates that she is not supposed to take this income into account in calculating the woman's eligibility, but she concludes that, "when you can pay for kitchen renovations, you can pay for a lawyer ... You're at the limit of what I accept. Legal aid is a service of last resort, it's for people who don't have any money."

> *Client:* But that spending was personal!
>
> *Lawyer:* Twenty-five thousand dollars for a kitchen is pushing it. We're publicly funded here.
>
> *Client:* That's a value judgment.
>
> *Lawyer:* It's not a value judgment. If I were deciding, you wouldn't be eligible ... There's a monthly inspection to ensure that we are taking people who meet the criteria. The inspector is going to say that isn't why they made a law on legal aid.[8]

As this tense discussion shows, differentiating between clients goes beyond official rules: similar to certain employees of French Caisses d'allocations familiales (Family Benefit Offices) described by Vincent Dubois (2010), Pineault openly expressed her disapproval ("if I were deciding, you wouldn't be eligible") in the name of defending public morality ("legal aid is for people who don't have any money"). Several times, we observed attitudes and words setting a moral boundary between acceptable and unacceptable behaviours.

Not all professionals used this type of moralizing language with their clients. The previous chapter showed that judges' trajectories and their relationships with their positions, both in France and in Quebec, led to differences in their style of intervention. A similarly wide array of practices could also be observed among lawyers. Of the five legal aid lawyers whose appointments we observed, Pineault was the most openly moralizing. It must be noted that she occupies a relatively prominent position in her professional world (she is the director of her legal aid office), a position reinforced by her marriage since her husband is a judge. By contrast, other lawyers in legal aid offices had a more militant understanding of their professional practice, while others had developed close relationships with a rural population, leading them to adopt an attitude that was closer to the ground.

If variations among professionals were significant, it must be noted that the lower classes are consistently separated from other social groups in moralizing related to physical behaviours and appearances. Lawyers and judges were attentive to behavioural hints they observed in their clients' appointments and hearings, which they perceived as predictors of normal behaviour toward their ex-spouses and children. In particular, lawyers classified aggressiveness as a male behaviour and firmly rejected it in that it undermined their ability to police interactions. Showing aggression during a hearing tended to damage credibility, while remaining calm was taken as a positive sign, bolstering judges' trust even in cases where accusations of violence were at play. This attitude is clear in the words of two judges, one from France and one from Quebec.

> During a hearing in Belles, Anaïs Le Meur hears from a young baker who is living with his mother after staying in a hotel. He is asking for visitation and overnight rights for his three-year-old son, whom he hasn't seen in two years. He heaps insults on the head of his ex-partner, who is working on a fixed-term contract in food services: "Look at me when I'm talking to you! I'm not going to hurt him, my son!" The judge reacts immediately: "On the other hand, you are a bit impulsive, sir. You're going to need to calm down." The man then asks if he can take his child over vacation, in July. The judge warns him: "If everything goes well. But you stay very calm."

> During a hearing in Montreal, over two days, Carl Brown hears two parents, both of whom have lived marginal lives for a long time and who are fighting over the custody of their six-year-old daughter. The mother, who has gone back to school, accuses the father, who has just begun working as a concierge, of being violent. In our interview, the judge distanced himself from this accusation: "I'm not sure he's a dangerous individual. He may be dangerous when he's alone with her, but I'm not sure of it ... His testimony was calm ... He got a little bit frustrated at one point during the cross-examination but not that much. I found him pleasant."

Generally speaking, the legal professionals whom we encountered in our study considered people with lower-class status to be the most likely to fail in their roles during hearings and to engage in deviant behaviour in their private lives (Biland and Schütz 2014). It is common for lawyers defending a less privileged clientele, as is the case with French social workers (Serre 2017), to have a fatalistic attitude toward their clients, which justifies giving behavioural advice that is not proffered to other social groups. In the Albanel legal aid office, for example, France Paquin instructed her clients "not to show too much cleavage" and to call court personnel by the formal "*vous*" in a context where the informal "*tu*" is more widespread than in France.[9] In other words, professional constructions of bodily and emotional responsibility, in addition to being highly gendered (aggressiveness for men versus cleavage or tears for women), had a marked social bent. Whereas legal professionals appeared to think this went without saying for members of the upper and even the middle classes, they made physical behaviour and appearance the objects of specific efforts and interactions with members of the lower class. Legal professionals justified this extension of their power to the supervision of bodies because they thought it was likely that clients from lower-class backgrounds would stray from dominant behavioural norms.

More broadly, what came through in interviews was the social remove that lawyers felt from the publics they served. In general, it was the members of the professional elite (those sitting on the bench of the Superior Court of Quebec or in the French courts of appeal) or professionals working with clients in reduced circumstances (such as in legal aid offices) who perceived the greatest distance between themselves and the publics they served: references to the gap between "us" and "them" were more explicit in these instances. Indeed, the similarities are striking between the words of Brigitte Cigliano, the presiding judge in a chamber of a French court of appeal and the daughter of a high-ranking civil servant and a teacher, who expressed great attachment to her rural roots, and those of Paul Émond, a judge in the Superior Court of a remote region and the son of the owner of a building company and a teacher. Both were born in the mid-1950s and were significantly older than most of the parties they heard, and, in both cases, this caused them to place even more emphasis on their efforts to make a connection in situations where they did not share – and even disapproved of – the parties' practices.

> A Portuguese man and his old lady. The wife had been parked in the garden shed. And then I asked my good man about his garden: "Sir, do you grow vegetables in your garden? ... You are an excellent gardener if you're managing to grow eggplants in X [a suburban town].

I can't get them to grow in Y [another suburban town nearby]!" He tells me: "Yes, your honour, sometimes I have a good year, sometimes not." Well, if you can believe it, everything got resolved after this discussion! ... It's often things like that, about life on the land. With a Kabyle couple, we had a real laugh about cantaloupe and things like that. I tell them: "You wouldn't be Kabyle, the two of you?" "Yes, yes, but how could you tell?" "It's very simple, you look like you come from the Auvergne [a rural French region]" ... And after that, we made inroads with them, not with everything, but with a certain number of things.

— Brigitte Cigliano

A hairdresser from Quebec ... who barely knows how to read: we'll translate what's at stake to something down to earth. Over the years, in my practice, I've forgotten that side of things. You're never too far from the plow and the land ... I come from a fairly poor family, but in the end we moved upwards, you become more important and perhaps a little bit above these kinds of affairs ... I'll give you an example: Native peoples. A lady who had uprooted her young child, three times, from school. That's very unhealthy. I told the lady: "Madame, you are close to nature. You know that you don't transplant plants. You don't uproot a tree. You have to give it time to grow so it can put down roots in the soil in the right way. You know that. That's not what you're doing with your child. You've switched schools three times in the same year. You're able to understand that: stability."

— Paul Émond

In these examples, the judges drew symbolic links between the parties and nature or the land, which reveals a process of othering that is constitutive of racism (Guillaumin 1995). In three of the four examples given, terms that demonstrated an alleged distance from the national social majority were used to describe the parties: "Native peoples" for Émond and "Portuguese" and "Kabyle" immigrants for Cigliano. Remarkably, Cigliano described masculine violence anecdotally. In doing so, she underplayed its seriousness in the interest of reconciling the ex-spouses: we will see this mechanism at work again in Chapter 4 when we look more closely at how family violence is underestimated or ignored by some judges. In this case, the judge's reaction to the man's treatment of his wife could also be explained by the fact that she saw this couple as being far removed from French norms of gender equality.

Thus, in both legal contexts, the ways in which professionals distanced themselves from certain groups typically involved setting the "cultures" of these minority groups at a remove from national norms. In some cases, this mobilization of cultural references to describe supposed disparities with dominant social norms could go as far as racializing certain individuals or couples (Bessière et al. 2018) – that is, assigning them a naturalized belonging based on presumed cultural and/or physical traits (Murji and Solomos 2005).

This culture-based discourse was not always stigmatizing. In Quebec, a lawyer of West African origin whose work in immigration law brought him to family law used differentializing language to underscore his ability to defend immigrants from Africa. This lawyer, who was in his thirties and had been practising law only for a short time, had designed marketing tools – particularly on social media – to reach out to immigrant populations. In our first meeting, he was defending a man who had arrived from a country neighbouring his own seven years previously.[10] In our interview, he explained to us that this client "really wanted someone he could trust, who wouldn't judge him. And with that, I think my skin colour helped, because there are things, a cultural context, that someone from Quebec, a quote-unquote white person, wouldn't have understood."[11] Here, being Black and an immigrant was thought of positively, as a kind of professional skill; proximity to clients' own experiences made it possible for this lawyer to avoid "judging," as he put it, and to treat his clients fairly, without racially stereotyping them. By contrast, certain lawyers who belonged to the majority culture expressed distance from certain types of individuals and associated their ethnoracial profiling with derogatory representations (Fassin 2013). It was in these situations that racializing attitudes could be found, such as in the words of a colleague of Cigliano who asserted that "Southern peoples,

Portuguese, North African, or Jewish, have views on divorce that are thirty years out of date!"[12]

In sum, judges in Quebec regularly displayed the types of paternalistic attitudes that have been described in colonial studies, in which foreign men are perceived as threatening and foreign women are seen as victims to be protected and emancipated (McClintock 1995). In France, judges' cultural perceptions pushed them to draw inspiration from non-legal knowledge such as ethno-psychiatry, which ascribes the psychological difficulties that migrants may encounter to their remove from the majority of society. This differentialist perception was dependent on social stratification: lower-class populations were more often dealt with in psycho-social terms than people from more privileged backgrounds.

Indeed, the assignment of ethno-racial traits occurred almost exclusively among members of the lower and working classes (who are often less well educated), which reinforces a differentializing treatment. On meeting a Black woman, the mother of four children with traditionally French names, who fit neither social nor racial stereotypes, a French judge expressed surprise in an aside to us during a hearing: "She seems very integrated ... She doesn't seem 'African' in the way I imagine them. No, really, she expresses herself very well!"[13] By contrast, the international mobility of upper-class Western "expatriates" was not questioned from a cultural angle. Instead, it was dealt with in purely legal terms through international private law. In other words, the professional production of social judgment that we observed was consistently indexed on several orders of differentiation and hierarchy: social class, gender, and race, which were interdependent and co-constructed in legal professionals' representations and in their attitudes toward laypeople.

What is more, we noted that parties mobilized these categories themselves during conflicts with each other. Seizing on the use of identity in more or less strategic ways was a means for people of lower-class status and/or minority groups to resist becoming passive receptacles of institutional power. Like gender, racialization can be a way of operating difference even within couples – between the more racialized partner and the less racialized one – and lending credibility to some of these lay labels, while rejecting others, allowing professionals to exercise power over conjugal relationships. In doing so, they legitimize certain forms of othering, erecting a moral barrier between acceptable otherness and otherness that goes against majority norms.

The interaction between Pineault and her North African client described earlier in this chapter deserves further attention. The client explained to Pineault in their meeting that she had been married in her country of origin in 2005 but that her husband had actually been living in Quebec since 1986. She offered Pineault a differentialist account of her marital problems: "Where we come from, you aren't supposed to get divorced. We don't have the same traditions as the Quebecois. I am not a spineless woman. No! But for us, balance for children is having two parents together ... I know the Arab mentality. He wants to be shown he's a man." Searching for arguments against the ex-husband's request for shared custody, Pineault attempted to apply a religious angle to the woman's story:

> *Lawyer:* You are of the Muslim faith. Is there anything like polygamy? Several wives?
>
> *Client:* Yes, in our religion you can have four wives, but you have to treat them the same; otherwise you can't. He isn't a ladies' man, he doesn't have that problem.
>
> *Lawyer:* And you don't veil ...
>
> *Client:* No, I was like this when he married me, that's the way it is.
>
> *Lawyer:* Do you think he could force your daughter to veil?
>
> *Client:* No, he doesn't know the basics of the religion. He doesn't know how to say the prayers. The submission of women isn't the religion; it's him, the man.

This conversation took place at a time of ongoing public debate over the *Quebec Charter of Values,* which, significantly, sought to limit the display of any symbols of religious affiliation (Koussens 2020).[14] The lawyer was searching for a strategic argument that could help her client to draw a link between the Muslim faith and male domination. The client, by dismissing this attempt to instrumentalize her religion, displayed her autonomy by limiting the lawyer's power to define her circumstances. In doing so, however, at the same time she was abandoning the argument most likely to go in her favour, rejecting what the majority of society considers the most illegitimate form of male domination over women.

Women in the Know; Men in Retreat

As this woman's opposition to the religious framing of her story shows, members of less advantaged classes are not "'empty vessels' waiting to be filled with the attitudes and potentialities prescribed for them by dominant discourses" (Barnes and Prior 2009, 22). I have already evoked situations of non-compliance – in body and in language – to describe power as a reciprocal social relationship. But until now I have focused on obvious prejudices in the form of prompts to behave or appear in certain ways or moralizing discourses. Is it possible to imagine more positive ways of limiting professional power or of even taking advantage of it?

The Canadian-born sociologist Erving Goffman (1961) described the distinction between contained adjustments and disruptive adjustments, which is a good way of accounting for the polarized manner in which men and women from less advantaged backgrounds played with judges' and lawyers' expectations in the interactions that we observed. Women tended to make contained adjustments, in which they strayed only slightly from their prescribed roles. As they encountered legal professionals during the courses of their separations, these women acquired a practical understanding of these institutions. This kind of contact with professionals who claimed to be the repositories of legitimate codes and norms gave them hope not only that they would come out ahead in litigation but also that, eventually, they would obtain better control over their lives. They found a degree of comfort in their ability to organize their lives post-separation and to build responsible, positive identities as divorced people.

In a case recounted earlier in this chapter, Claire Robin represented a woman who was about forty and appearing in court for a ruling on visitation rights with, and child support from, the father of her three children. The father was a tradesman, and the mother had worked with him until their separation six years before. The father's violent behaviour toward one of their daughters had put an end to shared custody. On the day of the hearing, her monthly salary was a little under seventeen hundred euros, while he earned twenty-four hundred euros. The ex-husband's lawyer had not submitted any conclusions before the hearing, so, on the day, Robin requested time to examine them with her client. Over the next hour, in a conversation that strayed far from the asymmetrical power relations and moralizing stances observed in other cases, Robin let her client know that she was within her rights, while the client expressed support for Robin when she criticized her colleague's manoeuvring. They went over the case's more technical aspects together (who was paying for supplemental health insurance, potentially under-declared income, and so on). Robin handed the conclusions over to her client so that she could check the supporting documents herself. The client suggested they request two hundred euros per child per month from the father; Robin proposed €160; ultimately, they agreed to the woman's second proposal of €180.[15]

The conditions that made this discussion between Robin and her client possible cannot be analyzed fully here, as we do not know the frequency or the tenor of their interactions before the encounter we observed. Nevertheless, this conversation shows the proficiency gained by this lower-middle-class woman over the long course of her divorce: she provides valuable information to her lawyer and negotiates demands with Robin that the lawyer then takes into account a few minutes later as she pleads for her client in the courtroom. In the lingering tension in the aftermath of divorce, it seems clear that Robin's professional support helped this mother to gain confidence in her recently made plans to care for her children full time.

At the other end of the spectrum, and as demonstrated in another case that Robin had heard, which was described earlier, men are more likely to retreat from an active role in proceedings, by choosing to forgo a lawyer, by refusing to respond when papers are served, or by failing to appear in court. In France, one out of every ten men does not show up for family court hearings (compared with one woman in twenty). Unemployed people are the least likely to be present, and, among them, men are once again less likely to appear than women (82 percent and 89 percent, respectively).[16] This non-compliance with professionals' expectations is disruptive in the sense that it radically undermines the institutional norm of negotiated divorce settlements. In these cases, the judges' work of conciliation is rendered impossible by the absence of one of the parties.

These men are the contemporary embodiment of the removal of less privileged classes from the world of "them," as the British academic Richard Hoggart (1957) called it in the middle of the past century, with "them" being legal professionals. Some men refuse to lower their expectations as their lawyers wish them to and, in this way, run the risk of ending up without any lawyer at all. Moreover, they distance themselves from the norm of co-parenting, which assumes that both parents will be involved in the lives of their children. They make little to no use of their visitation rights and may not even pay child support. In Canada, "fathers earning less than $30,000 annually are likely to see their children less often than those earning $50,000 or more per year" (Swiss and Le Bourdais 2009, 641). In France, 30 percent of separated fathers earning lower than minimum wage never see their children, compared with 8 percent of fathers with a monthly revenue of three thousand euros. Furthermore, fathers who have children with another partner see children from previous partnerships less often (Régnier-Loilier 2016, 42). Indeed, in several cases, women reported that their ex-spouses had entered new relationships and had other children, the implication being that fathers gave more priority to their current family ties than to past ones.

These gendered attitudes may be difficult to sustain over the long term. For the women we observed, familiarity with institutions did not equal autonomy: professionals were difficult to avoid and did not necessarily adopt the benevolent and supportive posture expected of them. Of course, fees are a regular obstacle for disadvantaged clients: spending little time with counsel does limit costs, but it also limits the scope of available services. Moreover, we have seen that lawyers and judges did not reliably provide the support women sought: some appreciated their role as teachers of the law, but others remained closed to it, preferring to maintain a bureaucratic identity and refusing to engage in anything that might resemble social work.

The French judge Pierre Terreau, whom we met in Chapter 2, was one of these individuals. Ill at ease in the encounters with private life that came with his work as a family judge, he reported that he sought out as little information as possible about families' histories. In an interview, he openly criticized "legal consumers" seeking advice on how to lead their private lives:

> They shouldn't see the court system as what I'd call a normal, an ordinary way of functioning. It's like doctors. You go see doctors when you're sick ... [The judge] doesn't have to understand [the person], but, well, try to set things straight. And also, I'd say, you shouldn't ... how can I put it, overstep your role as a family judge.[17]

As for men, their avoidance of institutions was often only provisional, and they were often haunted by the consequences of their avoidance when the institutions did catch up with them. The contrast between men's inexperience and women's competence in legal procedures, which the latter acquire in their many interactions with public services, was striking in many of the cases we observed (Perrin-Heredia 2009; Siblot 2006).

During the hearing presided over by Catherine Blanchard, a female judge in her fifties, the woman displayed what French sociologist Vincent Dubois (2010) has called "tactical docility," while the man behaved aggressively in the face of private and institutional reproach. This difference in their behaviours was most likely also connected to how each member of the divorcing couple was positioned in the labour market. The mother, who was a pharmacy technician, was the party filing the motion. Her ex-husband had recently found temporary employment doing roadwork, and the family benefit office had stopped paying the family's child support allowance and requested that she file a claim with the court to set an amount for child support. The mother had taken pains to inform herself about the judicial proceedings under way and put together her file very carefully, including documentation of her revenue and a spreadsheet of her expenses, which perhaps were prepared with the help of someone in the family benefit office. Before the judge, she opens a neatly arranged file folder in front of her and asks "would you like the paperwork? I brought everything."

The man, by contrast, seems to be caught short. He has come without his pay stubs and apologizes to the judge: "I didn't bring anything, I'm sorry." Growing angry, he accuses his ex-wife of being the person behind the procedure: "She's doing all this paperwork to keep being shitty with me, pardon the expression!" The judge explains that the claim originated with the family benefit office, but this does not mollify him: "I feel like I'm the one on trial here! I'm dying here, but I can pay. I'm living somewhere else, that's all, but I haven't abandoned my kids. I feel like I'm getting sued!" (Collectif Onze 2013, 110).[18] This man's irritation at a procedure he does not understand underlines how ambivalent this attitude of detachment really can be: it can be a positive experience only for men who do actually reject the norm of paternal involvement and, even then, only if there is limited institutional pressure to comply with this norm. It is important to note that non-compliance with the dominant view of post-divorce fatherhood, which is mostly focused on exercising visitation rights and paying child support, should not be confused with the refusal to engage in fathering. What was observed in the hearing above is more likely to be a feedback loop of distance from – and sometimes mistrust of – institutions and deviation from the dominant model of fatherhood.

By contrast, for women targeted by social services, familiarity with bureaucratic encounters is a resource for ensuring that their rights and their social status (as mothers) are respected – a status that remains difficult for them to escape. Among the lower classes, the ways in which women's and men's relationships are polarized with regard to the legal system's institutions and professionals are particularly striking in how they reinforce the gendered division of labour in child-rearing.

Among the Privileged
The relations between legal professionals and laypeople that we observed at the other end of the class spectrum were very different. Asymmetries were much less marked as the laypeople in this category were middle to upper class and sometimes even enjoyed higher socioeconomic status than the professionals with whom they were consulting. In the United States and Canada, the literature has observed that they

tend to occupy a "position of advantage" in courts because they have access to more resources for establishing evidence that judges find admissible (Galanter 1974,103). Moreover, because of their own social privilege, judges are more likely to rule in their favour (Leckey 2014). Their more frequent access to higher courts even allows them to help shape the normative principles that are applied to the population as a whole (Ferguson 2013). In France, sociologists have observed that economic and social capital favour access to the judicial elite as well as access to arrangements largely unavailable to people in other social categories (Spire and Weidenfeld 2011). Members of the privileged classes are able to play with legal constraints and be involved with the production of norms as well as ensure that their economic capital is protected from legal and tax institutions (Bessière and Gollac 2023).

Mastering Every Angle of the Case

As Muriel Mille and I discussed in an article that examined divorces among the wealthy in Quebec, the first notable characteristic of these privileged relationships with the law is that there is no pressure to lower expectations (Biland and Mille 2017). As is also true with taxation (Spire 2012), this flexibility comes from the ability of the public in question to mobilize multiple types of professionals, who advise them differently with regard to their histories and provide a wider range of information on available options. Not only are lawyers less hesitant to undertake procedures with uncertain outcomes, but they may also even encourage high expectations with regard to relations with ex-spouses. We were able to observe this in a meeting we sat in on with Elisabeth Buckley, the activist lawyer in Montreal who worked mainly with women married to wealthy men. Her client was a fifty-four-year-old woman, the mother of two adult daughters, who was seeking a divorce after thirty years of marriage. Her husband, who worked in the insurance business, earned $245,000 annually and owned business assets worth about two million dollars. The client had spent most of her married life in the home and currently had no personal income. She intended to ask for spousal support, and she and Buckley were preparing her budget.

Buckley, observing that "three thousand dollars isn't much clothing in a year," encouraged her client to up the amount. "You're accustomed to being able to be generous, and that is part of your standard of living," she explained to help her justify the demand. The client confirmed that she helped her daughters, particularly the eldest, who had four children and whose husband had only recently moved to Canada. In the end, Buckley estimated that her client would need $10,600 per month, to the astonishment of the client herself: "Oh boy! ... Oh my God, if I got that!" she exclaimed. To clinch her argument, Buckley involved the sociologist Muriel Mille in the conversation and remarked that "if you don't go high in the beginning, we'll end up in a bad position [for the negotiations that follow]. In reality, $120,000 [a year], I'm sorry, Miss Mille, it's nothing!"[19] Buckley's recommendations do not constitute the rule in all the cases we observed where women were divorcing rich men. In France in general and in Quebec among less specialized, less political lawyers, these women are not looked on so kindly by many legal professionals – a point to which we will return. However, the above conversation does help to shed light on the gulf dividing professional perceptions of divorce among the upper and lower classes.

Separations among the less privileged are often seen by lawyers as impoverishing both parties, as we saw above: their general attitude is that it is useless – and financially unrealistic – to engage in extensive legal battles. By contrast, as we saw in the meeting between Buckley and her client, in divorces between members of a high social status and high-income groups, lawyers often argue in favour of maintaining their lifestyle and, therefore, social status in order to justify their demands and undertake potentially longer and more controversial legal proceedings. Intergenerational social reproduction, which may become fragile in cases of separation, is never so explicit as when it is featured in debates between wealthy parents over child support (Collectif Onze 2013, 222–23). Lawyers' fatalistic attitudes toward the financial straits of members of the lower classes are transformed when they work with the more privileged. Sometimes it is their clients who demand this proactive attitude; sometimes it is the lawyers who encourage it, particularly with clients who may be ill-informed or unsure of their rights, as with the woman Buckley was advising. This shared belief in the utility of action and their ability to undertake it spurs mobilization on all fronts: inside and outside the legal system, ordinary and extraordinary, amicable and contested.

We also observed that members of elite classes were more likely to appeal. Their tendency to do so was strongly linked to the money at stake and, thus, to the parties' financial resources, as this judge at the Quebec Court of Appeal suggested to us: "Grounds for appeal are so narrow that most people don't do it, except possibly for financial issues. Issues of assets. Or child support in ultra-rich people's cases. But for ordinary folk, the Court of Appeal isn't a way to go."[20] The two divorces presented below, both involving couples in their fifties (one in France and one in Quebec), reveal the scope of the financial and legal resources mobilized by this type of divorce. The cases differed in terms of the amounts at stake and the tones of the decisions. In Quebec, the decision was a bold one, and referred to the system's loftiest legal principles, while the French decision was more routine. But they resembled each other in the number of specialized, recognized, and interested professionals who were involved.

In the case consulted in Besson, an executive in a multinational corporation, with a monthly salary of fifteen thousand euros and two high-school-age daughters, is divorcing his wife of fifteen years. The interim divorce order requires him to pay thirteen hundred euros in child support for his daughters (he has been asking for one thousand euros) and two thousand euros to his wife in duty of support (he has proposed five hundred euros). The man is appealing the decision. Each spouse is using two lawyers – one specialized in appeals procedure and one who will appear in court. In his hefty file (23 pages of conclusions, 133 pages of supporting documentation), the man reiterates his financial demands and includes a child welfare investigation (he has been concerned that one of his daughters has been oriented toward a vocational high school and that both have been arrested and held in police custody for theft). Finally, he requests that a small car be returned to him. The Court of Appeal grants him the automobile and the smaller amount of child support, but not his other demands, deeming his financial situation "not as disastrous as he is attempting to make it seem."

In the Montreal case described in the previous chapter, the couple had been married for twenty-five years. Up until the 2008 financial crisis, the man worked for a European bank and made more than a million dollars a year. The wife remained at home to raise their four children, now aged fourteen to twenty-three, who attended private schools and universities. Their dispute concerns the distribution of their financial assets and the man's financial contribution. To limit the loss of lifestyle resulting from the man's job loss, the judge decides to send the family back to Canada, where the cost of living is lower than in a European capital. But the ex-spouses are appealing. The wife, who up to now has been represented by respected family lawyers, is seeking counsel from a firm specializing in the defence of personal freedoms. The man is keeping his lawyer, nick-named "the legal pitbull." The Court of Appeal rejects this forced move, invoking the Universal Declaration of Human Rights and the *Canadian Charter of Rights and Freedoms.*

These two cases were both characterized by major financial inequalities between men and women and revealed gendered social relations that were different from those observed among the lower classes. Here, the fathers were neither disengaged nor present in the everyday lives of their children; they were above all attentive to their economic investments in their children's education, eager to ensure that their children's social status would be maintained but uncomfortable with leaving their ex-wives in charge of transmitting it (Fillod-Chabaud 2017). This desire for control encouraged them to turn to the legal system and to spend considerable money there: at the time of the hearing, the former banker had already paid $120,000 for his ex-wife's lawyers and appraisers.

Once again, economic capital is not the only thing at play in cases like these. Cultural and social capital are also essential keys to understanding how the privileged make use of legal procedures. Clearly, not all of them have studied the law, but, as our observations show, they have more personal and/or relational resources to find their way through the legal landscape, to choose respected lawyers, and to influence the ways in which their cases are represented. A telephone conversation we observed between Buckley and the brother of one of her clients, a tax lawyer, is evidence of this observation. The two lawyers agreed that the client should accept the shared custody being proposed for their seventeen-year-old daughter, their hope being that this would keep the case out of court. Over the course of the call, the brother warned Buckley that his sister had just inherited two million dollars and pushed for the inheritance to be left out of financial negotiations.[21]

Their understanding of codes and procedures – their procedural capital, in the words of Alexis Spire and Kathia Weidenfeld (2011) – and the desire for control among members of the upper class are particularly salient when it comes to their private lives, which they seek to keep from their ex-spouses and judges and often from their peers and the media. The professionals we observed tended to be relatively understanding of this concern. On the phone with one of her clients, Buckley mentioned the client's daughter's anorexia, a topic that the client refused to have brought up in the courtroom, explaining that not even her brother knew about it. In our observation of the trial of the former banker, Judge Madeleine Lagacé cut off the ex-wife when she raised the issue of her husband's depression and bipolar disorder, considering that it had nothing to do with the division of their assets. It is to be concluded that, if people of privileged status feel free to assert the right to preserve their privacy, even in the most intrusive of procedures, and if in general lawyers respect their desires, it is because of their social proximity, which leads them to share practices and representations.

Proximity and Complicity

Among women in the lower class, we recall that instances of cooperation between professionals and separating people relied on laypeople's bureaucratic proficiency. Among the upper class, cooperation tended to be based on shared social experiences. This class solidarity was even more likely to emerge when people shared the same gender identity or belonged to the same age group. "You saw how friendly things are with her!" Grace Dupont-Bernard, a lawyer, declared with pleasure after a long conversation with a woman university professor of the same age, who was in the process of divorcing an architect.[22] In the first place, we remarked that these lawyers were less likely to discourage their clients from calling on them, for example, and more likely to provide them with a mobile phone number. This does not mean that no filtering occurred: high hourly rates help to curb clients' enthusiasm. "When they see the bill and the number of minutes we spent explaining something over the phone, generally it stops," explained Marie-Josée Besnard, one of the lawyers of the former banker's ex-wife.[23] More than that, though, and in contrast to lawyers in solo practice or working in legal aid, these lawyers had access to teams of associates and secretaries. They shared the work of representing clients (such as preparing for and attending hearings or writing documents) and were able to call on several types of professionals to build their cases (financial or real estate appraisers, psychologists). Professional support such as this is essential in helping to confirm the elite individual's tendency to make the law a manageable instrument for negotiations and arrangements – to play with the law, as Ewick and Silbey (1998) put it.

Lawyers consider these clients to be demanding and may make strategic use of their clients' social proximity as a way of showcasing their qualifications as well as a means of encouraging clients to follow their advice. This type of dynamic was present in a meeting between Caroline Sourice and a man she introduced to me as a "country doctor," recounted in part in Chapter 2. The client was considerably older than Sourice, and she showed him an almost ostentatious deference, a stance that made it easier for her to call him into line when she needed to. They called each other by their honorifics – *maître* for her; *docteur* for him. Sourice did not interrupt the doctor when he spoke at length but also did not hesitate to reframe the discussion when he expressed too much rancour toward his ex-wife. When he mentioned "bloody interfering women," she retorted "there are all kinds of men and women. You have to listen to your daughter's wishes for shared custody."[24]

To grasp the state of her client's medical practice, Sourice drew on her personal experience with business structures used in law practice. To give her an idea of his work schedule, the doctor handed her a sheet of paper with the call schedule of the four doctors in his practice. The lawyer thanked him: "Doctor P., over the years, you've learned that some kinds of evidence aren't admissible. That's great!" Her client did not react to her sarcasm. Instead, he turned the discussion to how difficult it is to recruit doctors in rural areas and explained the financial structure of his practice to her. The lawyer's reactions signalled her understanding of independent professionals: "They don't want to be tied down," she noted, referring to young doctors who preferred not to buy into the practice. The man then took out his twelve-year-old daughter's vaccine schedule and mentioned his lawyer's son, as if to verify that he, too, was up to date with his vaccinations. The conversation that followed was brief and allusive, but it illustrated the symmetry the client was attempting to establish with his lawyer, asserting his own professional qualifications to intervene in her private life.

This last element in Sourice's conversation with this doctor indicates a third dimension of social proximity, which is sharing a similar lifestyle. Working-class clients, although they were careful to protect their private lives, nevertheless ended up discussing them with their lawyers – in detail that often went beyond procedural demands and suggested a shared lifestyle. Lawyers who felt removed from such clients tended to put up a "wall of privacy" with them. With more elite clients, by contrast, lawyers tended to behave more reciprocally, speaking of their own lives as a way to build trust through social bonding.

During her discussions with an executive in the financial industry (see Chapter 1), Montreal lawyer Marie-Josée Besnard remembered to include the cost of pool maintenance in his expenses because she had a pool herself. Moreover, she asked him to recommend hotels and places to go out in New York, where she would be travelling soon. Such conversations show that these lawyers share interests, patterns of consumption, and cultural practices with their clients and that they see it as part of their work in doing what it takes to ensure that they maintain their lifestyles after divorce. We noted that bonding was strongest when lawyers and laypeople also shared gender and generational identities, leading them to discuss highly personal topics with no connection to the legal issues at hand. Half an hour into an appointment with a fifty-year-old woman client, for example, Buckley observed "you must be hot, at your age" – a reference to menopause. The woman replied that she had had an operation a year earlier, and Buckley heaped praise on an expensive private clinic where one of her friends had had a hysterectomy, mentioning that the friend had been able to get in because her daughter was the director of a multinational tech company.[25]

In the small community of Albanel, where lawyers had a more socially diverse clientele and did not spend as much time with the wealthiest among them, their conversations nevertheless exhibited shared knowledge of people and places, revealing much about unequal social status in the community. François Charland reported finding clients through mutual acquaintances, showing that sensibilities were structured by social proximity within this local space: he identified a hairdresser because her father was a lawyer in a neighbouring town; when a cleaning lady arrived in his office, he mentioned that he knew her employer well.[26] For the judges we observed who encounter divorcing couples in a material and relational context that is both more formal and generally more infrequent, this social proximity was expressed in undertones, particularly in Quebec, where it is important to show neutrality.

We spoke to Madeleine Lagacé, the head of the family court, as she was reviewing files before they were assigned to judges. She was eager to take on the case of the former banker, which she found especially interesting both for herself and for the sociologists: "The financial stakes are very high; it's unusual to have cases of this scale." She considered the two parties to have "the best lawyers in Montreal, excellent appraisers," and, indeed, a few years later, one of their lawyers would be named to the Superior Court.[27] Having taken on the case, she spent five days hearing the parties, including two devoted to testimony from their financial and real estate appraisers, whose reports she had studied over the weekend. The hearings were highly technical and held in English (which was not her native language). Frequently, she interrupted the conversation to request explanations of arguments and to ensure that they lined up with the evidence that had been submitted. When I consulted the court files in her office, she called attention to the length of the lawyers' written arguments (several dozen pages, accompanied by hundreds of pages of evidence). She mentioned the time spent on her decision, which was long, including most of the Christmas holidays and two weeks in January. The case had allowed her to test her legal prowess and had brought her into contact with an internationally elite clientele, which seemed to interest her a great deal. She noted the properties they owned in several countries, the prestigious universities that were attended by their children, and so on.

In France, the social standing of family judges is considerably lower than that of members of the Quebec Superior Court, and their working conditions do not allow them to delve so deeply into these types of cases. Members of the wealthy upper class in France clearly have a superior social status to judges, who keep their distance. This changes in the Court of Appeal and the Court of Cassation, whose judges hold the highest position in their professional hierarchy and have more time to study cases. In these courts, we observed reactions similar to those of their peers in Quebec. In the Valin trial court, for example, I told Judge Mathilde Tabarès that we were "particularly interested in the issue of assets in divorces" and asked whether some of her cases might be useful to us. Immediately, she suggested "the biggest fish in the county," a divorce between a business entrepreneur in his fifties with an annual revenue of several million euros and a *polytechnique* graduate fifteen years his junior who had been the director of his company.[28] Legally and financially, this case was even more complicated than the one in Montreal since it involved the division of two large family-owned companies. At the same time, the procedure was radically different: most such proceedings are written, and the judges spend little time with the parties. Moreover, because they deal with so many cases, family judges limit their involvement in each one of them. What is more, they have little opportunity to receive training in dealing with cases of this financial complexity. Tabarès was the third judge in eighteen months to be involved with the case, and she noted with apparent relief that she would not yet have to rule on its contents.[29]

At the Paris Court of Appeal, by contrast, Brigitte Cigliano seemed fascinated by the case of a Middle Eastern dignitary and his European wife. Similar to her peers in Quebec, she praised the human qualities of this exceptional couple, which were indissociably linked to her legal interest in the case: "It was extremely interesting. They were very nice people, very simple, very likable. Very agreeable, you see. Very agreeable parties, how can I say this to you – very respectful. Really quality people. Both of them."[30] Comparing how judges treat cases in the two contexts shows that judges in Quebec were more likely than their French counterparts (with the exception of judges in the French courts of appeal) to show empathy and involvement in the divorces of wealthy couples. French trial judges did not treat these cases like "just anyone's"; the outcome of Tabarès's case, for example, would likely be a *jugement collégial* – a ruling by a group of three judges – which is unusual in family cases. As cultivated members of the upper class, these judges showed considerable respect for spending related to children's education (Collectif Onze 2013, 224). By contrast, they looked less favourably on "conspicuous consumption," interpreting costly travel, luxury cars, and so on as badges of privilege signalling their parties' belonging to the wealthiest echelons of the upper class (Veblen [1899] 1953). While brief, this comparison of different types of judges shows that heterogeneity within the upper class, as well as variations in the institutional roles of judges and their working conditions, do weigh on the family morality that they convey to parties.

Overconfident Men and Dependent Women

This comparison also reminds us that one should not assume that all upper-class parties meet the expectations of legal professionals all the time. In response to the changing fortunes of the former banker struggling to hang on to his social status, Lagacé expressed her thoughts on the family's lifestyle in her ruling, opining that "the parties are unrealistic and are engaged in an escalating battle of expenses and demands," words that aligned this out-of-the-ordinary case with those of less wealthy people. Gender also structures lawyers' expectations and deviations from them. As observed among people from less privileged classes, professionals do not generally reproach women and men with the same things. Upper-class men tended to show non-compliance in attitudes taken toward professionals, and, in turn, professionals remonstrated with or even called these men into line when they thought their exclusive knowledge or routines were being called into question.

Sourice's gently mocking reaction to the country doctor who had finally managed to correctly assemble the documents needed for the proceedings sheds light on a typically masculine way of failing to meet professionals' expectations. In general, men from the middle and upper echelons of society were more invested in their cases than men from more precarious and less advantaged social strata. Some of them nevertheless continued to display a lack of seriousness in their willingness to follow procedure: lawyers reported that they ran late, did not submit the necessary documents, and so on. This non-compliance could be specifically identified with the upper class in cases where it came accompanied by tremendous ease in speaking and even a desire to be proactive in the course of proceedings. In their professional relations with these clients, these ways of being gave rise to lively exchanges, where legal counsel alternated between explaining the law and irony – or even light rebukes – when men's words were perceived as deviating from institutional expectations.

In the course of the day spent with the executive in the financial industry, Besnard took the time to list all of his expenses in detail. Annoyed by the time it was taking, the client exclaimed: "This is ridiculous!" The lawyer replied: "For child support, the judge has to know what you're spending." A little later, when the man declared "I don't care about money!" she observed ironically "that's because you have a lot of it!" And when he mentioned changing jobs, she warned him: "Don't say that! The court can very easily set your revenue if you leave your job voluntarily." This non-compliance was sometimes even more problematic in the presence of judges, who were not being paid by these men to have their interests represented but, rather, to be the impartial authorities expected to rule in their cases. Judges showed irritation at behaviour that called into question their monopoly on knowledge and decision-making power. To them, these overconfident men were overstepping the bounds of their role as laypeople, as seen in these two hearings, involving a French judge and a dentist and a Quebecois judge and a lawyer.

A dentist and a speech therapist arrive in Sandrine Cabernet's courtroom in Valin. Both are in their forties, and both appear to be upper middle class. The woman is asking that they share custody of their nine-year-old son, who has lived with her for the past four years. "I want him to have the structuring presence of a father, because he has violent outbursts," she explains, insinuating that the father takes little care of his son, even neglecting his teeth. The father seems unenthusiastic: "I start at 7:30 in the morning. I'm going to have to lose an hour and a half of work a day." Solemnly, he explains that he would like to be allowed to call his son at the mother's house. "I'm asking for a probationary period ... It's my last line of defence to assert my rights as a father, which have been totally disregarded." He has brought no proof of revenue because he failed to pick up the summons from the post office: "Send them to my work address," he requests. None of this sits well with the thirty-year-old judge, who is married to a sales executive: a probationary period "doesn't make sense legally," she replies. She concludes that shared custody is an unlikely outcome if the parents cannot agree with each other.

Marc Lachance, a judge in Quebec City, is presiding over a hearing involving a lawyer and a director of communications. The couple, who are both in their early forties, were sharing custody of their two teenage children until a year ago, when the husband moved overseas. The father is asking to see his younger son each time he returns to Quebec. The older daughter, who suffers from bipolar disorder, refuses to see him, and he is worried about her. He is requesting an evaluation, which irritates the judge, who is himself from a family of lawyers.

> *Man:* My daughter is fairly emotionally fragile. She gets that from her mother's side ...
>
> *Judge:* I also have a seventeen-year-old daughter who decided to live with her mother. I can listen to you all afternoon, and I'm going to. But I am not going to order a psycho-social evaluation for a seventeen year old who decides to live with her mother. There's no reason to bring up genetics. Monsieur is not a geneticist. He is a lawyer. He is not being heard as an expert but based on the facts.

The words of both of these judges illustrate the tensions that their social proximity to litigants may provoke. In their dealings with men who did not fully understand their independence as judges and their power to decide, judges were sometimes stinging in their responses: Lachance declared right away that he would not order an evaluation, which is rare in a hearing in Quebec. The fact remains, however, that judges may sometimes be constrained by the resources that these parties deploy. As Lachance observed, "I can listen to you all afternoon, and I'm going to." As for Cabernet, she would have been hard put to actually challenge the decisions of the "hard-headed" dentist (as she described him after the hearing). In France, shared physical custody is uncommon in cases where parents cannot come to an agreement (Guillonneau and Moreau 2013). Ultimately, the dentist got what he wanted: the child stayed with the mother, who was the one penalized by his unwillingness to cooperate.

In contrast to men, women in the upper class whom we observed mostly complied with legal professionals' procedural and behavioural expectations. The problems that did emerge tended to arise among stay-at-home mothers. Most middle- and upper-class mothers now follow the model of working outside the home (Collins 2019; Hochschild and Machung 1990). This model is built on norms of individual autonomy, which are particularly significant in the context of divorce, wherein the parties are is supposed to "rebuild" their lives as they see fit. Lawyers' reactions to more privileged women who deviated from this norm were revealing of class and gender traits and the ways in which these traits informed their understandings of the economic disparities between men and women.

In France, a "compensatory benefit" (*prestation compensatoire*) exists to compensate for the negative impact of divorce on women's standard of living, particularly in cases where women have left the labour market to support their spouses' careers and raise their children. It is awarded in one out of five divorces and nearly always to the woman (Belmokhtar and Mansuy 2016). Nonetheless, we regularly observed family judges expressing doubts about whether the benefit was justified. Yves Defert, a judge in his forties in Belles, provided such an example: "The compensatory benefit is very sexist ... In modern couples, both people work, and one person's career shouldn't happen to the detriment of the other's – or maybe only in exceptional cases."[31]

Defert's formulation was much firmer and more outspoken than those of most of his colleagues. All the same, reservations about the validity of the compensatory benefit are widespread in France. Several feminist politicians have suggested that it maintains women's dependence on men: Yvette Roudy, the minister for women's rights in the early 1980s, as well as members of Parliament from the Delegation on Women's Rights in 2000 have publicly expressed this viewpoint. As a result, it was decided that the benefit would be awarded in a lump sum rather than as an allowance (Revillard 2009).[32] This argument is still prominent in contemporary debate. At a conference organized by the French Ministère de la justice (Ministry of Justice) in 2016, Cécile Bourreau-Dubois and Myriam Doriat-Duban (2016), the economists whose work on the subject is most widely recognized, asked this question: "Why maintain the compensatory benefit when there are so many reasons to think it is outdated?"[33] The political, academic, and activist segments of France are clearly reluctant to ask that men compensate for the lack of gender equality in professional and household labour, which continues to be a characteristic of many couples.

In our observations, the professional positions of judges appeared to make them even less sensitive to the costs of domestic specialization for divorcing women. Most French family judges, as we have seen, are women who excelled in school to achieve a respected professional status. Their position does not mean that they are free from gender inequalities in the home: several of the judges with whom we spoke lived with executives working long hours in the private sector and had chosen a career as a family judge to balance their work and family lives (Bessière and Mille 2014). Nevertheless, their lives contrast starkly with those of women who stayed home to support their husbands' careers. In our observations, it appeared that these women's cases tended to reinforce judges' support for the norm of women living active professional lives.

Middle- and upper-class women have more access to this benefit than women from less privileged backgrounds. Because it must – with certain exceptions – be paid out as a lump sum, the compensatory benefit is accessible only to married couples with assets. We noted nonetheless that the women requesting it were often perceived as making excessive demands, despite the fact that the inequalities inherent in their investment in the domestic sphere would doubtless persist from the time of divorce all the way through to retirement. In a contested divorce ruling that we observed in Marjac in 2007, a man and a woman, both aged forty-five and married for sixteen years with three children, were in disagreement over the amount of the compensatory benefit to be paid out. The woman was requesting thirty thousand euros. The man, a high school teacher making thirty-two hundred euros per month, proposed twelve thousand euros. The judge settled on eighteen thousand euros, an amount significantly closer to the man's request than the woman's. No precise calculations were given to justify this in the ruling, only a series of observations:

> Madame took parental leave after the birth of their [third] child, after which she did not see fit to find another job, despite the fact that she had obtained a degree as a childcare assistant in 1994 and never made any professional use of it and that her two older children were going to school full time, and childcare for the third child would be easy once she started school. She therefore chose not to work during these years of marriage and easily found work when she needed to. By all assumptions, and independent of her living choices, which should not be the financial burden of the husband, it is clear that her pension will be lower than her husband's. Given that she is in good health, she can still work for some twenty years and is currently employed as a domestic aide [work that is paid at minimum wage]. (Collectif Onze 2013, 241–42)

By characterizing this woman's withdrawal from the labour market as a personal "life choice" rather than concluding that it had been the result of a series of complex arrangements between her and her ex-husband – and by underestimating the degree to which her long absence from the labour market would place her at a lasting disadvantage, this judge's ruling ignored the deeply gendered division of labour in couples of different sexes: when one of them remains in the home, it is still almost always the woman.

The Legal Encounter as a Situated Nexus of Power   147

In Quebec, we found that women who had dedicated themselves to family life during their marriages or domestic partnerships were not perceived as negatively as they are in France. Feminist movements in the 1980s fought hard against the economic inequalities of divorce. Unlike in France, they succeeded in asserting the view that economic transfers from men to their ex-spouses were a way of fostering autonomy among divorced women (Revillard 2009). Moreover, we observed that judges tended to consider the specialization of feminine and masculine roles to be most financially viable in wealthy circles. There is also a wider range of allocative mechanisms available in Quebec than in France, such as the partition of family patrimony, spousal support, and compensatory allowance; furthermore, and in contrast to France, the partnership of acquests is the default regime for marriages and civil unions.[34] Let us recall that some of the Quebec judges we spoke with were men in their sixties and seventies whose wives had also stayed at home. Furthermore, it is probable that both their economic resources, which are much greater than those of French family judges, and their social capital as members of the political and legal elite led them to socialize with more couples for whom this marked gender specialization continues to exist.

Finally, in Quebec, certain lawyers, such as Buckley, remained highly mobilized in their professional practices in the fight against economic inequalities between men and women. One of her clients, for example, had raised four children over the course of a thirty-year marriage, while her husband worked to grow the family business, a chain of supermarkets that at the time of our observation was worth an estimated twelve million dollars. In her motion, this woman, who was considered to be a housewife, claimed to have worked in one of the supermarkets for seven years, doing accounting, replacing absent workers, writing her husband's speeches, and helping him with store openings. "I completely fulfilled my role as the wife of a businessman ... I took care of the housework so that the defendant could devote himself to growing his businesses," she concluded, requesting one-third of the company's value. In her interim ruling, Judge Gisèle Fontaine concluded that "none of the amounts [suggested by the woman] is unreasonable, given the standard of living of both parties during the marriage." She ordered the man to pay fifty-five hundred dollars per month in spousal support (he had requested two thousand dollars). In her motivations, the judge regretted the way in which the father had "completely minimized the mother's contribution to their marriage" and observed that he was late in divulging his assets, suggesting that he had perhaps even hidden some them.[35]

It should be noted that Fontaine's recognition of the labour contributed by the businessman's ex-wife was not the typical Quebecois view of women partners in the privileged classes who had put their careers on hold. First, as in France, options for compensation are reserved for married couples. Because of the decline of the marriage rate for individuals under fifty, the increasing prevalence of couples in which both partners work, and the fact that the length of partnership is a consideration in the calculation of benefits, economic transfers are less important to divorcing and separating couples in their thirties and forties (Jarry et al. 2016). Moreover, we observed that lawyers tended to uphold the norm of women working more firmly for women under fifty. The legitimacy of compensatory mechanisms is clearly waning among generations most exposed to separations. Finally, the ability to seek a lawyer who is both competent and invested in this issue is essential to the success of such procedures: proving the revenue and the assets of these men, who are generally business leaders, is a complex and daunting task. In our study, lawyers varied significantly in their attitudes and behaviours regarding this aspect of divorce depending on their place of residence. The lawyers in Albanel, for example, who encountered wealthy couples much more rarely, were much less committed to these issues than the specialized lawyers we met in Montreal. Even in the same national context and the same social group, geographical and generational attachments also help to structure the relationships of lawyers and laypeople.

***

Variations in power relations between legal professionals and separating couples reveal a second dimension that characterizes the regulation of families post-breakup. Alongside unequal access to law and justice, their very interactions with legal professionals help to differentiate social groups and organize them into hierarchies. As divorce has liberalized, couples continue to depend on professionals to help them assert their rights. Moralizing attitudes remained the norm in situations where there was a significant social gap between the two groups. Our documentations of the ways in which lawyers seek to influence separating couples' expectations attest to the triumph of government by consensus and speech, as has been noted in relationships between doctors and patients (Memmi 2003, 447). These interactions are moments of socialization of the law, in which lawyers and judges give ex-partners keys to appropriating the institutional order and, in doing so, give shape to the futures of their families. Spoken (and unspoken) language also lies at the heart of the symbolic violence displayed by these professionals. Not revealing parties' rights or leading them to understand that they are unattainable, preventing parties from speaking, speaking in their place, and inferring from their verbal abilities their capacity to make it through certain types of procedures are all ways to exert control over speech as well as through it.

This chapter has shown the extent of the class privilege enjoyed by members of the upper class in their relationships with the legal profession. It has also given us the opportunity to reflect on the effects of behavioural and speech norms on gender relations. Among the lower class, women seem to be more compliant with these norms than men. The latter's absence or aggressiveness tends to penalize them in legal proceedings. But, among the upper class, variations in behaviour are less clear-cut, and men may find some advantage in curtailing their communications (by making it more difficult to assess their resources, for example) or in delegating their lawyers to do the speaking.

The next chapter will continue to explore the ramifications of this privilege, showing the strong degree of variation in parental roles depending on gender and social class. Whereas I noted few national differences in the realm of interactions, we will see that they stand out when we turn to lifestyle and standards of living after separation.

How Family Justice Frames Unequal Parenthoods

4

The surveillance of intimate relationships by the law is on the wane. Now, separating couples tend to seek lawyers and judges for help settling issues related to the care of their children, which is where contemporary legal professionals spend the bulk of their time. Most of our observations in the courtroom and in law offices involved custody or child support. Interventions in this arena have become a key vantage point for observing the parenting models that they relay and the ways in which these models are appropriated by parents. On the surface, a single, succinct term describes contemporary parenting norms: "co-parenting" (*coparentalité*) emerged in Quebec at the end of the 1970s (Lachance 1979, 146) and was quickly and widely adopted in France (Commaille 1982, 144). In both places, it rapidly became a central fixture of public debate). As a category of public action, it has come to inflect and influence public policy related to parenting – notably social policy – far beyond private law (Martin 2015).

The stated goal of co-parenting is simple enough: to ensure that both parents are involved in the lives of their children and even to encourage parental equality when it comes to their care. Co-parenting therefore plays a part in policies related to gender equality. Positive law testifies to this: Title IX of the *French Civil Code,* regarding parental authority, is "neutral overall with regard to gender" (Dionisi-Peyrusse and Pichard 2014, 488). While the terms "father" and "mother" are still employed in the *Civil Code of Quebec,* both parents are subject to the same laws, and the *Civil Code* has recognized same-sex parental couples since 2002.[1] In the political world, the use of the non-gendered term "parent" is widespread – for example, the terms "father" and "mother" have more or less disappeared from debates among members of the Assemblée nationale of Quebec (Bouchard, Fortin, and Hautval 2017, 25).

In both national contexts, four legal tools have been designed to foster the involvement of both parents following a separation. The first tool – joint parental authority, which is also known as joint legal custody – is typical of civil law jurisdictions: under it, both parents share responsibility for bringing up the children they have together, cooperating to decide on questions such as health, schooling, or religious education, whether or not they live in the same place. The second tool is visitation rights, which allow the non-custodial parent to maintain regular, but not daily, contact with his or her children (usually on weekends and school holidays). The third tool is joint physical custody, in which children receive practical care on a day-to-day basis from both parents. The fourth tool is child support or transfers of money between parents to cover their upkeep.

Despite the veneer of legitimacy provided by their egalitarian rhetoric, this chapter will show the very concrete ways in which these four legal tools actually serve to entrench intertwined disparities of gender, social class, and race. Far from effacing differences between the paternal and maternal roles, or bringing some measure of uniform practice to child-rearing across social classes, the strongly differential use of these tools reinforces inequalities already at work in parenting, both between genders and among families. Even in cases where the father and the mother are both involved, expectations of them and their contributions remain quite different, and their appropriations of these expectations are different as well. In practical terms, most parents agree that mothers will be assigned the bulk of day-to-day responsibility for the care of their children and that fathers will maintain more episodic and elective relationships with them.

In this context, encouraging co-parenting implies heteronormative gender roles. More than thirty years ago, the American legal scholar Karen Czapanskiy (1991, 1415–16) described the law and its practice by legal professionals as imbued by an "ideology of gendered parenting": "Fathers are given support and reinforcement for being volunteer parents, people whose duties toward their children are limited, but whose autonomy about parenting is broadly protected. Mothers are defined as draftees, people whose duties toward their children are extensive, but whose autonomy about parenting receives little protection." Today, the obligation of day-to-day care remains with mothers, who, after separation, end up with the additional obligation to make way for fathers when they demand it.

Our research shows that this gendered structuring of parental roles cannot be disentangled from class structuring. Parents of different social classes do not adopt the same child-rearing arrangements, and these divergences are encouraged by professionals. "Co-parenting" does not prescribe a single norm across the board; rather, it opens up certain realms of possibility for parenting for some families more than others. The norm of co-parenting is not just socially differentiated, however. It is also strongly linked to national context. In France, our research found, its definition is largely symbolic, and it devalues practical and financial responsibility for children. In Quebec, these responsibilities are assigned more significance, leading to partially distinct modes for managing parental roles.

Mandatory Mothering, Optional Fathering

I begin by noting the outcome of most separations: although decisions in favour of joint physical custody are far more common than they were in the 1980s, court proceedings are still more likely to end up awarding physical custody of children to mothers than to fathers (Table 5). This fact contradicts the claims of fathers' groups, which have argued that courts are biased toward women and award custody to children's mothers against their fathers' wishes (Fillod-Chabaud 2017). While it

TABLE 5 Types of physical custody awarded by judicial rulings

Type of custody	France (%)		Quebec (%)	
	1985[a]	2012[b]	1982[c]	2008[d]
Mother	85	71	77	61
Joint	5	17	7	20
Both parents[e]			16	5
Father	9	12		13
Other	1			1
Total	100	100	100	100

Sources:
a Statistics based on divorce rulings (Festy 1988, 530).
b All statutory rulings related to physical custody handed down by French Family Court judges on June 4–15, 2012, throughout France ($N = 6,042$) (Guillonneau and Moreau 2013, 5).
c Judges' rulings with no further detail (Beaudry 1988, 435).
d Random sample of statutory child support orders issued in 2008 throughout Quebec ($N = 2,000$) (Biland and Schütz 2015a, 3).
e In France, rulings are for individual children and in Quebec for sibling groups, which explain cases where some members of a sibling group live with the father and others with the mother.

is true that fathers are awarded physical custody less often, it is because they request it less often. In cases where only one parent expresses the desire for physical custody, it is usually the mother: 69 percent of the time in Quebec[2] and 83 percent of the time in France (Guillonneau and Moreau 2013, 36). Only a minority of parents are actually in open conflict over where their children should live. Just 8 percent of judgments in Quebec and 11 percent in France record disagreement over custody.[3] In the vast majority of cases, judges' decisions merely ratify existing agreements: in more than 90 percent of French cases, both parents' wishes are met.[4]

Anchoring Parenting in Class and Gender

The gendered division of work, and even of family life, is central to understanding why the majority of children of separated parents live mostly with their mothers. Mothers still perform the bulk of domestic and child-rearing labour in a couple (Brousse 2015; Champagne, Pailhé, and Solaz 2015; Crespo 2018), and they still have fewer prospects in the job market (Beaujot, Liu, and Ravanera 2015; Meurs, Pailhé, and Ponthieux 2010). During the process of separation, it is often easier for them to assert the value of their greater experience in the daily care of their children. Men, by contrast, are generally more invested in the labour market and less in the home; only rarely do they think of themselves in the role of solo parent (Martial 2016; Piesen 2016). They may fear they are not qualified or, similar to the dentist we encountered in Chapter 3, may be reluctant to sacrifice work time outside the home.

When legal professionals push for "co-parenting" because it is "in the best interests of the child" – linking together the two guiding principles of contemporary family law – it is crucial to remember that they are doing so within a still deeply unequal context. Nevertheless, connecting co-parenting and the best interests of the child is a matter of consensus among professionals, as we found. They mobilized this connection regularly in their work. As Céline Paquette, a judge in Quebec, put it, "seeing both parents, and that both parents have a decent home environment, is in the vital interest of the child."[5] When a young mother remarked that her ex-partner "did nothing but contribute the sperm ... and doesn't even deserve his son," French judge Anaïs Le Meur reproached the mother that such words could "wreck" the child and advised that she read books on psychology to help her understand the harmful effects of such speech on her child.[6] It is no coincidence that the judge was addressing a mother here and not a father: the goal of co-parenting discourse is to make space for fathers, even in cases where mothers are reluctant to step into that space (Collectif Onze 2013, 178). When we asked about potential obstacles to co-parenting, legal professionals often mentioned a lack of cooperation from mothers. Brigitte Lévesque, another judge in Quebec, noted that she was obliged to remain "vigilant" when a woman who remarried "intentionally eliminates her former partner." She explained that "you have to leave room for the father in there."[7]

This issue has sparked particularly heated debate over whether mothers with sole custody can move away from the father of their child(ren). In 1996, the Supreme Court of Canada set the criteria for evaluating requests to change custody arrangements in cases where one parent was relocating.[8] In 2019, Canadian divorce law was modified to include provisions related to parental relocations.[9] A parent who wishes to relocate must now notify the other parent at least sixty days before the expected date of relocation. On receiving notice, if the other parent opposes the move, he or she has thirty days to file an objection with the courts. Currently, French law is not quite so extreme, but the question of relocation has been the subject of equally intense debate. In 2014, Socialist deputies to the Assemblée nationale (National Assembly) submitted a draft law to establish the legal principle of joint physical custody, even in cases where children stayed with one of the parents only episodically.[10] The judge charged with examining the law at the French Ministère de la justice (Ministry of Justice) confided in me that she was in favour of this kind of change: "Symbolically, requiring joint physical custody is a way to help mentalities evolve."[11]

The draft legislation also proposed that a parent planning to relocate be obliged to obtain the authorization of the other parent or to petition the courts. This clause was contested on the grounds of freedom of movement and the mobility increasingly demanded by the job market. Ultimately, the draft legislation did not reach a Senate vote, and custody laws remained unchanged in this regard. This episode in the law reveals an ongoing political controversy in France between the left and the feminist movement, notably, that extends to legal professionals. Judge Brigitte Cigliano expressed outrage over judges whom she called "Zorros" when she described being called to hand down appellate court rulings on decisions by her colleagues in the trial courts. "Zorros" was her term for judges whom she perceived as seeing themselves as "vigilantes" and attempting to sanction women who had legitimate reasons to relocate.[12] Moreover, legal professionals tended to privilege "stability" and "routine" for very young children (under the age of two or three), which contributed to maintaining mothers in the primary parenting role in the early childhood years.

Finally, the norm of co-parenting limits the degree to which judges are able to account for the issue of family violence, particularly as fault divorce has become rare. In both France and Quebec, legal professionals carefully distinguish between violence against children and partner violence (usually against women), giving more importance to the former than to the latter. In 2019, a research team involving the Quebec Fédération des maisons d'hébergement pour femmes (Federation of Women's Shelters) analyzed 250 family law rulings from the Quebec Superior Court and the Quebec Court of Appeal between 2000 and 2016 that included considerations of family violence. In total, 96 percent of these rulings related to at least one child, and 82 percent had to do with custody (Bernier and Gagnon 2019, 13–14). These decisions used the language of "conflict" far more frequently than the language of "violence." In 73 percent of these cases, women were the only reported adult victims (men accounted for just 4 percent). Despite these stark figures, the language in these rulings consistently assigned responsibility to both partners. Moreover, judges had a tendency to ascribe violent behaviour to circumstances (relating it to the separation, for example) rather than to enduring and structural conditions (15–16).

The 2019 amendment to the *Canadian Divorce Act* included a definition of family violence and provisions for it to be addressed in court. In Quebec, in 2021 and 2022, two bills were adopted to improve the way in which courts handle issues related to family violence.[13] However, the expansion of out-of-court legal services and the diversification of the types of professionals involved in separation make it difficult to establish any unitary policy on family violence. In an interview in November 2020, a lawyer who had been practising family mediation in a remote area for the past sixteen years surmised that many of the women he worked with did not dare to reveal that they had been the victims of domestic partner violence.[14] He suspected that they preferred to keep this information under wraps to ensure that the separation process went smoothly. He further noted, that when he advised women who did speak up to drop mediation and consult a lawyer, many of them chose not to, fearing it would make matters with their ex-partners even worse.

Family judges in France are even more tolerant of so-called ordinary violence against children than their counterparts in Quebec. Moreover, they tend to "oppose 'partner violence' and 'partner conflict,'" considering certain acts such as "light" physical violence or psychological harassment to be "acceptable" during the separation process (Jouanneau and Matteoli 2018, 319). This observation was made by a sociologist and a legal scholar in 2018, despite the fact that family judges' powers with regard to post-separation violence had been reinforced eight years prior in 2010, when the law was modified to include provisions that allowed judges to issue a protection order, for example, forbidding a partner from having any contact with the ex-partner.[15] These orders remain rare, however: they comprise less than 1 percent of the new cases opened in family courts (Guillonneau 2019). In the autumn of 2019, a national forum on intimate partner violence (Le Grenelle des violences conjugales) brought new visibility to this issue. Notably, it led to a reform of the protection order and the introduction of protective bracelets to help keep abusive ex-partners away from their victims.

The legal professionals we encountered in the course of researching this book appeared to have little awareness of their role as protectors, as the following two observations will show. In the first, a Court of Appeal judge successively interviewed three children whose father was contesting the protection order obtained by their mother. The judge explained to each of them in turn that he was not interested in the father's violence against their mother. When the eldest of the siblings, who was the age of twelve, began his testimony with the statement "he hits my mother," the judge replied "yes, but what about you? That's couple stuff, but what about you?"[16] A few months later, in a trial court, we observed a lawyer defending a known victim of intimate partner violence. Although she did argue that it was grounds for awarding the mother full physical custody of their daughter, she sounded apologetic, promising that "we won't get into the whole coercive control thing."[17]

In both of these cases, intimate partner violence was relegated to the wings, as if it were not the concern of judges presiding over separations (or, rather, as if it were only their concern in very specific cases under a set of conditions that were rarely all met). Indeed, men's violence against women and children was never discussed as a structural mechanism. Instead, it was left to coexist alongside other factors in a more vast and more vague universe of parental deviance – a universe that legal professionals generally approach using gender stereotypes. As I have shown with my colleague Gabrielle Schütz, faults ascribed to mothers are different from those ascribed to fathers (see Table 6), and legal professionals

TABLE 6 The gender of post-separation deviance

Women	*Men*
Manipulative: plays the victim, makes false accusations to get what she wants	Violent (physically and/or verbally): toward the ex-partner, their children, and even other people
Unstable and/or disorderly: bad relationships that endanger children, frequent relocations, a rotation of new partners	Controlling and/or jealous: toward the ex-partner and even toward professionals caring for their children
Venal and lazy: desires an unreasonable lifestyle, has not actively looked for work since the separation, seeks to keep the family home	Stingy or spendthrift: requests joint physical custody to avoid paying child support, refuses to pay for children's upkeep but makes extravagant purchases (car, TV)
Demanding, clingy, alienating: interferes in the father's relationship with the children, opposes visitation rights, does not communicate information, excludes him from decisions	Absent: does not exercise visitation rights, disappears from the children's lives, is unavailable to them
Negligent: does not provide appropriate care to children, does not oversee their education closely enough, leaves them alone	Incompetent: does not look after children on a daily basis or see to their everyday needs (cooking, care, schedules, and so on)
Does not stimulate the children: does not play with them, does not take them out	Is only good for fun: does not set any rules or boundaries

Source: Biland and Schütz (2014)

are much more likely to give credence to them when they fall in line with gender stereotypes (Biland and Schütz 2014, 38).

In our observations, instances in which explicit restrictions were placed on a couple's co-parenting hewed to these categories of parental deviance. For the majority of situations, encouraging prolonged contact with both parents was the norm, and bounding the mother's territory was the main tactic for achieving this scenario. In contrast to this restrictive approach to the maternal role, professionals showed a marked benevolence toward paternal involvement. François Charland, the experienced lawyer in Albanel, remarked approvingly to us that, "today, more and more fathers take an interest in caring for their children and really try to paint a picture of themselves that is different from what the mother is saying. And that's a good thing for the child to have both sides of the story."[18]

In reality, this ideal of co-parenting plays out in deeply asymmetrical ways because separated fathers who actively seek involvement in the daily lives of their children are the exception, not the rule. Thus, mothers are assigned the duty of making space for fathers, whereas fathers maintain the right – not the obligation – to take responsibility for their children. Gérard Boyer, a judge in Quebec, acknowledged to us that this version of paternal involvement was voluntary, explaining that joint custody happens "if the father wants to be involved." As he put it, "if the father shows up, and the father wants to be involved, I'll encourage it."[19] If the father does not express such a desire, co-parenting is usually limited to joint legal custody with visitation rights. Granted to the vast majority of fathers, the sharing of parental authority is a way of allowing them to maintain their power to decide over their children's education. But, in purely practical terms, when visitation rights are limited to every second weekend and half of school holidays – as they most commonly are – fathering becomes something "discontinuous, occasional, extraordinary in the strict sense of that word" (Collectif Onze 2013, 165). The routine of granting sole custody to the mother with visitation rights for the father, in keeping with the parents' own informal practices, was evident in multiple hearings.

Custody Hearing in Marjac, France

A health aide and an unemployed worker, who are both around the age of twenty-five, appear before Judge Pierre Terreau without a lawyer, regarding their daughter, A., aged six. The judge reminds them that they hold joint legal custody: "That is the rule." The parties nod their agreement, with no questions, appearing not to understand exactly what he means. The judge asks: "Where does A. live?" The mother replies: "With me." The judge asks whether physical custody should be assigned to the mother. "Yes," she answers, and the father mutters "yeah, sure, no choice about it!" The judge then informs the father of his visitation rights, every second weekend and half of school holidays, quickly adding "that's what's generally done." They nod their agreement a second time, remarking that this is what they already do. The hearing lasts three minutes. (Collectif Onze 2013, 172)[20]

Hearing in Quebec City

A nineteen-year-old woman and her lawyer appear before Judge Brigitte Lévesque. Her ex-partner, who has just completed a vocational degree, is absent. The young woman is questioned for five minutes by her lawyer:

> Lawyer: "Who takes care of the child?"
> Woman: "Me."
> Lawyer: "Does the father have visitation rights?"
> Woman: "Yes, when he wants, he calls me."
> Lawyer: "It's worked out amicably?"
> Woman: "Yes ..."
> Lawyer: "He never keeps her for long?"
> Woman: "No."

At this, the judge dictates her decision to the clerk: "The parties are the parents of T., born in September 2009. They separated in December 2010, and the mother has taken responsibility for the child's care ... On these grounds, the court grants sole custody of the child T. to the plaintiff, with visitation on agreement by the two parties."[21]

These two hearings reflect two different histories. By his very absence, the father in Quebec City was consenting to the mother's full custody, confirming the correlation observed in the previous chapter between withdrawal from legal proceedings and distance from the socially accepted paternal role. By contrast, the French father was resigning himself to this agreement after a long domestic partnership: he grumbled his acceptance of the mother's full custody because he had "no choice about it." The barriers to his involvement as a father were partly socioeconomic: he was a recipient of a means-tested social benefit (known as the Revenu de Solidarité Active [RSA]), and his low income made caring for his daughter more complicated.[22] Significantly, these two cases involved lower-class fathers, who as a social group are far more constrained in the job market by irregular and unpredictable work schedules than their middle- and upper-class counterparts (Lesnard 2009). Fathers in this socio-economic category are more likely to be living in economically precarious situations, with little access to lawyers or aid from the state, which can be an obstacle to exercising their visitation rights, particularly if they do not have adequate housing for their children. These factors limit the opportunities that these fathers may have to engage in "co-parenting."

In contrast to fathers, mothers are more likely to be reminded by social services, lawyers, and ex-partners that they are the only ones capable of caring for their children. Interactions with professionals reinforce the gendered division of parenting roles already manifest in the family arrangements of manual labourers (Schwartz 2012) and low-level employees (Le Pape 2009) during cohabitation. Legal professionals rarely question such unequal practices: perhaps because they assume these men have significant social difficulties, they do not question their avoidance of their role as fathers and reaffirm the assignment of women to their role as mothers. A minority of women are disqualified from this role by certain specific failings such as extreme violence, severe negligence, or mental illness (Bernheim and Lebecke 2014; Cardi 2007). In such cases, custody is awarded to the father, or the children are put in foster care. But, as clear-cut examples of feminine deviance, they serve to uphold the norm rather than weaken it.

In addition, as we saw in the previous chapter, legal professionals tend to assume that families from non-Western backgrounds do not follow norms of gender equality and are therefore unlikely to engage in "co-parenting." These assumptions upheld the normative stances they took in interactions with parents, while also lowering the likelihood that custody would actually be shared. Significantly, during the two days of hearings that sociologists observed with family judge Anna de Mattéi, she nearly always asked parties from Sub-Saharan Africa about their grasp of joint legal custody (a complex notion that many parents have trouble understanding), while asking only one "white" couple the same questions.[23]

In Quebec, allegations of violence are made more frequently by parties hailing from non-European countries than by people born in Canada (Biland and Schütz 2014, 40). Legal professionals tend to believe them more and to register their disapproval under the banner of their position as members of the majority culture. Thus, speaking in an interview with a father born in Quebec who had accused his ex-wife's new partner, who was from Latin America, of violence, Lévesque explained to our team that "it isn't acceptable for a parent to beat a child in Quebec, even if it's part of their culture. For me, that's always going to be a 'no.' And you have to pay attention to the difference in the way men treat women." She did not mention this kind of attention when it came to pure laine French Canadians.[24] When legal professionals work with people from economically disadvantaged backgrounds, particularly when these people are racialized, their work includes reminding clients of the supposedly unfamiliar norm of co-parenting, while assuming that its application will generally be minimal. Moving up the social scale as well as when they are working with members of the cultural majority, the situation changes: professionals encourage co-parenting in interactions with upper- and middle-class parents, assuming they will be more able, willing, and likely to embrace it.

As a consequence, as American and Australian studies have also shown (Cashmore et al. 2010; Donnelly and Finkelhor 1993), joint physical custody is more frequent among middle- and upper-class parents who have advanced degrees and both work outside the home (Bloch 2021; Pelletier 2016). These parents are also more likely to be homeowners, with more spacious living arrangements than most single-parent households (Algava, Penant, and Yankan 2019, 3). By contrast, compared to the average, the number of French children living in joint custody drops by a factor of two when their household income is in the bottom 30 percent (2). Of course, socio-economic factors are not the only ones to determine child custody. The child's age is also a factor – joint custody remains rare in early childhood – as are location and housing costs: the proximity of parental homes (Cretin 2015) and lower housing costs (Algava, Penant, and Yankan 2019, 3) are both factors that favour joint custody.

Be that as it may, employment status remains a crucial factor: parents with stable and relatively well-paid jobs are far more likely to share physical custody (Brunet, Kertudo, and Malsan 2008). There are fewer inequalities in the distribution of domestic labour when women are more invested and better paid in the labour market and when men have higher qualifications and flexible work schedules (Brugeilles and Sébille 2009). When such couples separate, joint physical custody may indeed be a promising solution for both parents. In France, unsurprisingly, divorce by mutual consent, where middle- and upper-class couples are over-represented (see Chapter 1), has the highest incidence of joint physical custody: it reached 30 percent in 2012 (Guillonneau and Moreau 2013, 20). The impact of revenue is most noticeable among men: 40 percent of fathers in the top income quartile in Quebec (the wealthiest, in other words) request physical custody (potentially joint) compared with 20 percent of fathers in the bottom quartile.[25]

Nonetheless, we should refrain from believing that joint physical custody is the result of a pre-existing equality that the justice system limits itself to upholding. In fact, the demands of these fathers seem to be more acceptable both to mothers and to legal professionals because their resources as parents are more credible than those of men from less advantaged backgrounds. In addition to possessing the financial resources to delegate a part of the labour of childcare to professionals, the men we observed in this category evoked child-rearing practices that resemble the "concerted cultivation" observed by sociologist Annette Lareau (2011, 1) among the American middle class. They reported carefully choosing their children's schools, planning extracurricular activities that helped to foster their skills and talents, and maintaining close relationships with educational professionals. All of these activities bear witness to their capacity to pass on their privileged social status to their children.

Fathers with lower-class status also described being involved with their children: they frequently mentioned teaching manual skills, giving them a feel for the land (in rural parts of Quebec, this often meant going out into the forest to cut wood), as well as informal sporting activities (playing hockey in the backyard, for example). But such parenting practices are far removed from the world of school and education; they are informal modes of generational teaching and less directly oriented toward performance. By contrast, fathers in upper-class settings described their parental involvement with reference to practices that are both monetized and culturally legitimate. Before separation, the occasional investments they made in their children's lives were often decisive in terms of social reproduction, serving to demonstrate the value of their involvement as fathers and to convince others of the worth of intensifying this involvement post-separation (Biland and Mille 2017).

One of our observations, for example, involved the head of a Montreal marketing company (with an income of over four hundred thousand dollars per year) and his ex-wife, who worked in his company. They could not agree on custody arrangements for their youngest children, aged eleven and sixteen. In her motion, the father's lawyer affirmed he was "able to provide the intellectual and social stimulation the children need and to help them with their studies, has already done homework with them, and is involved in their social activities (sports, among others)."[26] This is a far cry from the fast-food meals and evenings in front of the television that nearly all fathers from lower-class backgrounds described to us, which were not perceived by professionals as contributing as much to the work of child-rearing and further discredited them as "only good for fun" with their children. In general, less privileged parents were questioned much more frequently about their day-to-day lives and the routine aspects of childcare (meal preparation, bedtime, personal hygiene, and so on). By taking these things for granted in their interactions with upper- and middle-class parents, legal professionals left those fathers the space and time to showcase the kinds of elective and even distinctive activities – two months in Europe for one Quebecois father, for example – that fit better with their schedules and their social skills.

These fathers' strategies for highlighting their parenting skills are directly linked to gender relations among the upper and middle classes: for these men, the implicit or expressed goal was to avoid giving mothers "control" over child-rearing during the separation, to borrow a term used by lawyer Marie-Josée Bénard in a sworn affidavit she prepared with a financial executive to request joint physical custody of his children, aged five and eight, even though his ex-wife had stayed at home to care for them during their marriage.[27] Overall, the post-separation parental practices that we observed were connected to expectations constructed before the separation as well as to behaviours that were perceived as likely or unlikely, valued or discredited, by legal professionals. Rights and responsibilities were connected for fathers and mothers based on two interlocking systems of domination: class and gender. Lower-class women were propelled toward their duties as mothers, while their ex-partners encountered great difficulty in asserting their rights. Upper- and middle-class women were assigned the duty of making way for the fathers of their children, while their ex-partners enjoyed great latitude in choosing how they would be involved. These practical variations, which are co-constructed by parents and legal professionals, form the bedrock of the inequalities that play out in each socially situated configuration. Thus, although they are far from uniform, practices of joint custody nearly always place the bulk of child-rearing and financial responsibilities on mothers (Cadolle 2011).

Parental Roles as National Constructs

Our research revealed that these mechanisms of class and gender were present on both sides of the Atlantic but not in the same form and not with the same intensity. Table 4 provides an initial, statistical hint of these differences, showing that joint custody is a more common outcome in Quebec than in France (25 percent versus 17 percent of rulings); what is more, dual residence for children is more widespread in Quebec than in other Canadian provinces (Pelletier 2017, 120). If joint custody is more common in Quebec, it is first of all because parents have come to an agreement about it. When parents come to an agreement on the custody of their child(ren) in France, it is joint in one out of five cases (Guillonneau and Moreau 2013, 19), compared to two out of five cases in Quebec.[28] This preference for joint physical custody in Quebec can be explained in part by the fact that it is valued by professionals: we found that court and psycho-social interventions encouraged it there much more than they did in France.

Given that France adopted a law promoting joint physical custody in 2002, this may seem surprising.[29] No such law exists in Quebec, where the 2019 amendment to the federal divorce act affirms that, "in allocating parenting time, the court shall give effect to the principle that a child should have as much time with each spouse as is consistent with the best interests of the child."[30] In a context where appellate courts have more political clout, this promotion of joint physical custody by the legal system is jurisprudential. As early as 1993, the Supreme Court of Canada interpreted the *Divorce Act* as allowing joint physical custody but rejected the notion that the law presumed in favour of it.[31] Since the 2000s, the Court of Appeal has handed down a series of decisions clarifying its applicability.[32]

In line with their professional mandate both in their rulings and in our interviews with them, judges underlined to us that they believed it was imperative to hand down decisions on a "case-by-case basis." As Lévesque explained, "joint custody happens when all the stars are aligned!" since so many different dimensions must be taken into consideration in assigning custody. The relatively vague and multi-faceted notion of "the best interests of the child" upholds judges' discretionary power and helps to justify their "tailor-made" decisions.[33] The fact remains, however, that judges in Quebec spoke of joint custody more frequently, more spontaneously, and more enthusiastically than their French counterparts. Philippe Nadeau, who had sat on the bench for twenty-one years at the time of our interview, told us he believed that joint custody has been "the big, big, major change" since he was appointed in 1991. He added that "if the father is also a good father and has good parenting skills, it's normal to have ... joint custody."[34]

Valuing joint custody was not only the purview of male judges making arguments favourable to their gender, however. Nadeau did mention his own experience as a divorced father with primary custody of his teenage children when we spoke of it. But the attitudes of women judges were very similar: by the late 1990s, their view of joint custody had become very favourable (Quéniart and Joyal 2001), and recent interviews confirm that this remains the case (Godbout, Parent, and Saint-Jacques 2015). For the most part, we noted that professionals involved with families during the course of separation relayed this supposed judicial preference for joint custody. Michel Tétrault (2004), a legal aid attorney and a law professor at the Université de Sherbrooke who has authored numerous publications on the subject, titled a section of one of his books "Presumption of Joint Custody: Legal? No! Factual? Yes!" Claudette Guilmaine (2009, 21), a social worker and a mediator who has published extensively on the topic since the 1990s, opened a 2009 book with the assertion that joint custody "is basically the norm now," which is a point of view broadly echoed in the media (Goyer 2016; Leduc 2013). This body of work does not argue for joint custody in each and every circumstance, but it does present it as an option that is often preferable for children and regularly favoured by judges. Today, this perspective seems to be widespread in Quebec. In a survey of 1,200 people (of whom 28 percent had personal experience with separation), the majority responded that joint custody was the "ideal" solution for children over the age of three (Godbout, Saint-Jacques, and Ivers 2018, 404–6).

Family therapists and social workers are in large part responsible for helping to disseminate these representations so widely over the past thirty years, and their influence has grown as the public recognition of the role of family mediation has increased. After Canada ratified the 1991 United Nations Convention on the Rights of the Child, which introduced the concept of "the best interests of the child" to international law, the Quebec government asked a group of experts to "propose ways to prevent the emergence of severe problems in youths" (Groupe de travail pour les jeunes 1991, 9).[35] Headed by Camil Bouchard, a professor of psychology at the Université du Quebec à Montréal, the group, most of whose members were directors of psycho-social services teams, published a report in 1991 titled *Un Québec fou de ses enfants (Quebec Treasures Its Children)*. The report underlined the importance of father-child relationships, mentioning the childhood risks associated with parental separations (mental health, learning difficulties, depression) (42). It also deplored the frequent absence of fathers from their young children's lives and concluded with a plea to expand family mediation, which encouraged joint custody (89, 146).

Although the movement of fathers' groups was in its nascent phase at that time, the "cause of fathers" was taken up by many psycho-social and legal professionals in their work with families in the name of a supposedly scientific understanding of the best interests of the child.[36] This academic legitimation of joint custody has been an important phenomenon in North America. Psychological and even psychiatric categories have informed Canadian and Quebecois jurisprudence much more than French law. Judicial recognition of parental alienation syndrome (PAS), which began much earlier in Quebec than in France, is evidence of this awareness.[37] The diagnosis was developed in the 1980s by Richard A. Gardner, an American child psychiatrist, to describe situations in which a child is manipulated by one parent into refusing contact with the other. The upholding of this pathology by judges indicates the importance assigned to maintaining ties to both parents and the suspicion with which mothers are viewed, in that they are more often custodial parents and therefore more likely to express these potentially "alienating" views (Caplan 2007).

An analysis of custody rulings handed down in 2016 by the Superior Court and the Court of Appeal confirms that mothers are suspected of this behaviour much more often than fathers (forty-five cases versus twenty-one or 68 percent) and that the very broad definition of parental alienation, which is much broader than the criteria used by psychologists, is used to their detriment (Zaccour 2018). In a context where the feminist movement has mobilized strongly to reduce economic inequalities post-separation (see Chapter 5), feminist critiques of custody rulings are much less common than in France, where PAS has been denounced as a way of obscuring male violence (Romito and Crisma 2009), or the United States, where "family court and abuse professionals have long been polarized over the use of parental alienation claims to discredit a mother alleging the father has been abusive or is unsafe for the children" (Meier 2020).

It must be said that social workers and psychologists enjoy far more recognition professionally and institutionally in Canada than in France. The existence of court psycho-social evaluation services is symbolic of their significance in the separation process and means that they are much more likely to interact with legal professionals. Furthermore, psycho-social interventions with families in Quebec are characterized by a behaviourist approach to family issues and child development, which is particularly visible in the frequency of diagnoses of attention-deficit hyperactivity disorder: in Canada, youth in Quebec are the greatest consumers of medication for this disorder (Tremblay and Daigle 2017, 5).

In the field of separations, American research has inspired the use of a range of instruments for measuring parental conflict and practical approaches to "co-parenting." Tétrault (2004, 496) describes "models for responsibility-sharing agreements" that offer several ways to organize joint custody. Guilmaine (2009, 411–12) provides a list of "preventive parenting attitudes" intended to ensure healthy child development. This shared belief in joint custody among judges and psycho-social workers fosters second-order belief among lawyers, attesting to their work "in the shadow of the law" (Mnookin and Kornhauser 1979, 950). Convinced that judges and therapists prefer joint custody arrangements, attorneys end up promoting this belief by supporting fathers who request it and encouraging mothers to accept it. "It has become much easier now for the courts to grant shared custody," Charland affirmed to us. You will recall that he is the lawyer who in Chapter 3 advised his client not to seek sole custody because she was "not strong enough."[38] A few months after this meeting, we observed Charland's meeting with a truck driver in his mid-thirties whose three children ranged in age from five to nine years old. He had been sharing physical custody with their mother for a few weeks, following an agreement reached in mediation. Charland asked whether "monsieur can do everything [with the children]," and the father assured him of his involvement prior to the separation: "I gave them baths, I did homework with them." The lawyer then inquired whether he also prepared evening meals, to which the father replied that "that was more unusual" since he often came home late from work. Charland did not react to this last statement and agreed to go ahead with the father's request and prepare a motion to make joint custody official.[39]

Indeed, given the level of evidence required to obtain sole custody, lawyers often conclude that mothers have little alternative but to accept fathers' demands. Middle-class mothers, whose ex-partners are more likely to request joint custody but who hardly have the means to seek an expert opinion to counter their claims, are the most likely to come under pressure to make these sorts of concessions. Instead of "quibbling," they are expected to recognize that the person who was more involved with the children's lives during the course of the domestic partnership should not have priority and to accept that fathers will raise their children differently from the way they would themselves (Mille and Zimmermann 2017). This kind of discourse affects parents' expectations: in contested cases, mothers in Quebec request joint custody more frequently than French mothers do (16 percent compared to 7 percent), and they request sole custody less often (71 percent compared to 90 percent) (Guillonneau and Moreau 2013, 26).[40] Concretely, the tools offered by "manuals" and the time permitted by free mediation sessions help parents and lawyers to work out joint custody in a way that appears satisfying to both parties. Furthermore, in Quebec, custody is considered to be joint when each parent takes care of a child at least 40 percent of the time. Consent is facilitated by relatively flexible and varied arrangements, which are not necessarily equal in quantitative terms.

So why is joint custody sought less often in France? Maria Flores, a judge in Quebec City, offered us this comparative viewpoint: "French psychiatrists are really opposed to joint custody. Personally, I think you need to look at every situation, every case – there's no dogma for it."[41] This view of "French psychiatrists" appears to be widely held. While they are hardly unanimous on the subject, their mobilization against joint custody received a great deal of media attention in the 2000s (Neyrand and Zaouche Gaudron 2014; Tena 2012). *Le livre noir de la résidence alternée (The Dark Side of Joint Custody)* is emblematic of this form of expert critique. The book, published in 2006 and coordinated by a midwife who founded a non-profit organization to raise awareness of the pitfalls of the 2002 custody law, includes contributions from three lawyers, a psychotherapist, and three child psychiatrists who are also psychoanalysts (Phélip 2006). The legal and psychological professions working with families in France share a very different understanding of custody than the one observed in Quebec.

Broadly speaking, their perspective, which draws from the field of psychoanalysis, sees children as needing to "attach" themselves to the parent who cares for them in a continuous way – generally the mother – in order to build a sense of emotional security and to pursue healthy emotional development. Being separated from this "primary attachment figure" is a major psychological risk, one that is considered to be definitive due to the cognitive and emotional immaturity of young children. As a result, they argue, joint custody should be excluded as an option before the age of six (in Quebec, the thinking tends more toward splitting it up over short periods of time) and adopted with caution for older children. A key figure in the origin of this approach was the daughter of Sigmund Freud, Anna, who used it in cases of separation and adoption and whose influence on American court decisions was significant at the time (Goldstein, Freud, and Solnit 1973). Respect for psychoanalysis has waned over the years in North America while remaining strong in France, where it still exerts considerable influence over family policy and the way in which judges address separation.

French psychoanalyst Françoise Dolto holds the greatest sway in this matter, and she participated in the drafting of public policy from the 1960s to the 1980s (Garcia 2011; Robcis 2013). Inspired by Jacques Lacan, she assigned considerable importance to fathers both because she saw them as holding the symbolic function of "the Father" and because of the importance she assigned to sexual differentiation as a structuring factor in socialization. While Dolto did reach out to certain fathers' groups, she never fully supported the idea of joint custody. Monique Pelletier, who was secretary of state for family affairs and the status of women under French president Valéry Giscard d'Estaing, included Dolto in a working group on issues related to divorce and custody (Robcis 2013, 135). Pelletier also cited Dolto in her opposition to joint custody "If Françoise Dolto ... after thirty years of experience ... says,

I notice that such and such solutions have serious drawbacks, it is important for judges to know that. Judges are not psychologists, and they do not have to be, but they need to be informed on these questions," she declared in an interview (136).

By the 1990s, risks perceived as being associated with the absence of fathers (in particular, those related to juvenile delinquency) were thought of in similar terms in France and Quebec. Nevertheless, in France, the concepts of filiation, legal custody, and visitation rights were prioritized over fathers' day-to-day involvement in their children's lives as solutions in official reports (see, in particular, Bruel 1998). Indeed, the idea of joint legal custody maps exactly onto Dolto's understanding of fatherhood: the father is perceived as a symbolic figure whose authority is affirmed and takes effect through visitation rights. Even today, when faced with factors limiting the involvement of both parents (for example, the father's work schedule, distance between family homes, or housing costs), French legal professionals tend to fall back on a symbolic understanding of co-parenting. We observed this in a hearing in Valin in which Judge Sandrine Cabernet reminded two parents of their rights and obligations related to decisions about their children rather than their practical care.

The woman, a welfare recipient in her mid-thirties, was appearing alongside her former partner, who was somewhat older than she was and spoke poor French. To "make it legal," the mother was requesting "sole custody" of their child, with overnight visitation rights for the father every other weekend. Cabernet, on hearing the mother say "I don't want to have to run after him to make decisions," asked if she was also requesting sole legal custody and added a warning: "Sole legal custody requires grounds, it's not just for your administrative convenience." She then turned to the father: "Do you want to let her have sole legal custody?" The mother explained to the father: "If I want to enrol her in private school, I don't ask for your opinion." He remained silent, seemingly lost. After Cabernet repeated her line of questioning several times – "What would you like? Do you want to make decisions for your child?" – the father acquiesced and accepted the visitation rights proposed by the mother. Cabernet brought the hearing to a close with no further comment on the matter.[42]

Litigation over physical custody reveals the intersecting representations of child-rearing held by therapists, social workers, and legal professionals. In cases resembling the one described above, family judges regularly order psycho-social evaluations. These reports, made by psychologists and social workers, show the enduring influence of psychoanalysis on professionals' understanding of family problems. In them, experts often mobilize PAS as a way to undermine mothers while, at the same time, calling on attachment theory to naturalize mothers' day-to-day investment in children's lives. Mothers should be "enfolding, calming to children," while fathers must show above all that they are responsible – for example, by not unexpectedly quitting their jobs (Minoc 2017, 79). These reports, when we examined them, showed the eminently gendered way in which psycho-social professionals' expectations were structured with regard to parents. While judges did form their own opinions about these reports, of course, they were nevertheless exposed to these psychoanalytically inspired norms by the psycho-social workers who authored them. Parents, we noted, were also confronted with these norms in their encounters with lawyers and even when seeking information and advice from popular psychology literature. This exposure was often evident in our interviews and observations.

Karine Morel, a lawyer, mobilized these psychoanalytical terms in a meeting with a forty-one-year-old executive with a monthly income of four thousand euros who had left the family home a year earlier. When he recounted to Morel that his eleven-year-old daughter "took her mother's side," the attorney retorted that he had "really messed up the Oedipal aspect of things" by leaving his family and starting a new relationship.[43] Discussing a different case with us, Catherine Blanchard, who has been a family judge for over ten years, mentioned two parents in conflict over physical custody of their five-year-old son. Both of them, she recalled, had tried to give her books to support their claims: the mother, in an attempt to keep the child, offered Blanchard *Le livre noir de la résidence alternée*, while the father recommended a book that took a more open view of joint custody. Blanchard cut them off at the pass, she told us: she had already read both of the books.[44]

This symbolic definition of co-parenting has limited the development of tools that might encourage it in actual, practical terms. Parental "communication notebooks," used widely in Quebec, are still unusual in France, for example. Moreover, as we know, French judges have very little time to spend on any one case, giving them a tendency to fall back on currently existing arrangements rather than taking the time to identify and propose custody arrangements tailored to fit the practical and sometimes complex demands of day-to-day care. In the discourse of family judges, and in clerks' notes, we frequently observed them using the expression "the usual overnight visitation rights" ("every second weekend and half of school holidays"), which shows just how routine their practice can be. In reality, of course, "the usual" is not the only option – far from it – and some parents do choose more original ways to organize their joint custody. For example, 11 percent of divorces provide for "extended" overnight visitation (Carrasco and Dufour 2015, 3). Nevertheless, judges rarely promote other options and are merely content to commend parents – usually middle- to upper-class parents – for having availed themselves of the right professional advice in order to arrive at their own satisfactory and practical arrangement.

Later in the meeting between Karine Morel and the father that was described earlier, the father remarked to Morel that his work prevented him from taking the children every second week. She suggested that he come up with other options: "There are lots of extended overnight visitation options ... You can extend Friday night to Monday morning school drop-off, which allows you to stay in contact with schools, or you can do mid-week stays, from Tuesday night to Thursday morning, or you can do two out of three weekends." When the father admitted that he had not yet given it much thought, she encouraged him to do so. Similarly, in another hearing, Le Meur praised two parents in their thirties for finding an atypical joint physical custody arrangement (two days, three days, three days, rather than every other week) on the advice of a child psychiatrist. "OK, perfect," she remarked to the father in their ultra-rapid, ten-minute hearing: "It's going well, that's the main thing. When the parents can maintain dialogue, that's ideal."[45]

Although both jurisdictions uphold a standard of co-parenting, the roles of parents are understood very differently in France and Quebec, due to the very different ways in which politics, activism, and professional approaches intersect in the two places. In neither place have fathers' groups achieved their goal of having shared physical custody granted any time a parent requests it.[46] They have managed, however, to sow doubt regarding the work of judges: "Lawyers representing men complain that judges systematically favour the mother in custody agreements," a former judge of the Quebec Court of Appeal reported to us.[47] Across the Atlantic, French fathers' groups also regularly accuse judges of favouring mothers. Although it is not enough to confirm these allegations, high-ranking judges do often display an essentialist understanding of the careers and professional approaches of men and women judges (Bessière, Gollac, and Mille 2016). Although they are in the majority in their field, women judges still feel obliged to allay suspicions of partiality, leaving little room to embrace feminist stances.

Although judges and high-ranking civil servants do perceive fathers' groups as being extreme in their positions, the lobbying pressure exerted by these groups has had a certain measure of success, particularly in their demand for "parental equality," which they define as the sharing of physical custody rather than as the sharing of child-rearing duties before separation (Fillod-Chabaud 2016). In contrast, because so far the most credible feminist argument mobilized against acceding to this pressure has to do with risks related to family violence and because reducing family violence is still not a priority in family courts, feminist critiques of the stances taken by these fathers' groups have had little impact on "run-of-the-mill" cases (Côté 2004). Our research has shown that the tension between these two activist approaches is present in both countries and that, despite widespread perceptions to the contrary, it is not certain that women in Quebec are more mobilized or listened to on this issue than French women. National differences may be better explained by the way in which professionals understand parenting roles. The dominant schools of psychology and their appropriation by legal professionals are determining factors here. In both places, there is a marked tendency to psychologize the law and family justice, but the way this is done differs from one context to the other (Grossman and Friedman 2011).

Women in France, particularly when they come from lower socioeconomic classes, are assigned a mothering role for which they receive little to no social recognition. The same is true of less advantaged women in Quebec since their ex-partners are very unlikely to demand physical custody. Among the middle and upper classes, by contrast, pressure on mothers to compromise with fathers is weaker in France than it is in Quebec, where fathers are far more likely to be encouraged to be involved in their children's daily lives post-separation. Can the same patterns of difference be perceived in financial contributions to children's upkeep when it comes to organizing economic solidarity between parents?

Co-Parenting: Who Pays the Price?

Remarkably, professionals across the board agree that sharing the financial costs of child-rearing is less important than sharing custody. In an interview, French lawyer Sophie Carlasade used an aphorism to explain the way she ranked these issues: "Cases where there are really deep issues at play, [they're] the child's physical custody. Already, well, I guess I'd say, money can't buy happiness, you're not going to argue over numbers forever."[48] In Quebec, Judge Marc Lachance expressed a similar sentiment to us and concluded with similarly casual language: "Child custody is the central issue in family cases. I don't see any other. The rest is just moolah."[49]

And, yet, the two jurisdictions' *Civil Codes* hardly neglect the matter of money. Both define the obligation of support for "relatives in the direct line in the first degree" and specify that each parent has material obligations toward the children.[50] The *Civil Code of Quebec* stipulates that upkeep "is presumed to meet the needs of the child and to be in proportion to the means of the parents."[51] The *French Civil Code* indicates that "each parent must contribute to the upkeep and education of their children in proportion to their means, to those of the other parent, and to the needs of the child."[52] Child support is the main instrument of intergenerational financial solidarity post-separation, and it is calculated according to similar principles in the two jurisdictions (children's needs and parents' means).

Despite professionals' perceptions to the contrary, we found that financial issues were a frequent concern and regularly raised by parents. In more than half of non–mutual consent hearings observed in France, parents were in disagreement over child support and petitioned for a decision from the court. In Quebec, the subject was raised in 80 percent of the meetings we observed with lawyers. Parents' social status and gender inequality affect the financial aspects of separation as much as they do the issues related to custody. Fathers, since they generally earn more and spend less time caring for their children post-separation, are most often designated to pay child support, in line with the male bread-winner model.[53] Although women suffer greater financial losses in the wake of a separation, it is up to them to advocate for the economic rights of their children (see Textbox 2).

TEXTBOX 2 The gendering of poverty post-separation

> Single-parent households are more affected by poverty. Calculated as 50 percent of median household income, their poverty rate is 31 percent in Quebec and 22 percent in France (Haut Conseil de la famille 2014, 130). Since mothers are awarded physical custody of their children in most cases, this means that 84 percent of these households in France[54] and 74 percent in Quebec[55] are headed by women. The gendering of poverty is reinforced by the fact that women are less present in the workforce and are paid less: separated mothers are exposed to greater risk of poverty than separated fathers (Belleau et al. 2022).
>
> While it is most marked among lower social strata, gender inequality is perceptible in all social groups. French fiscal data on divorced households indicate that, among women, divorce leads to a 19 percent drop in standard of living, compared with just 2 percent among men (Bonnet, Solaz, and Garbinti 2021). In Quebec, the gap between mothers and fathers with children under the age of fourteen is even greater: in the two years following the separation of a de facto couple, the mother's disposable income drops by an average of 28.5 percent (24.5 percent for divorced women). By contrast, de facto fathers' incomes rise by 12.5 percent after a separation (11.5 percent for divorced fathers) (Belleau et al. 2022).

Inescapable Needs, Escapable Payments

Child support constitutes a significant portion of separated mothers' incomes, accounting for 18 percent of median declared income in France (Bonnet, Garbinti, and Solaz 2015, 3) and 17 percent of their mean income in Quebec (Belleau et al. 2022). The importance of this contribution to their revenue regularly leads them to seek the help of legal professionals in matters related to it. Social services also play a significant role in women's requests: recall that, in order to obtain welfare payments from the state, parents must prove that they have followed the proper steps. These administrative procedures allow lawyers to see how women spend their money and, more broadly, to observe the economic arrangements in their households.

Played out through socialization to the law as well as through re-proof, we shall see that the relational asymmetries explored in Chapter 3 return here in full force. When budgets are tight, family arrangements and patterns of consumption come under careful scrutiny, as we observed in a meeting between Séverine Pineault, a legal aid attorney in Quebec City, and a client. The woman, aged fifty-six, was the mother of two daughters, aged eighteen and twenty-three. She received seven hundred dollars in child support from their father. She would have liked him to pay the money to the daughters directly so that it did not count in her income, which was threatening to lower the amount of state aid she was receiving. She is working part-time in the fast-food industry and earning eighteen thousand dollars per year. Her health problems sometimes keep her from working for three or four months at a time, and because of this she receives an annual disability payment of eight thousand dollars. Her youngest daughter is working at a paid internship and contributes to rent, while the eldest, unable to find a job after completing her studies, has returned home to live with her mother. "I've spent the past five years [since the oldest daughter turned eighteen] fighting for him to quit paying child support ... He doesn't want to, it drives him nuts ... He's scared of paying more. He doesn't want to get a lawyer. I can't take it anymore," she says tiredly.

She explains a second financial problem to the lawyer: unable to obtain a regular lease to pay for her car, she has signed for a high-interest one and has been unable to pay it in full. Although the car has been seized, the lender keeps demanding payment. Reading over the lease agreement, Pineault notes that there is a cancellation fee. "When you signed it, did you really read it?" she inquires. "Well, it was guys from a garage," the woman replies. "Guys from a garage? With 29 percent monthly interest – that's just not good sense! But you signed?" The lawyer explains that some of her wages can be garnished, but not her disability payment, and suggests she take the issue to small claims court. Regarding the child support payment, she suggests the woman ask her daughters to speak to their father to convince him to pay for her legal aid expenses: "It'll cost him less money than a private lawyer."

This encounter reveals the administrative work many women must do as the primary figures in their children's daily lives. It is also up to these mothers to convince judges of their children's "needs," notably when children are pursuing their studies, as may be seen in the following two cases, both involving teenagers.

Post-Divorce Case in Marjac

An accounting assistant and a company director, who have been divorced for two years, petition judge Pierre Terreau regarding child support payments for their nineteen-year-old son, who began a tertiary degree six months earlier. The mother, who makes sixteen hundred euros per month, describes the new costs associated with his studies, which he is pursuing in a city far from the family home, meaning that he must now cover rent, transportation, and so on. She asks that child support payments be raised from €150 to €400 per month. The father, who makes twenty-six hundred euros per month, describes his other expenses (his new partner is expecting a child and does not work outside the home). Arguing that his son could have asked for a room in a student dormitory (less costly) and that he should be working during school holidays, he agrees to raising the support payments to two hundred euros. The mother has already specified that the son's application for student housing was refused and that he spends "most of his vacations studying." The judge decides to raise child support payments to €240, considering that housing costs could be "significantly reduced" and that the young man "could earn some money by doing the usual type of student job (childcare, tutoring, and so on)."[56]

Contested Divorce Hearing in Albanel

"While Madame's ambitions are praiseworthy, one's ambitions must fit one's means," Judge Gabriel Forest dictates to the court clerk in a ruling in which he refuses to order a truck driver to pay for the purchase of a

> computer and for the horseback riding lessons that the mother, who works in the food service industry, is requesting for their three daughters, aged eleven to nineteen. "The reality of the situation is that both parents earn modest incomes [thirty thousand dollars and twenty-one thousand dollars, respectively], which should not be spent thoughtlessly," he adds. Rejecting the requests for help with horseback riding and the computer, the judge upholds the request for help with enrolment in an intensive English program: "This kind of learning is desirable in the context of globalization, where we already know that people without a second language have far fewer opportunities."[57]

In cases where working fathers do not declare or under-declare their income and assets, it is up to mothers to establish the existence of these hidden resources. "That's expensive," Daniel Morel, an experienced Quebec-area lawyer, explained to a supermarket employee earning twenty-six thousand dollars per year, in an attempt to discourage her from undertaking a certain procedure against her ex-partner, who was a mechanic.[58] In addition to their costs in terms of time, energy, and money, procedures of this kind place mothers in direct confrontation with their ex-partners. Often, fearing that conflict will escalate, mothers "are ready to pay for peace at any price," reports Charles Lavoie, a legal aid attorney in Albanel.[59]

These cases underline the ways in which the challenges raised by the power asymmetries between caregiver mothers and provider fathers place less privileged mothers at even greater disadvantage than mothers in more advantaged settings. Professionals, as we have seen, express much more doubt about the legitimacy of educational expenses undertaken by these mothers than they do about those undertaken by middle- and upper-class mothers. That being said, even women with better access to financial resources are not free from all these constraints: fathers who are wealthy business leaders go to great lengths using complex financial operations to lower their taxable income (Bessière and Gollac 2022, 3), and a great deal of technical expertise is required from elite legal professionals to expose them (Biland and Mille 2017).

Nor do men escape this professional scrutiny of their lifestyles. When they experience a drop in their income, they also turn to the courts to reduce their child support payments. Half of all pension review cases in Quebec are filed by the debtor of support, compared to one-quarter of requests from the creditor of support.[60] In France, a little over half of pension review cases filed in the two years following divorce are submitted by fathers (Belmokhtar 2016, 5). However, legal professionals' attitudes toward those who are owed child support and those who owe it are not the same: while the former must modify their spending to fit their often modest means, the latter are more likely to be asked to show that their modes of consumption are not out of line with their duty to provide. Thus, French judge Mathilde Tabarès explained to us that "if Monsieur has a BMW and doesn't want to pay child support, if someone on welfare has an iPhone," she makes sure to question them about their spending.[61] In a meeting between Pineault and a twenty-nine-year-old secretary who was the mother of a baby, the mother explained to Pineault that the father, who worked as a window washer in summer and cleared snow in winter, now owned a horse and had told her "you won't get a cent." Pineault assured the mother: "We'll prove that in court. You don't pay for your horse before your child."[62]

Not all fathers are treated the same when it comes to their duties as providers. Methods for calculating child support, and the way in which they are used by legal professionals, contribute to the social stratification of fatherhood. Indigent fathers in both places are exempt from paying child support. In Quebec, the child support guidelines, known as the Basic Parental Contribution Determination Table, provide for a basic deduction of $12,215 (a little more than half of the annual minimum wage),[63] while its French equivalent sets a "subsistence minimum" of €565 per month, which is the amount of the monthly basic welfare benefit for a single person, known as the RSA.[64] Men undertake administrative procedures to prove their lack of means in order to pay nothing, while women must do the same amount of work to request support, only to receive nothing in the end.

As economic capital rises, the question of what the father can pay takes precedence over the child's needs. Significantly, the more children a father has, the smaller the amount he pays per child, a sign that children's "needs" are not calculated individually but, rather, in standardized ways based on a double assumption of economies of scale and of fathers' limited ability to pay. With certain exceptions (a child with a disability, for example), spending on children increases only when parents belong to the middle and upper classes: their solvency as well as the legitimacy of their distinctive educational practices (such as private school and costly leisure activities) combine to make child support into an instrument of social reproduction.

Both jurisdictions' calculation methods stipulate that, above a certain revenue threshold, child support remains at the judge's discretion. In Quebec, when a parent earns more than two hundred thousand dollars annually, the Child Support Determination Form sets a standard amount ($14,510 per year for one child) along with a percentage of earnings, which "is shown for information purposes only." In France, there is no formula for calculating child support if the debtor parent makes more than five thousand euros per month. In other words, for the wealthy, lawyers are decisive in determining children's needs and convincing judges to set amounts that fit with the sometimes uncertain, controversial, or declining social status of the debtor parent. Our observation of the following hearing offers an illustration of this process.

In the Belles family court, a couple filing for divorce after eighteen years of marriage were in conflict over child support for their two teenage children. The mother makes twenty-eight hundred euros per month as an air traffic controller after twelve years at home caring for the children. The father is an airline pilot on medical leave for depression; his monthly income has dropped from twelve thousand euros to forty-six hundred euros. In her argument, the mother's lawyer requests one thousand euros per month per daughter, justifying the amount by explaining that both children attend "specialized schools" (a program for gifted children for the daughter; a special needs program for the son) and adding that there are additional costs for speech therapy and orthodontics. She mentions their extracurricular activities: the daughter plays piano; the son practises archery, goes swimming, and builds model airplanes. More broadly, she evokes the "lifestyle" that her client wishes to provide for the children. Earlier, she indicated to the judge that she is "trying to keep life materially normal" for the children by organizing birthday parties and outings. The father's lawyer replies by highlighting his client's illness and the potentially irreversible decline in his income. "Given his intellectual capacities, he is very attentive to the children's education, he is present," the lawyer adds, calculating that he can only afford five hundred euros per month per child.[65]

Depending on their own resources, women are more or less dependent on public and private financial transfers and are therefore unequally exposed to surveillance of their lifestyles by professionals. Familiarity with institutions among women from the least privileged backgrounds discussed in the previous chapter has much to do with these domestic survival strategies. Child support also reveals socio-economic differentiation among men. While the poorest among them are unable to play the role of provider and are the most likely to lose contact with their children, the wealthiest (particularly business owners) are able to play on their unreliable incomes as well as on their children's "needs" to control their financial involvement with them. They also benefit from the fact that, with few exceptions, property and financial assets are not taken into account in the calculation of child support, while the cost of child-rearing is assessed narrowly, without accounting for the negative impact that day-to-day childcare may have on women's careers.

The Economics of Childhood: National Patterns

While the situations in France and in Quebec are similar in their broad strokes, our research showed that economic practices and norms are not identical. Lachance, the Quebec judge who noted that custody was a more challenging issue than child support, went on in the same interview to temper his words on the subject: "It's important that child support be sufficient for the children, in meeting their needs. I'm not minimizing that." By contrast, the French lawyer who pointed out that "money can't buy happiness" was speaking within a national context where the financial side of parental roles is far less prominent than in Quebec.

Significantly, rules to determine child support were standardized much earlier in Quebec. Since 1997, parental contributions have been set using mandatory guidelines. A form issued by the Ministère de la justice must be filled out in order to obtain a court ruling, meaning that its use is widespread. These tools are more sophisticated than their French equivalents: the guide published by the Quebec Ministère de la justice is fifty-two pages long, compared to just six pages in France, and Quebec lawyers have two dedicated software programs to use in their offices. These tools bolster professional prerogative since professionals are the ones best qualified to use them; at the same time, they make it possible to adjust contributions more precisely to the actual circumstances of parents and children – similar to the instruments used to help determine custody arrangements that I discussed earlier in this chapter.

By contrast, the guidelines provided by the French Ministère de la justice since 2010 are extremely simple: it is possible to calculate the amount of a parental contribution in a few clicks on several institutional or professional websites. These guidelines are far from universally applied, however. In the interactions that we observed, parents tended to refer to them more than professionals, who often expressed their mistrust of them. When a client appearing in court to obtain a child support order mentioned to Claire Robin that she had used the guidelines, the lawyer cut her off: "You can't trust those guidelines." Her client did not bring them up again.

Approaches that favour standardization and predictability thus receive far less attention in France than in Quebec. In the many cases consulted in the course of this research, the financial information available varied greatly, naming gross and net salaries or simply citing income with no further details given, generally but not consistently referring to benefits received from the state. This wide variation in practice is certainly due in part to judges' long-expressed reluctance to trust this tool (a matter to which we will return in Chapter 5) as well as to the fact that less significance is ascribed to financial obligation overall. Consider the judge in Besson, recounted earlier in Chapter 3, who approved a divorce agreement in which the father was to pay fifty euros in child support for his daughter, when the guidelines recommended one hundred and thirty-two euros "It's symbolic," she observed, without asking for any explanation or questioning the arrangement.[66] In Quebec, a judge would not have heard parents in this kind of divorce case since the parents were both in agreement, but, if she had, she would have asked how an amount that was so much lower than the recommended one could be justified by the specific circumstances of the parties.

These national differences are also perceptible in the proportion of cases in which no amount at all is set for child support: 15 percent in Quebec[67] compared to 32 percent in France (Carrasco and Dufour 2015). This gap may be explained by different understandings of the economic contributions of fathers from less privileged backgrounds. In France, the obligation to pay child support or exemption from it is strongly linked to the existence of a form of social welfare payment called the Allocation de Soutien Familial (ASF) (Family Support Allowance), a public child support allowance that in some cases replaces child support payments from a parent unable to fulfill the support obligation. Many judges are hesitant to set a contribution lower than this amount, preferring that women receive the public benefit instead: in 2007, just 7 percent of child support payments were set at amounts lower than the ASF (Collectif Onze 2013, 214). The amount of the ASF corresponds to the contribution of a debtor of support making eleven hundred euros per month. Practically speaking, then, the obligation to pay child support actually goes into effect above the threshold of minimum wage rather than above the threshold of the RSA.

Judges' reluctance to order "low" child support payments goes beyond accounting for state aid, however: it is also linked to the importance they assign to men working and, more specifically, to men in precarious situations returning to work. We observed in the French case below that the judge did not believe returning to work should automatically imply higher child support payments, considering that it would deprive these men of the fruits of their labour. The Quebec case presented alongside it stands in sharp contrast: there, the judge encouraged the mother to request a parental contribution as soon as the father had found work.

Hearing in Belles, France

A municipal employee making twenty-two hundred euros per month is seeking sole custody of her children, who are aged nine and eleven. She expresses surprise that her ex-partner, an electrician working on a fixed-term contract for thirteen hundred euros per month, is able to avoid paying child support. "If he's unable to cover half of the costs, it's up to me to do it?" Judge Anna de Mattéi, irked by this party who is "clearly very well-informed" about the law (as she puts it to the sociologists after the hearing), dismisses the case: "It is also in the best interests of the children to see their father managed to get it together when he was on minimum unemployment benefits. He got it together; Monsieur isn't unworthy." (Collectif Onze 2013, 215)[68]

Hearing in Albanel, Quebec

A twenty-one-year-old woman, a hospital worker and mother of a six-month-old infant, appears before Judge Brigitte Lévesque. Her ex-partner is absent, but his lawyer explains that "for the moment he does not wish to have visitation rights and is not working." The mother left the father when the baby was ten days old and filed a complaint against him for family violence. The father never asked to see the child again. At the end of the hearing, the judge encourages the mother to file charges again when he has found work: "As soon as he's working, file a support claim."[69]

There are significant contrasts between these two cases: the French father was in regular contact with his children, whereas the Quebecois father was entirely absent, both from the life of his own child and from the hearing. The French judge assigned more priority to the father's parental role than to his financial contribution, while, in Quebec, the father's non-involvement heightened the judge's sense that the mother should be vigilant about his return to work. Nevertheless, some conclusions can be drawn from these two scenarios that are applicable beyond their specific circumstances. In Quebec, we found that judges overall tended to be more attentive than their French counterparts to fathers' strategic attempts to lower their parental contributions, such as reducing their working hours, under-reporting income, or requesting shared physical custody.

Child support payment methods are further evidence of this greater vigilance. Starting in 1995, the Quebec government implemented a public system of deduction at the source, through which child support payments are collected directly from the debtor parent's pay. This means that support payments to the creditor parent are transferred through the Quebec tax authority. Parents may agree together to opt out of this system, and nearly one separated couple in five choose to do so (Haut Conseil de la famille 2014, 137).[70] However, the exemption can be revoked in the case of non-payment, and penalties are levied on debtors of support who do not make child support payments to the tax authorities in a timely manner.

In both courts and lawyers' offices, these provisions are often cited by professionals, both to encourage women to assert their rights and to remind fathers of their obligations, but the cost of these procedures is often prohibitive for mothers. Nor are fathers exempt from administrative procedures: until 2014, any change to child support requires a court ruling – a process costlier than what can be observed in France. The contrast between the two jurisdictions is even more striking when we recall that direct collection is all but non-existent in France and that we found most French legal professionals believed child support to be a "small" issue. Overall, they expressed the attitude that it was better not to push things too hard: there was no guarantee that judges' rulings would be followed, and they were seen as potentially discouraging fathers from being involved in their children's upbringing.

The two jurisdictions also differ in their approach to child support among the middle and upper classes. Proportionally speaking, wealthier fathers are not the ones paying the highest child support in either country. Nevertheless, high-income parents are more consistently held to their obligation to provide support in Quebec than in France. The Quebec guidelines specify a lower proportion of revenue to be paid in child support by parents with higher incomes than by lower-income parents. The percentage applied in the table increases sharply once parents' incomes rise from one salary that is half the median to two median salaries: for one child, it goes from 5.5 percent to 11.5 percent of income.[71] In other words, it is at the threshold between the lower and middle classes that the weight of child support in parental income grows the most.

It must be recalled that the Quebec Ministère de la justice table only determines the "basic parental contribution"; other amounts may be added for infant care, higher education, health, schooling, or extra-curricular activities. A quarter of the cases examined include provisions for such costs, for which the annual median amount is fourteen hundred dollars.[72] All other things being equal, these specific costs are more likely to be added to support payments from wealthier parents than to less wealthy ones. These amounts do balance somewhat the lower proportional support payments of wealthier debtors of support. The two contexts differ in terms of taxation as well: unlike in France, child support payments in Quebec are not deductible expenses. There is no tax benefit given to fathers in Quebec for paying child support, which mechanically adds to its cost; this is not the case for wealthier fathers in France.

Under French guidelines, child support is calculated as a constant proportion, no matter the debtor of support's income. But this percentage is calculated once the "subsistence minimum" has been deducted. The proportion of income paid in child support thus increases as income increases: set at 7 percent for a monthly income of one thousand euros, it rises to 12 percent for a monthly income of five thousand euros. However, trial courts generally reduce this progression. In cases of conflict between parents, family judges set amounts that are relatively close to the table provided in the guidelines unless the debtor of support earns more than four thousand euros per month: in these cases, payments tend to be proportionally much lower (Bourreau-Dubois and Sayn 2011, 123).

Our observations show a tendency to cap child support due to judges' reluctance to order high payments. Earlier in this chapter, I noted one example of this situation in our observation of Judge Pierre Terreau in a hearing with a father from a wealthy family. French family judges, as noted in Chapter 2, tend to come from the educated ranks of the upper middle class, and, here again, we found that their social position affected their attitudes. If judges do not perceive their educational benefit, they tend to see the costly "needs" of wealthy, upper-class children as luxuries or whims and even as going against the "best interests of the child" (Collectif Onze 2013, 222–23). Judges in the Superior Court of Quebec have a much higher social standing, which manifests most notably in their high incomes. It stood out in our research that their lifestyles resemble those of the wealthy parties they hear in court (they described vacation homes in the Laurentides or in Charlevoix, travel to Europe or "the South," and so on). Spending that French judges might consider superfluous or ostentatious they tended to see as justified.

From one end of the social scale to the other, the rules of the child maintenance system for calculation, collection, and taxation mean that payments vary much more as a function of income in Quebec. In France, half of the child support payments ordered in 2012 were between $145 and $290 per month (Belmokhtar 2014).[73] In Quebec in 2008, the range was much greater: half of the basic monthly child support payments were between $52 and $260.[74] Higher child support payments were also more frequent: 12 percent of "basic" child support payments were greater than $520 per month per child; in France, by contrast, just 10 percent of monthly child support payments were higher than $435 (Collectif Onze 2013, 209). This more marked variation in child support payments among different social classes in Quebec cannot be ascribed to overall income structure since the gap between the bottom and the top deciles is similar in the two jurisdictions (3.6 in France and 3.7 in Quebec) (Ministère des Finances 2016, 57). Rather, it is linked to the greater value assigned to the economic role of fathers in Quebec.

The two calculation methods also differ in the ways in which they account for gender inequality. The reference table in France is based solely on the debtor of support's income, whereas the reference table in Quebec is based on the "disposable income of [both] parents." In this way, the French calculation method turns a blind eye to the level of financial contribution of the custodial parent and, thus, to structural inequalities between fathers and mothers. This system reflects a widespread practice of French family judges, who, when determining child support amounts, look primarily at the non-custodial parent's income.

Econometric studies show that this income – in other words, the father's ability to pay – is the key factor determining the amount of child support to be paid (Bourreau-Dubois and Deffains 2003). This method of calculation is particularly problematic in situations where the income of one or both parents changes, as it adjusts support payments only with regard to the income of the debtor of support and not the custodial parent.

This approach is also inadequate in cases where parents share physical custody. The guidelines state that child support should still be paid in these cases; in reality, however, it rarely is. In 2013, child support payments were included in one-quarter of cases where joint physical custody was assigned.[75] Generally speaking, judges assume that parents will split costs, even in situations where their incomes are unequal, and they do not systematically include an order for child support in cases with major income disparities. In one of the cases consulted in Besson, for example, a judge assigned joint custody of a couple's nine-year-old son to a mother working part-time as a salesperson in a bakery earning €420 per month and a quantity surveyor earning €3,060 per month. The mother had requested two hundred euros per month in child support, which was lower than the €224 suggested in the guidelines. But the judge ordered no child support payment at all, considering that her expenses were limited (she lived in a home owned by her new partner) and that the father had agreed to pay for his son's schooling, presuming he attended a private secondary school later on.[76]

Consequently, the rise of joint physical custody has led to a decline in the incidence and in the amount of child support payments. Between 2003 and 2012, the proportion of cases in which child support was ordered went down by five percentage points among unmarried separating couples; the amounts paid decreased by 10 percent (Carrasco and Dufour 2015, 5). The growing emphasis on co-parenting in child-rearing has not extended to financial co-parenting – when women make way for fathers in their children's day-to-day activities, they often lose out financially. By contrast, the calculation method used in Quebec explicitly provides for the sharing of expenses related to the child based on the income of both parents. In theory, no child support is owed if and only if parents share physical custody equally and earn the same income. In reality, not all decisions adhere to the amount specified in the table: half the time, parents agree to child support that is 10 percent lower than the amount stipulated in the table.[77]

Even as the rising incidence of shared physical custody has lowered the amount of child support payments, and caused a drop in the number of cases in which support payments are set, the contrast with the French situation remains stark: child support is ordered in three-quarters of joint custody cases,[78] which is three times as many as in France. In other words, involvement in the daily life of a child does not exempt parents from their financial obligations. The system in Quebec does much more to organize economic solidarity between men and women. Taking into account the financial compensations provided to divorcing spouses discussed in Chapter 3, it is clear that, in Quebec, the private economy of marriage better accounts for gender inequality overall. In France, by contrast, the calculation of child support payments, similar to the calculation of compensatory benefits for ex-spouses, is based on "reverse accounting, in which the result comes first and computation comes after" (Bessière 2019). Starting with what men will agree to pay, rather than starting with their actual resources or the concrete needs of women and children, these calculation methods are blind to gender inequalities and perpetuate the gender wealth gap.

Although these divergences in calculation methods for private transfers of child support in the two jurisdictions are significant, let us recall one major similarity between France and Quebec: in both places, financial obligations between spouses are a consideration for married couples only. Since de facto spousal relationships are just as common on either side of the Atlantic, this choice is equally debatable in both contexts. It should be noted that, while the Supreme Court of Canada upheld a first challenge to Quebec's restriction of economic rights and obligations to married ex-spouses, a second challenge is currently under way in Quebec; the issue has never been brought before the court in France.[79] French blindness to gender inequalities stands out once again.

**

Our research confirmed that parental roles are deeply gendered and intimately linked to parents' social positions. The poorest men tended

TABLE 7 **National variations in the norm of co-parenting**

	France: Symbolic co-parenting		Quebec: Practical co-parenting	
	Role in care	*Economic role*	*Role in care*	*Economic role*
Mothers	Obligation to include fathers in decisions and to leave them leeway to participate occasionally	Obligation to actively request child support, which is sometimes non-existent, often reduced, and comes with no assurance that payment will be enforced	Obligation to include fathers in children's daily lives if they request it (and except in cases of reprehensible behaviour)	Obligation to request child support, with high chances of it being granted and paid
Fathers	Encouragement to exercise their right to make decisions jointly and to participate occasionally or even daily among the middle and upper classes	Expectation that they will pay child support if they belong to the middle and upper classes, with little to no enforcement	Encouragement to exercise their rights to day-to-day involvement, exercised differently depending on social status	Obligation to pay child support, with the exception of the poorest among them

to distance themselves from the norm of co-parenting not only because of their position in the job market but also because of their distance from institutions. Their ex-partners played the central role in caring for their children and could not escape this role when the father was absent. Higher up on the social ladder, men were more likely to be encouraged to be involved in their children's lives, both because of their relative financial stability and because of the resources they offered in terms of child-rearing, which were looked on favourably by professionals. In these cases, women were asked to make a place for fathers, although these men's practical involvement in their children's lives remained highly variable, in terms of both personal presence and finances It is here that the differences between France and Quebec really stand out (see Table 7). In Quebec, we found that the practical dimension of the norm of co-parenting was more affirmed, including with regard to financial transfers between parents. Middle- and upper-class women in Quebec had far more reason to hope that fathers would respect their obligation to participate in a child's upkeep than in France.

We may conclude from this overview that the current value placed on "co-parenting," both by the law and by legal professionals, does not in any way help to achieve symmetry between maternal and paternal roles. It is true that, while obligations continue to weigh disproportionately on mothers after separation, these obligations are largely consented to. However, as our study showed, these expressions of consent are anchored in gendered socialization and in divisions of labour pre-separation. Supported by judges' and lawyers' observations about making way for fathers, marked by unequal financial circumstances, and warped by the presence of male violence, the parental norms that emerged as we examined separation in both jurisdictions were more constraining to women than they were encouraging to men – all the more so because men were so rarely sanctioned when they violated these norms.

Family Law and the Welfare State: Intertwining Economic Inequalities

5

When we compared the impact that different ways of governing separation had on people's lives in France and Quebec, the most significant differences to emerge were economic. Key among these economic differences are the ways in which the two jurisdictions address private transfers of child support, as we saw in the previous chapter. The obligation to pay child support is more strongly enforced in Quebec than in France. On the surface, it might be inferred that, in their pursuit of the same goals – supporting the children of separated parents and reducing gender inequalities – Quebec prioritizes private transfers while France prefers public redistribution.

Once the many points of similarity between the two jurisdictions have been taken into account, this interpretation proves to be too simplistic: in both contexts, the economic impact of separation is softened by social policy; both places consider poverty in single-parent families to be a matter of public concern, and both have implemented a number of redistributive mechanisms to ameliorate it. In 2012, France and Quebec spent a similar proportion of their gross domestic product on family policy (around 3 percent), and, in both places, the child poverty rate is lower than the minimum set by the Organisation for Economic Co-operation and Development as well as by Canada's other provinces

(7.5 percent in France, 10 percent in Quebec) (Régie des rentes du Québec 2012, 28). The existence of these redistributive policies means that neither jurisdiction governs separations through private law alone or solely through legal professionals: in both places, they are also targeted by social and tax policies.

This chapter will study the ways in which public and private forms of solidarity in both France and Quebec are intertwined when it comes to financial support for children with parents in different households. According to a comparative study of child maintenance policies in fourteen countries in Europe and North America, "countries organized their child maintenance in quite different ways. History, culture, and socio-economic institutions all affect the nature of child support leading to cross-national divergence" (Skinner and Davidson 2009, 33). A comparative analysis of France and Quebec makes it possible to go beyond a synchronic comparison of the existing mechanisms, which until now has been the preferred methodology for studies that examine a wide range of cases. To that end, this chapter will explore both their emergence over the long term, beginning in the 1970s, and their implementation up to and including recent years.

In each national context, child maintenance systems depend on established relationships among three fields of action: women's rights, social and family policy, and the law. The first of these, which French sociologist Laure Bereni (2021, 208) has called "the women's cause field," comprises "the relational structure of groups mostly devoted to the advancement of women in a variety of social settings, cutting across the line between civil society and political institutions." Her term highlights the location of this field between feminism as a social movement and state feminism, as it is inscribed and expressed in public institutions and policies. In the case of Quebec, women's groups within civil society mobilized to push for reforms in economic and family law; this effort was then taken up by women's policy agencies (Mazur and McBride 2008), and, as a result, these issues were placed on political agendas (Revillard 2016). Women's rights are not the only consideration in political agendas concerning economic and family law, however; since the early 2000s, counter-pressure from fathers' groups has changed the way families are represented in civil society.

State policy regarding child maintenance does not depend on women's policy agencies alone; it also depends on the way welfare states are structured. According to British social scientist Jane Lewis (1992), a specialist in the feminist analysis of welfare states, the French and Quebecois systems have a modified form of the male breadwinner model baked into them and thus consider women both as mothers and as workers. France, however, has a longer history of family policy (Kempeneers and Dandurand 2002; Lenoir 1992), and, until recently, neoliberal thinking had less of an influence on public policy there, meaning that the country has, on the whole, maintained a more protectionist approach to public support for mothers (Revillard 2009). Quebec, by contrast, has tended to prefer combinations of private transfer and public redistribution. How are these family policies linked to the work of legal professionals? Looking back to Chapter 1, where we examined how court proceedings for separations have been lightened or made optional, we recall how child support payment systems have served as instruments for reforming the justice system, modifying the role of professionals in the public and private sectors and shifting power toward the latter group.

In Quebec, these three fields – feminist, social, and legal – have come together to build a system of child support that stresses male responsibility. Public interventionism in Quebec is a relatively recent phenomenon in its political history: the historiography shows that the Quebecois welfare state only emerged in the early 1960s in a period known as the "Quiet Revolution" (Linteau et al. 1986). Starting in the 1990s, it went through a series of neoliberal reforms, which included improving the child support payment system in order to reduce the cost of state welfare benefits. Neoliberalism was not the only force at play, however; it was counterbalanced by the growth of family policy, which focused on single-parent households as a major target of income redistribution. Overall, this configuration promoted both private transfer and public solidarity, with an emphasis on the former over the latter, meaning that the poorest mothers saw their access to state welfare benefits diminish.

In France, there has never been this kind of convergence among the fields of feminism, social policy, and the law. The relative weakness of the women's movement, combined with the institutional strength of the family branch of the social security system and a focus on streamlining court procedures, has meant that solo-parent households became a focus of public policy earlier on to the detriment of enforcing private obligations. Even more than in Quebec, separated women from less privileged backgrounds depend on social services to weather the financial storms of life post-separation.

Quebec: Private Fairness and Social Policy Reform

In Quebec, as we saw in the previous chapter, child support is calculated according to standardized and mandatory guidelines. Unless parents apply for an exemption, child support payments are debited directly from the paycheques of debtor parents by the tax authorities, who then pay them to creditor parents. Furthermore, child support payment is tax neutral: according to the Quebec Ministère de la justice (Ministry of Justice), "the person making a child support payment does not deduct it from his or her income, and the person receiving a child support does not add it to his or her income."[1] These three pillars of the Quebec child support system went into effect twenty-five years ago between 1995 and 1997. They are the product of a consensus built progressively among an institutionally and ideologically diverse range of actors to promote the economic rights of women, while also reforming social and legal policy.

Promoting the Economic Rights of Women and Children

The women's rights movement played a major role in building this consensus, which led to several reforms to the *Civil Code of Quebec*. These reforms were intended not only to establish legal equality between partners but also to improve the economic circumstances of divorced women (compensatory allowance in 1980, family patrimony in 1989). The last legislative reform to emerge from this mobilization was the "support-payment collection program," through which the public tax authority was empowered to directly debit child support payments from debtor parents in order to improve the payment of child support. This mobilization occurred during a period when the divorce rate was rising rapidly: in 1991, 22 percent of households with children in Quebec were headed by a single parent (Lindsay 1992, 18). Moreover, mothers of young children were largely absent from the job market, and family policy was still rudimentary.[2] While universal government assistance to families in the form of the family allowance has existed since 1967, with roots stretching back to 1945 (Quebec is actually the only province in Canada to provide this allowance), the amount paid to families through this program is low. At the beginning of the 1990s, families received ten dollars per month per child, the equivalent of seventeen dollars today (Régie des rentes du Québec 2006, 12). This system led to the mass impoverishment of single-parent households: two-thirds of children living in single-parent households lived below the poverty line at the time (Groupe de travail pour les jeunes 1991, 27, 69).

In 1980, as a response to this, thirty-one organizations formed an umbrella group to push for the reform of the child support payment system, known as the Front commun pour un véritable service de perception des pensions (United Movement for a Real Child Support Collection Service) (Revillard 2016, 162). Two organizations were driving forces within this umbrella group. The first was the Association féministe d'éducation et d'action sociale (AFEAS) (Feminist Association for Education and Social Action). Founded in 1966 and led in its early years by the wives of farmers and small businessmen for whom the lack of recognition of women's work within family-run enterprises was a huge problem if they divorced, the AFEAS was perceived as being moderate. The second organization was a province-wide group representing single-parent families founded in 1974. Since 1995, it has been known as the Fédération des Associations de Familles Monoparentales et Recomposées du Québec (FAFMRQ) (Federation of Associations of Single-Parent and Blended Families). The FAFMRQ comprised thirty-nine local groups when it was founded, providing legal advice, social activities, and mutual aid for its seventy-five hundred members.[3] It took part in a combination of grassroots organizing and mutual aid that characterized feminism in Quebec in the second half of the 1970s and helped to anchor the cause of women's rights in broader society (Lamoureux 2000).

It appears that this pragmatic approach and institutionalization (via public funding) created a certain distance in the feminist movement from the more radical approach taken by other groups in the 1960s, without making it any less political. Indeed, quite to the contrary, the FAFMRQ articulated and helped to communicate political demands to the Quebec government, notably with regard to the direct collection of child support payments. These women's movements found political allies in women's policy agencies (WPAs). The Conseil du statut de la femme (Council on the Status of Women), a government consultative and review body founded in 1973, served as a key link between institutional politics and the social movement, bringing together representatives from various women's groups and contributing to the construction of a body of feminist expertise. The Conseil du statut de la femme first proposed direct debit for child support in 1978 in its first major report, titled *Pour les Québécoises: Égalité et indépendance (For Quebecois Women: Equality and Independence)* (Conseil du statut de la femme 1978, 186). The second women's policy agency, the Secrétariat à la condition féminine (Women's Secretariat) was launched in 1979. It was essentially a ministry for women and ultimately would be responsible for drafting the legislation establishing direct debit child support payments.

Two other factors contributed to the adoption of this policy by the Quebec government. The first factor was the establishment of ties between the women's movement and the Parti Québécois, which was behind two referenda for Quebec's independence, one in 1980 and one in 1995.[4] Early women's liberation groups in the 1970s sought to show that "the oppression of women is a political issue as important as the oppression of Quebec as a nation" (Lamoureux 2016, 57). Following the failure of the first referendum, Pauline Marois, the minister responsible for the status of women, advised René Lévesque, the Parti Québécois premier of Quebec, to help women become financially independent in order to rally them behind the project of national sovereignty (Revillard 2016, 154). The Parti Québécois followed her advice in 1994 when it made child support reform a part of its campaign platform, with the goal of "improving women's economic status" and "ending discrimination" (Parti Québécois 1994, 50, 53). According to the lawyer who served as the adviser on family law to the Ministère de la justice from 1986 to 2015, preparing for the second referendum was a major impetus behind this partisan agenda setting.[5]

In 1994, the Parti Québécois' electoral victory brought several feminists into the Assemblée nationale (National Assembly). Céline Signori, a neonatal nurse by training, was a key Parti Québécois member of the National Assembly (MNA) involved in the direct debit law; earlier in her life, she had directed the FAFMRQ from 1985 to 1992 and had served as president of the Quebec Women's Federation from 1992 to 1994. Jeanne Blackburn, the minister responsible for the status of women, who introduced the bill to the Assemblée nationale, was a former teacher and regional director of the AFEAS. These two politicians played a decisive role in rallying first MNAs from the Liberal Party and then a broad base of politicians, and, as one of them recalls, "we did it with MNAs from the opposition ... We promised each other: 'You work with your people, I'll work with mine.'"[6] The bill ultimately passed unanimously; party discipline, it must be said, is strong in the Assemblée nationale of Quebec.

The role of the feminist movement and of WPAs was thus essential in setting up a child support collection and enforcement system in Quebec. They were responsible for the widespread publication of public data that revealed the impoverishment of single-parent families and the inadequacy of child support collection. The Conseil du statut de la femme reported that, between 1981 and 1983, just 44 percent of separations were accompanied by a child support order, less than half of which were actually paid as ordered (Conseil du statut de la femme 1995, 8–9). These groups called on academics and professionals in the field to build their own expertise, mobilizing examples from outside Canada, including the Child Support Assurance System, which had been in force in the state of Wisconsin in the United States since 1983, and its Australian equivalent, which was put in place in 1989 and analyzed in-depth in 1994 (FAFMRQ 1994). The FAFMRQ also mobilized statistics from elsewhere in Canada, pointing out that the system established in Ontario in 1992 had made it possible to increase the number of single-parent families receiving child support and that, furthermore, the system had allowed the province to save twenty-eight million dollars in social benefit payments (FAFMRQ 1993, 13).

Finally, these groups also played an important role in the definition of the system's goals. In addition to fighting poverty among women and children, it was thought of as a stepping stone to women's liberation. A former FAFMRQ staff member from 1994 to 2015 explained the argument for economic independence made by women's groups in an interview with us in 2014: the direct collection of child support disentangles it from the power relations at play in separating couples:

> What we did with the law was to flip the power relationship: before direct collection, the father would show up with his cheque and hold it over the mother's head: "If you don't do this or that, I won't give it to you." Sometimes he brought it, sometimes he didn't. We wanted to sidestep that kind of power play, so that there were no more negotiations, so it's the government collecting, and the government paying.[7]

Along with providing expertise, the mobilization of these groups turned out to be key in the last phase of the project. Just days before the bill was to be voted on, a women's March for Bread and Roses took place. One of its demands was for the direct collection of child support: 850 women marched from Montreal to Quebec City, where they were joined in front of the Assemblée nationale by a crowd of fifteen thousand people. This march was a "site of convergence" that bore witness to the fact that women's groups were united behind this cause, making it more visible to the general public (Bereni 2021, 209).

At the same time, at the beginning of the 1990s, the impoverishment of single-parent households was embraced as an issue outside the feminist movement as well. The report entitled *Un Québec fou de ses enfants*, which was cited in Chapter 4 for promoting the involvement of fathers in their children's lives post-separation, made the promotion of children's economic rights, rather than of mothers', the focus of its argument in favour of direct debit (Groupe de travail pour les jeunes 1991). Let us recall that Article 27(2) of the United Nations Convention on the

Rights of the Child, adopted in 1989 and frequently cited by these professionals, states that "the parent(s) and others responsible for the child have the primary responsibility to secure, within their abilities and financial capacities, the conditions of living necessary for the child's development."[8] *Un Québec fou de ses enfants* called for essentially the same thing as the women's movement, "an absolute necessity: reducing poverty," along with a solution: "Implement a system for setting and directly collecting child support" (Groupe de travail pour les jeunes 1991, 64, 74). In other words, psycho-social professionals rallied behind this feminist cause in the name of the best interests of the child.

The Battleground of Public Interventionism

Nevertheless, it would be more than fifteen years before Quebec's government took up these demands, and the clinching arguments for implementing reform were not those of women's groups: as early as January 1981, the Ministère de la justice set up a collection system but only for "bad payers."[9] Child support inspectors, who were lawyers working for the Ministère de la justice, took legal action against debtor parents in arrears. But collection-related problems persisted: in the early 1990s, 55 percent of child support orders required intervention from the court or an inspector before they were paid (Rémillard 1993). Processing cases took several months; one-quarter of these proceedings led nowhere; and one-quarter of creditor parents had to appeal to a child support inspector multiple times (S. Pelletier 1987, 131–48).

Women's groups condemned this legal framework as inadequate. In February 1992, the FAFMRQ began promoting the establishment of an "automatic, universal, and obligatory system for collecting child support" (Sommet de la Justice 1993). However, the Liberal minister of justice opposed such a system, calling direct collection "socialist" (Rémillard 1993). Over the summer of 1993, the FAFMRQ continued its campaign, drawing up a list of the proposed system's supporters and detractors (FAFMRQ 1993). In this context, including a new child support collection system in its campaign platform was an excellent way for the Parti Québécois to set itself apart from its Liberal adversary, which sustained heavy criticism over the issue.

In addition to competition among political parties, different ministries vied for responsibility for the new system. The government formed by the Parti Québécois in 1994 relieved the Ministère de la Justice of its responsibility for collection, placing it in the hands of the tax services with the promise of greater efficiency at a lower cost. The system was also attractive to the Ministère de la Sécurité du Revenu (Ministry of Income Security), which saw the direct collection of child support as a means to reduce the payment of last-resort financial assistance, which half of single-parent families received at that time (FAFMRQ 2003, 7). Prioritizing family solidarity over public redistribution was widely accepted, as this comment by Judge Maria Flores confirms:

> When a debtor parent stops [paying child support] and the mother has no income, that means that she has no resources, and must rely on minimum welfare payments, which are help from the state. It's too easy for a debtor parent to come to an agreement with the mother and say "listen ... Let's look the other way. We'll organize it between us: don't show up and then apply for welfare" ... If everyone did that, there wouldn't be enough money to really give to those who need it, and that's a social issue.[10]

Her words echo one of the key arguments of the prevailing attitude toward reform: making men responsible for paying child support is not merely a way to bring justice to women; it is also an opportunity to limit public welfare payments to them.

As legal scholar Elizabeth Stuart Perry (2019, 21) notes, the child maintenance system is based on "each society's fundamental assumptions and beliefs about the proper relationships between parents, children, and the welfare state." In Quebec and across North America, prioritizing family solidarity over public solidarity reveals a liberal – and even a neoliberal – understanding of the relationship between a state and its citizens. This explains why the Ministère des solidarités et de la santé was also interested in the amounts paid for child support, seeking to ensure that they were high enough to keep women from applying for aid. Tellingly, in 1994, more than half of single mothers (55 percent) were welfare recipients (Emond 1996, 113). Child support calculation methods were developed first and foremost by the state, specifically by the Ministère des solidarités et de la santé and the Ministère de la justice.

Three mid-level employees of the Ministère des solidarités et de la santé – all trained economists – succeeded each other as linchpins in the creation of Quebec's child support guidelines. They used data from the 1986 Canadian census to compare the spending habits of households with and without children to determine the cost of child-rearing. To define the scope of application for the basic parental contribution, they included nine "essential needs" to establish the amount to be paid in minimum welfare benefits.[11] It was less obvious why the Ministère de la justice, which did not share these clear-cut financial motivations, would show such support for this new double-barrelled approach. Part of it can be explained by a desire to see court decisions applied, as the ministry was well aware of the inefficacy of the earlier approach to child support order enforcement. Added to that was the shared belief that private payments should come before public aid. As the lawyer who headed up a task force on the issue confided to us, "as a taxpayer, I was saying 'I'm going to pay instead of the debtor parent? That's out of the question."[12]

Already in 1986, the desire to expand the practice of family mediation provided another good reason to set guidelines for child support payments. The two subjects were officially linked during the 1992 Sommet de la Justice (Justice Summit), and draft Bill 65 on the public financing of family mediation became law six months after the guidelines were put into effect.[13] Reducing the cost of separation by limiting conflict and avoiding litigation were mobilized as arguments in favour of mediation. The guidelines were seen as a tool that would help separating couples reach an agreement more easily. They laid objective ground rules for debate and were accessible to mediators without legal training. The compartmentalization that was at work in court reform in Quebec was confirmed here: the ministry, unable to change the traditional court procedure (the adversarial system) instead worked to remove at least some of the litigation from the courtroom. Indeed, the guidelines functioned as a tool for promoting joint physical custody (in that they recommended less child support when custody was shared) – it was a way of governing without passing laws.

This approach was not unique to Quebec: most common law countries at that time were in the process of putting guidelines in place to streamline child support payments, and Canada was no exception (Dewar 2000). In 1989, the Federal-Provincial-Territorial Family Law Committee began working on federal child support guidelines. However, following the failure of the Meech Lake Accord, which was supposed to recognize Quebec as a "distinct society" within Canada, Quebec's Liberal government withdrew from the committee for the next two years from 1990 to 1992. On its return, it sought to assert its own calculation methods, which were different from those that had been set up at the federal level, in the name of the particularities of Quebec law (its *Civil Code* and its civil law tradition), its population (there are more unmarried couples in Quebec than elsewhere in Canada, and federal guidelines do not address them), and its family and social policy (Department of Justice Canada 1995, 104). The federal government accepted this demand but weakened its power – the guidelines were to be presumptive, rather than indicative, and could not be applied to parents who were not residents of Quebec.[14]

The origins of these guidelines confirm that reforms to Quebec family law were vectors for the affirmation of national sovereignty (Revillard 2007b). This position certainly did not inspire consensus among lawyers, some of whom were members of the Canadian Bar Association, which had helped to set up the federal guidelines. They let it be known that the Quebec model was vulnerable to lawsuits in that it would lead to child support payments being set below the recommendations of the federal guidelines (Barreau du Québec 1996, 42–43).[15] These lawyers also condemned the initial choice to consider a parent as holding joint physical custody starting at a 30/70 percent time split. Ultimately, they succeeded in raising the minimum threshold to 40 percent (Goubau, Fortin, and Grassby 1997). Nevertheless, a preference for guidelines adapted to the legal, social, and political specificities of Quebec was shared by the Liberal government in 1985–94 and the Parti Québécois government in 1994–96, and, in December 1996, the law on the determination of child support was adopted unanimously.[16]

Although there was public consultation regarding the guidelines, there was little room for the women's movement in their creation. It is possible that the rather technical nature of the project did not facilitate its appropriation beyond the realm of professional statisticians and *Civil Code* specialists. Moreover, support for the guidelines from groups and organizations representing the women's movement was only lukewarm. The FAFMRQ considered that the new system fostered more "equity" (FAFMRQ 1995) in the sense that it ensured fewer variations in the child support payments that judges set and gave a precise basis for apportioning the cost of child maintenance between two parents. But, in its parliamentary brief, the Conseil du statut de la femme (1996, 19) spelled out the system's limits in no uncertain terms:

> It is an illusion to think that child support alone can resolve the problem of the impoverishment of women and children when families separate. Improving private law is only part of the improvement of families' economic circumstances; greater equality for women in the workplace, better distribution of family responsibilities, and more robust state support to families are avenues that are just as important to explore if we wish to establish more justice and equality between women and men and among families.

By calling for greater state involvement, the organization was critiquing the neoliberal leanings of the Quebec child support system, which justified public intervention with the goal of reducing the cost of separation to the public. Elisabeth Buckley, a feminist lawyer and a supporter of the federal guidelines, was even more direct in our interview with her: "It's the government that wanted welfare recipients to get their child support. We were doing the government's job to make sure that the poorest men got even poorer."[17]

Feminists in Quebec were aware of the class bias of this reform, which, above all, affected men who earned just enough income to be required to pay child support. Women's groups and governments nevertheless came together over the third part of the reform, which was tax neutrality, an issue with a greater effect on middle- and upper-class parents. Here, again, they differed in their reasoning. Women's groups sought to improve women's financial status, which had been negatively affected by child support orders. As for the provincial and federal governments, although the Superior Court had upheld their right to continue the taxation of child support in a key equality rights case, the governments at both levels preferred tax neutrality as a means to increase tax revenue.[18] The lawyer advising the Ministère de la justice on this issue underlined this motivation, pointing out that tax neutrality for child support "gave more financial resources to the state" and added that "we were just waiting for the Superior Court decision so we could say 'you'll win de facto,' because it put seventy-five million [dollars] in our pocket."[19] Here, then, was the clinching argument: because, on average, debtor parents are wealthier than creditor parents, there was a considerable amount for the state to gain in ceasing to make child support tax deductible for those paying it while it stopped taxing those receiving it. The Quebec child support system, by promoting gender equality through private law, was forging a compromise between two separate goals: promoting women's liberation and protecting the public purse. What impact did this have on the inequalities within and among families?

Restricting Welfare Benefits, Developing Family Policy

Enforcing child support payment comes at a significant cost: sixty-two million dollars or the equivalent of 713 full-time jobs in 2014 (Commission de révision permanente des programmes 2015, 43–44). The government's hope, though, was that the cost of enforcement would be compensated by a decrease in the number of people receiving welfare benefits, and, indeed, between 1995 and 2015, this number was nearly halved, dropping from 802,000 to 449,000 (Ministère des Finances 2016, 53). These decisions in Quebec were part of a general trend in North America to intensify private responsibility with the goal of restricting public aid to the poorest segment of the population. Similar motivations may be observed in the United States (Grossman and Friedman 2011, 225–28) and across Canada, where a report to the federal Department of Justice referred to the "heavy burden on social assistance programs" that resulted from the avoidance of child support (MacDonald 1997). In reality, at the end of the 1980s, the federal government lowered its financial contributions to provincial social welfare programs, which led to reforms in Quebec that were "designed in a manner that was punitive and stigmatizing for recipients" (Dumais 2012, 385).

At the same time, it was possible to allocate the new tax revenue generated by the tax neutrality of child support to new out-of-court services such as mediation, special clerks, social benefits, and family services such as childcare centres. The inspiration here was not to be found in other Anglo-American jurisdictions but, rather, in social-democratic Scandinavia, which is known for its promotion of gender equality and redistributive policies (Paquin and Lévesque 2014). Nor did these reforms reflect government disengagement; rather, they sought to reallocate resources and redefine the populations targeted by social and family policies. The Quebec government became harsher with regard to recipients of welfare benefits while, at the same time, strengthening its family services, particularly for single-parent families. Significantly, the poverty rate dropped for single-parent households (although it was still high), but it stagnated for people living alone (Dumais 2012, 90). Parallel reforms to child support and welfare benefits thus led to horizontal redistribution among the most precarious low-income households, from people living alone (including separated fathers) to mothers in single-parent families.

The reforms also led to vertical redistribution among families to the benefit of the middle and upper classes. In the years following these reforms, public aid to parents was reduced across the board, but it was the poorest parents who lost the most: taxes were lowered for wealthier parents (Rose 2001). Moreover, separated middle-class women with jobs could now count on more reliable private transfers: child support payments improved considerably after direct collection was put in place by the tax authorities. The number of child support orders grew, as did the collection rate; the latter reached 80 percent in 2014 (Commission de révision permanente des programmes 2015, 44). However, this rate was twice as high for child support collected directly from the debtor parent's salary than for child support paid from a bank account (Ministère de la famille et de l'enfance 2001, 4). In other words, the tax authorities were most effective when debtor parents were salaried employees and much less so when they were self-employed.

It should be added that the establishment of a flat rate for government-subsidized childcare facilities – of five dollars per child per day (a key measure of this new family policy) – also mostly benefited middle- and high-income families. Single-parent families with household incomes of less than twenty thousand dollars paid more for childcare under the new system (Conseil du statut de la femme 1997, 51). The same is true for family mediation, which is still used most by couples in the middle- and high-income brackets as we saw in Chapter 1. Adding to this situation, the threshold for legal aid qualification stayed frozen during this period, meaning that people earning minimum wage could no longer benefit from it.

The tax and social system reform of 2005 attempted to correct these anti-redistributive effects: family benefits were integrated into the taxation system in the form of a tax credit that was accessible to all families. Public aid increased for single-parent families across the board but particularly for those families whose earnings were only slightly higher than social benefit payments (Rose 2009, 17). If the 1990s were characterized by the shrinking of social programs, the 2000s and the 2010s saw a return to public investment in favour of families. Nevertheless, the poorest and most precarious people remained the target of restrictive measures. The quest to cap basic welfare benefits intensified, weighing on single-parent families who benefited from various forms of government aid. Access to the last-resort financial assistance program became even more conditional in 2016. Recipients who could not demonstrate that they were making sufficient efforts to search for a job saw their payments reduced in an effort to shrink the number of people receiving them.[20]

Furthermore, the last-resort financial assistance program collects child support payments directly and only pays a portion of them directly to the creditor parent (one hundred dollars per child since 2011). Women's groups and organizations representing "persons receiving social aid" have contested this policy in court on two separate occasions (in 2003 and in 2009–12) but so far with no success. Opposition MNAs (from the Parti Québécois or Québec Solidaire, the most left-leaning party in the Assemblée nationale) have also unsuccessfully proposed legislation to bring this policy to an end. Child support is also calculated as revenue in applications to four different aid programs, a further limit on access to public benefits: last-resort financial assistance, student loans and aid, housing subsidies, and legal aid. In November 2019, the Coalition Avenir Québec government announced that a portion of child support would no longer be counted as income in applications for housing subsidies. The Coalition contre le détournement des pensions alimentaires pour enfants (Coalition against Child Support Misappropriation), an umbrella group for numerous citizen-sector groups, mobilized against the inclusion of child support in the calculation of government aid but were only partially successful.

The past twenty years have shown that, in Quebec, as in the rest of Canada, the focus of family and social policy remains on private transfers (Bercuson, Granatstein, and Young 1986, 103; Gorlick and Brethour 1998, 11). Let us recall that, until 2014, a court order was necessary to modify child support payments, and fathers whose incomes had dropped, as well as mothers whose ex-partners had become wealthier, incurred significant costs to see to it that child support payments were adapted to their new financial circumstances. Since 2014, the Service administratif de rajustement des pensions alimentaires pour enfants (Child Support Recalculation Service) has made it possible to modify child support payments out of court. This service has not been as successful as was hoped: in 2020, in its sixth year of operation, it received just 754 requests (Commission des services juridiques 2021, 78) – a tiny proportion of the 284,600 requests for child support collection received by Revenu Québec the same year.[21]

Today, the belief persists that child support payments are difficult to change, leading some parents to avoid making their separation and divorce agreements official in order to avoid the support payment collection program. Interviewed at the end of 2020, a lawyer working exclusively in family mediation explained that he advised parents who got along with each other not to use the program.[22] In his opinion, the Service administratif de rajustement des pensions alimentaires pour enfants was heavy on paperwork and difficult to use. He was just as critical of the Service d'aide à l'homologation (Homologation Assistance Service), which was designed to help parents make changes to court judgments. Because clients must access the service through legal aid offices before consulting with a lawyer or mediator, he believed that the process was too time-consuming and discouraging to potential users. And, yet, avoiding the collection program makes mothers more vulnerable to fathers who sidestep child support payments for one reason or another.

Overall, this child maintenance policy penalizes low-income mothers in precarious circumstances who cannot collect significant child support either because their ex-partners are unable to pay or because the administration withholds a portion of it. This penalization has been made more acute by the fact that the heightened value placed on individual responsibility has come hand in hand with cuts to social benefits, in a trend that is coming to resemble the American workfare model (Morel 2002). The neoliberal influence in this policy is undeniable, but it is not the only one since child support reform has been part of an expansive trend in family policy. This expansion indicates the force of the "Investing-in-Children Policy Paradigm" at both levels of government (Jenson 2004, 176). This paradigm stands out in *Un Québec fou de ses enfants* as well as in "early intervention" approaches. It gained considerable ground over this period (Parazelli, Lévesque, and Gélinas, 2012) and became a key priority for public policy targeting poverty reduction. Nevertheless, "the interests of children began to take precedence over that of the adults who were their parents" and, in particular, over the interests of women (Jenson 2004, 184). This sea change explains in large part why unmarried women, although their numbers are steadily rising, still have such reduced economic rights.

It also bears mentioning that, in 1996, two fathers' groups, the Association masculine d'entraide pour la famille (Men's Mutual Family Aid Association) and the Groupe d'entraide aux pères et de soutien à l'enfant (Society for Support and Mutual Aid for Fathers and Children) submitted briefs to the Assemblée nationale. But, as three members of my research team pointed out, the two briefs "expressed opposing points of view on the determination of child support. [Their] language [was] choppy, far less grammatically and syntactically correct than the language found in briefs from other groups" (Bouchard, Fortin, and Hautval 2017, 23). In 2004, these groups succeeded in obtaining the concession that the existence of children from another partnership justified lowering child support payments, but this law contributed little else in the course of debates over social benefits.[23] Concretely, fathers' groups have not been the main drivers of changes to the child support system. Declining engagement from women's groups in economic issues related to separation and divorce (Biland and Schütz 2015b), the rising importance of considerations related to the issue of children's rights, and government finances were the key determining factors in the decades during which Quebec was fortifying its family policy, which today most favours children whose parents both earn steady incomes.

France: Ineffective Rights and Gender Inequality

A very different relationship between private transfer and public redistribution exists in France. First, the state began acting as an intermediary in the collection and payment of child support only recently, in January 2021, and participation in the system is not obligatory in any way, meaning that the rate of default and non-enforcement is much higher than in Quebec. At the same time, a social benefit of €118 per month per child is, in principle, guaranteed to those raising their child(ren) on their own, until each child turns twenty. Child support also counts as income for taxation purposes, meaning that it costs less to the person paying it and more to the person receiving it. Although this tax advantage structurally favours men (at least those who pay taxes) over women, it went unquestioned for many years, a form of what has been called "unconscious sexism" by two sociologists (Bessière and Gollac 2022). Finally, child support payments are set at a judge's discretion: the guidelines published by the French Ministère de la justice – thirteen years after Quebec's guidelines – are merely indicative. As we saw in Chapter 4, these calculation methods mean that French judges set lower child support payments for the wealthy than their counterparts in Quebec.

To understand these differences, it must be recalled that France developed its family policies much earlier than Quebec did. Political belief in the social and moral value of the family nourished one of the most powerful "state ideologies" from the end of the nineteenth century to the beginning of the 1960s (Lenoir 2003). In the period following the

Second World War – which was much earlier than in Quebec – France "set up family policy independent of the other branches of social policy" through dedicated organizations, notably the family branch of the social security system (Lenoir 1992, 27). Women were the main targets of this social policy from the beginning, and they have remained so, particularly those who fit the modern template of the isolated, impoverished mother in distress (Kniebiehler 1997). In the absence of significant feminist mobilization, private transfers between ex-partners have long remained a lesser priority. The issue of child support re-emerged in the 2000s, but more in relation to the efficiency of the court system than as a way to combat inequality. Today, it is largely in the purview of the family branch of the social security system, whose handling of it has not called into question the protectionist approach to mothers that France has shown over the past decades.

Providing for Women Instead of Making Men Pay
The impoverishment that follows separation became a problem in the public eye a bit earlier in France than it did in Quebec. Growing awareness led to the institutionalization of several approaches intended to improve the payment of child support. Overseen by the first secretary of state for the condition of women, legislation to authorize the public collection of child support was first proposed in 1975.[24] It allowed women to whom child support was owed to file a claim with the Procureur de la République (Prosecutor of the Republic), which would then instruct the tax authorities to collect the payments. The law also made it possible for the Caisses d'Allocations Familiales (CAF) (Family Benefit Offices) to advance child support payments to women in need. These policies came on the heels of another law, passed two years earlier, which made it possible to call on a bailiff to collect unpaid child support.[25] If France adopted these kinds of measures so early, how to explain the very different path it quickly began to follow?

The first major contrast between France and Quebec may be observed in differences between their feminist movements: feminism in France is less structured, has less political clout, and has taken a less active role in public debate over family law (Revillard 2016, 189). While a divorced women's movement – the Fédération syndicale des femmes chefs de famille (Federation of Women Heads of Household) – did emerge in 1963, its orientations were and are very different from those of the FAFMRQ on the other side of the Atlantic (Friedli 2015). As a member of the powerful, corporatist, and somewhat conservative Union nationale des associations familiales (National Union of Family Associations), the French federation does not define itself as feminist and has little weight in the public policy arena (Martin-Papineau 2003, 12; Minonzio and Vallat 2006). "Isolated mothers," as they are known in France, have a little more voice in the progressive feminist movement than they do in the traditional family values movement, which advocates on behalf of large families and for universal family benefits.

As for political parties, the alliance forged in Quebec between sovereigntists and feminists, as we saw in the previous chapter, succeeded in placing the direct collection of child support on the political agenda. But, in France, the opinion held among many socialists and communists that family law was "bourgeois law" from which individuals ought to be liberated led to the perception that "injustices in the private sphere [were] less important than inequalities in the work world" (Revillard 2007a, 420, 422). There was a certain degree of parliamentary opposition from the left on this issue: a group of communist as well as socialist deputies proposed legislation to create a "guarantee fund" for child support.

The right, which held power in the 1970s, found itself caught between the supporters of traditional familialism and a new generation that sought to promote itself as a modernizing force. Françoise Giroud, the secretary of state for the condition of women in 1974–76, and Monique Pelletier, who held the same position in 1978–81, both belonged to the more liberal wing of the French right, but they were forced to compromise with their more conservative allies, who were opposed to the legalization of abortion and unenthusiastic about the 1975 divorce reform. Though she supported legislation in favour of child support collection, Giroud rejected a proposal by the left wing of Parliament at the time to establish a guarantee fund on the grounds that its cost to the public would be too high and that it risked encouraging "debtors' negligence and the government taking over their obligations" (Revillard 2007a, 430). In her subsequent proposals, Pelletier did not call into question the targeting of "bad payers" or "isolated mothers" who received tax benefits. A Catholic mother of seven children and the daughter and wife of a banker, Pelletier was also a juvenile court judge and the director of a non-profit network dedicated to teaching parenting skills (R. Lenoir 2003, 464). She expanded the power of the CAF to advance child support payments and authorized it to petition the tax authorities to collect them.[26]

When the left took power in 1981, it did not diverge from this rather timid approach. The creation of a "guarantee fund for the collection of child support payments" was one of the 110 promises in François Mitterrand's campaign platform. Once elected, he gave the task of implementing the fund to Yvette Roudy, whom he had appointed minister for women's rights, a position she held until 1986. However, the law she orchestrated that was passed on December 22, 1984, merely expanded the role of the CAF without implementing any new policy mechanisms.[27] In an interview she gave in 2005, Roudy did not remember where the idea for the project had come from, nor did she mention any women's groups supporting it. Moreover, her entourage was hardly unanimous on the issue: her first chief of staff opposed it, and his successor promoted a mechanism far less ambitious than the campaign promise. Roudy's interest in this issue was mostly eclipsed by other issues at the top of the feminist agenda (equality in the workplace, contraception, abortion) (Revillard 2007a, 437–46).

At the least, the law of 1984 did lead the Caisse nationale des allocations familiales (CNAF) (National Family Benefits Offices) to finance studies on the economic impact of separation and divorce. These studies highlighted the ways in which separation led to impoverishment as well as to the volume of outstanding child support payments. In her summary report, one CNAF manager pointed out that "separation, for two thirds of single-parent families, translates to lower income" and that "among poor families who are recipients [of aid from a CAF in Southern France], one in two is a single-parent family with a child" (Blanc 1990, 9, 11). She added that only half of divorced women (and even fewer separated ones) reported receiving child support. Child support payments were "unreliable, both in amount and in regularity" (11): every month, 40 percent of them went unpaid (Festy 1986). These statistics were somewhat less alarming than their Quebecois equivalents: child support was paid more regularly, and the poverty rate for single mothers was lower. Single mothers in France tended to work more than both their counterparts in Quebec and French women living in couples (Martin 1997, 59). Moreover, there were half as many single-parent households in France than in Quebec at the time of the Quebec reforms (11 percent, according to Lefaucheur 1986, 173).

Above all, the administrative interpretation of these figures was very different. The manager at the CNAF believed that "impoverishment is experienced by both ex-partners" and that the problem of unpaid child support was linked "to the precarious circumstances in which many divorced fathers end up because of unemployment or professional difficulties" (Blanc 1990, 8, 10).[28] Unlike the FAFMRQ, which made efforts to disseminate the government's research findings, the French women's movement did little with them. Research was produced, but the administration's interpretation of it did not recognize private transfers as participating in gender inequality, meaning that little to no public action was taken. No evaluations of the different methods of collection were circulated publicly, and they remained unchanged for thirty years.

However, unlike the Quebec Ministère du Revenu (Department of Revenue), the family branch of the French social security system had considerable margin for action, meaning that public redistribution was the main solution pursued to improve the circumstances of single-parent families (R. Lenoir 1992). Two benefits became key in the maintenance of children following separation, neither of which had any direct equivalent in Quebec. Both of them sought to reduce the impoverishment of separated mothers in France by expanding a public protection approach to a new category of the population known as an "isolated mother" or a "monoparental head of household." The first benefit, known as the Allocation Parent Isolé (API) (Isolated Parent Benefit), was established in 1976. It was emblematic of the centrist reform that was the focus of then-president Valéry Giscard d'Estaing's mandate. More precisely, it was the result of a growing awareness of the failures of the social welfare system as it then existed, raised in large part by reformist politicians such as presidential adviser Lionel Stoléru (1974) and René Lenoir (1974), who was secretary of state for social action.

New leaders were appointed to the CNAF during the same period, with profiles that differed considerably from the pillars of familialism that had directed it in previous eras. These new leaders, who had been drawn from the highest ranks of the financial branches of the French government, recommended means testing to define the populations to be targeted by the social policies (R. Lenoir 1992). Fighting poverty in France became a largely technocratic affair, whereas, in Quebec, it remained an object of political activism. Among the "new poor" identified by these modernizing economists (Dulong 1997), "isolated mothers" were a key group (Martin-Papineau 2003, 14).

Bertrand Fragonard is considered to have been the "father" of this benefit (Martin-Papineau 2003, 7). Trained at France's prestigious École nationale d'administration, he began his career at the French Cour des comptes in 1964 and served as chief of staff for the Ministère des solidarités et de la santé, first under René Lenoir and then Simone Veil. Thirty years later, he recalled that citizen sector organizations were consulted very little as the benefit was created: "First of all, there's no lobby for single young women!" he joked (Helfter 2010, 137). This public policy intervention was thought of as a technocratic tool in the fight against poverty rather than as a lever for women's liberation. And, indeed, the API retained a familialist cast: it was intended only for the poorest mothers; eligibility lasted only a year or up to the first three years of a child's life; and the benefit was lost if the parent beneficiary ceased to be single. Nevertheless, the API was a part of a broad expansion of minimum social benefits (the number of recipients doubled between 1995 and 2015), as opposed to in Quebec where the payment of welfare benefits diminished.[29]

Moreover, along with several other countries in continental Europe, France progressively implemented a social benefit specifically for children whose non-resident parents could not or would not pay child support (Skinner and Davidson 2009, 46). Created in 1970, this benefit was initially limited to children who had lost one of their parents or who had been recognized by only one parent.[30] Five years later, the passage of a new and more liberal divorce law led to a rapid increase in the number of separations (Prost 1999, 79). This in turn raised the question of whether this benefit should be extended to children whose parents no longer lived together. In 1975, a decree was issued stating that children with one parent who "declines or is unable to uphold their duty of maintenance" were eligible to receive this benefit.[31] The following year, the amount of the benefit increased by 50 percent (Helfter 2010, 137). In 1984, the Roudy bill, as it was commonly known after its initiator, Yvette Roudy, gave the benefit its current name – the Allocation de soutien familial (ASF) (Family Support Allowance) – and made it need-blind. The ASF was still limited to parents who remained single, however, confirming that "isolated mothers," rather than all children whose parents did not live together, were the targets of this form of public redistribution.

In reality, this benefit played two distinct roles. The first one had to do with combating poverty: the ASF stepped in for the parent who did not earn enough income to pay child support. But the ASF could also be paid out as an advance on child support in cases where child support went unpaid, with the expectation that the outstanding amounts would then be collected from the debtor parents.[32] Both benefits expanded the role of the CAF in the lives of single-parent families. It should be noted that Bertrand Fragonard worked as the head of the CAF from 1980 to 1987 and was a major figure of the "welfare elite" driving French family policy at that time (Hassenteufel et al. 1999). Political parties came and went, but these high-ranking public officials asserted a "centrist" and financial vision of these issues throughout, which explains why these benefits were targeted and means tested (Martin 2001, 106–7). It also shows why paternal responsibility remained a non-priority. In an interview, Bertrand Fragonard noted that the guarantee fund promoted by Roudy was the subject of a great deal of criticism within the minister's entourage and that he himself was opposed to it:

> A lot of people were saying "you're giving the mother too much power, in the sense that, if she is sure she will receive child support, she can sideline the guy or even sabotage his visitation rights and so on" ... When you chatted with lawyers, people like that ... I was divorced. I paid my child support with no trouble. But when she [Yvette Roudy] told me: "now you'll pay the fund and not your wife," I found that shocking. And I was deeply opposed to it.[33]

In short, the administration in France was far more reluctant than the one in Quebec to use public pressure to constrain fathers to pay child support. The weakness of women's groups, the priorities pursued by WPAs, and the predominance of men among high-ranking civil servants and elected officials all led to a situation where child support payments had to be worked out within the power imbalance between ex-partners, placing women at a structural disadvantage. For these men at the helm of government, social benefits offered the advantage of preserving existing social relations between genders, forcing women to rely on the goodwill of men or meet the requirements of the administrative bodies.

Conservative Child Support Guidelines for the Sake of Court Efficiency

Another feature of the French system that may come as a surprise to anyone for whom Quebec is a reference is that the Ministère de la justice has little to do with debates over child support. This disengagement persisted until the 2010s, as can be seen in this interview with the magistrate working as the director of the Bureau du droit des personnes et de la famille (Bureau of Individual and Family Rights) in the Ministère de la justice at the time: "Enforcement? No, once the judge has issued the child support order, enforcing it isn't up to us. In fact, it's done by bailiffs. We don't have any numbers on payment defaults, for example, because that comes after the litigation in court."[34] If family law and family courts pay little attention to this issue, it might be assumed that matters would be different in the criminal justice system since the French Penal Code considers failure to pay child support for more than two months as "*abandon de famille*" (family desertion), which constitutes a criminal offence: those found guilty of it are liable for up to two years in prison and a fine of up to fifteen thousand euros.[35] But many judges consider this procedure to be inadequate, as may be observed in the following conversation between two judges and a lawyer during a conference on child support.

A juvenile prosecutor had been asked to give a presentation on family desertion, but she opened with the caution that she was "not a specialist on this infraction." Her presentation was extremely short. Noting that the "charges are not very serious," she described conditions under which they can be dismissed, pointing out that mediation is a frequent recourse in criminal cases as an alternative to prosecution. The lawyer who had organized the conference expressed concern over the "significant default rate for child support payments" and the "impoverishment of single-parent families" and raised the question of "why there is not an apposite criminal policy." The prosecutor explained that there is a certain reluctance to consider these bad payers as "ordinary delinquents." Mentioning her own experience as a family judge, she suggested that failure to pay is the result of a "broader context" (conflict, trouble seeing the children). "Litigation won't do anything!" she affirmed. The lawyer spoke of filing multiple claims and then abandoning the effort: "The prosecution ends up defending the interests of the father for failing to pay." A family judge asked whether there were any data available at the national level on the number of cases filed and heard. The prosecutor admitted that she did not know the statistics.[36]

In an era when amicable divorce is the norm, it is perhaps to be expected that this prosecutor would consider the enforcement of child support payments through the criminal justice system to be an inadequate response. Statistics on this topic do exist, and they show that divorced couples are unlikely to resort to this option: only a small minority (12 percent) of people who have not received the child support provided for in their divorce rulings report filing suit for family desertion (Belmokhtar 2016, 4). What is most surprising about the exchanges presented above is the lack of interest and knowledge expressed by the two judges, both of whom work in family courts. Yet again, prevailing suspicions about mothers (are they preventing the fathers from seeing their children? are they being unaccommodating?) make it difficult to perceive child support as an instrument of gender equality.

Since the 2000s, although continuing to neglect the question of child support enforcement, the Ministère de la justice has taken a strong interest in calculating it, and, in 2010, it published a set of optional guidelines. The two reports that oriented family law reform over this period, which I discussed in Chapter 1, both recommended the creation of these guidelines. In her report, Françoise Dekeuwer-Défossez (1999, 142) underscored the "necessity of more transparence and unity in setting the amount of these payments," calling for "reflection on the possibility of creating reference guidelines." The Ministère de la justice followed up on this report by forming its first working group to address the topic. But it was only nine years later, following a report by Serge Guinchard (2008), that the guidelines became a concrete reality. This professor of private law advocated for the publication of guidelines in several areas in order to "impel a strong decrease in litigation," to "support the development of amicable processes for settling differences," and to lighten the load of "agreement approval procedures" (51–52). He explained that the main goal of the guidelines was to enhance the efficiency of the court system by improving its management.

Both reports bear witness to the fact that arguments in favour of the guidelines are much narrower in France than in Quebec. Nowhere is the prospect raised of increasing the amount of child support paid or fighting inequality; instead, the goal is to reduce variations in decisions from one judge to another, and from one jurisdiction to another, by providing family judges with a "decision-making tool" that saves them time. Isabelle Sayn (2014, 1, 7), a legal scholar involved in reflections on the guidelines since 1999, emphasized the argument for the "efficiency of the legal or court decision" as the "source of the creation of the guidelines." The family judge Jean-Claude Bardout also has highlighted the utility of this tool in his practice: "Personally, I don't think that the judge does, or should, fill his work time with calculations. For me, child support litigation has really been simplified ... Pretty often, the lawyers come and say 'we came to an agreement based on the guidelines.' I save time in hearings, thanks to those guidelines."[37]

Évelyne Serverin, a long-time legal adviser to the Ministère de la justice, observed much the same thing; in her opinion, the guidelines "stop the haggling [and] protect judges."[38] As these quotations make clear, guidelines are above all a tool for family judges, contrary to the situation in Quebec, where judges in the Superior Court rarely deal with them directly. The ministry has now set guidelines that essentially reflect the existing practices of judges and are directly inspired by the calculation tool that Bardout created for himself and tested in his own court. Moreover, the economists involved in designing the guidelines sought to stay close to the amounts ordered in trial courts and in courts of appeal (Sayn, Jeandidier, and Bourreau-Dubois 2012). Clearly, the goal here was not to upset existing practice – unlike in Quebec, where child support payments were seen as being too low – but, rather, to encourage judges to adopt the guidelines by limiting the changes they imposed.

This recognition of what was already in place was also a way of reproducing judges' representations of child support calculations. The fact that the table in the guidelines refers only to debtor parents' income is a reflection of the habitual practices of judges, as is its infrequent use in cases of joint custody (already noted in Chapter 4). Bardout reported to us that he tended to favour dividing the costs in half, without attempting to account for income disparities between men and women: "I think that the lawmaker didn't particularly intend for there to be child support when there is joint custody, because apparently it seems logical to split things down the middle ... There, people who get along often say 'we split things down the middle' ... If the parents agree, I don't step in." Even though the guidelines did not seek to change the amount of child support payments, judges were reluctant to begin using them as they were perceived to be a form of managerialization. In 1999, Dekeuwer-Défossez's report called for guidelines to be indicative, rather than mandatory, in order to preserve the autonomy of family judges. "If all we had to do was blindly apply guidelines, what use would we be anymore?" a family judge remarked in an interview in 2009.[39] In 2013, the Court of Cassation ruled that child support could not be set using the guidelines alone: judges needed grounds for each specific case.[40] In so doing, France's highest law court confirmed the small role that the guidelines were to play in judges' considerations: these guidelines ranked last in the hierarchy of legal norms, far lower than in Quebec.

The process by which the guidelines were created shows the ways in which calculation methods were set apart from other dimensions of child support: the tool was above all built to respond to the concerns of the Ministère de la justice and of trial judges. While its managerialist bent is clear, the courts' approach to it and their use of it have been rather conservative, both because this calculation method basically reproduces existing practices (including in its blindness to economic inequalities between parents) and because the guidelines, consigned as they are to the margins of the law, do not meaningfully change the work of judges.

Path Dependency and the Implementation Gap

In the decade that followed the establishment of guidelines in France, the question of child support moved outside the purview of the Ministère de la justice. A handful of high-ranking civil servants in the social policy sector and a group emerging from within the women's movement began to take an interest in the guidelines for reasons that were very different from those of the ministry. For them, the guidelines were a way to place the links between private transfers and state solidarity back on the agenda. Between 2012 and 2021, a series of reforms was passed whose stated goal was to improve the payment of child support while increasing public redistribution to single-parent families. But these reforms were built on forty years of assumptions and decisions: institutionally, the family branch of the social security system remained the central actor in the child support system. Furthermore, the definition of solidarity that it mobilized was not driven, as it had been in Canada, by concern for the economic rights of women and children, which meant that power struggles between ex-partners remained decisive in the determination of post-separation arrangements. What does this remobilization over such a long-dormant issue mean? And why did it lead to reforms with such modest goals and patchy implementation?

High-ranking civil servants played a central role both in the creation of the reform agendas and in the limited goals that they pursued. The first set of reforms, undertaken during the presidency of François Hollande between 2012 and 2017, was the result of joint interventions by Fragonard, the former head of the CAF who, as mentioned earlier, had been a central figure in family policies, and a young feminist official named Élizabeth Le Hot. Fragonard, then in his seventies, had headed the Haut Conseil de la famille (High Council on Family Affairs) since 2009.[41] The consultative body worked closely with the prime minister and included many young social policy specialists. Le Hot was one of them for a time. Admitted to the École Nationale d'Administration in 2008, at a time in her life when she herself was, as she put it, "a single-parent family," she frequently described her experiences as motivating her involvement with this issue. She had spent the first years of her career in the civil administration in various branches of the welfare state: the Direction de la Sécurité Sociale (Social Security Administration) (2010–12); the Haut Conseil de la famille (High Family Council) (2012–13); the staff of the Ministère des Droits des Femmes (Ministry for Women's Rights) (2013–14); and the staff of the Secrétariat d'Etat à la famille (Secretary of State for Families) (2014–16). This young government feminist and this senior functionary both called for expanding public redistribution for single-parent families and for an improvement in child support payments.

The first series of changes concerned the ASF, which, most significantly, was raised by 25 percent. At the same time, a new instrument, known as the supplementary payment, was progressively included in the ASF. Child support payments that were lower than the ASF could now be supplemented by family benefits, up to the amount of the ASF itself. This instrument was intended to encourage judges to set "small" child support amounts (rather than the widespread practice of exonerating the poorest fathers altogether, which we observed in the previous chapter). Child maintenance obligations were thus reinforced among fathers from less privileged backgrounds, in exchange for increased government support to mothers. This mechanism, which Le Hot dubbed "minimum child support," was part of a socially minded tax reform to benefit poorer families that was put in place during Hollande's mandate. As Le Hot explained, "the major advance is minimum child support. Which is a real help. An estimated one hundred thousand families could be affected by it. We know that child support in these families averages forty-nine euros, meaning that the average benefit per child per month received by these families will be fifty-one euros ... It's Robin Hood."[40]

Overall, the social welfare and tax system did indeed become more beneficial to single-parent families: public aid raised their median standard of living from one-half to three-quarters of that of single people (Bodier et al. 2015, 18). It is far from certain, however, if improving the links between child support and family benefits actually raised the amounts intended for children. Indeed, for the decisions that we analyzed that were handed down in 2013, around 17 percent of the child support orders for minors were lower than the ASF – a ten-point increase compared with child support orders in 2007.[43] In other words, judges seem to have rapidly taken on board the idea that some creditor parents would be able to round out their "small" child support payments with public aid.

Nevertheless, this public aid is far from systematic. It took eight years to reach the goal of one hundred thousand recipients of ASF supplementary payments, a number that is still lower than the estimated number of child support payments inferior to the ASF.[44] It must be noted that no direct transmission of data from the courts to the CAF has been planned so that custodial parents can rapidly and easily receive payments. Yet again, it is the most financially vulnerable mothers who end up having to undertake lengthy procedures with courts and benefit offices. Moreover, mothers who move in with new partners are no longer eligible for ASF supplementary payments, which are reserved for "isolated mothers." Overall, implementing a combination of private transfer and public aid, which is crucial for poorer families, has not yet gone far enough.

And what of the payment of child support today? Although Fragonard and Le Hot converged in their thinking when it came to the ASF, they were more hesitant, and even found themselves in disagreement, over how the government ought to address the problem of outstanding child support payments. Nearly eight hundred thousand families receive the ASF, at an annual cost of 1.7 billion euros (CNAF 2018, 28). The payment of child support is a significant matter for the public coffers. Both Fragonard and Le Hot agreed that the CAF's enforcement system was unsatisfactory, and they asked that the CAF be afforded more resources so that they could engage in routine monitoring of parents considered "unable" to pay. However, the two were unable to agree on a unified payment system. Fragonard, although he was no longer opposed to it in principle, remained circumspect. Data had not been updated since the 1980s, and so he sought quantitative information that might back a favourable decision about it. However, his attempts to mobilize the administration and professional groups to provide that information failed: the data available from the CNAF and the Ministère de la justice were only for a portion of the people who would be affected by such a system (recipients or divorced people). The tax authority refused to cooperate, meaning that no enforcement data from the public treasury were made available. The national bailiffs' association undertook a survey of its members, to which only 3 percent of them responded (Haut Conseil de la famille 2016, 120). Finally, a major survey on separation-related statistics undertaken by Fragonard was blocked by Claude Thélot (2016), his counterpart at the Cour des Comptes (French Court of Accounts).

Research in the sociology of ignorance has shown that a lack of knowledge can serve as an argument for inaction (see, for example, McGoey 2014). This was certainly the case in the French situation: far from being inevitable, failure to move forward with a universal payment system resulted from inadequate investment by the central institutions and weakened the reformist momentum of the most committed actors. In 2016, Fragonard described himself as still "hesitant" about the desirability of an agency tasked with collecting and distributing all child support payments. He still preferred an optional system, which would be a kind of insurance that parents would pay for their own "security." He doubted that it would be possible to produce the one hundred million euros needed for such a system and deemed it improbable that tax rules would ever evolve in France.

Le Hot took a much firmer position, at least in the speech she wrote for Najat Vallaud-Belkacem. During a parliamentary debate over the draft legislation on gender equality in 2014, the minister clearly mobilized an argument of "gender justice":

> Who is not aware that the face of vulnerability today is all too often that of a lone woman heading a single-parent household, all too often deprived of the vital resource of child support, despite the fact that it is her right to receive it? ... The goal of [this] new system for securing child support is to put an end to the long, hard struggle of isolated mothers dealing with unpaid child support.[45]

The tone of this discourse closely echoed the tone that was heard in Quebec twenty years earlier. There, as in France, the matter of public savings was raised alongside the goal of advancing women's rights: "Family Benefit Offices recovered just €15 million out of €75 million" in ASF benefits advanced for unpaid child support, lamented Vallaud-Belkacem.[46] Off camera, Le Hot was far less confident, admitting that creating a universal collection system seemed highly improbable to her.

The actual reforms to the child support payment system implemented during Hollande's term of office were a far cry from this model. The first reform, called the Garantie contre les impayés de pension alimentaire (GIPA) (Child Support Enforcement Guarantee), made only minor changes to the system: the waiting period required before a parent could apply for an advance on unpaid child support was shortened from two months to one, and the period of collection for child support enforcement was raised from six to twenty-four months. These changes had little impact on creditors, who rarely sought the help these reforms purported to offer: in 2017, only one creditor parent in ten who had been the victim of a payment default applied to the CAF (Union des Caisses nationales de sécurité sociale 2017, 4). It would seem that some parents are dissuaded from action by the application process, which is complicated, and by the extensive documentation required by the administration (Mathivet et al. 2014).

While the impact of the GIPA was minimal for separated parents, its effects were clear at the institutional level, where it strengthened the role played by the family branch of the social security system in the lives of separated families. From the 1980s to the time of these reforms, the CAF had put less and less effort into collection and enforcement, which demanded more legal competence and time than most other issues. Aurélie Schaaf, who has been in charge of child support collection for the CNAF since September 2019, was the head of a local CAF in the early 2000s, and she recalled the "big files" related to collection in an interview:

> We dealt with [collection files] when we had time ... We were no good. We didn't have much competence ... You need time, you need to be able to concentrate. When you're good, you can handle three or four files in a day, whereas when you're dealing with other services, like housing subsidies, you can process twenty to thirty files a day.[47]

In addition to the onerousness of the files, collecting unpaid child support implies a coercive role in relation to fathers, which is not customary for these services as they are habitually concerned with monitoring mothers. Monitoring mostly consists of verifying that these women are well and truly "isolated" through family visits, which are now supplemented by data mining to detect fraud (Dubois, Paris, and Weill 2018). In the words of Daniel Lenoir, who was the director of the CNAF from 2013 to 2017, "it's not the Family Benefit Office's job to go collect money. The job of the Family Benefit Office is to pay."[48] Child support collection requires cooperation with the courts as well as with employers and even with the tax authorities – work with which the CAF is unaccustomed and for which it is poorly equipped.

So why was the CNAF asking that its role be expanded in this arena and for the state to entrust it with this work rather than the tax authorities? First, because it fit with the organization's own plans: the ASF was launched as a part of a broader initiative to pool services and benefits among the CAF. As a result of this initiative, certain offices were empowered to manage the allocation of benefits for others and, therefore, to train specialized agents to process more complex cases. Second, since the 2000s, family services had been investing in parenting support programs (Minonzio 2007). The CNAF thought that it had a broad vision of all the challenges faced by separated parents, meaning that it was uniquely qualified to intervene in matters involving them. As a result, in 2017, the GIPA was replaced by what was, on paper at least, a more ambitious system. The Agence de recouvrement des impayés des pensions alimentaires (Child Support Collection Agency) opened under the direction of the family branch. The change was purely cosmetic, according to Daniel Lenoir (2019), who oversaw its rollout: "It's putting a label on something that already exists." The CAF's power to collect unpaid child support was more or less the same, and there was still no question of its acting as an intermediary between parents in the collection and payment of upkeep for their children.

One thing has evolved in all of this: as of 2020, the family branch was empowered to participate in setting child support payment amounts, in the name of its own budget concerns and the Ministère de la justice's goal of reducing litigation. More specifically, the family branch is now authorized to make amicable child support agreements between unmarried parents binding as long as the parents respect the guidelines. However, when this change went into effect, these guidelines were not the same as the ones published by the Ministère de la justice. The amount they set was not indicative but, rather, imperative: it was the minimum amount required to receive a supplementary payment from the ASF. Moreover, it required that a child support payment be set in cases of joint physical custody, which, as we saw earlier, are not the norm in French court decisions. Finally, payment amounts rose more steeply since the number of children rose. The existence of two distinct calculation methods – one for the court system and one for the social security system – has institutionalized differentiation based on marital status (the CAF are not empowered to decide alone in the case of divorce) and on income (people earning lower incomes are more likely to receive family benefits). For the social security system, the guidelines were a discreet way to lower the financial cost of the supplementary ASF payment by raising the amount of child support owed by poorer fathers. As Daniel Lenoir openly revealed, "the Family Benefit Office guidelines – I wanted them because I wanted to avoid fraud."[49]

So why does France continue to have such a patchy child support system? The first factor has to do with the difficulties encountered by the small number of high-ranking officials in their efforts to convince their colleagues to make reform a priority. The second factor has to do with the challenge of bringing the court system on board. The third factor lies in the feminist movement's failure to rally behind the cause. Although these high-ranking officials knew each other well, often working closely with one another in the same institutions, they were unable to unite around this issue. Certainly, within the administration, there was no convergence behind the goal of improving private payments, notably among experts in social policy. State feminists such as Le Hot were convinced of the importance of mobilizing family solidarity as a means of improving the status of women, while high-ranking civil servants continued to see the job market as the main vector of equality.

Finally, there were those who dismissed the whole idea of the state intervening in financial transfers between parents because of their own family situations. In 2015, a study by France Stratégie, a public organization advising the prime minister, undertook to assess the effects of the guidelines using "typical cases" imagined by the study's authors (Ben Jelloul and Cusset 2015). Instigated by a research coordinator incensed at having to pay child support to an ex-partner who earned more money than he did, the study concluded that, because of France's tax and social system, the decrease in standard of living for non-custodial parents (most often fathers) post-separation was more significant than that of custodial parents. The study, which paid no attention to structural inequalities between men and women, drew criticism from the Haut Conseil de la famille (2015) and the Secrétariat d'Etat aux droits des femmes (Ministry for Women's Rights) (Rossignol 2015) and proved that there was real resistance within the government to improving the child maintenance system. Daniel Lenoir affirmed the existence of this type of resistance, explaining that he believed certain CAF directors, who were themselves debtor fathers, were reluctant to give more muscle to the child support payment system. He added, however, that personal convictions were not the only reason for inaction. In 2017, the main priority of the minister of social affairs was the launch of a new benefit for low-income workers known as the employment bonus (*prime pour l'emploi*). Improving the child support collection system was a secondary goal, and the resources mobilized to reach it were insufficient.

The second obstacle to the goal of a unified support payment system was the court system: collaboration between the family services branch and the Ministère de la justice was not nearly comprehensive enough. Discussions about combining the two guidelines began only in 2020. Before that, the first collection system to mediate between debtor and creditor parents, launched in 2014, had ended in failure due to a lack of cooperation from the courts. That system had been intended only for violent debtor parents, who until that time could be exempted from paying child support as a way of keeping them from contact of any kind with their victims (most often women). Theoretically, the family services branch could now act as an intermediary so that child support could be paid with no contact between parents, presuming that the family services branch was alerted to violent situations observed during court proceedings. Schaaf, the current director of the Agence de recouvrement des impayés des pensions alimentaires, told me that it appeared this information was rarely transmitted: "For reasons I do not know, family judges do not avail themselves of this possibility. We have had very few requests."[50] Here, once again, the lack of communication between family courts and the CAF makes vulnerable women even more vulnerable. It should be noted that, during the same period, the Ministère de la justice was seeking a response to the demands of fathers who thought they were at a disadvantage in custody-related court decisions: in 2013, some of these fathers climbed onto cranes to make themselves heard, a gesture that received broad media attention. It was in this context that the ministry launched the reform to legal custody that was discussed in Chapter 4 rather than undertaking any serious reflection on the economic impact of separations.

Finally, in contrast to Quebec in the 1990s, French feminist groups have only recently become involved in the issue and only in a limited way. The first organization to form behind this cause, Abandon de famille tolérance zéro (Family Desertion Zero Tolerance), was only founded in 2013. An informal group that communicates through social media, its only public spokesperson is its founder, Stéphanie Lamy. Despite being the only organization to have publicly taken up this cause, it has not been included in official exchanges with the relevant administrations. In the past, the highest-profile women's groups have concentrated their efforts on issues related to violence against women. Another organization, SOS Les Mamans (SOS for Moms), which was founded in 2008 and counts 180 members, was consulted by the Ministère de la justice on the subject of reforming legal custody, but its president indicated that economic issues took second place behind the problem of violence against women. Although she was in her fifties and had experienced discontinuous employment, she still affirmed the importance of independence through work in words that recalled the historical priorities of French feminists (Revillard 2016, 143):

> Child support, I'll tell you very honestly, it's important, but for me it comes second. When you have children who aren't mistreated, when the other parent isn't toxic, a pedophile, or whatever. So it's true that it's not good, it's true. But me, I tell myself, and it's what I tell mothers every time: "We don't need anyone to raise our kids. We

work, we have a salary, if we have to raise them without child support, we'll do it."[51]

At the other end of the spectrum in the women's movement are the institutionalized and professionalized structures of the Centre d'information sur les droits des femmes et des familles (Centre for Information on Women's and Family Rights). The topic of child support comes up regularly in requests to their local centres, but the national offices rarely pass these requests for information on to the public authorities. The public authorities, in turn, have not sought their opinion on this issue, as one of the national centre's technical advisers explained: "[The Child Support Enforcement Guarantee] was managed exclusively by the Family Benefit Offices. And no one came to us beforehand either. Because sometimes we are solicited beforehand ... but not much on this kind of subject, really."[52] Because of these internal dynamics, and because of the role that its members are assigned by public administrations, the feminist movement has remained in the background when it comes to the economic impact of separation and divorce.

Surprisingly, the Yellow Vest movement, which was active in 2018 and 2019, was the first large-scale social movement in France to bring any real visibility to this issue. Women were very present on the roundabouts occupied by these activists, and they achieved a level of visibility – notably in the media – that is rarely seen in mixed-gender movements. Many of these women came from poorer and lower-middle-class backgrounds, and many worked in undervalued and poorly paid jobs while raising children alone (Gallot 2019). In protests organized within the movement on behalf of women, they spoke out against their working conditions and their standards of living, highlighting the financial difficulties they encountered after separating from their partners.

While noting that they were not feminists (this kind of distancing from the feminist movement can often be observed among members of the working class), they made demands that had to do with the economic impact of separation and the ways in which it amplified gender inequality. The expression "economic violence," previously heard in the mouths of Le Hot and Lamy, gained unprecedented currency. The concerns expressed by these women reached all the way to the upper echelons of the French government: in March 2019, during the great debate initiated by the executive branch to engage with the protest movement, Marlène Schiappa, secretary of state for gender equality, organized a meeting with single mothers in Seine Saint Denis, France's poorest *département*, located on the outskirts of Paris. Soon after this meeting, the prime minister announced that the CAF could collect child support directly from the salaries of debtor parents and pay it to creditor parents – a service that finally went into effect in January 2021.

For the first time in several decades, a social movement had exerted direct influence on child maintenance policy in France. It must be said that giving priority to private payments meshed with the social policy stances of President Emmanuel Macron, who was elected in 2017. The social security and tax measures taken at the beginning of his mandate have led to a deepening of inequalities in the standard of living, with decreased housing subsidies having the greatest impact on poorer households (Delmas and Guillaneuf 2020). Significantly, a review of the ASF undertaken under Hollande in view of increasing payments was put on hold. The inclusion of child support in the calculation of social welfare benefits still has not been called into question, and two feminist economists have warned that improving child support collection may actually have a negative impact on single mothers' standard of living by reducing their eligibility for government benefits (Périvier and Pucci 2019).

Now that there is agreement among stakeholders on the figures – more than one-third of child support payments remain outstanding (Auvigne et al. 2016) – systems are gradually being put in place to improve collection: the CAF now have access to the income that debtor parents declare to the tax authorities; collection rates are now included in the performance indicators for the family services branch, which must be reported yearly to the Ministère des solidarités et de la santé and Parliament; 450 collection agents were recruited in 2020; and a system for sharing information between the family services branch and legal professionals was put in place in 2021 so that legal professionals could communicate child support amounts agreed on by parents to family services, along with debtor parents' contact information.

Other issues, however, although central to the lives of women raising children on their own, have remained on the sidelines. Though the collection rate has improved – reaching 69 percent in 2020 (Direction de la sécurité sociale 2021, 79) we should not forget that the family branch handles only a small proportion of outstanding child support payments. As of mid-2021, there were around seventy thousand child support collection cases open (Schaff 2022), and over three hundred thousand parents appear to be victims of default (Auvigne et al. 2016, 7). Similarly, tax rules for child support, which put middle-class women at a structural disadvantage, began to be debated only in 2019 at the initiative of the Assemblée nationale's women's rights delegation and the Haut Conseil de la famille, without any clear recommendations being made.

Viewed from Quebec, these numerous and modest reforms may seem more surprising given the frequency with which French reformers have held up Quebec's child maintenance policy as an example. In 2013–14, Fragonard travelled to Sweden, the United Kingdom, and Germany. He also spent two days in Quebec and returned from his trip with the idea that the Quebecois system was "the most comprehensive one of all, the most methodical," noting, in particular, that it was less costly than the English child maintenance system.[53] Daniel Lenoir (2019, 7) proposed a dedicated agency "based on the Quebecois example" to assure the payment of all child support orders. But evoking Quebec's approach has produced little in the way of concrete results: starting in 2021, some twenty years after Quebec's system was put in place, the French CAF was permitted to serve as intermediaries for child support payment, if the writ of divorce (or separation) orders it or if a parent asks for it. This is in no way a default rule for all child support orders.

This opt-in system runs a considerable risk of creating implementation gaps, given the challenges of meeting all the conditions for its success, both for legal professionals and social services (who are not accustomed to working together) and for parents: if the current enforcement system is used so little, why would another voluntary system work any better? True, not everyone uses the direct debit service in Quebec, but, because France has placed less value on private transfers in the past few decades and more value on parents' payment "choices," power struggles between ex-partners play a more significant role there than they do in Quebec. In February 2022, a year after it was rolled out, fifty-two thousand people were participating in it – not even a quarter of the target number set by the government.[54] Over the same period, only fourteen hundred requests for intermediation were registered from the court to the CAF,[55] confirming that relations between the judiciary and the social services remain tenuous. In response to these manifest inadequacies, and shortly before the 2022 presidential elections, the government undertook a new reform effort: in 2023, twenty-eight years after Quebec's system was put in place, new child support payments in France will be collected by the CAF, except in cases where both parents agree to opt out.[56]

Several factors explain the slowness of policy transfer from Quebec to France. Most reformers have little familiarity with the nuts and bolts of the Quebec system: in certain government reports, the task of documenting approaches outside France is left to a single intern. Moreover, there is only limited interest in Quebec within France's social administrations. It is true that, for the past several years, Quebec's commitment to promoting family mediation has been held up as inspiration, particularly its "information sessions on parenting after separation" (launched in Quebec in 2012 and in France in 2014). But it is rare to find a French judge who has heard of Quebec's child support guidelines or a French tax official who knows of Quebec's collection system and even rarer still to find anyone who thinks it can be adapted to France. Finally, given the limited budget of the French child maintenance system, Quebec's system seems too costly. It should be recalled that, in 2014, over seven hundred Quebec tax employees worked in the child support collection service. In France, that number reached eight hundred in 2021 – for a population nine times larger.

Obviously, this chapter cannot draw any definitive conclusions about a system that is only now being put into effect. But, at the time of writing, it was impossible to ignore the fact that the creation of a mediated collection service for child support payment was, above all, a handy communication tool: showing concern for women's financial difficulties, especially during an economic crisis linked to a public health crisis, is a good way for a president perceived as leaning more and more to the right to shine a positive light on his social policies. As in Quebec nearly thirty years earlier, this greater focus on private transfers has taken place in a context of declining commitment to public redistribution.

***

"Social policies define and enforce particular definitions of family obligation," Jane Millar (1996, 181) wrote of England's and Australia's child support systems. The French and Quebecois cases confirm her analysis. Given that women are far more likely to care for children following a separation, and to have fewer resources, they are far more affected by the bureaucratic constraints inherent in public redistribution. It is also mothers who suffer the consequences when the child maintenance system is not used in situations where their ex-partners do not fulfill their obligations. Nevertheless, despite these broad similarities, political configurations in France and Quebec have long been very different and explain why protectionist attitudes remain stronger in France (see Table 8).

TABLE 8 National differences in child support policies

	France	Quebec
Determination guidelines	Optional (2010–)	Mandatory (1997–)
Tax rule	Child support counts as income	Tax neutral (1996–)
Mediated collection	Opt out (2023–)	Opt out (1995–)
Enforcement	Family benefits offices, criminal courts, bailiffs, tax services (1975–)	Tax services (1995–)
Maintenance guarantee	Yes, for single-parent households (1975–)	None
Social benefits	Child support counts as income	Child support counts as income (except for housing program eligibility)

In France, as we have seen, outstanding child support payments have long been a low-priority issue and have not provoked any kind of scandal or political crisis. This lack of pressure means that governmental administrations have put other preoccupations first, using institutional needs and approaches to build the existing system. Recent reforms to French collection and enforcement policies confirm that the French administration continues to target lower-income populations. Mothers from these backgrounds continue to face intrusions into their private lives because the payment of their benefits is contingent on their "isolation." The setting of child support payments by the CAF extends some similar administrative constraints to lower-income fathers. By contrast, middle- and upper-class women, who are less likely to receive family benefits, are less able to rely on private transfers than their Quebecois counterparts. Middle- and upper-class fathers benefit from legal professionals' reluctance to oblige them to pay, which is more marked in France than in Quebec. This is due to the fact that, in Quebec, the problem of unpaid child support was publicized earlier and more widely, which encouraged the decompartmentalization of advocacy movements. Quebec's system benefits middle-class women the most, and the state has benefited from the high value placed on family solidarity, to the detriment of lower-income families.

Conclusion

Lest we forget, in the thirty years that followed its legalization (1884–1914), divorce remained inaccessible to many couples in France. In the words of historian Anne-Marie Sohn (1981, 607), "[d]ivorce was not for the proletarian: even with legal aid, the cost of the procedure and the law's complexity were dissuasive to less educated couples ... Half of divorces occurred among the bourgeoisie, one third among blue-collar workers, and then the rest were employees." Female infidelity was more severely punished than male misdemeanours and even family violence, which was most often committed by men. In Quebec, where the influence of the Catholic Church was stronger and the right to divorce even more restricted, this situation remained true until after the Second World War: the double standard for adultery set out in the *Civil Code of Quebec* was not changed until 1954 (Dandurand 1985, 89).[1] Until 1968, divorce remained "the privilege of a minority, as it required costly proceedings and a decision from the Federal Parliament" (Collectif Clio 1982, 428).

These historical facts should remind us that the liberalization of civil law did not produce the intertwining inequalities of class and gender that structure the long history of marriage and domestic partnership. Incontestably, the legal recognition of the equality of men and women as well as redistributive policies designed to benefit single-parent families have helped to soften inequality in its harshest forms. But true equality is still a long way off. As this study has shown, the "private ordering" of separation is actually making socio-economic inequalities in access to law and rights more acute again. Acknowledging that men and women are equal under the law does not put an end to the gendering of parenting roles, economic status, or exposure to violence. It is crucial to recall that this private ordering of separation and the slide back toward inequality that it has set in motion are occurring at the same time that the legitimacy, the power, and even the very existence of the welfare state are being called into question. The power of public redistribution to correct inequalities has been undermined by decades of neoliberal policies. While the huge rise in separation and divorce numbers would seem to be a clear marker of the individualism that characterizes our era, we should not mistake this phenomenon as the product of individual relationships alone. Institutions, whose norms and practices justify and participate in the contemporary renewal of age-old inequalities, play a central role.

The Institutional Production of Private Inequalities

The regulation of separation is not the regulatory field in which state intervention has dwindled. Reproductive rights and end-of-life decisions are other realms where "the withdrawal of authority has taken place by the removal of the penalty" (Memmi 2003, 645). A close examination of the ways in which contemporary private life is governed shows how the state's power over its populations is now masked and directed. This masking is evident in the diffuse and even negotiable nature of constraint as well as in the waning of decision-making power as a mode of domination: most often today, constraint operates by structuring expectations and the production of consent. But the way in which the state masks the constraints that it imposes depends on the population it is targeting; constraint does not take the same form, produce the same effects, or have the same intensity depending on the class and the gender of the separating couples as well as their self-proclaimed or externally assigned origins.

Justifications for this transformation in the institutional reproduction of social relations fall into three different registers. The first justification comes from approaches to public management that oriented administrative reforms starting in the 1980s and blurred the boundary between the public and private sectors. The second comes from "increasing reference to rights in public policy," one of which was the right to divorce (Baudot and Revillard 2015, 11). The third may be found in the growth of the concept of "the best interests of the child," a vague but omnipresent theme deployed to maintain state intervention into (certain) private lives.

The goal of efficiency in the allocation of public resources is rooted in market-oriented values such as reducing the "public cost" of separations. This has created more and more porousness between public and private interventions, as they have come under pressure from the commodification of the legal profession, the weakening of the welfare state, and the managerialization of the court system. The contribution of legal professionals to political life and public action over the past several centuries has been documented (Garneau 2016; Karpik 1995). Contemporary systems that have institutionalized their presence at different stages of the public policy process have made their contributions all the more important. Legal professionals participate in the drafting of public policy, aid in promoting or dismissing it, and then implement it through their work with clients. And, although other professionals such as psychologists or social workers play an increasingly prominent role in divorces and separations, which has somewhat reduced the predominant place of lawyers, they (and notaries to a lesser degree) still play an integral role in family law policy. The recognition of individual rights and freedoms maps easily onto this market-oriented world view. All separating couples do not have the same "needs" and therefore ought to have a "choice" in the ways they go about their separations. This makes the "market" (of more or less costly lawyers, more or less rapid procedures), with its promise of many options, appear to be an appropriate response. This market-based approach, however, coupled with a sharper emphasis on individual responsibility (achieving a "successful" divorce by making "the right choices"), has accentuated disparities between different populations.

When they separate, members of the upper classes work with private professionals whose services they choose and pay for themselves. In court, their cases receive more attention from judges. Members of the lower classes must make do with public services – or private ones that are paid for by public funding – for legal, psychological, and social matters. The result of this situation is that public/private boundaries for family interventions also function as social barriers. The differences between these populations stand out in myriad ways: from wait times and care taken over family histories to the number, the qualifications, and the reputations of the professionals involved and the size and the content of the cases. There is a world of difference between a separation handled by a lawyer in a legal aid office that is decided without judicial intervention and a divorce that requires a multi-day trial involving highly paid lawyers and experts. These socio-economic inequalities are linked to gender inequalities: men from poorer backgrounds are less likely to have legal representation than women from the same backgrounds. Legal representation for these women, however, is bound up with demands from social services administrations. In other words, non-litigious paths to separation have organized formal equality among separated couples: while theoretically they can "choose" from a menu of different options, the legal services they receive and the likely outcome of their procedures vary greatly depending on their social status.

Across social classes, it is true that professional intervention does help certain women and certain men to achieve more control over their lives following the breakup of their domestic partnerships. But others are dispossessed of this control by professionals or called to order if they do not demonstrate the "right" expectations. In structural terms, social status has a tremendous impact on the likelihood that a person will be able to take advantage of any flexibility in the law. The growing menu of separation options favours those who are able to master the workings of the system, either using their cognitive and institutional resources or thanks to the legal advice to which they have recourse.

These inequalities of access lead to the "unequal regulation of the private sphere ... or the increased autonomy of some [among the middle and upper classes] is accompanied by a return to the 'government of populations' for others [members of the lower class]" (Commaille 2006, 96, 102). Depending on their social position, separated people must contend with more or less intrusive procedures (contested divorce versus mutual consent), in which institutional oversight may reach into various aspects of their private lives. This oversight is largely financial among the upper class; among the lower class, it is more likely to extend to child-rearing and education. The form and intensity of the government of private life also depends on gender: women are surveilled as mothers, men as workers. It also depends on the real or supposed national backgrounds of the people involved: racialized individuals are more likely to be labelled as deviant, both as parents and sexually.

The "best interests of the child" has become the central maxim of family morality in the past decades. As it has become easier for couples to sever – and, thus, to retie – the bonds of domestic partnership, heteroparental families have remained the privileged targets of public interventions aimed at maintaining them as the "basic building block" of society. Nearly thirty years ago, French sociologist Irène Théry ([1993] 2001, 432) sounded the alarm about this issue: "[C]hildren's rights are nothing but a Trojan horse for unbelievable state interference in families and private life." However, the question of whether her fears were justified remains open. What is true is that the most intrusive state interventions, such as social worker home visits, are carried out for the sake of children; however, not all subjects targeted by these interventions are currently treated from the perspective of their own "best interests."

The idea that agreement between parents is the best measure taken for the best interests of the child is widespread, and it has encouraged many French professionals to take a hands-off approach to family issues. Often, with laypeople, these professionals refer back to socially constructed expectations rather than attempting to shift the power relationships between ex-partners, to the detriment of women (Collectif Onze 2013, 52–56). Lawyers in Quebec are less likely to simply accept the status quo. They do, however, strongly encourage compromise, which also runs the risk of ignoring the asymmetries of power that characterize so many domestic partnerships. Moreover, in both contexts, redistributive devices between ex-partners (compensatory benefits in France, family patrimony and spouse alimony in Quebec) have grown weaker over the past decades, even though they have remained necessary given the continuing inequalities in both the job market and the family sphere. Unlike in other jurisdictions (notably in Canada), only divorced couples have access to these devices. Since the number of common law partnerships is on the rise, it has resulted in increased financial inequalities between men and women. Moreover, as working outside the home has become the norm for women, legal professionals have come to view these redistributive devices between partners as less legitimate.

Overall, in both contexts, professionals contribute to the continued production of distinctly gendered parenting. Indeed, in most cases, the mother cares for the children on a daily basis, while the father looks after them episodically and (theoretically at least) pays child support. This gendered parenting, constructed over the course of the couple's domestic partnership through the unequal apportioning of labour inside and outside the home, is affirmed, even amplified, post-separation. While this configuration may still be said to be the classic version, it has ceased to be the most legitimate. The norm of co-parenting encourages both parents to be involved in their children's lives after they separate, and even on a daily basis, through shared physical custody. The gap between this norm and actual practices, which remain mired in the norms of the past, can be attributed to the unequal distribution of childcare along gender lines, which begins while couples are still living together.

It must also be perceived as being based in social stratification: shared physical custody occurs most in family situations where the father is (relatively) well off and the mother is employed in the labour market. By contrast, the growing precariousness of the job market and the cost of housing are tending to reinforce the gendered division of parenting roles within the lower class. The distribution of labour in the home during the COVID-19 pandemic has shown just how fragile a hold these norms have even among the more well off: among mothers and fathers both working remotely from their jobs, the burden of home- and house-related tasks fell squarely on women, further accentuating gender inequalities (Pailhé, Reynaud, and Solaz 2020).

If the emancipation of women is defined as their power to break free from constraints linked to their gender – chief among these the constraints of violence and economic disadvantage – or measured by the degree to which it is possible for them to transcend gendered roles (beginning with that of the mother), then it cannot be said that the way family law is put in action is inadequate to foster this emancipation. Arguably, from this perspective, the regulation of separation actually helps to reproduce current social relations. Professionals and institutions take action in situations that are already unequal; depending on their representations of the families they are working with and on their ability to take action in conjunction with the privileges enjoyed by some and the disadvantages faced by others, they in effect help to give these already unequal situations standing under the law. This perpetuation of inequalities between and among families can in large part be attributed to a lack of awareness among the people working with them, which is unfortunate given that these professionals are in a key position to actually fight these mechanisms.

The "Convergent Divergence" of Judicial Policies

The class-based, gender-based, and race-based regulation of separations is a similarity shared between the French and the Quebecois systems, and it appears to be a feature of numerous other Western jurisdictions. In both places, divorce is widespread; in both places, (neo) liberal thinking has shifted the regulation of domestic partnership away from conjugal relations and into the realm of parenting, and it has set limits on the use of long, intrusive procedures. At the same time, our analysis has shown myriad differences between the two contexts. Quebec offers more options to separating couples than France does, making inequalities of access to law and justice more marked there. The social position of judges is higher in Quebec, and their institutional role is quite different, which is particularly evident in the fact that their power to speak out is less explicit than their power to rule (Biland and Steinmetz 2017). There is also greater emphasis in Quebec on the practical dimension of "co-parenting," to the extent that public policy is more focused on combining private transfer and public redistribution. These differences are more or less marked depending on the subject (types of litigation, characteristics of professionals, institutional interactions, childcare, and distribution of public and private obligations), but they are not independent of one another, and, in the two contexts, they lead to at least two partially different regimes of inequality.

The Quebecois configuration gives rise to more marked class inequalities than the French configuration. In Quebec, economic capital plays an even more decisive role in access to the most "unusual" procedures (such as long, contested divorce trials), and it is a decisive resource for capturing the attention of lawyers, who themselves are located at the top of the professional hierarchy. By contrast, the Quebecois approach does more to account for gender inequalities – in particular in the private financial dimension. As a result, middle- and upper-class mothers in Quebec tend to lose less financially during separations than their French counterparts: child support is more common and better paid. To a certain extent, mothers in Quebec are also able to rely more on the day-to-day involvement of fathers since shared physical custody is also more common there. At the same time, women in the lowest class suffer from the neoliberal turn of social policy, as evidenced by the fact that single-parent households are more afflicted by poverty in Quebec than in France.

This book has explored several factors that explain these differences: legal cultures (the functioning of the court system, procedural models, and professionals' patterns), political configurations (the ways in which the state is linked to social movements as well as the degree of interconnectedness between courts and the welfare state), and social norms (the social definition of relations between the sexes and among generations). The possibility of transnational circulation across the two jurisdictions was suggested multiple times by my study subjects in Quebec as soon as they noticed my French accent. This question deserves to be explored briefly here since France and Quebec, as I wrote with my colleague Fabien Desage, sit "across from each other, in comparative terms," a position from which "civil servants, activists, politicians, journalists tend to compare themselves to one another" (Biland and Desage 2017, 9).

"Convergent divergence" might be a good way to characterize the differences and similarities that we observed between the two jurisdictions during this binational study. Research on the regulation of capitalism, from which our study draws, uses this expression, which "describes the process of diffusion as one in which agents simultaneously converge on a fashion and distinguish themselves from others" (Levi-Faur and Jordana 2005, 194). The researchers who coined this term identify a "transnational similarity of public policy" – which stands out to a certain extent in comparisons of France and Quebec – in international transfer processes, which presuppose explicit circulations that mobilize actors and institutions (Bennett 1991, 231). These actors and institutions play a limited role in the government of private life, however. Certainly, the International Convention on the Rights of the Child (ratified by France and Canada in 1989) contributed to the rising influence of the ideology of the best interests of the child (Théry [1993] 2001, 430).[2] Certainly, European institutions (such as the European Commission, the European Court of Human Rights, or the Council of Europe) have produced conventions, handed down rulings, and formulated resolutions that orient French family law. Certainly, private international law exists; indeed, those who practise it are seen as legal virtuosos by top-ranking judges (Bessière et al. 2018). But, in their daily practice, trial judges and family lawyers refer first and largely exclusively to nationally constructed norms.

The similarities between the two contexts may be better explained by the idea of "parallel problem pressures" (Holzinger and Knill 2005, 786). The huge growth in the number of separations is of central concern in both places, and, in both places, this growth has taken place in a context of managerialization of public policy and growing emphasis on individual autonomy and rights. In comparatist language, "cognitive convergence" can be observed in the sense that the increasing incidence of separation and divorce is perceived in very similar terms in the two jurisdictions because of the analogous, but not coordinated, evolution of norms related to public intervention in private life (Bennett 1991). Comparative studies show that this uncoordinated convergence is weaker than coordination that is imposed or that arises from regulatory competition or even transnational communication (Holzinger and Knill 2005, 792–93). Is this the reason that such significant differences exist between France and Quebec?

It should be noted that some transnational circulation in the regulation of separation does take place. In constructing its public policies, Quebec often looks abroad for inspiration. Quebec has a strong orientation toward comparative approaches both because it belongs to the Canadian Confederation and because of the desire of many of its leaders to set Quebec apart from the rest of Canada, and professional orders and activist groups tend to follow in this strong orientation by dint of their privileged access to the state administration. While France was once a source of inspiration to Quebec in terms of family law and social policy, this influence has waned considerably. Today, both activists and administrators are more likely to look to other Canadian provinces or to Anglo-American jurisdictions than they are to continental Europe.

In the course of our fieldwork, we often found ourselves explaining the differences between the two legal systems in which the legal professionals we were interviewing worked. For practical reasons, circulations between France and Quebec by family law professionals are very limited. For judges, they are nearly impossible, given the social and institutional differences between their positions in the two contexts. Historical ties do exist between the two bars, and mutual recognition agreements, put in place in 2008, allow professional qualifications to be recognized across the two jurisdictions, meaning that, technically, lawyers are able to move from one job market to the other. Few take advantage of this possibility, though, due to demographic differences between the two places and the importance of local networks in the legal world.[3]

In France, by contrast, Quebec is frequently mentioned when family law reform is on the agenda, particularly when it comes to child support (Garapon, Perdriolle, and Barnabé 2013; Lenoir 2019) and family mediation (Sassier 2001). Since the 1990s, professionals from Quebec have been travelling to France to promote family mediation and, more recently, collaborative law and parenting workshops. By the same token, high-ranking French civil servants and judges travel to Quebec for training or to collect information about Quebecois approaches. Because of the shared language, Quebec is a highly practical option for France as it seeks international comparisons in the realm of public policy, which is a precious tool for inspiring, identifying, and legitimizing policy. Quebec, in a way, is France's North America in miniature – far easier to explore for someone who is not fluent in English or who is seeking an extra-European point of comparison that is more socially acceptable than the United States. Nevertheless, public policies targeting separated couples in France remain far more state-centred than in Quebec and have involved neither civil society nor France's international partners to any great degree. The "Quebec model" has received a great deal of attention in France, but it took a long time for this attention to translate into any concrete impact on the child support payment system. The institutions, the reformers, and the representations of the problem at hand were simply too different.

Put another way, international references and even examples held up as models do not determine the actual contents of transnational transfers (Dumoulin and Saurugger 2010): the circulation process involves the selection, the alteration, and even the neutralization of approaches employed outside a given national system. Those seeking to import models from abroad have a difficult time letting go of simplified and even rosy visions of "other places." Their desire to legitimate such models as well as their often distant understanding of them – the result of internet research and short stays – make it unlikely that professionals will encounter, let alone gain any deep insight into, critiques or internal dynamics of change (Bérard and Chantraine 2017). It was precisely in order to avoid the pitfall of a comparison oriented toward identifying "the example to follow" that this study was conducted over several years in both places (Spurk 2003, 75), using fieldwork that made it possible to grasp different practices and "to reconstruct foreign ways of thinking and reasoning" (Hassenteufel 2005, 117). I hope that this approach will inspire comparatists to make more use of ethnography in their work and ethnographers to undertake more international comparisons. This kind of empirical approach was the key to moving beyond a study of the design of public policies in order to interrogate how those policies actually affect people in their private lives.

***

It is no coincidence that the "democratization" of divorce followed closely on the "democratization" of secondary schools. France and Quebec both attempted to broaden access to secondary school at around the same time: France stopped requiring entrance examinations before the sixth grade in 1959, and Quebec did away with classical colleges in 1964. The liberalization of family law followed in the same vein as an attempt to put an end to the most glaring inequalities among different social classes. It also took a step toward ending institutional gender inequalities. But just as the unprecedented rise in the number of teenagers enrolled in secondary school did not eradicate educational inequalities, the increase in separations merely reconfigured inequalities related to the law and the justice system. Widespread separation does not mean equal access to legal professionals or to the courts; the right to choose when and how one enters and leaves a domestic partnership is no guarantee of equality within couples. It is even likely that many separations are the result, at least in part, of frustrations related to inequalities between partners (Lambert 2009). Within couples as in society as a whole, inequality fractures social bonds and impedes the democratization of family relationships (Savage 2021). Unexpectedly, in that it recognizes the right to join and part ways at will, separation and divorce law might even offer a kind of response to an aspiration (rarely fulfilled) for equality in intimate partnerships. All too often, in an era of increasingly fragile welfare states, public mechanisms designed to counteract private inequalities come with a price to pay in terms of surveillance and even moral injunctions.

The social sciences can, and should, empower us to transform our lives. This book, by examining the institutional (re)production of private inequalities in the realm of marriage, separation, and families, has shown that, while personal freedoms and equality before the law are necessary conditions for meeting our individual and collective aspirations for human liberation, they are not enough. If we do not strive for substantive equality, and if we do not undertake to truly transform intimate relationships and parental roles, we cannot hope to advance down the path of freedom. The goal of this book is to invite readers to imagine new ways – in both the public and the private spheres – to help the politics of rights keep its emancipatory promises.

Notes

Introduction

1 The studies presented in this book began before marriage equality became law in France. As a result, the scope of our work was limited to the private lives of hetero-sexual, cisgender couples, despite the fact that the slow recognition of non-hetero-, non-cis-normative relationship configurations is a major perspective from which contemporary transformations in family and law can be explored. My current research explores this topic.

2 ECtHR, *L.L. v France*, application no. 7508/02, October 10, 2006.

3 Convention for the Protection of Human Rights and Fundamental Freedoms, 1950, 213 UNTS 222; Conseil constitutionnel, Decision no. 99-416 DC, July 23, 1999.

4 *Nouvelle-Écosse (Procureur général) c Walsh*, [2002] 4 RCS 325; *Miglin c Miglin*, [2003] 1 RCS 303, inf. (2001) 53 OR (3d) 641, conf. (1999) 3 RFL (5th) 106; *Hartshorne c Hartshorne*, [2004] 1 RCS 550, inf. [2002] BCJ no. 2416 (QL) (CACB), conf. [2001] BCJ no. 409 (QL) (CSCB).

5 *Québec (Procureur général) c A*, 2013 CSC 5; *Canadian Charter of Rights and Freedoms*, Part 1 of the *Constitution Act, 1982*, being Schedule B to the *Canada Act 1982* (UK), 1982, c. 11.

6 In addition to me, the members of the Collectif Onze are Céline Bessière, Benoit Coquard, Aurélie Fillod-Chabaud, Sibylle Gollac, Wilfried Lignier, Muriel Mille, Julie Minoc, Samuel Neuberg, Sabrina Nouiri-Mangold, and Hélène Steinmetz.

Notes to pages 13–25 251

7 A social process of categorization through which groups are designated as "other" in a hierarchical relationship based on the naturalization of their presumed cultural and/or physical traits.

8 In defining social classes, this book has relied on research in French sociology (for example, Lamont and Duvoux 2014), which generally distinguishes among three major groups: lower, middle, and upper classes. This definition takes several dimensions into account (economic resources, cultural capital, employment status). It aims to counter a trend, common in North America that consists of over-expansively defining the middle class in a way that distinguishes only the statistical minorities of the very poor and the super rich. This definition of the lower class is much broader and includes not only people living in poverty and precariousness but also low-level workers and employees in steady jobs – for example, low-level public employees such as bus drivers or street sweepers. Symmetrically, our definition of the upper class includes more than just the super rich, extending to business executives, doctors, lawyers, university professors, and so on.

9 Maude Benoit, Joanie Bouchard, Baudoin Cadet, Martin Chabert, Dominic Drouin, Jessika Drouin, Aurélie Fillod-Chabaud, Maxim Fortin, Jessica Garant, Marie Hautval, Maxime Huot-Couture, Paul Levesque, Muriel Mille, Catherine Rainville, Arnaud Sawadogo, Gabrielle Schütz, and Hélène Zimmermann.

10 Including Catherine Achin, Abigail Bourguignon, Marion Flécher, Hélène Oehmichen, Camille Phé, Lus Prauthois, Nicolas Rafin, Gabrielle Schütz, and Alan Tymen.

11 In Quebec, legal competence in matters of family law is shared between the provincial and the federal levels of government. Marriage and divorce laws are federal, but laws related to unmarried couples are set by the National Assembly of Quebec, as are those pertaining to the obligations between parents and children and to civil procedures.

12 "OECD Family Database," *Organisation for Economic Co-operation and Development*, http://www.oecd.org/els/family/database.htm.

13 "Live Births, by Marital Status of Mother," *Statistics Canada*, https://www150.statcan. gc.ca/t1/tbl1/en/tv.action?pid=1310041901&request_locale=en.

14 Data sets from the French Justice Ministerial Statistical Department, http://www. justice.gouv.fr/statistiques.html.

15 All research conducted in Quebec was approved by the Université Laval Ethics Committee (Approval Codes nos. 2010-238 A-2 R-3 / 12-02-2015; 2012-129 R-1 / 18-09-2014; 2020-183 R-1 / 10-09-2021). Research in France did not require this step.

Chapter 1: Why the Liberalization of Divorce Leads to Unequal Access to Justice

1 Law no. 2016-1547, November 18, 2016.

2 "Divorces," *Institut National d'Études Démographiques*, 2022, https://www.ined.fr/fr/ tout-savoir-population/chiffres/france/mariages-divorces-pacs/divorces/.

252 Notes to pages 25–31

3 *Divorce Act,* RSC 1985, c. 3; Law no. 2004-439, May 26, 2004.

4 Data set Q-SC-1981-2011.

5 Data set Q-SC-1981-2011; "Table 2: Divorces and Crude Divorce Rates, Canada, Provinces and Territories, 1981 to 2008," *Statistics Canada,* 2015, https://www150.statcan.gc.ca/n1/pub/91-209-x/2013001/article/11788/tbl/tbl2-eng.htm.

6 Divorce by mutual consent (*French Civil Code,* arts. 230–32) and three forms of contested divorce: uncontested divorce (arts. 233–34), fault divorce (art. 242), and default divorce (arts. 237–38). In 2010, a little over half of divorces were by mutual consent. One-quarter of cases were uncontested, with the remaining cases divided about evenly between the two other procedures (Belmokhtar 2012).

7 Separation of unmarried couples and hearings to modify the agreements of already divorced or separated couples.

8 In the three forms of contested divorce, divorces are pronounced as the outcomes of written proceedings. Lawyers file their cases with the family court judge and may testify briefly; the parties are not present. Some judges may order a second hearing for parents who are under investigation by social services, but such procedures are rare.

9 Living separate and apart for at least one year, adultery, or "physical or mental cruelty of such a kind as to render intolerable the continued cohabitation of the spouses." *Divorce Act,* RSC 1985, c. 3 (2nd Supp.).

10 Starting on January 1, 2021, conciliation hearings were replaced by a hearing for provisional measures. Law no. 2019-222, March 23, 2019; Decree no. 2019-1380, December 17, 2019.

11 Hearing observed by the author and Rémi Audot, Valin, March 2010. With the exception of the public figures described in Chapter 5, all names in this book have been changed in order to protect the privacy of the respondents.

12 Observation by the author and Baudoin Cadet, Quebec City, April 2011.

13 *Code of Civil Procedure,* CQLR, c. C-25.01.

14 *An Act to Institute, under the Code of Civil Procedure, Pre-Hearing Mediation in Family Law Cases and to Amend Other Provisions of the Code,* SQ 1997, c. 4.

15 Data set Q-CSO-2008.

16 Regulation Respecting the Application of the *Act to Promote Access to Justice through the Establishment of the Service administratif de rajustement des pensions alimentaires pour enfants,* c. A-2.02, rule 1.

17 *An Act to Promote Access to Justice in Family Matters,* SQ 2012, c. 20, arts. 29–41.

18 M.C. Saint-Jacques et al., "Enquête longitudinale auprès des parents séparés et recomposés du Québec" [Longitudinal Study of Separated and Blended Families in Quebec], *Scholars Portal Dataverse,* 2020, https://doi.org/10.5683/SP2/SJWLPK.

19 To become a state-certified mediator, applicants must belong to an approved professional association and follow a basic training course. *Code of Civil Procedure,* rule 0.7.

20 Interview with a lawyer working for the Associate Chief Justice of Quebec by Gabrielle Schütz and Sabrina Nouiri-Mangold, Quebec City, October 2011.

21 Interview with the author, Joanie Bouchard, Maxim Fortin, and Marie Hautval, Quebec City, February 2014. The following quotations attributed to the same person are all drawn from the same interview.

22 Telephone interview with a social worker who was a pioneer in the use of mediation by the author, May 2017.

23 *Divorce Act.*

24 *Code of Civil Procedure.*

25 Telephone interview with a pioneer in the use of mediation by the author, May 2017.

26 *Canadian Charter of Rights and Freedoms,* Part 1 of the *Constitution Act, 1982,* being Schedule B to the *Canada Act 1982* (UK), 1982, c. 11, art. 11.

27 In criminal matters, this means that prosecutors are lawyers employed by the minister of justice, not magistrates.

28 *R. v Jordan,* 2016 SCC 27; *R. v Cody,* 2017 CSC 31.

29 We should also bear in mind that the civil union, a legal relationship similar to marriage enacted by Quebec in 2002, can be dissolved by a joint declaration before a notary. *Civil Code of Quebec,* SQ 1991, c. 64, arts. 521.13, 521.17.

30 Data set F-TC-2013.

31 Data set Q-SC-1981-2011.

32 See, for example, ECtHR, *Pretto v. Italie,* application no. 7984/77, December 8, 1983; ECtHR, *Pélissier and Sassi v. France,* application no. 25444/94, March 25, 1999.

33 Conversation with Jérémy Mandin and Hélène Steinmetz, Carly, December 2008.

34 Participant observation with Céline Bessière, Muriel Mille, Julie Minoc, and Hélène Steinmetz, Carly, January 2012.

35 *Rapport d'activité des députés du Front de gauche,* 15th Legislature, 2016, http://oise.pcf.fr/sites/default/files/rapport_dactivite_14eme_legislature.pdf.

36 On May 9, 2016, twenty feminist groups published a press release titled "Divorce 'by Mutual Consent' without a Judge Is a Serious Threat to Women's Rights," http://www.collectifdroitsdesfemmes.org/spip.php?article457.

37 Decree no. 2018-655, July 24, 2018, regarding the allocation of family benefits and the delivery of official agreements, as provided for by the *Social Security Code,* art. L582–2.

38 Data set Q-PHD-2013.

39 In 2018, 270 of the 400 lawyers working in legal aid offices were women (68 percent), and 44 percent were under the age of thirty-five (Commission des services juridiques 2018, 92).

40 Data set Q-PHD-2013.

41 Video conference interview with the author, October 2021.

42 Data set Q-CSO-2008.

43 Data set Q-CSO-2008.

44 Data set Q-PHD-2013.

45 Observation by Muriel Mille, Montreal, September 2013.

46 Interview with Hélène Zimmermann, Albanel, April 2013.

47 Interview by the author and Gabrielle Schütz, Montreal, April 2012.

48 Interview by Aurélie Fillod-Chabaud and Catherine Rainville, Quebec City, June 2011.

49 The mission of these centres was defined in the *Youth Protection Act*, CQLR, c. P-34.1: "[t]o protect children whose security or development is or may be considered to be in danger."

50 In total, 7 percent of men, but only 1 percent of women, make one hundred thousand dollars or more per year [Q-CSO-2008].

51 *Civil Code of Quebec*, art. 588.

52 Video conference interview with the author and Hélène Zimmermann, France and Quebec, January 2021.

53 Observation by Muriel Mille, Montreal, September 2013.

54 These settlement conferences are an alternative to arbitration and have been advocated for by certain judges for the past decade or so (see Chapter 2).

55 Data set Q-CSO-2008.

56 Observation by the author and Catherine Rainville, Albanel, 2011.

57 Data set F-TC-2013.

58 In 2005, people with at least two years of post-secondary education were more likely to be living in common law partnerships. Age, however, remains the greatest determining factor, and it is likely that employees and workers are, on average, younger than professionals (Prioux 2009).

59 In France, having a dependent child is recognized as a favourable argument for immigration status.

60 Data set F-TC-2013.

61 Interview with Céline Bessière and Aurélie Fillod-Chabaud, Marjac, February 2009.

62 Data set F-TC-2013.

63 Data set F-TC-2013.

64 Data set F-TC-2013.

65 Interview and observation by the author and Pierre de Larminat, Marjac, February 2009.

66 Data set F-TC-2013.

67 *French Civil Code*, art. 373-2-12.

68 *French Civil Code*, art. 2062 on agreements for collaborative procedures.

69 Interview with Céline Bessière and Camille Phé, Besson, February 2014.

70 Statistics Canada, "A Fifty-Year Look at Divorces in Canada, 1970 to 2020," 2022, https://www150.statcan.gc.ca/n1/daily-quotidien/220309/dq220309a-eng.htm; Ministère français de la Justice, "Références Statistiques Justice," 2021, http://www.justice.gouv.fr/art_pix/PARTIE-1_Annuaire_ministere-justice_2020_16x24.pdf.

Notes to pages 61–82 255

71 Video conference interview with the author and Hélène Zimmermann, France and Quebec, November 2020.

72 For example, *Droit de la famille – 20474*, 2020 QCCS 1051 (March 27, 2020).

Chapter 2: How Gender and National Context Shape the Legal Profession

1 Of the 169 judges whose birthplaces were known, 93 percent had been born in Quebec and only 3 percent abroad (in the United States or in Europe). Of the 192 judges whose undergraduate degrees were known, 84 percent had studied in Quebec, and 15 percent at the University of Ottawa (whose Faculty of Law has a civil law section). Only one judge had studied elsewhere in Canada.

2 Interview with the author, Aurélie Fillod-Chabaud, and Catherine Rainville, Quebec City, May 2011.

3 "Women in the Judiciary Working towards a Legal System Reflective of Society," *Organisation for the Economic Co-operation and Development*, 2017, https://www.oecd.org/gender/data/women-in-the-judiciary-working-towards-a-legal-system-reflective-of-society.htm.

4 Interview with Wilfried Lignier and Benoit Coquard, Valin, March 2010.

5 Data set F-TC-2013.

6 Observation by and interview with the author and Pierre de Larminat, Marjac, February 2009.

7 Code de l'organisation judiciaire, art. R123-13, https://www.legifrance.gouv.fr/codes/texte_lc/LEGITEXT000006071164/2020-01-01/.

8 Observation by Hélène Steinmetz and Alina Surubaru, Valin, March 2010.

9 Interview with the author, Aurélie Fillod-Chabaud, and Catherine Rainville, Quebec City, May 2011.

10 Interview with the author and Catherine Rainville, Quebec City, July 2011.

11 Pierre Bourdieu defined *illusio* as a "tacit recognition of the value of the stakes of the game and ... practical mastery of its rules" (Bourdieu and Wacquant 1992, 107).

12 Interview with the author and Catherine Rainville, Quebec City, July 2011.

13 Interview with the author and Catherine Rainville, Quebec City, July 2011.

14 Informal discussion with and observation by the author in a regional court, October 2021.

15 Interview with the author and Gabrielle Schütz, Montreal, January 2012.

16 Interview with Aurélie Fillod-Chabaud and Catherine Rainville, Quebec City, May 2011.

17 Observation by and interview with the author and Catherine Rainville, Albanel, June 2011.

18 Interview with Jérémy Mandin, Carly, February 2009.

19 Observation by Sibylle Gollac and Raphaële Salem, Marjac, February 2009.

20 Interview with the author and Pierre de Larminat, Marjac, February 2009.

21 *Ruffo v. Conseil de la magistrature*, [1995] 4 SCR 267.

22 "Ethical Principles for Judges," *Canadian Judicial Council*, https://cjc-ccm.ca/cmslib/general/news_pub_judicialconduct_Principles_en.pdf.

23 Ad Hoc Committee on the Appointment of Supreme Court of Canada Justices, October 4, 2012, https://www.justice.gc.ca/eng/news-nouv/ja-nj/2012/doc_32800.html.

24 Interview with Aurélie Fillod-Chabaud and Catherine Rainville, Quebec City, May 2011.

25 Interview with the author and Catherine Rainville, Montreal, 2012.

26 Discussion with Aurélie Fillod-Chabaud and Gabrielle Schütz, Montreal, November 2011.

27 Video conference interview with the author, France and Quebec, April 2021.

28 Translator's note: *maître* is an honorific term for a lawyer, equivalent to "esquire" in English. While the honorific would not be used in this context in English, it is worth noting that it is systematically used in the French-speaking context.

29 Interview with the author, Besson, February 2016.

30 Interview with the author and Muriel Mille, Albanel, March 2013.

31 Interview with Igor Rolemberg and Nicolas Rafin, Besson, February 2014.

32 Partners are considered to be the heads of law firms. They are both the firms' co-owners and their directors.

33 Interview with Céline Bessière, Aurore Koechlin, and Camille Phé, Paris, November 2014.

34 *Pro bono* legal practice offers legal defence and other legal services to persons or organizations whose cause is valued either politically or legally (Cummings 2004).

35 Interview with the author, Marie Hautval, and Muriel Mille, Montreal, October 2014.

36 In France, associate lawyers (*collaborateurs*) are self-employed professionals, but the firm they work for pays them a set monthly fee. Most of an associate lawyer's clients come from partners in the firm. This is a junior position in the French legal profession.

37 Observation by the author, Besson, February 2016.

38 Discussion with the author and Hélène Oehmichen, Besson, February 2016.

39 Interview with Muriel Mille, Besson, April 2014.

40 Interview with Céline Bessière, Montreal, February 2015.

41 Interview with the author and Muriel Mille, Albanel, March 2013.

42 Interview with the author, Joanie Bouchard, and Maxim Fortin, Quebec City, April 2014. Since 2017, notaries in Quebec have been allowed to represent clients for non-contentious proceedings.

43 Observation by Muriel Mille, Albanel, November 2013.

44 Observation by the author and Aurélie Fillod-Chabaud, Quebec City, March 2011.

45 Interview with Catherine Rainville and Hélène Zimmermann, Albanel, April 2013.

46 Interview with Muriel Mille, Montreal, May 2013.

Notes to pages 110–47   257

Chapter 3: The Legal Encounter as a Situated Nexus of Power

1 Observation by the author and Elodie Hennequin, Belles, December 2009.

2 Observation by Hélène Zimmermann, Albanel, July 2013.

3 Observation by the author and Baudoin Cadet, Quebec City, April 2011.

4 Observation by the author and Baudoin Cadet, Quebec City, April 2011.

5 Interview with Aurélie Fillod-Chabaud and Catherine Rainville, Quebec City, May 2011.

6 Observation by the author and Hélène Oehmichen, Besson, February 2016.

7 Observation by the author, Quebec City, October 2013.

8 Observation by the author, Quebec City, September 2013.

9 Interview with Muriel Mille and Hélène Zimmermann, Albanel, April 2013.

10 Observation of a hearing by Catherine Rainville and Gabrielle Schütz, Quebec City, September 2011.

11 Interview with the author and Hélène Zimmermann, Quebec City, November 2012.

12 Conversation with Céline Bessière, Paris, January 2015.

13 Observation by Benjamin Faure and Julie Minoc, Valin, March 2010.

14 This Charter was never adopted. However, civil servants in positions of authority, as well as public school teachers, are prohibited from wearing symbols of their religion by a law adopted in 2019, which remains in force. Bill 21, *An Act Respecting the Laicity of the State*, SQ 2019, c. 12.

15 Observation by the author, Besson, January 2016.

16 Data set F-TC-2013.

17 Interview with the author and Pierre de Larminat, Marjac, February 2009.

18 Observation by Céline Bessière and Sabrina Nouiri-Mangold, Carly, December 2009.

19 Observation by Muriel Mille, Montreal, October 2013.

20 Interview with the author, Quebec City, May 2017.

21 Observation by Muriel Mille, Montreal, October 2013.

22 Observation by Céline Bessière and Camille Phé, Besson, February 2014.

23 Interview with Muriel Mille, Montreal, July 2013.

24 Observation by the author, Besson, February 2016.

25 Observation by Muriel Mille, Montreal, October 2013.

26 Observations by Hélène Zimmermann, Albanel, July and October 2013.

27 Conversation with the author and Catherine Rainville, Montreal, December 2011.

28 Case accessed by the author and Céline Bessière, Valin, March 2010.

29 Conversation with the author and Rémi Audot, Besson, March 2010.

30 Interview with the author and Hélène Steinmetz, Paris, June 2016.

31 Interview with the author and Jérémy Mandin, Belles, March 2009.

32 Law no. 2000-596, June 30, 2000.

33 Participant observation by the author, Paris, October 2016.

34 Under a partnership of acquests, which is a regime of both marriage and civil unions, each spouse retains his or her own private property, while acquests (anything

258 *Notes to pages 148–60*

acquired in the course of the union) are shared equally between the spouses. The division of the family patrimony implies an equal division of principal and secondary residences, furniture, and retirement plans. Spousal support has a social basis (avoiding one parent's dependence on public welfare), a contractual basis (good faith of both parties), and a compensatory basis (when one parent left the labour market for the sake of the family, resulting in negative economic consequences). The compensatory allowance may be awarded when one spouse contributed money, goods, or services that allowed the other spouse to become wealthier, to her or his detriment. The compensatory allowance therefore has a meaning and a scope different from the French compensatory benefit.

35 Case accessed by Muriel Mille, Montreal area, August 2015.

Chapter 4: How Family Justice Frames Unequal Parenthoods

1 See, for example, *Civil Code of Quebec,* SQ 1991, c. 64, arts. 597–612.
2 Data set Q-CSO-2008.
3 Data set Q-CSO-2008; Data set F-TC-2013.
4 Data set F-TC-2013.
5 Interview with Catherine Rainville and Gabrielle Schütz, Quebec City, November 2011.
6 Observation by the author and Arnaud Cogez, Belles, December 2009.
7 Interview with Aurélie Fillod-Chabaud and Catherine Rainville, Quebec City, June 2011.
8 *Gordon v Goertz,* [1996] 2 SCR 27.
9 *Divorce Act,* RSC 1985, c. 3; Bill C-78, *An Act to amend the Divorce Act, the Family Orders and Agreements Enforcement Assistance Act and the Garnishment, Attachment and Pension Diversion Act and to make consequential amendments to another Act,* SC 2019, c. 16, s. 16.8.
10 Draft Law on Parental Authority and the Best Interests of the Child, June 27, 2014.
11 Interview with the author, Paris, November 2015.
12 Interview with the author and Hélène Steinmetz, Paris, June 2016.
13 Bill 92, *An Act to Create a Court Specialized in Sexual Violence and Domestic Violence,* November 2021; Bill 2, *An Act Respecting Family Law Reform with Regard to Filiation and Amending the Civil Code in Relation to Personality Rights and Civil Status,* June 2022.
14 Video conference interview with the author and Hélène Zimmermann, France and Quebec, November 2020.
15 Law no. 2010-769, July 9, 2010.
16 Observation by the author, Paris, November 2015.
17 Observation by the author, Besson, February 2016.
18 Interview with Catherine Rainville and Hélène Zimmermann, Albanel, April 2013.
19 Interview with the author and Catherine Rainville, Quebec City, 2011.
20 Observation by Céline Bessière and Shahideh Noorolahian, Marjac, February 2009.

21 Observation by the author and Catherine Rainville, Quebec City, May 2011.

22 The Revenu de Solidarité Active is a French social benefit that provides a monthly minimum payment to recipients who meet certain conditions, notably of unemployment or under-employment. The monthly payment, which is allocated on a sliding scale depending on the recipient's revenue, is well below minimum wage.

23 Observation by Marion Azuelos and Hélène Steinmetz, Belles, March 2009; observation by Céline Bessière and Jérémy Mandin, Belles, April 2009.

24 Observation by and interview with Aurélie Fillod-Chabaud and Catherine Rainville, Quebec City, May and June 2011.

25 Data set Q-CSO-2008.

26 Hearing observed and case file accessed by Catherine Rainville and Gabrielle Schütz, Montreal, January 2012.

27 Observation by Muriel Mille, Montreal, 2013.

28 Data set Q-CSO-2008.

29 Law no. 2002-305, March 4, 2002.

30 Bill C-78, *An Act to amend the Divorce Act, the Family Orders and Agreements Enforcement Assistance Act and the Garnishment, Attachment and Pension Diversion Act and to make consequential amendments to another Act.*

31 *Young v Young,* [1993] 4 SCR, 3.

32 Beginning with *L. (T.) c A.P. (L.),* [2002] RJQ 2627.

33 In defining a child's best interests, art. 33 of the *Civil Code of Quebec* states that "consideration is given, in addition to the moral, intellectual, emotional and physical needs of the child, to the child's age, health, personality and family environment, and to the other aspects of his situation."

34 Interview with the author and Catherine Rainville, Montreal, January 2012.

35 Convention on the Rights of the Child, 1989, 1577 UNTS 3.

36 In 2005, Camil Bouchard, a deputy of the Parti Québécois, made himself a spokesperson for fathers' groups in the National Assembly, relaying their conclusions that there was "systematic discrimination against men in the courts with regard to child custody" (Assemblée nationale du Québec 2005). Whether he had any direct links to them and when these links might have been developed remain to be examined.

37 A Quebec Court of Appeal decision recognized it in 1994. *R.M. c B.R.,* [1994] AQ no. 947. In France, it was recognized two decades later. Court of Cassation, First Civil Chamber June 26, 2013, no. 12/14392.

38 Interview with Catherine Rainville and Hélène Zimmermann, Albanel, April 2013.

39 Observation by Hélène Zimmermann, Albanel, October 2013.

40 Data set Q-CSO-2008.

41 Interview with Jessika Drouin and Gabrielle Schütz, Quebec City, April 2012.

42 Observation by the author and Pierre de Larminat, Valin, March 2010.

43 Observation by Céline Bessière and Sibylle Gollac, near Besson, February 2016.

44 Interview with Jérémy Mandin and Hélène Steinmetz, Belles, December 2008.

45 Observation by the author and Elodie Hennequin, Belles, December 2009.

46 In 2009, conservative deputies in the French National Assembly and in the Canadian House of Commons submitted draft legislation in support of this idea (Draft Law no. 1531 in France and Bill C-422, *An Act to amend the Divorce Act, (equal parenting) and to make consequential amendments to other Acts*, in Canada). Neither passed. A 2016 petition submitted to the website of the National Assembly of Quebec demanding that shared custody be the default option for children if their parents separate was also tabled, despite support from the Action des nouvelles conjointes et des nouveaux conjoints du Québec (Quebec New Spouses Action Committee) and the Association des grands-parents du Québec (Quebec Grandparents' Association).

47 Interview with Marie Hautval and Hélène Zimmermann, Quebec City, September 2015.

48 Interview with Sibylle Gollac and Raphaëlle Salem, Marjac, February 2009.

49 Interview with the author, Aurélie Fillod-Chabaud, and Catherine Rainville, Quebec City, May 2011.

50 *Civil Code of Quebec,* art. 585; *French Civil Code,* art. 203.

51 *Civil Code of Quebec,* art. 587-1.

52 *French Civil Code,* art. 371-2.

53 This expression describes a social model in which the man works outside the home and brings in all or most of the household's revenue. Many welfare states, including France, were built on this model and made social protections dependent on employment. This model has declined as women have entered the job market in ever-greater numbers, but it has not disappeared, as can be seen in the persistence of gender disparities in pay (Lewis 2001).

54 Tableaux de l'économie française, 2020, https://www.insee.fr/fr/statistiques/42776 30?sommaire=4318291.

55 Census in Brief, "Portrait of Children's Family Life in Canada in 2016," https://www12.statcan.gc.ca/census-recensement/2016/as-sa/98-200-x/2016006/98-200 -x2016006-eng.cfm.

56 Case file accessed by Sibylle Gollac, Marjac, Februray 2009.

57 Observation by the author and Catherine Rainville, Albanel, June 2011.

58 Observation by Hélène Zimmermann, near Quebec City, May 2013.

59 Interview with Hélène Zimmermann, Albanel, April 2013.

60 Data set Q-CSO-2008.

61 Observation by the author and Rémi Audot, Valin, March 2010.

62 Observation by the author, Quebec City, September 2013.

63 "Annex 1: Table de fixation de la contribution alimentaire parentale de base," January 1, 2022, https://www.justice.gouv.qc.ca/fileadmin/user_upload/contenu/documents/En__Anglais_/centredoc/publications/couple-famille/TA_tablefix_parent _2022_EN_MJQ.pdf.

64 "Barème des pensions alimentaires", June 1, 2020, https://www.justice.fr/simulateurs/pensions/bareme.

65 Observation of a conciliation hearing by Aurélie Fillod-Chabaud and Sibylle Gollac, Belles, April 2009.

66 Observation by the author, Besson, February 2016.

67 Data set Q-CSO-2008.

68 Observation by Marion Azuelos and Hélène Steinmetz, Belles, March 2009.

69 Observation by the author and Gabrielle Schütz, Albanel, October 2011.

70 Exemption requires the debtor of support to pay a "deposit" of one month's child support to the tax authorities (or to provide a guarantee from her or his bank).

71 This calculation, which uses data collected from the Haut Conseil de la Famille (2014, 134), considers the child support provided for in the case of sole custody, with the usual visitation rights, and considers median parental income to be equal to fifty-six thousand dollars pear year (twenty-three thousand dollars for women and thirty-three thousand dollars for men) (Conseil du Statut de la Femme 2016, 70).

72 Data set Q-CSO-2008.

73 At an exchange rate of $1.45 to €1.

74 Data set Q-CSO-2008.

75 Data set F-TC-2013.

76 Case file accessed by the author, Besson, July 2016.

77 Data set Q-CSO-2008.

78 Data set Q-CSO-2008.

79 After a first ruling handed down by the Supreme Court of Canada in 2013 (*Québec (Procureur général) c A*, 2013 CSC 5), a new case was brought to the Superior Court of Quebec in the spring of 2021. See the press conference held by the law firm representing the ex–de facto partner in March 2021. "Goldwater, Dubé Challenges the Government of Quebec to Protect Unmarried Couples and Their Children," https://goldwaterdube.com/en/blog/2021/goldwater-dube-challenges-the-government-of-quebec-to-protect-unmarried-couples-and-their-children.

Chapter 5: Family Law and the Welfare State

1 "Child Support. Support Payments," https://www.justice.gouv.qc.ca/en/couples-and-families/separation-and-divorce/children-a-joint-responsibility/child-support/.

2 Their employment rate climbed from 30 percent in 1976 to 61 percent in 1990, but the gap continued to grow between mothers living in couples, who were more often professionally active, and single mothers (Rose 2014).

3 "Fédération des Associations de Familles Monoparentales et Recomposées du Québec," http://www.fafmrq.org/wp-content/uploads/2014/11/8-Atelier6_LD_Colloque2014.pdf.

4 The Parti Québécois, a nationalist, sovereigntist political party founded in 1968, has held seats in Quebec's government since 1970 and first won government in

the province in 1976. Founded as a social-democratic party, it has become less interventionist and more budget conscious since the latter half of the 1990s. There are currently two other parties in Quebec's government, the Liberal Party, a centre-right federalist party founded in 1867, and the Coalition Avenir Québec (CAQ), founded in 2011, which leans right on economic issues and holds a nationalist, autonomist stance in the debate over Quebec's independence. The CAQ has held the majority since 2018.

5 Interview with the author and Marie Hautval, Quebec City, July 2014. The following quotations attributed to the same person are all drawn from the same interview.

6 Interview with Joanie Bouchard, Saguenay region, July 2014.

7 Interview with Joanie Bouchard and Maxim Fortin, Montreal, May 2014.

8 Convention on the Rights of the Child, 1989, 1577 UNTS 3.

9 *Law to Favour the Enforcement of Child Support Orders,* LQ 1980, c. 21.

10 Interview with Jessika Drouin and Gabrielle Schütz, Quebec City, April 2012.

11 Food, housing, communications, household cleaning, personal hygiene, clothing, furnishings, transportation, and leisure activities. "Child Support. Support Payments," https://www.justice.gouv.qc.ca/en/couples-and-families/separation-and-divorce/children-a-joint-responsibility/child-support/.

12 Interview with the author and Marie Hautval, Quebec City, July 2014.

13 Bill 65, An Act to Institute, under the *Code of Civil Procedure,* Pre-Hearing Mediation in Family Law Cases and to Amend Other Provisions of the Code, 1997.

14 Order Designating the Province of Quebec for the Purposes of the Definition of "Applicable Guidelines" in Subsection 2(1) of the *Divorce Act,* SOR/97-237, 1997.

15 Between 2010 and 2013, a class action suit brought by the ex-spouses of wealthy men challenged the constitutionality of the Quebec calculation model, on the grounds that the sums it calculated were lower than those set by the federal guidelines. The Court of Appeals ruled that the Quebec model was nonetheless not discriminatory. *Droit de la famille – 139,* 2013 QCCA 15.

16 *An Act to Amend the Civil Code of Quebec and the Code of Civil Procedure as Regards the Determination of Child Support Payments,* SQ 1996, c. 68.

17 Interview with Joanie Bouchard and Maxim Fortin, Montreal, June 2014.

18 *Thibaudeau v Canada,* [1995] 2 SCR 627.

19 Interview with the author and Marie Hautval, Quebec City, July 2014.

20 Bill 70, *An Act to Allow a Better Match between Training and Jobs and to Facilitate Labour Market Entry,* 2016.

21 "Revenu Québec en un coup d'œil," https://www.revenuquebec.ca/fr/salle-de-presse/statistiques/revenu-quebec-en-un-coup-doeil/.

22 Video conference interview with the author and Hélène Zimmermann, France and Quebec, November 2020.

23 *An Act to Amend the Civil Code and the Code of Civil Procedure as Regards the Determination of Child Support Payments,* SQ 2004, c. 5.

24 Law no. 75-618, July 11, 1975.

25 Law no. 73-5, January 2, 1973.

26 *Corrective Finance Law*, Law no. 80-1039, December 23, 1980, art. 15.

27 Law no. 84-1171, December 22, 1984.

28 This despite the fact that unemployment was lower in France than in Quebec at the time (8.5 percent compared with 12 percent). "Principaux indices et séries chronologiques", *Insee*, 2022, https://www.insee.fr/fr/statistiques/3532158?sommaire=3530678.

29 "Les effectifs d'allocataires des minima sociaux", 2020, https://drees.solidarites-sante.gouv.fr/sites/default/files/2021-01/Fiche%2006%20-%20Les%20effectifs%20d%E2%80%99allocataires%20de%20minima%20sociaux.pdf.

30 Law no. 70-1218, December 23, 1970.

31 Decree no. 75-244, April 14, 1975, for the application of Law no. 75-6, January 3, 1975.

32 Decree no. 82-534, June 23, 1982, for the application of Law no. 70-1218, December 23, 1970.

33 Interview with the author, Paris, April 2016.

34 Interview with the author, Paris, November 2015.

35 *French Penal Code*, March 1, 1994.

36 Participant observation by Céline Bessière and Muriel Mille, Toulouse, October 2014.

37 Interview with the author and Aurélie Fillod-Chabaud, Toulouse, June 2015.

38 Interview with the author, Paris, April 2016.

39 Interview with Jérémy Mandin, Carly, February 2009.

40 Court of Cassation, First Civil Chamber, October 23, 2013, no. 12/25301.

41 In December 2016, it became the Haut Conseil de la famille de l'enfance et de l'âge (High Council on Family, Childhood, and Aging).

42 Interview with the author, Paris, May 2016.

43 Data set F-TC-2013.

44 In 2020, 96,000 children received this benefit, according to figures given to the author by the director of the child support collection agency for the Caisse nationale des allocations familiales (National Family Benefits Office) in September 2021.

45 Speech to the National Assembly, January 20, 2014, http://www.assemblee-nationale.fr/14/cri/2013-2014/20140135.asp.

46 "Najat Vallaud-Belkacem annonce une réforme des pensions alimentaires," June 30, 2013, http://www.la-croix.com/Actualite/France/Najat-Vallaud-Belkacem-annonce-une-reforme-des-pensions-alimentaires-2013-06-20-976234.

47 Video conference interview with the author, France, November 2020.

48 Interview with the author, Paris, September 2020.

49 Interview with the author, Paris, September 2020.

50 Video conference interview with the author, France, November 2020.

51 Video conference interview with the author, France, March 2016.

52 Interview with the author, Paris, February 2016.

53 Interview with the author, Paris, April 2016.
54 "Ce qui a changé dans votre département, famille – santé – handicap, 2022" ("What's Changed in Your *département*: Family – Health – Disability), https://www.gouvernement.fr/les-actions-du-gouvernement/resultats.
55 Webinar organized by the French National Bar Association, March 18, 2022, https://youtube/BqyCeqyaArw.
56 Law no. 2021-1754, December 23, 2021, art. 100. Decree no. 2022-259 of February 25, 2022, regarding the systematic application of financial intermediation for the payment of child support.

Conclusion
1 *Civil Code of Quebec,* SQ 1991, c. 64.
2 Convention on the Rights of the Child, 1989, 1577 UNTS 3.
3 In the first four years, only eighty such mutual recognition agreements were signed. "Qu'est-ce que les ARM ont changé pour les avocats au Québec?," 2016, https://montreal.consulfrance.org/Qu-est-ce-que-les-ARM-ont-change.

References

Abbas, Hicham, and Bertrand Garbinti. 2019. "De la rupture conjugale à une éventuelle remise en couple: L'évolution des niveaux de vie des familles monoparentales entre 2010 et 2015." In *France portrait social,* edited by Insee, 99–113. Paris: Insee Références.

Abel, Richard L., and Philip S.C. Lewis. 1989. *Lawyers in Society: Comparative Theories.* Los Angeles: University of California Press.

Action Committee on Access to Justice in Civil and Family Matters. 2013. *Access to Civil and Family Justice: A Roadmap for Change.* Ottawa: Justice Canada. https://www.cfcj-fcjc.org/sites/default/files/docs/2013/AC_Report_English_Final.pdf.

Algava, Élisabeth, Sandrine Penant, and Leslie Yankan. 2019. "En 2016, 400 000 enfants alternent entre les deux domiciles de leurs parents séparés." *Insee Première* 1728.

Arens, Chantal. 2020. "Pour une transformation profonde de la justice." *Le point,* May 7.

Assemblée nationale du Québec. 2005. *Consultation générale sur le document intitulé: Vers un nouveau contrat social pour l'égalité entre les femmes et les hommes.* http://www.assnat.qc.ca/en/travaux-parlementaires/commissions/cas/mandats/Mandat-2937/index.html.

Auvigne, François, François Dumuis, Laurence Pecaut-Rivolier, Jérôme Guedj, Catherine Sueur, Marie-Bénédicte Maizy, Irène Domenjoz, and Isabelle Bignalet. 2016. *Création d'une agence de recouvrement des pensions alimentaires: Rapport de l'Inspection des finances, de l'Inspection générale des affaires sociales et de l'Inspection générale des services judiciaires.* Paris: IGS, IGAS, IGSJ.

Auyero, Javier. 2012. *Patients of the State: The Politics of Waiting in Argentina*. Durham, NC: Duke University Press.

Baillon, Denis, Nelly Costecalde, Georges Godin, and Brigitte Munoz-Perez. 1981. *Le divorce en France*. Vol. 2. Paris: Insee.

Baril, Hélène. 2013. "Sondage: des riches? Où ça?" *La Presse,* December 6.

Barnes, Marian, and David Prior, eds. 2009. *Subversive Citizens: Power, Agency and Resistance Public Services*. Bristol, UK: Policy Press.

Barreau du Québec. 1996. *Mémoire sur le modèle québécois de fixation des pensions alimentaires pour enfants,* présenté à la Commission des affaires sociales de l'Assemblée nationale du Québec, Quebec. http://numerique.banq.qc.ca/patrimoine/details/52327/60753.

–. 2015. *Barreau-mètre 2015: La profession en chiffres*. https://www.barreau.qc.ca/media/1240/barreau-metre-2015-maj.pdf.

–. 2022. *Rapport annuel 2021–2022*. https://www.barreau.qc.ca/media/3089/barreau-metre-2022.pdf.

Barreau du Québec/Centre interuniversitaire de recherché en analyse des organisations. 2009. "Enquête socio-économique auprès des membres du barreau du Québec 2008." *Journal du Barreau du Québec* 41: 29–32.

Bas, Philippe, and Bruno Retailleau. 2016. "Le divorce par consentement mutuel sans juge: Une fausse bonne idée?" *Le Monde,* June 14.

Bastard, Benoit, David Delvaux, Christian Mouhanna, and Frédéric Schoenaers. 2014. "Maîtriser le temps? L'accélération du traitement judiciaire du divorce en France et en Belgique." *Temporalités* 19. https://journals.openedition.org/temporalites/2795.

Bastard, Benoit, and Christian Mouhanna. 2007. *Une justice dans l'urgence. Le traitement en temps réel des affaires pénales*. Paris: Presses Universitaires de France.

Baudot, Pierre-Yves, and Anne Revillard. 2015. "Introduction. Une sociologie de l'État par les droits." In *L'État des droits. Politiques des droits et pratiques des institutions,* edited by Pierre-Yves Baudot and Anne Revillard, 11–58. Paris: Presses de Sciences Po.

Beaudry, Madeleine. 1988. "La garde des enfants suite au divorce: Contexte historique, courants actuels et perspectives empiriques." *Service social* 37 (3): 435–54.

Beaujot, Roderic, Liu Jianye, and Zenaida R. Ravanera. 2015. "The Converging Gender Trends: Earning and Caring in Canada." *Document de travail du Réseau stratégique de connaissances: Changements de population et parcours de vie* 3 (3): 1–10.

Beck, Ulrich. 2007. "The Cosmopolitan Condition: Why Methodological Nationalism Fails." *Theory, Culture and Society* 24 (7–8): 286–90.

Belleau, Hélène. 2015. "D'un mythe à l'autre: De l'ignorance des lois à la présomption du choix éclairé chez les conjoints en union libre." *Canadian Journal of Women and the Law* 27 (1): 1–21.

Belleau, Hélène, Marie Connolly, Marie Mélanie Fontaine, Marion Goussé, and Sylvie Lévesque. 2022. "Répercussions économiques des ruptures conjugales." In *La séparation parentale et la recomposition familiale dans la société québécoise: Les premiers moments*, edited by Marie-Christine Saint-Jacques. Quebec City: Presses de l'Université Laval.

Belmokhtar, Zakia. 2012. "Divorces: Une procédure à deux vitesses." *Infostat justice* 117.

–. 2014. "Une pension alimentaire fixée par les juges pour deux tiers des enfants de parents séparés." *Infostat justice* 128.

–. 2016. "La contribution à l'entretien et l'éducation de l'enfant, deux ans après le divorce." *Infostat justice* 141.

Belmokhtar, Zakia, and Julie Mansuy. 2016. "En 2013, neuf prestations compensatoires sur dix sous forme de capital." *Infostat justice* 144.

Ben Jelloul, Mohammed, and Pierre-Yves Cusset. 2015. *Comment partager équitablement le coût des enfants après la séparation?* Document de travail, France Stratégie. https://www.strategie.gouv.fr/sites/strategie.gouv.fr/files/atoms/files/04-doc_cout_separations_17juin.pdf.

Bennett, Colin J. 1991. "What Is Policy Convergence and What Causes It?" *British Journal of Political Science* 21 (2): 215–33.

Bérard, Jean, and Gilles Chantraine. 2017. "Chercher son modèle et trouver son double? Les usages de l'exemple québécois/canadien dans la conception des réformes pénales et pénitentiaires françaises depuis les années 2000." *Politix* 120: 87–111.

Bercuson, David J., Jack L. Granatstein, and William R. Young. 1986. *Sacred Trust? Brian Mulroney and the Conservative Party in Power*. Toronto: Doubleday.

Bereni, Laure. 2021. "The Women's Cause in a Field: Rethinking the Architecture of Collective Protest in the Era of Movement Institutionalization." *Social Movement Studies* 20 (2): 208–23.

Bernard, Vincent, Gabrielle Gallic, Olivier Léon, and Catherine Sourd. 2020. "Logements suroccupés, personnes âgées isolées ... des conditions de confinement diverses selon les territoires." *Insee focus* 189. https://www.insee.fr/fr/statistiques/4478728.

Bernheim, Emmanuelle, and Claire Lebecke. 2014. "De la mère 'normale.' Normes, expertises et justice en protection de la jeunesse." *Enfants, familles, générations*. https://journals.openedition.org/efg/532.

Bernier, Dominique, and Catherine Gagnon. 2019. "Violence conjugale devant les tribunaux de la famille: Enjeux et pistes de solution." Mémoire soumis à la consultation sur la réforme du droit de la famille organisée par le Ministère de la justice du Québec. Montreal: Fédération des maisons d'hébergement pour femmes.

Bessière, Céline. 2008. "Se marier pour aller jusqu'au bout ensemble? Ruptures conjugales et transmission des exploitations agricoles dans la lignée." *Revue d'études en agriculture et environnement* 3 (88): 47–70.

–. 2019. "Reversed Accounting: Legal Professionals, Families and the Gender Wealth Gap in France." *Socio-Economic Review*. https://academic.oup.com/ser/advance-article-abstract/doi/10.1093/ser/mwz036/5536821.

Bessière, Céline, Emilie Biland, Abigail Bourguignon, Sibylle Gollac, Muriel Mille, and Hélène Steinmetz. 2018. "'Faut s'adapter aux cultures, Maître!' La racialisation des publics de la justice familiale en France métropolitaine." *Ethnologie française* 24 (1): 131–40.

Bessière, Céline, Emilie Biland, and Hélène Oehmichen. 2020. "Justice familiale: Tribunaux à l'arrêt, inégalités aggravées." *Dalloz actualité*. https://www.dalloz-actualite.fr/node/justice-familiale-tribunaux-l-arret-inegalites-aggravees.

Bessière, Céline, and Sibylle Gollac. 2023. *The Gender of Capital: How Families Perpetuate Wealth Inequality*. Translated by Juliette Rogers. Cambridge, MA: Harvard University Press.

Bessière, Céline, Sibylle Gollac, and Muriel Mille. 2016. "Féminisation de la magistrature: Quel est le problème?" *Travail, genre et sociétés* 36: 175–80.

Bessière, Céline, and Muriel Mille. 2014. "The Judge Is Often a Woman: Professional Perceptions and Practices of Male and Female Family Court Judges in France." *Sociologie du travail* 56 (1): 43–68.

Bessière, Céline, Muriel Mille, and Gabrielle Schütz. 2020. "Les avocat·es en droit de la famille face à leur clientèle. Variations sociales dans la normalisation de la vie privée." *Sociologie du travail* 62 (3). http://journals.openedition.org/sdt/33401.

Bessy, Christian. 2016. "Transformation du marché du travail des avocats et nouveaux intermédiaires du recrutement." *Droit et société* 92: 201–27.

Biland, Émilie. 2019. *Gouverner la vie privée. L'encadrement inégalitaire des separations conjugales en France et au Québec*. Lyon: ENS Éditions.

Biland, Émilie, and Fabien Desage. 2017. "Vers un enracinement cosmopolite. Sciences et pratiques de la comparaison international." *Politix* 120: 9–35.

Biland, Émilie, Sibylle Gollac, Hélène Oehmichen, Nicolas Rafin, and Hélène Steinmetz. 2020. "La classe, le genre, le territoire: Les inégalités procédurales dans la justice familiale." *Droit et société* 106: 547–66.

Biland, Émilie, and Muriel Mille. 2016. "Selon que vous serez puissant ou misérable ... Les inégalités sociales et genrées dans l'accès à la justice familiale." *Nouveaux cahiers du socialisme* 16: 70–78.

–. 2017. "Ruptures de riches. Privilèges de classe et inégalités de genre au sein de la justice québécoise." *Sociétés contemporaines* 108: 97–124.

Biland, Émilie, and Gabrielle Schütz. 2014. "Tels pères, telles mères? La production des déviances parentales par la justice familiale québécoise." *Genèses* 97: 26–46.

–. 2015a. "Physical Custody of Children in the Province of Québec: A Quantitative Analysis of Court Records." *Collection que savons-nous?*. https://www.arucfamille.ulaval.ca/sites/arucfamille.ulaval.ca/files/que_savons-nous_5-ang_en_ligne.pdf.

–. 2015b. "Les couples non-mariés ont-ils des droits? Comment juristes, intellectuels et journalistes ont construit l'affaire 'Éric c Lola.'" *Canadian Journal of Law and Society* 30 (3): 323–43.

Biland, Émilie, and Hélène Steinmetz. 2017. "Are Judges Street-Level Bureaucrats? Evidence from French and Canadian Family Courts." *Law and Social Inquiry* 42 (2): 298–324.

Bilge, Sirma, and Patricia Hill Collins. 2016. *Intersectionality*. Cambridge, UK: Polity Press.

Blanc, Catherine. 1990. "Les principaux résultats." *Recherches et prévisions* 21: 7–16.

Bloch, Kilian. 2021. "En 2020, 12 % des enfants dont les parents sont séparés vivent en résidence alternée." *Insee Première* 1841.

Bodier, Marceline, Guillemette Buisson, Aude Lapinte, and Isabelle Robert-Bobée. 2015. "Couples et familles: Entre permanences et ruptures." *Insee références* 9–23.

Boigeol, Anne, and Jacques Commaille. 1974. "Divorce, milieu social et situation de la femme." *Économie et statistique* 53: 3–21.

Boltanski, Luc. 1969. *Prime éducation et morale de classe*. Paris: Mouton.

Bonnet, Carole, Bertrand Garbinti, and Anne Solaz. 2015. "Les conditions de vie des enfants après le divorce." *Insee Première* 1536.

–. 2021. "The Flip Side of Marital Specialization: The Gendered Effect of Divorce on Living Standards and Labor Supply." *Journal of Population Economics* 34 (2): 515–73.

Bouchard, Joanie, Maxim Fortin, and Marie Hautval. 2017. "Des droits des mères à ceux des enfants? Les réformes du régime québécois de pensions alimentaires pour enfants." *Droit et société* 95: 13–26.

Bourdieu, Pierre. 1987. "The Force of Law: Toward a Sociology of the Juridical Field." *Hastings Law Journal* 38: 814–53.

–. 1993a. "À propos de la famille comme catégorie réalisée." *Actes de la recherche en sciences sociales* 100: 32–36.

–. 1993b. *Language and Symbolic Power*. Cambridge, MA: Harvard University Press.

–. 2012. *Sur l'état*. Paris: Seuil.

Bourdieu, Pierre, and Loïc J.D. Wacquant. 1992. *An Invitation to Reflexive Sociology*. Chicago: University of Chicago Press.

Bourreau-Dubois, Cécile, and Bruno Deffains. 2003. "Les obligations alimentaires vis-à-vis des enfants de parents divorcés: Une analyse économique au service du droit." Research report for the Mission de recherche Droit et Justice, Université Nancy 2 and Centre National de la Recherche Scientifique.

Bourreau-Dubois, Cécile, and Isabelle Sayn. 2011. "Évaluation de la mise en place d'une table de référence pour le calcul de la contribution à l'entretien et à l'éducation des enfants." *Dossiers d'études CNAF* 141.

Boussard, Valérie, Ornela Mato, and Jiyoung Kim. 2022. "La tentative de médiation familiale préalable obligatoire: Une obligation qui n'arrive pas à ses fins." *Informations sociales* 207: forthcoming.

Brousse, Cécile. 2015. "Travail professionnel, tâches domestiques, temps 'libre': Quelques déterminants sociaux de la vie quotidienne." *Économie et statistique* 478: 119–54.

Brown, Elizabeth, Alice Debauche, Christelle Hamel, and Magali Mazuy, eds. 2021. *Violences et rapports de genre. Enquête sur les violences de genre en France*. Paris: INED Éditions.

Bruel, Alain. 1998. "Assurer les bases de l'autorité parentale pour rendre les parents plus responsables." Report to the Department of Employment and Solidarity, Paris.

Brugeilles, Carole, and Sebille Pascal. 2009. "La participation des pères aux soins et à l'éducation des enfants. L'influence des rapports sociaux de sexe entre les parents et entre les générations." *Politiques sociales et familiales* 95: 19–32.

Brunet, Florence, Pauline Kertudo, and Sylvie Malsan. 2008. *Étude sociologique sur la résidence en alternance des enfants de parents séparés*. Dossiers d'études, Caisse nationale d'allocations familiales no. 109. https://www.caf.fr/sites/default/files/cnaf/Documents/Dser/dossier_etudes/Dossier%20109%20-%20R%E9sidence%20Altern%E9e.pdf.

Cacouault-Bitaud, Marlaine. 2001. "La féminisation d'une profession est-elle le signe d'une baisse de prestige?" *Travail, genre et sociétés* 5: 91–115.

Cadolle, Sylvie. 2011. "Partages entre pères et mères pour la résidence en alternance des enfants et recomposition des rôles de genre." In *Aimer et compter? Droits et pratiques des solidarités conjugales dans les nouvelles trajectoires familiales,* edited by Hélène Belleau and Agnès Martial, 163–82. Montreal: Presses de l'Université du Québec.

Caplan, Paula J. 2007. "Le syndrome d'aliénation parentale." *Recherches et prévisions* 89: 59–63.

Cardi, Coline. 2007. "La 'mauvaise mère': Figure féminine du danger." *Mouvements* 49: 27–37.

Carlson, Marcia J., and Paula England, eds. 2011. *Social Class and Changing Families in an Unequal America*. Palo Alto, CA: Stanford University Press.

Carrasco, Valérie, and Clément Dufour. 2015. "Les décisions des juges concernant les enfants de parents séparés ont fortement évolué dans les années 2000." *Infostat Justice* 132.

Cashmore, Judy, Patrick Parkinson, Ruth Weston, Roger Patulny, Gerry Redmond, Lixia Qu, Jennifer Baxter, Marianne Rajkovic, Tomasz Sitek, and Ilan Katz. 2010. *Shared Care Parenting Arrangements since the 2006 Family Law Reforms*. Report to the Australian Government Attorney-General's Department, Social Policy Research Centre, University of New South Wales. https://www.arts.unsw.edu.au/sites/default/files/documents/2_AG_Shared_Care.pdf.

Champagne, Clara, Ariane Pailhé, and Anne Solaz. 2015. "25 ans de participation des hommes et des femmes au travail domestique: Quels facteurs d'évolutions?" *Économie et statistique* 478: 209–41.

CNAF (Caisse nationale des allocations familiales). 2018. *Rapport d'activité*. Paris: CNAF. https://www.caf.fr/sites/default/files/cnaf/Documents/DCom/Quisommesns/Presentation/Rapport_dactivite/RA-2018.pdf.

Collectif Clio. 1982. *L'histoire des femmes au Québec depuis quatre siècles*. Montreal: Quinze.

Le Collectif Onze. 2013. *Au tribunal des couples. Enquête sur des affaires familiales*. Paris: Odile Jacob.

Collins, Caitlyn. 2019. *Making Motherhood Work: How Women Manage Careers and Caregiving*. Princeton, NJ: Princeton University Press.

Commaille, Jacques. 1982. *Familles sans justice. Le droit et la justice face aux transformations de la famille*. Paris: Le Centurion.

–. 2006. "L'économie socio-politique des liens familiaux." *Dialogue* 174: 95–105.

–. 2015. *À quoi nous sert le droit?* Paris: Gallimard.

Commaille, Jacques, Pierre Strobel, and Michel Villac. 2002. *La politique de la famille*. Paris: La Découverte.

Commission de révision permanente des programmes. 2015. *Rapport: Cap sur la performance*. Quebec City: Gouvernement du Québec.

Commission des services juridiques. 2018. *46e rapport annuel de gestion 2017–2018*. Montreal: Commission des services juridiques. https://www.csj.qc.ca/Intranet Uploads/CSJ/Francais/Fichiers/final_Rapport_Annuel_18-06_LR.PDF.

–. 2021. *49e rapport annuel de gestion 2020–2021*. Montreal: Commission des services juridiques. https://www.csj.qc.ca/IntranetUploads/CSJ/Francais/Fichiers/49e%20 Rap.%20annuel%20CSJ%202020-2021-Final_-web2_OK.pdf.

Conseil de modernisation des politiques publiques. 2008. *La révision générale des politiques publiques (RGPP): 1er rapport d'étape*. Paris: Conseil de modernisation des politiques publiques. https://www.vie-publique.fr/sites/default/files/rapport/pdf/084000755.pdf.

Conseil du statut de la femme. 1978. *Pour les Québécoises: Égalité et indépendance*. Quebec City: Gouvernement du Québec.

–. 1995. *Avis sur la perception des pensions alimentaires*. Quebec City: Gouvernement du Québec.

–. 1997. *La société et les familles: Miser sur l'égalité et la solidarité. Avis sur les nouvelles dispositions de la politique familiale et sur la fiscalité des familles*. Quebec City: Gouvernement du Québec.

–. 2016. *Mémoire sur le projet de loi n° 70, Loi visant à permettre une meilleure adéquation entre la formation et l'emploi ainsi qu'à favoriser l'intégration en emploi*. Quebec City: Gouvernement du Québec.

Corriveau, Patrice. 2011. *Judging Homosexuals: A History of Gay Persecution in Quebec and France*. Vancouver: UBC Press.

Côté, Denyse. 2004. "La garde partagée des enfants: Nouvelles solidarités parentales ou renouveau patriarcal?" *Nouvelles questions féministes* 23 (3): 80–95.

Crespo, Stéphane. 2018. "L'emploi du temps professionnel et domestique des personnes âgées de 15 ans et plus." In *Coup d'œil sociodémographique*, Institut de la statistique du Québec 62.

Cretin, Laurette. 2015. "Résidence et pension alimentaire des enfants de parents séparés: Décisions initiales et évolutions." *Insee résultats, couples et familles* 2015 édition: 41–49. https://www.insee.fr/fr/statistiques/2017528.

Cummings, Scott L. 2004. "The Politics of Pro Bono." *University of California Los Angeles Law Review* 52: 1–149.

Czapanskiy, Karen. 1991. "Volunteers and Draftees: The Struggle for Parental Equality." *University of California Los Angeles Law Review* 38: 1415–81.

Dandurand, Renée. 1985. "Les dissolutions matrimoniales, un phénomène latent dans le Québec des années 60." *Anthropologie et sociétés* 93: 87–114.

Défenseur des droits. 2018. *Enquête: Conditions de travail et expériences des discriminations dans la profession d'avocate en France.* https://www.defenseurdesdroits.fr/sites/default/files/atoms/files/rapp-enq-avocats-a4-num-02.05.2018.pdf.

Dekeuwer-Défossez, Françoise. 1999. *Rénover le droit de la famille. Propositions pour un droit adapté aux réalités et aux aspirations de notre temps. Rapport au garde des Sceaux, Ministre de la justice.* Paris: La Documentation française. https://www.vie-publique.fr/sites/default/files/rapport/pdf/994001755.pdf.

Delmas, Fabien, and Jorick Guillaneuf. 2020. "En 2018, les inégalités de niveau de vie augmentent." *Insee Première* 1813.

Delphy, Christine. 2013. *L'ennemi principal.* Vol. 1: *Économie politique du patriarcat.* Paris: Syllepses.

Department of Justice Canada. 1995. *Federal/Provincial/Territorial Family Law Committee's Report and Recommendations on Child Support.* Ottawa: Department of Justice Canada. http://publications.gc.ca/site/eng/9.645780/publication.html.

–. 2001. *Expanding Horizons: Rethinking Access to Justice in Canada.* Ottawa: Research and Statistics Division.

Desmond, Matthew. 2016. *Evicted: Poverty and Profit in the American City.* New York: Crown.

Dewar, John. 2000. "Family Law and Its Discontents." *International Journal of Law, Policy and the Family* 14 (1): 59–85.

Dezalay, Yves. 1990. "Juristes purs et marchands de droit. Division du travail de domination symbolique et aggiornamento dans le champ du droit." *Politix* 3 (10–11): 70–91.

Dionisi-Peyrusse, Amélie, and Marc Pichard. 2014. "L'autorité parentale et la persistance des inégalités de genre." In *La loi et le genre. Études critiques en droit français,* edited by Stéphanie Hennette-Vauchez, Marc Pichard, and Diane Roman, 485–502. Paris: CNRS Éditions.

Direction de la sécurité sociale, 2021, *Rapport d'évaluation des politiques de sécurité sociale – Famille. PLFSS 2022*.

Donnelly, Denise, and David Finkelhor. 1993. "Who Has Joint Custody? Class Differences in the Determination of Custody Arrangements." *Family Relations* 42 (1): 57–60.

Douillet, Anne-Cécile, Thomas Soubiran, Thomas Léonard, and Helena Yazdanpanah. 2015. *Logiques, contraintes, et effets du recours aux comparutions immédiates. Étude de cinq juridictions de la cour d'appel de Douai*. Paris: Mission de recherche droit et justice.

Dubois, Vincent. 2010. *The Bureaucrat and the Poor: Encounters in French Welfare Offices*. London: Routledge.

–. 2019. "Welfare Fraud Inspectors between Standardization and Discretion." In *Inspectors and Enforcement at the Front Line of Government*, edited by Steven Van de Walle and Nadine Raaphorst, 167–86. Cham, Switzerland: Palgrave Macmillan.

Dubois, Vincent, Marine Paris, and Pierre-Édouard Weill. 2018. "Des chiffres et des droits. Le data mining ou la statistique au service du contrôle des allocataires." *Revue de politiques sociales et familiales* 126: 35–46.

Dulong, Delphine. 1997. *Moderniser la politique, aux origines de la Ve République*. Paris: L'Harmattan.

Dumais, Lucie. 2012. "L'état et les politiques sociales. Dispositifs de protection, solidarités et autres mutations." In *L'administration contemporaine de l'état*, edited by P. Tremblay, 369–93. Montreal: Presses de l'université du Québec.

Dumont, Fernand. 1993. *Genèse de la société québécoise*. Montreal: Boréal.

Dumoulin, Laurence, and Sabine Saurugger. 2010. "Les *policy transfer studies*: Analyse critique et perspectives." *Critique internationale* 48 (3): 9–24.

Eekelaar, John, and Mavis Maclean. 2013. *Family Justice: The Work of Family Judges in Uncertain Times*. London: Hart.

Eekelaar, John, Mavis Maclean, and Sarah Beinart. 2000. *Family Lawyers: The Divorce Work of Solicitors*. London: Hart.

Ehrmann, Henry W. 1976. *Comparative Legal Cultures*. Englewood Cliffs, NJ: Prentice-Hall.

Emond, Ariane. 1996. "Aux yeux des mères." In *Recueil de réflexions sur la stabilité des couples-parents*, edited by Conseil de la famille, 111–25. Quebec City: Gouvernement du Québec.

Enquête québécoise sur la santé de la population. 2021. *Répercussions de la pandémie sur la vie sociale, la santé mentale, les habitudes de vie et la réalité du travail des Québécois*. Quebec City: Institut de la statistique du Québec.

European Commission for the Efficiency of Justice. 2020. *European Judicial Systems, CEPEJ Evaluation Report*. Council of Europe. https://rm.coe.int/rapport-evaluation-partie-1-francais/16809fc058.

Evetts, Julia. 2003. "The Sociological Analysis of Professionalism: Occupational Change in the Modern World." *International Sociology* 18 (2): 395–415.

Ewick, Patricia, and Susan Silbey. 1998. *The Common Place of Law: Stories from Everyday Life*. Chicago: University of Chicago Press.

FAFMRQ (Fédération des associations de familles monoparentales et recomposées du Québec). 1993. "Pour une perception automatique des pensions alimentaires avec retenue à la source." *Bulletin de liaison* 19 (1). http://bv.cdeacf.ca/CF_PDF/1993_12_p2954_1993v19n01.pdf.

–. 1994. *Nous réclamons un système de perception automatique des pensions alimentaires avec retenue à la source. Analyse du système australien et recommandations pour le Québec*. http://bv.cdeacf.ca/bvdoc.php?no=1999_09_0105&col=CF&format=htm&ver=old.

–. 1995. "Les pensions alimentaires volent la vedette." *L'entre-nous* 2 (5): 1–2.

–. 2003. *Mémoire présenté à la Commission des institutions, Projet de loi 21 modifiant les règles de fixation des pensions alimentaires pour enfants*. https://www.fafmrq.org/wp-content/uploads/2014/05/2003-11MemFixationPAE-Pl21.pdf.

Farrow, Trevor, and Lesley Jacobs, eds. 2020. *The Justice Crisis: The Cost and Value of Accessing Law*. Vancouver: UBC Press.

Fassin, Didier. 2013. *Enforcing Order: An Anthropology of Urban Policing*. Cambridge, UK: Polity Press.

–. 2015. "Introduction. Governing Precarity." In *At the Heart of the State: The Moral World of Institutions*, edited by Didier Fassin, Yasmine Bouagga, Isabelle Coutant, Jean-Sébastien Eideliman, Fabrice Fernandez, Nicolas Fischer, Carolina Kobelinsky, Chowra Makaremi, Sarah Mazouz, and Sébastien Roux, 1–10. London: Pluto Press.

Ferguson, Lucinda. 2013. "Arbitration in Financial Dispute Resolution: The Final Step to Reconstructing the Default(s) and Exception(s)?" *Journal of Social Welfare and Family Law* 35 (1): 115–38.

Festy, Patrick. 1986. "Le paiement des pensions alimentaires aux femmes divorcées." *Recherches et prévisions* 4: 23–26.

–. 1988. "Après la séparation: Diversité et stabilité des comportements." *Population* 3: 517–35.

Fillod-Chabaud, Aurélie. 2016. "Les usages du droit par le mouvement des pères séparés. Une comparaison France-Québec." *Genre, sexualité and société* 15. http://journals.openedition.org/gss/3746.

–. 2017. "La prise en charge des enfants par les membres de SOS PAPA: Une analyse des conditions matérielles de la transmission culturelle." *Droit et société* 95: 27–41.

Fineman, Martha. 1991. *The Illusion of Equality: The Rhetoric and Reality of Divorce Reform*. Chicago: University of Chicago Press.

Fiss, Owen M. 1983. "The Bureaucratization of the Judiciary." *Yale Law Journal* 92: 1442–68.

Foucault, Michel. 2009. *Security, Territory, Population: Lectures at the Collège de France, 1977–1978*. New York: Picador/Palgrave Macmillan.

Freidson, Eliot. 1970. *Profession of Medicine: A Study of the Sociology of Applied Knowledge*. Chicago: University of Chicago Press.

Friedli, Fiona. 2015. "Redéfinir la famille pour en faire partie. Les mobilisations des 'femmes chefs de famille' (France, 1963–1982)." *Genre and histoire* 16. http://journals.openedition.org/genrehistoire/2337.

Galanter, Marc. 1974. "Why the Haves Come Out Ahead: Speculations on the Limits of Legal Change." *Law and Society Review* 9 (1): 95–160.

Gallot, Fanny. 2019. "Les femmes Gilets jaunes: Révolte de classe, transgression de genre, histoire longue." In *Manuel indocile de sciences sociales. Pour des savoirs résistants*, edited by Fondation Copernic, 538–43. Paris: La Découverte.

Garapon, Antoine, Sylvie Perdriolle, and Boris Barnabé. 2013. *La prudence et l'autorité. L'office du juge au XXIe siècle, Rapport de la mission de réflexion confiée par Madame Christiane Taubira, garde des Sceaux, à l'Institut des hautes études sur la justice, sur l'évolution de l'office du juge et son périmètre d'intervention*. Paris: Ministère de la justice. https://www.ihej.org/wp-content/uploads/2013/07/rapport_office_du_juge_mai_2013.pdf.

Garcia, Sandrine. 2011. *Mères sous influence. De la cause des femmes à la cause des enfants*. Paris: La Découverte.

Garneau, Jean-Pierre. 2016. "Devenir porte-parole durant l'ère des révolutions: Le lent et (parfois) difficile parcours des avocats du Québec colonial." *Criminocorpus*. http://journals.openedition.org/criminocorpus/3391.

Giddens, Anthony. 1991. *Modernity and Self Identity: Self and Society in the Late Modern Age*. Cambridge, UK: Polity Press.

Girard, Chantal. 2018. "Les naissances au Québec et dans les régions en 2017." In *Coup d'œil sociodémographique* 65. https://bdso.gouv.qc.ca/docs-ken/multimedia/PB01600FR_coup_doeil_65_2018H00F00.pdf.

Giurge, Laura M., Ashley V. Whillans, and Ayse Yemiscigil. 2021. "A Multicountry Perspective on Gender Differences in Time Use during COVID-19." *Proceedings of the National Academy of Sciences* 118 (12): 1–7.

Godbout, Élisabeth, Claudine Parent, and Marie-Christine Saint-Jacques. 2015. "Positions Taken by Judges and Custody Experts on Issues Relating to the Best Interests of Children Custody Disputes Québec." *International Journal of Law, Policy, and the Family* 29 (3): 272–300.

Godbout, Élisabeth, Marie-Christine Saint-Jacques, and Hans Ivers. 2018. "Après la séparation, avec qui les enfants devraient-ils vivre? Une analyse de l'opinion québécoise." *L'année sociologique* 68 (2): 393–422.

Goffman, Erving. 1961. *Asylums: Essays on the Social Situation of Mental Patients and Other Inmates*. New York: Vintage Books.

Goldstein, Joseph, Anna Freud, and Albert J. Solnit. 1973. *Beyond the Best Interests of the Child*. New York: Free Press.

Gorlick, Carolyne, and Guy Brethour. 1998. *Welfare-to-Work Programs in Canada: A Discussion Paper*. Ottawa: Canadian Council on Social Development.

Goubau, Dominique, Jean-Marie Fortin, and Miriam Grassby. 1997. "Un système de fixation des pensions alimentaires dans l'intérêt des enfants?" *Le journal du Barreau* 29: 20–21.

Gouron-Mazel, Annie. 2002. "Juge de la famille et homosexualité." *Jurisclasseur* 1: 4–10.

Goyer, Maude. 2016. "La garde partagée sous toutes ses formes est en train de devenir la nouvelle norme *Le Devoir*, June 6.

Grossman, Joanna L., and Lawrence M. Friedman. 2011. *Inside the Castle: Law and the Family in Twentieth Century America*. Princeton, NJ: Princeton University Press.

Groupe de travail pour les jeunes. 1991. *Un Québec fou de ses enfants*. Quebec City: Gouvernement du Québec. https://publications.msss.gouv.qc.ca/msss/fichiers/1994/94-849.pdf.

Guillaumin, Colette. 1995. *Racism, Sexism, Power and Ideology*. London: Routledge.

Guillonneau, Maud. 2019. "Les décisions d'ordonnance de protection prononcées en 2016." *Infostat Justice* 171.

Guillonneau, Maud, and Caroline Moreau. 2013. *La résidence des enfants de parents séparés. De la demande des parents à la décision du juge. Exploitation des décisions définitives reçues par les juges aux affaires familiales au cours de la période comprise entre le 4 juin et le 15 juin 2012*. Paris: Ministère de la justice. https://www.ladocumentationfrancaise.fr/rapportspublics/134000796/index.shtml.

Guilmaine, Claudette. 2009. *Vivre en garde partagée. Une histoire d'engagement parental*. Montreal: Les Éditions du CRAM/Centre Hospitalier Universiaire Saint-Justice.

Guinchard, Serge, ed. 2008. *L'ambition raisonnée d'une justice apaisée, rapport de la Commission sur la répartition des contentieux remis au garde des Sceaux*. Paris: Documentation française.

Hassenteufel, Patrick. 2005. "De la comparaison internationale à la comparaison transnationale. Les déplacements de la construction d'objets comparatifs en matière de politiques publiques." *Revue française de science politique* 55 (1): 113–32.

Hassenteufel, Patrick, Myriam Bachir, Virginie Bussat, William Genieys, Claude Martin, and Marina Serré. 1999. *L'émergence d'une "élite du welfare"? Sociologie des sommets de l'État en interaction*. Rapport de recherche pour la Mire. https://hal.archives-ouvertes.fr/hal-01166215/document.

Hausegger, Lori, Troy Riddell, Matthew Hennigar, and Emmanuelle Richez. 2010. "Exploring the Links between Party and Appointment: Canadian Federal Judicial Appointments from 1989 to 2003." *Canadian Journal of Political Science* 43 (3): 633–59.

Haut Conseil de la famille. 2014. *Les ruptures familiales. État des lieux et propositions*. Paris: Haut Conseil de la famille. https://www.hcfea.fr/IMG/pdf/2014_04_LES_RUPTURES_FAMILIALES.pdf.

–. 2016. *Actes du colloque du Haut Conseil de la famille: Les ruptures familiales: Affaire publique, affaire privée?* Paris: Haut Conseil de la famille. https://www.strategie.gouv.fr/actualites/actes–colloque–rupturesfamiliales–affaire–publique–affaire–privee.

Haynes, John. 1981. *Divorce Mediation: A Practical Guide for Therapists and Counselors.* New York: Springer.

Heinz, John P., and Edward O. Laumann. 1982. *Chicago Lawyers: The Social Structure of the Bar.* New York: Russell Sage Foundation and American Bar Foundation.

Helfter, Clémence. 2010. "La création de l'allocation de parent isolé. Entretien avec Bertrand Fragonard." *Informations sociales* 157: 134–41.

Hochschild, Arlie R., with Anne Machung. 1990. *The Second Shift: Working Parents and the Revolution at Home.* New York: Avon Books.

Hoggart, Richard. 1957. *The Uses of Literacy: Aspects of Working Class Life.* London: Chatto and Windus.

Holzinger, Katharina, and Christoph Knill. 2005. "Causes and Conditions of Cross-National Policy Convergence." *Journal of European Public Policy* 12 (5): 775–96.

Honnorat, Pascale. 2018. *Divorce par consentement mutual. Retours d'expérience.* Paris: Conseil national des barreaux.

Illouz, Eva. 2019. *The End of Love: A Sociology of Negative Relations.* New York: Oxford University Press.

Institut de la Statistique du Québec. 2021. *État du marché du travail au Québec. Bilan de l'année 2020.* Quebec City: Gouvernement du Québec. https://statistique.quebec.ca/fr/fichier/etat-du-marche-du-travail-au-quebec-bilan-de-lannee-2020.pdf.

Israël, Liora, and Rachel Vanneuville. 2017. "Legal Training and the Reshaping of French Elite. Lessons from an Ethnography of Law Classes in Two French Elite Education Institutions." *Journal of Education and Work* 30 (2): 156–67.

Jarry, Jocelyne, Evelyne Lapierre-Adamcyk, Céline Le Bourdais, and Alain Roy. 2016. "Lignes directrices facultatives en matière de pension alimentaire pour époux. Pertinence de leur application au Québec?" *Canadian Journal of Law and Society* 31 (2): 243–65.

Jenson, Jane. 2004. "Changing the Paradigm: Family Responsibility or Investing in Children?" *Canadian Journal of Sociology* 29 (2): 169–92.

Jeune Barreau de Montréal. 2016. *Rapport du JBM sur le système d'aide juridique québécois.* Montreal: Jeune Barreau de Montréal. https://ajbm.qc.ca/wpcontent/uploads/2015/08/rapportaidejuridiquevf.compressed.pdf.

Jolowicz, John A. 2003. "Adversarial and Inquisitorial Models of Civil Procedure." *International and Comparative Law Quarterly* 52 (2): 281–95.

Jouanneau, Solenne, and Anna Matteoli. 2018. "Les violences au sein du couple au prisme de la justice familiale. Invention et mise en oeuvre de l'ordonnance de protection." *Droit et société* 99: 305–21.

Judicial Compensation and Benefits Commission. 2016. *Report and Recommendations Submitted to the Minister of Justice of Canada.* Ottawa: Judicial Compensation and Benefits Commission. http://quadcom.gc.ca/archives/2015/Media/Pdf/2016/FinalReport.pdf.

Justice pour tous. 2018. *Sondage Justice pour tous.* http://adaj.ca/justicepourtous/sondage.

Karpik, Lucien. 1995. *Les avocats. Entre l'état, le public et le marché XIIIe–XXe siècle.* Paris: Gallimard.

–. 2003. "Les avocats: Entre le renouveau et le déclin." *Hermès* 35: 203–11.

Kay, Fiona. 2009. "Intraprofessional Competition and Earnings: Inequalities across a Professional Chasm: The Case of the Legal Profession in Québec, Canada." *Law and Society Review* 43 (4): 901–38.

Kelly, Mary Bess. 2012. "Divorce Cases in Civil Court, 2010/2011." *Juristat.* Statistics Canada catalogue no. 85-002-X. https://www150.statcan.gc.ca/n1/pub/85-002-x/2012001/article/11634-eng.pdf.

Kempeneers, Marianne, and Renée Dandurand. 2002. "Pour une analyse comparative et contextuelle de la politique familiale au Québec." *Recherches sociographiques* 431: 49–78.

Kniebiehler, Yvonne. 1997. *La révolution maternelle depuis 1945: Femmes, maternité, citoyenneté.* Paris: Perrin.

Koussens, David. 2020. "Nationalistic Secularism and the Critique of Canadian Multiculturalism in Quebec." In *Citizenship and Belonging in France and North America: Multicultural Perspectives on Political, Cultural and Artistic Representations of Immigration,* edited by Ramona Mielusel and Simona Pruteanu, 17–32. London: Palgrave Macmillan.

Lachance, Micheline. 1979. *Les enfants du divorce.* Montreal: Éditions de l'Homme.

Lamari, Moktar, Pierre Noreau, and Marylène Leduc. 2020. "Measuring Justice System Performance in Quebec and Canada: Indicators for Benchmarking Systems and Highlighting Best Practices." In *The Justice Crisis: The Cost and Value of Accessing Law,* edited by Trevor Farrow and Lesley Jacobs, 41–68. Vancouver: UBC Press.

Lambert, Anne. 2009. "Des causes aux conséquences du divorce: Histoire critique d'un champ d'analyse et principales orientations de recherche en France." *Population* 64: 155–82.

Lamont, Michèle, and Nicolas Duvoux. 2014. "How Neo-Liberalism Has Transformed France's Symbolic Boundaries?." *French Politics, Culture and Society* 32 (2): 57–75.

Lamoureux, Diane. 2000. "Services ou politique: Quelques dilemmes du mouvement des femmes au Québec." *Cahiers du genre* 28: 133–57.

–. 2016. *Les possibles du féminisme. Agir sans "nous."* Montreal: Remue-Ménage.

Langevin, Louise. 2009. "Liberté contractuelle et relations conjugales font-elles bon ménage?" *Nouvelles questions féministes* 28 (2): 24–35.

Laplante, Benoit, and Ana Fostik. 2017. "L'égalité, l'indépendance et l'union de fait. Le choix de l'union de fait et du mariage au Québec et en Ontario de 1986 à 2011." *Cahiers québécois de démographie* 46 (1): 11–45.

Lareau, Annette. 2011. *Unequal Childhoods: Class, Race and Family Life*. 2nd ed. Los Angeles: University of California Press.

Lascoumes, Pierre, and Carla Nagels. 2014. *Sociologie des élites délinquantes. De la criminalité en col blanc à la corruption politique*. Paris: Armand Colin.

Le Pape, Marie-Clémence. 2009. "Être parent dans les milieux populaires: Entre valeurs familiales traditionnelles et nouvelles normes éducatives." *Informations sociales* 154: 88–95.

Leckey, Robert. 2014. "Strange Bedfellows." *University of Toronto Law Journal* 64 (5): 641–68.

Leduc, Louise. 2013. "Garde partagée: Papa veut sa place." *La Presse*, November 25.

Lefaucheur, Nadine. 1986. "Les familles monoparentales: Des chiffres et des mots pour les dire, formes nouvelles ou mots nouveaux?" In *Les familles d'aujourd'hui*, edited by Association Internationale des Démographes de Langue Française, 173–81. Paris: Presses Universitaires de France/Institut National des Études Démographiques.

Lenoir, Daniel. 2019. "Pensions alimentaires: En finir avec les impayés." *Terra nova*. http://tnova.fr/system/contents/files/000/001/717/original/Terra–Nova_Note –pensionsalimentaires_060319_%281%29.pdf?1551857674.

Lenoir, Rémi. 1992. "L'état et la construction de la famille." *Actes de la recherche en sciences sociales* 91: 20–37.

–. 2003. *Généalogie de la morale familiale*. Paris: Seuil/Liber.

Lenoir, René. 1974. *Les exclus. Un français sur dix*. Paris: Seuil.

Lesnard, Laurent. 2009. *La famille désarticulée. Les nouvelles contraintes de l'emploi du temps*. Paris: Presses Universitaires de France.

Levi-Faur, David, and Jacint Jordana. 2005. "Regulatory Capitalism: Policy Irritants and Convergent Divergence." *Annals of the American Academy of Political and Social Science* 598: 191–97.

Lewis, Jane. 1992. "Gender and the Development of Welfare Regimes." *Journal of European Social Policy* 2 (3): 159–73.

–. 2001. "The Decline of the Male Breadwinner Model: Implications for Work and Care." *Social Politics* 8 (2): 152–69.

Lindsay, Colin. 1992. *Les familles monoparentales au Canada*. Ottawa: Statistique Canada.

Linteau, Paul-André, François Ricard, and Jean-Claude Robert. 1986. *Histoire du Québec contemporain*. Vol. 2: *Le Québec depuis 1930*. Montreal: Boréal.

Lipsky, Michael. 1980. *Street Level Bureaucracy: Dilemmas of the Individual Public Services*. New York: Russell Sage Foundation.

MacDonald, Mary. 1997. *Expedited Child Support: An Overview of the Commonwealth Countries' and United States' Procedures for Establishing and Modifying Child Support*.

Ottawa: Department of Justice Canada. https://www.justice.gc.ca/eng/rp-pr/fl-lf/child-enfant/ecs-tapae/p1a.html.

Mack, Kathy, and Sharyn Roach Anleu. 2007. "Performing Impartiality: Judicial Demeanour and Legitimacy." *Law and Social Inquiry* 35 (1): 137–73.

Maclean, Mavis, and John Eekelaar. 2013. *Managing Family Justice in Diverse Societies*. London: Hart.

Maclean, Mavis, John Eekelaar, and Benoit Bastard, eds. 2015. *Delivering Family Justice in the 21st Century*. London: Hart.

Marin, Stéphanie. 2020. "Garde partagée: Un parent sans symptômes peut voir ses enfants, tranche la cour." *La Presse*, April 1.

Martial, Agnès. 2016. "Les temporalités plurielles de la paternité." In *Des pères "en solitaire"? Ruptures conjugales et paternité contemporaine,* edited by Agnès Martial, 79–93. Marseille: Presses Universitaires de Provence.

Martin, Claude. 1997. *L'après divorce. Lien familial et vulnérabilité*. Rennes: Presses Universitaires de Rennes.

–. 2001. *La régulation politique de la famille*. Mémoire pour l'HDR en sociologie. Paris: Université Paris 5.

–. 2015. "Parenting Support in France: Policy in an Ideological Battlefield." *Social Policy and Society* 14 (4): 609–20.

Martin-Papineau, Nathalie. 2003. "La construction paradoxale d'un problème politique: L'exemple des familles monoparentales (1968–1988)." *Recherches et prévisions* 72: 7–20.

Mather, Lynn, Craig McEwan, and Richard R. Maiman, eds. 2001. *Divorce Lawyers at Work: Varieties of Professionalism in Practice*. Oxford: Oxford University Press.

Mathivet, Amandine, Hélène Ceretto, Hayet Iguertsira, and Xavier Zunigo. 2014. "Étude sur l'allocation de soutien familial en lien avec la contribution à l'entretien et l'éducation de l'enfant." *Dossier d'études CNAF* 172.

Mazur, Amy G., and Dorothy E. McBride. 2008. "State Feminism." In *Politics, Gender, and Concepts: Theory and Methodology,* edited by Gary Goertz and Amy G. Mazur, 244–69. New York: Cambridge University Press.

McClintock, Anne. 1995. *Imperial Leather: Race, Gender and Sexuality in the Colonial Contest*. New York: Routledge.

McGoey, Linsey. 2014. *An Introduction to the Sociology of Ignorance: Essays on the Limits of Knowing*. New York: Routledge.

Memmi, Dominique. 2003. "Governing through Speech: The New State Administration of Bodies." *Social Research* 70 (2): 645–58.

Meier, Joan S. 2020. "U.S. Child Custody Outcomes in Cases Involving Parental Alienation and Abuse Allegations: What Do the Data Show?" *Journal of Social Welfare and Family Law* 42 (1): 92–105.

Menkel-Meadow, Carrie. 1985. "Portia in a Different Voice: Speculations on a Women's Lawyering Process." *Berkeley Women's Law Journal* 1 (1): 39–63.

Merle, Pierre. 2000. "Le concept de démocratisation d'une institution scolaire: Une typologie et sa mise à l'épreuve." *Population* 55 (1): 15–50.

Meurs, Dominique, Ariane Pailhé, and Sophie Ponthieux. 2010. "Enfants, interruptions d'activité des femmes et écart de salaire entre les sexes." *Revue de l'OFCE* (Observatoire français de la conjoncture économique) 114: 113–33.

Milan, Anne. 2013. *Marital Status: Overview, 2011, Report on the Demographic Situation in Canada*. Statistics Canada catalogue no. 91–209–X. https://www150.statcan.gc.ca/n1/pub/91-209-x/2013001/article/11788-eng.pdf.

Miles, Robert. 1993. *Racism after "Race Relations."* London: Routledge.

Millar, Jane. 1996. "Family Obligations and Social Policy: The Case of Child Support." *Policy Studies* 17 (3): 181–93.

Mille, Muriel, and Hélène Zimmermann. 2017. "Des avocats et des parents. Demandes profanes et conseils juridiques pour la prise en charge des enfants au Québec." *Droit et société* 95 (1): 43–56.

Ministère de la famille et de l'enfance. 2001. *Évaluation du programme de perception des pensions alimentaires. Volet "impacts psychosociaux."* Quebec City: Ministère de la famille et de l'enfance.

Ministère de la justice du Québec. 2012. *Note d'information concernant le programme de médiation familiale*. Quebec City: Ministère de la justice du Québec.

Ministère des Finances. 2016. *Budget 2016–2017. Régime québécois de soutien du revenu*. Quebec City: Gouvernement du Québec. http://www.budget.finances.gouv.qc.ca/budget/2016-2017/fr/documents/Revenu_Juin2016.pdf.

Minoc, Julie. 2017. "(Dés)ordres familiaux à la loupe. Les normes maternelles et paternelles au prisme de l'enquête sociale." *Droit et société* 95: 71–86.

Minonzio, Jérôme. 2007. "La médiation familiale dans les CAF. Un service dont l'efficacité varie selon les conflits traités." *Recherches et prévisions* 89: 71–80.

Minonzio, Jérôme, and Jean-Philippe Vallat. 2006. "L'Union nationale des associations familiales (UNAF) et les politiques familiales. Crises et transformations de la représentation des intérêts familiaux en France." *Revue française de science politique* 56 (2): 205–26.

Mnookin, Robert H., and Lewis Kornhauser. 1979. "Bargaining in the Shadow of the Law: The Case of Divorce." *Yale Law Journal* 5: 950–97.

Morel, Sophie. 2002. *Modèle du workfare ou modèle de l'insertion? La transformation de l'assistance sociale au Canada et au Québec*. Ottawa: Condition féminine Canada.

Morton, Frederick Lee, ed. 2002. *Law, Politics and the Judiciary in Canada*. Calgary: University of Calgary Press.

Mouhanna, Christian. 2012. "De la plume aristocratique à la plume gestionnaire. Le cas de la magistrature." In *Les paradoxes de l'écriture. Sociologie des écrits professionnels dans les institutions d'encadrement*, edited by Christel Coton and Laurence Proteau, 85–104. Rennes: Presses Universitaires de Rennes.

Mulcahy, Linda. 2011. *Legal Architecture: Justice, Due Process and the Place of Law*. London: Routledge.

Murji, Karim, and John Solomos. 2005. *Racialization: Studies in Theory and Practice*. Oxford: Oxford University Press.

Neyrand, Gérard, and Chantal Zaouche Gaudron, eds. 2014. *Le livre blanc de la résidence alternée*. Toulouse: Érès.

Noreau, Pierre. 1998. "La superposition des conflits: Limites de l'institution judiciaire comme espace de résolution." *Droit et société* 40: 585–612.

Noreau, Pierre, and Samia Amor. 2004. "Médiation familiale: De l'expérience sociale à la pratique judiciarisée." In *Famille en transformation, la vie après la séparation des parents*, Centre de recherche sur l'adaptation des jeunes et de la famille à risque, 269–97. Quebec City: Presses de l'Université Laval.

Normand, Silvio. 2011. "La culture juridique et l'acculturation du droit: Le Québec." *ISAIDAT Law Review* 1 (1): 779–816.

Pailhé, Ariane, Emilie Reynaud, and Anne Solaz. 2020. "Même quand elles travaillaient à l'extérieur, les femmes ont consacré plus de temps que les hommes aux tâches domestiques et à s'occuper des enfants." *Insee références*. https://www.insee.fr/fr/statistiques/4797670?sommaire=4928952.

Paillet, Anne, and Delphine Serre. 2014. "Les rouages du genre. La différenciation des pratiques de travail chez les juges des enfants." *Sociologie du travail* 56 (3): 342–64.

Papon, Sylvain. 2018. "770 000 bébés nés en France en 2017: Six sur dix sont nés hors mariage." *Insee focus* 124.

Paquin, Stéphane, and Pier-Luc Lévesque, eds. 2014. *Social-démocratie 2.0: Le Québec comparé aux pays scandinaves*. Montreal: Presses de l'Université de Montréal.

Parazelli, Michel, Sylvie Lévesque, and Carol Gélinas. 2012. "La prevention précoce en question." *Nouvelles pratiques sociales* 1: 1–15.

Parti Québécois. 1994. *Programme électoral du Parti Québécois*. Quebec City: Parti Québécois.

Pelletier, David. 2016. "Prévalence, déterminants et dynamique des arrangements de temps parental postséparation chez les enfants québécois nés à la fin des années 1990." PhD diss., Université de Montréal.

–. 2017. "Combien d'enfants en double résidence ou en garde partagée? Sources et mesures dans les contextes québécois et canadien." *Cahiers québécois de démographie* 46 (1): 101–27.

Pelletier, Sylvie. 1987. *Pensions alimentaires 1981 à 1986, attribution et perception*. Quebec City: Ministère de la justice.

Périvier, Hélène, and Muriel Pucci. 2019. "Le recouvrement des impayés de pensions alimentaires réduit les dépenses sociales mais réduit également le niveau de vie de certaines mères isolées." *Blog de l'OFCE (Observatoire français de la conjoncture economique)*. https://www.ofce.sciences-po.fr/blog/le-recouvrement-des

-impayes-de-pensions-alimentaires-reduit-les-depenses-sociales-mais-reduit-egalement-le-niveau-de-vie-de-certaines-meres-isolees/.

Perrin-Heredia, Ana. 2009. "Les logiques sociales de l'endettement: Gestion des comptes domestiques en milieux populaires." *Sociétés contemporaines* 76: 95–119.

Perry, Elizabeth Stuart. 2019. *Child Support Law in California and Sweden: A Comparison across Welfare State Models.* Umeå: Skrifter från Juridiska institutionen vid Umeå universitet.

Phélip, Jacqueline, ed. 2006. *Le livre noir de la garde alternée.* Paris: Dunod.

Piesen, Alexandra. 2016. "Une paternité à construire au quotidien: Le cas de la résidence au père." *Revue des politiques sociales et familiales* 122: 77–88.

Piketty, Thomas. 2014. *Capital in the Twenty-First Century.* Cambridge, MA: Belknap Press.

Poitras, Karine, Emilie Biland, Elisabeth Godbout, Johanne Clouet, and Marie-Hélène Filteau. 2022. "Aller en médiation ou consulter un·e avocat·e? Recours et non-recours aux services (para-)juridiques dans le processus de separation." In *La separation parentale et la recomposition familiale dans la société québécoise: Les premiers moments*, edited by Marie-Christine Saint-Jacques, Quebec City: Presses de l'Université Laval.

Portmann, Anne. 2016. "Divorce sans juge: Désaccord entre l'Ordre parisien et le Conseil national des barreaux." *Dalloz Actualité,* May 16.

Prioux, France. 2009. "Les couples non mariés en 2005: Quelles différences avec les couples mariés?" *Politiques sociales et familiales* 96: 87–95.

Prioux, France, and Magali Barbieri. 2012. "L'évolution démographique récente en France: Une mortalité relativement faible aux grands âges." *Population* 67 (4): 597–656.

Prost, Antoine. 1999. "Frontières et espaces du privé." In *Histoire de la vie privée 5. De la première guerre mondiale à nos jours,* edited by Paul Ariès and George Duby, 15–132. Paris: Seuil.

Protecteur du citoyen. 1996. *Le régime de perception des pensions alimentaires.* Quebec City: Québec Ombudsman.

–. 2012. *Brief Presented by the Québec Ombudsman before the Committee on Institutions as Part of the Special Consultations and Public Hearings on Bill 64: An Act to Promote Access to Justice in Family Matters.* Quebec City: Québec Ombudsman.

Quéniart, Anne, and Renée Joyal. 2001. "La garde contestée de l'enfant à la suite d'une rupture conjugale: Des juges de la Chambre de la famille s'expriment sur divers aspects de la question." *Prisme* 35: 116–30.

Régie des rentes du Québec. 2006. *Soutien aux enfants: Statistiques de l'année 2005.* Quebec City: Gouvernement du Québec. http://collections.banq.qc.ca/ark:/52327/bs20047.

–. 2012. *Le soutien aux enfants: Évolution de 2005 à 2012.* Quebec City: Gouvernement du Québec. http://collections.banq.qc.ca/ark:/52327/bs2268262.

Régnier-Loilier, Arnaud. 2016. "Séparation conjugale et rupture du lien père-enfants. Des causes multiples." In *Des pères "en solitaire"? Ruptures conjugales et paternité contemporaine,* edited by Agnès Martial, 29–47. Marseille: Presses Universitaires de Provence.

Regroupement provincial des maisons d'hébergement et de transition pour femmes victimes de violence conjugale, Fédération de ressources d'hébergement pour femmes violentées et en difficulté du Québec. 1997. *Mémoire sur le projet de loi no 65 en matière de médiation familiale.* Montreal. http://bv.cdeacf.ca/CF_PDF/ 2002_17_0066.pdf.

Rémillard, Gil. 1993. "Une responsabilité." *Le Soleil,* May 16.

Resnik, Judith. 1982. "Managerial Judges." *Harvard Law Review* 96: 374–448.

Revillard, Anne. 2007a. *La cause des femmes dans l'état: Une comparaison "France-Québec" (1965–2007).* PhD diss., École normale supérieure de Cachan.

–. 2007b. "Entre arène judiciaire et arène législative: Les stratégies juridiques des mouvements féministes au Canada." In *La fonction politique de la justice,* edited by Jacques Commaille and Martine Kaluszynski, 145–63. Paris: La Découverte.

–. 2009. "Le droit de la famille: Outil d'une justice de genre? Les défenseurs de la cause des femmes face au règlement juridique des conséquences financières du divorce en France et au Québec (1975–2000)." *L'année sociologique* 59: 345–70.

–. 2016. *La cause des femmes dans l'état. Une comparaison France-Québec.* Grenoble, France: Presses Universitaires de Grenoble.

Robcis, Camille. 2013. *The Law of Kinship: Anthropology, Psychoanalysis, and the Family in France.* Ithaca, NY: Cornell University Press.

Roman, Diane. 2014. "Les aides aux parents isolés: L'aide sociale au prisme d'une lecture féministe du droit." In *La loi et le genre. Études critiques en droit français,* edited by Stéphanie Hennette-Vauchez, Marc Pichard, and Diane Roman, 321–38. Paris: CNRS Éditions.

Romito, Patrizia, and Micaela Crisma. 2009. "Les violences masculines occultées: Le syndrome d'aliénation parentale." *Empan* 73 (1): 31–39.

Rose, Ruth. 2001. *La politique de soutien au revenu des familles du Québec: Une évaluation et une proposition.* Recherche effectuée dans le cadre du protocole d'entente UQAM – Relais-femmes pour le compte de la FAFMRQ. Montreal.

–. 2009. *Le traitement des pensions alimentaires pour enfants dans les programmes de soutien du revenu et la fiscalité, opinion d'expert déposée dans le cadre du recours Girard et al. c. Ministère de l'emploi et de la solidarité sociale.* Montreal.

–. 2014. "Conditions socio-économiques: Le sort des familles monoparentales s'est-il vraiment amélioré?" Communication au colloque Familles monoparentales et recomposées: Des victoires à célébrer et des actions à poursuivre. Montreal.

Rossignol, Laurence. 2015. "Les pensions alimentaires sont-elles trop élevées?" *Libération,* July 1.

Roussel, Violaine. 2003. "L'indépendance de la magistrature en France: L'émergence d'une notion à contenu variable." *Revue suisse de science politique* 9 (3): 113–53.

Sandefur, Rebecca. 2008. "Access to Civil Justice and Race, Class and Gender Inequality." *Annual Review of Sociology* 34: 339–58.

San Martin, Eva, and Marion Tillous. 2021. *Spatialité des violences conjugales and COVID-19*. https://anrcovico.hypotheses.org/110.

Sarat, Austin, and William L.F. Felstiner. 1995. *Divorce Lawyers and Their Clients: Power and Meaning of the Legal Process*. Oxford: Oxford University Press.

Sarat, Austin, and Stuart A. Scheingold, eds. 1998. *Cause Lawyering: Political Commitments and Professional Responsibilities*. Oxford: Oxford University Press.

Sassier, Monique. 2001. *Arguments et propositions pour un statut de la médiation familiale en France, rapport à la ministre déléguée à la famille*. Paris: Ministère de la famille. https://www.vie-publique.fr/sites/default/files/rapport/pdf/014000484. pdf.

Savage, Mike. 2021. *The Return of Inequality: Social Change and the Weight of the Past*. Cambridge, MA: Harvard University Press.

Sayn, Isabelle. 2014. "Les barèmes dans le fonctionnement du droit et de la justice." In *Le droit mis en barèmes?*, edited by Isabelle Sayn, 1–17. Paris: Dalloz.

Sayn, Isabelle, Bruno Jeandidier, and Cécile Bourreau-Dubois. 2012. "La fixation du montant des pensions alimentaires: Des pratiques et un barème." *Infostat Justice* 116.

Schaaf, Aurélie. 2022. "L'agence de recouvrement et d'intermédiation des pensions alimentaires au coeur de la couverture du risque séparation par la branche famille." *Informations sociales* 207: forthcoming.

Schwartz, Olivier. 2012. *Le monde privé des ouvriers*. Paris: Presses Universitaires de France.

Schultheis, Franz. 1992. "L'avenir de la famille au centre des antinomies de la modernité." In *Du politique et du social dans l'avenir de la famille*, edited by Haut Conseil de la population et de la famille, 49–55. Paris: Documentation française.

Schultz, Ulrike, and Gisela Shaw, eds. 2013. *Gender and Judging*. London: Hart.

Skinner, Christine, and Jacqueline Davidson. 2009. "Recent Trends in Child Maintenance Schemes in 14 Countries." *International Journal of Law, Policy and the Family* 23 (1): 25–52.

Sénat. 2010. *Étude d'impact. Projet de loi relatif à la répartition du contentieux et à l'allégement de certaines procédures juridictionnelles*. Paris: Sénat. https://www.senat.fr/leg/etudes–impact/pjl09–344–ei/pjl09–344–ei.html.

Serre, Delphine. 2017. "Class and Gender Relations in the Welfare State: The Contradictory Dictates of the Norm of Female Autonomy." *Social Sciences* 6 (2). https://doi.org/10.3390/socsci6020048.

Siblot, Yasmine. 2006. "'Je suis la secrétaire de la famille!' La prise en charge féminine des tâches administratives entre subordination et resource." *Genèses* 64: 46–66.

Siblot, Yasmine, Marie Cartier, Isabelle Coutant, Olivier Masclet, and Nicolas Renahy. 2015. *Sociologie des classes populaires contemporaines*. Paris: Armand Colin.

SOM. 2017. *Sondage sur les services de médiation familiale, rapport final présenté au Ministère de la justice*. Quebec City: Ministère de la justice du Québec. https://www.justice.gouv.qc.ca/fileadmin/user_upload/contenu/documents/Fr__francais_/centredoc/rapports/couple-famille/Rapport_SOM_Mediation_VF.pdf.

Sohn, Anne-Marie. 1981. "Les rôles féminins dans la vie privée. Approche méthodologique et bilan de recherches." *Revue d'histoire moderne et contemporaine* 4: 597–623.

Sommet de la justice. 1993. *La justice: Une responsabilité à partager: Les actes du Sommet de la justice tenu à Québec du 17 au 21 février 1992*. Quebec City: Ministère de la justice. https://cap.banq.qc.ca/notice?id=p%3A%3Ausmarcdef_0000338350&queryId=32.

Spire, Alexis. 2012. *Faibles et puissants face à l'impôt*. Paris: Raisons d'agir.

Spire, Alexis, and Kathia Weidenfeld. 2011. "Le tribunal administratif: Une affaire d'initiés? Les inégalités d'accès à la justice et la distribution du capital procédural." *Droit et société* 79: 689–713.

Spurk, Jan. 2003. "Épistémologie et politique de la comparaison internationale: Quelques réflexions dans une perspective européenne." In *Stratégies de la comparaison internationale*, edited by Michel Lallement and Jan Spurk, 71–82. Paris: Presses du CNRS (Centre national de la recherche scientifique).

Statistics Canada. 2019. "Family Matters: Being Common Law, Married, Separated or Divorced in Canada," Statistics Canada catalogue no. 11-001-X. https://www150.statcan.gc.ca/n1/daily-quotidien/190501/dq190501b-eng.htm.

Stoléru, Lionel. 1974. *Vaincre la pauvreté dans les pays riches*. Paris: Flammarion.

Swiss, Liam, and Céline Le Bourdais. 2009. "Father-Child Contact after Separation: The Influence of Living Arrangements." *Journal of Family Issues* 30 (5): 623–52.

Teisceira-Lessard, Philippe. 2017. "La justice n'a pas à choisir le parrain ou la marraine d'un bébé, tranche la cour." *La Presse*, January 16.

Tena, Marta de. 2012. *La garde alternée: Du sur-mesure pour nos enfants*. Paris: J.-C. Lattès.

Tétrault, Michel. 2004. *La garde partagée: De la légende urbaine à la réalité* (ebook). https://docplayer.fr/5862385-La-garde-partagee-de-la-legende-urbaine-a-la-realite-m-e-michel-tetrault.html.

Thélot, Claude. 2016. *Les ruptures familiales et leurs consequences: 30 recommandations pour en améliorer la connaissance*. Paris: Conseil national de l'information statistique. https://www.cnis.fr/wp-content/uploads/2017/10/RAPPORT-RUPTURES-FAMILIALES-_-nouvelle-version-29mai2017.pdf.

Théry, Irène. (1993) 2001. *Le démariage. Justice et vie privée*. Paris: Odile Jacob.

Thornton, Margaret. 2007. "Otherness on the Bench: How Merit Is Gendered." *Sydney Law Review* 29 (3): 396–413.

Tremblay, Éric, and Jean-Marc Daigle. 2017. *Prévalence de l'usage des médicaments spécifiques au trouble du déficit de l'attention avec ou sans hyperactivité (TDAH) chez les Canadiens de 25 ans et moins.* Quebec City: INESSS (Institut national d'excellence en santé et en services sociaux). https://www.inesss.qc.ca/fileadmin/doc/INESSS/Rapports/ServicesSociaux/INESSS_Portrait_TDAH_IMS.pdf.

Troper, Michel. 2007. "Judicial Power and Democracy." *European Journal of Legal Studies* 1 (2): 2–17.

Union des caisses nationales de sécurité sociale. 2017. *Instance nationale de concertation Branche Famille.* Paris: Union des caisses nationale des sécurité sociale.

Urvoas, Jean-Jacques. 2016. "Le Ministère de la justice n'a plus les moyens de payer ses factures." *Journal du Dimanche,* April 2.

Valois, Martine. 2012. "La mission de justice dans l'état moderne." In *L'administration contemporaine de l'état,* edited by Pierre Tremblay, 209–23. Montreal: Presses de L'Université du Québec.

Vaus, David, Matthew Gray, Lixia Qu, and David Stanton. 2017. "The Economic Consequences of Divorce in Six OECD Countries." *Australian Journal of Social Issues* 52 (2): 180–99.

Vigour, Cécile. 2006. "Justice: L'introduction d'une rationalité managériale comme euphémisation des enjeux politiques." *Droit et société* 63: 425–55.

–. 2018. *Les réformes de la justice en Europe. Entre politique et gestion.* Bruxelles: De Boeck.

Veblen, Thorstein. (1899) 1953. *The Theory of the Leisure Class: An Economic Study in the Evolution of Institutions.* New York: Macmillan.

Walzer, Susan. 2008. "Redoing Gender through Divorce." *Journal of Social and Personal Relationships* 25 (1): 5–21.

Watkins-Hayes, Celeste. 2009. *The New Welfare Bureaucrats: Entanglements of Race, Class, and Policy Reform.* Chicago: University of Chicago Press.

Weber, Max. 1978. *Economy and Society.* Los Angeles: University of California Press.

Webley, Lisa. 2011. "Solicitors as Imagined Masculine, Family Mediators as Fictive Feminine and the Hybridization of Divorce Solicitors." In *Alternative Perspectives on Lawyers and Legal Ethics,* edited by Francesca Bartlett, Reid Mortenson, and Kieran Tranter, 132–50. London: Routledge.

Weitzman, Lenore J. 1985. *The Divorce Revolution: The Unexpected Social and Economic Consequences for Women and Children in America.* New York: Free Press; London: Collier Macmillan.

Zaccour, Suzanne. 2018. "Parental Alienation in Quebec Custody Litigation." *Les cahiers de droit* 59 (4): 1073–1111.

Index

Abandon de famille tolérance zéro (Family Desertion Zero Tolerance) (France), 231

Action Committee on Access to Justice in Civil and Family Matters (Quebec), 32

AFEAS. *See* Association féministe d'éducation et d'action sociale (AFEAS) (Feminist Association for Education and Social Action)

Agence de recouvrement des impayés des pensions alimentaires (Child Support Collection Agency) (France), 228, 233–35

agreement(s): and avoidance of courtroom, 30–31; and best interests of the child, 242; on child support, 43, 47; and conciliation, 80–81; homologation by judges, 43; and joint custody, 166; mediation and, 31, 52; modification to, 107–8; nonagreement, and hearings, 26–27; non-agreement vs., in Canada, 26;

regarding shared custody, 144; tools for professionals, 31

Allocation Parent Isolé (API) (Isolated Parent Benefit) (France), 216, 217

Allocation de Soutien Familial (ASF) (Child Support Allowance) (France), 185, 217–18, 224–25, 228, 229, 233

alternative dispute resolution: collaborative law and, 93; COVID-19 pandemic and, 60; in France, 38, 98–101; litigation vs., 34, 104–5. *See also* out-of-court alternatives

API. *See* Allocation Parent Isolé (API) (Isolated Parent Benefit) (France)

arbitration, 37, 70, 71–73, 74–75, 83, 254n54

Arnou, Béatrice, 96–97, 98

ASF. *See* Allocation de Soutien Familial (ASF) (Child Support Allowance) (France)

associate lawyers (*collaborateurs*), 256n36

Association féministe d'éducation et d'action sociale (AFEAS) (Feminist Association for Education and Social Action), 198, 200

Association masculine d'entraide pour la famille (Men's Mutual Family Aid Association), 211

at-fault divorce, 8, 10–11, 18, 25

Barreau du Québec, 66, 94

Basic Parental Contribution Determination Table (Quebec), 181

Besnard, Marie-Josée, 49–50, 137, 138, 142, 165

best interests of the child: *Civil Code of Quebec* definition, 259*n*33; and co-parenting, 154; custody and, 48; fathers and, 168; and joint custody, 166; psychological/behavioural knowledge and, 9; psycho-social professionals and, 202; and public interventions, 242; and state interventions, 240; UN Convention on the Rights of the Child and, 167, 246; and visitation rights, 48

Bill 65 (Quebec), 204

Blackburn, Jeanne, 200

Blanchard, Catherine, 130–31, 173

Bouchard, Camil, 259*n*36; *Un Québec fou de ses enfants (Quebec Treasures Its Children)*, 167–68

Buckley, Elisabeth, 104–5, 132–33, 136, 138–39, 147, 206

Bureau du droit des personnes et de la famille (Bureau of Individual and Family Rights) (France), 219

Cabernet, Sandrine, 142–43, 144, 172

Caisse d'allocations familiales (CAF) (Family Benefit Office) (France), 53, 108, 120; advance of child support payments, 213, 215; and ASF, 225; child support agreements and, 43; child support collection, 228, 230, 233, 234, 235, 237; child support payment guidelines, 229; family court lack of communication with, 231; GIPA and, 227, 232; non-divorce family procedures and, 53; privatization of divorce and, 9; role in lives of single-parent families, 218; and tax authorities collecting child support payments, 215

Caisse nationale des allocations familiales (CNAF) (National Family Benefits Office) (France), 215, 216, 217, 225, 228

Canadian Judicial Council, Ethical Principles for Judges, 82

caseloads: and court management, 76; and duration of cases, 71; and duration of hearings, 96–97; judges (France) and, 38, 39; judges (Quebec) and, 39; lawyers (France) and, 97–98; legal aid (Quebec) lawyers and, 45; lightening of, 25–26, 29–30

Catholic Church, 84, 238

Centre d'information sur les droits des femmes et des familles (Center for Information on Women's and Family Rights) (France), 232

Charland, François, 103, 104, 113–14, 139, 159, 169–70

Charter of Rights and Freedoms (Canada), 11, 36, 37, 135

Charter of Values (Quebec), 126

child custody: best interests of the child and, 48; in Canada, 26; fathers in France and, 231; hearings, 29; judges (Quebec) and, 50; poorest mothers, and sole custody, 46; prior parental agreement, and judge's approval, 71; special clerks and, 30; upper classes and, 50; and violence,

156. *See also* joint custody; joint legal custody; joint physical custody

child physical custody: awarding to mothers, 152–53; fathers' groups and, 152–53; fathers requesting, 153; gender differences in requests for, 153; gendered division of work and, 153–54. *See also* joint physical custody; shared physical custody

child poverty. *See* poverty: child

child support: absence of lawyer in, 47; agreement vs. litigation regarding, 47; agreement regarding, 43; amounts vs. incomes, 189–90; Basic Parental Contribution Determination Table, 181; calculation of, 181, 183, 188–89, 190–91; Canadian federal guidelines, 205; caps on, 188–89; children's economic rights and, 201–2; children's needs and, 176, 179, 181–82, 183; in *Civil Codes*, 176; collection/enforcement system, 200–1; co-parenting and, 190–91; cost of procedures for collection of, 187; court rulings regarding changes in, 187; COVID-19 and, 4, 60; defined, 151; fathers and, 177, 180, 186–87, 190; financial issues as frequent parental concern, 176–77; in France vs. Quebec, 183–91, 193, 194, 234–35, 236(t), 245, 247–48; gender inequalities and, 189–90, 191; guidelines, 184–85; increase in payments, 179–80; indigence and, 181; intergenerational social reproduction and, 133; judges and, 71, 185, 186–87, 189; and justice system reform, 196; legal professionals and, 177, 187; lower-class fathers and, 185, 191, 193; maintenance policies, 195–96; mediation and, 105; and men's socio-economic

differences, 183; middle class and, 187–89, 193; mothers and, 177, 183; no amount set for, 185, 186; in Ontario, 200–1; parents' prior agreement on, 71; payment methods, 187; poorest mothers with sole custody, and, 46; power asymmetries in, 180, 201; proportionality to parents' needs, 176; recalculation, 33, 36–37; scrutiny/surveillance in, 119, 178–79, 181, 183; shared physical custody and, 190–91; social classes and, 180, 189; social services and, 177–78; special clerks and, 30; spending patterns and, 142, 178–79; subsistence minimum, 181; tax benefits, 188; in UK, 234; upper class and, 187–89, 193; upper-class men and, 55; welfare state structure and, 196

child support (France): Allocation de Soutien Familial and, 185; amounts, 224–26, 228–29; ASF and, 217–18, 224–25; authorities' own family situations and, 229–30; CAF and, 43, 228, 229, 230, 233, 234, 235, 237; CNAF and, 228; collection/enforcement, 225–26, 227–29, 233, 234, 235; courts and, 213, 228, 229, 230–31; familialism vs. modernization and, 214–15; family benefit supplement and, 224; family branch of social security system and, 223, 234; and family desertion, 219–20; family service branch and, 230–31; fathers' responsibility for, 218–19; feminist/women's groups and, 229, 231–32; and gender equality/inequality, 220, 221, 226; GIPA and, 227; guarantee fund, 214–15, 218; guidelines, 212, 220–23, 229; history, 213–19; and income disparities, 222; joint custody and, 222, 229;

judges and, 43, 212, 220, 224, 231; lack of prioritization of cases, 56, 236–37; lawyers and, 56; and living standards of non-custodial vs. custodial parents, 230; lower-class fathers and, 224, 229; as managerialization, 222; Ministère de la justice and, 219–23; optional payment system, 226; parental agreement regarding, 222; patchiness of, 223, 229–30; power imbalance/struggles and, 219, 223, 234–35; and public savings, 226–27; Quebec system as example for, 234; rates for wealthy, 212; reforms, 223–29, 236–37; state as intermediary in, 212; taxation and, 212, 226, 228, 234, 235; unified payment system, 225–27; unpaid/outstanding, 212, 215–16, 218, 220, 225–26, 228, 233, 234; upper-class men and, 55; Yellow Vest movement and, 232–33

child support (Quebec): amounts, 203; avoidance of system, 210–11; calculation methods/guidelines, 204–6; Child Support Determination Form, 182; children from other partnerships and, 212; collection/enforcement, 197, 199, 202, 207, 208, 235; cost, 235; as example in France, 234; family solidarity vs. public redistribution and, 203–4; fathers' groups and, 211–12; federal child support guidelines and, 205; judges and, 182–83; last-resort financial assistance program and, 209–10; male responsibility for, 196; modifications to, 210–11; neoliberalism and, 206, 211; penalization of low-income mothers, 211; reform, 198–212; and single-mother family poverty, 206; tax neutrality of, 197, 206–7, 208; tax services

and, 203; three pillars of, 197; and welfare benefits, 203–4, 206, 207–8, 209; women's rights movement and, 197

Cigliano, Brigitte, 122–24, 140–41, 155

Civil Code (France). See *French Civil Code*

Civil Code of Quebec, 197; best interests of the child in, 259*n*33; on child support, 176; double standard for adultery, 238; family law in, 17; parents under, 151; and same-sex parental couples, 151

civil justice: and inequality, 23; judges/courts and intervention, 13

civil law system: and Federal-Provincial-Territorial Family Law Committee, 205; and joint parental authority, 151; judges under, 64, 71

class. See social classes

class inequalities. See socio-economic inequalities

CNAF. *See* Caisse nationale des allocations familiales (CNAF) (National Family Benefits Office) (France)

Coalition Avenir Québec, 210

Coalition contre le détournement des pensions alimentaires pour enfants (Coalition against Child Support Misappropriation), 210

Code of Civil Procedure (Quebec), 30, 35, 37, 76

Code de l'organisation judiciaire (*Code of Judicial Organization*) (France), 72

collaborative law, 58, 60, 93, 99, 247. *See also* mediation

Commission sur la repartition du contentieux (Commission on the Distribution of Court Litigation) (France), 41

292   Index

common law legal system: caseloads in, 76; child support in, 205; judges in, 66, 76, 83, 85; judges in, vs. in civil law, 64

common law partnerships. *See* de facto spousal relationships

conciliation: adversarial system and, 78; and agreement, 80–81; court absences and, 129; French hearings, 27, 28, 252*n*10; impartiality and, 78; judges (France) and, 70–71, 73; judges (Quebec) and, 75, 76–78; judges and, 70, 83; paternalism and, 85; *procès-verbal d'acceptation*, 70; settlement conferences, 77–78

Conseil de modernisation des politiques publiques (Council for the Modernization of Public Policies) (France), 42

Conseil du statut de la femme (Council on the Status of Women) (Quebec), 199, 200, 206; *Pour les Québécoises: égalité et indépendance (For Quebecois Women: Equality and Independence)*, 199

contested divorces: in France, 252*n*6, 252*n*8; non-representation in, 33

convergent divergence, 245–46

co-parenting: about, 150; asymmetry in, 159, 193; best interests of the child and, 154; and child support, 190–91; duration of cases and, 174; family violence and, 155–57; and fuzzy government, 15; and gender equality, 150–51; and gendered expectations, 151–52; goal, 150–51; and inequalities, 151–52; legal tools, 151; lower classes and, 161, 162; men's distancing from, 129; middle classes and, 162; national context and, 152; non-Western families and, 162; as norm, 15; parental communi-

cation notebooks, 173–74; parental deviance and, 159; psychological/behavioural knowledge and, 9; and public policy, 150; in Quebec vs. France, 19, 152, 174–75, 192(t), 193, 244, 247; racialized people and, 162; and shared physical custody, 243; and social inequalities, 15; space for fathers in discourse of, 154; symbolic understanding of, 19, 152, 172, 173–74; upper classes and, 162; upper-class men and, 193; US research regarding, 169

costs: litigation, 33, 51; mediation, 51–52; mediation (Canada), 32–33; mediation (France), 38; private mediation, 60. *See also* earnings; fees

Cour des Comptes (Court of Account) (France), 226

courts: agreement, and avoidance of, 30–31; behavioural norms, 104–5; decorum, 121–22; and economic inequalities, 11; economic/cultural inequalities and access to, 11; in family law, 25; in France vs. Quebec, 64; gender, and absence from hearings, 128–29; judicial ritual Quebec vs. France, 102–3; management/managerialization, 32, 39, 75–76, 240; and professional/institutional intervention, 13; reserved for long trials, 36; roles, 24, 64; and social reproduction, 12; and surveillance of private lives, 14. *See also* hearings

courts (Canada): decorum, 73–74; spatial organization, 74; unreasonable delay in, 37, 40

courts (France): accessibility of, 73; budget, 39; case flow, 39–40; and child support, 213, 228, 229, 230–31; COVID-19 pandemic and, 60; efficiency, 213, 221; fewer procedural requirements, 38–39; "immediate appearance" in, 39–40; in-person vs. digital technology, 60; as inquisitorial vs. adversarial, 38; lower classes and time spent in, 59; management/managerialization, 42–43, 221; as "public service," 40–41; unreasonable delay and, 40

courts (Quebec): dockets, 27; and family violence, 156; legal aid recipients and, 47–48; litigation costs, 32; lower classes and, 48; middle classes and, 50–51; unreasonable delay in, 37, 40; upper classes and, 50–51; waiting time for dates, 33

COVID-19 pandemic: and alternative conflict resolution, 60; and courts, 60; and distribution of labour in home, 243; effects of, 3–4; impact in Quebec vs. France, 61; and inequalities, 59–61; and legal professionals, 60–61; lockdowns, 60; and parental duties, 61; and remote services, 60–61; and role of law, 4

custody. *See* child custody

custody sharing. *See* shared custody

de facto spousal relationships: civil union dissolution, 253*n*29; education levels and, 254*n*58; increasing number, 242–43; legal disadvantage of, 11; legal representation in France, 38; and right to equality, 11

Défenseur des Droits (Ombudsman) (France), 42

Dekeuwer-Défossez, Françoise, 42, 220–21, 222

Delegation on Women's Rights, 145

deviance, parental, 158–59

divorce: federal vs. provincial responsibilities for, 35–36; in France, 26; liberalization of, 6; no-fault, and law

practice, 89; non-contested, and state intervention in private life, 8; private ordering of, 8–9; in Quebec, 26–27; rates of, 17; rates in Quebec, 26, 197–98; rise in non-contested, 8; social classes in France and, 238

Divorce Act (Canada), 25, 156, 166

Divorce Act (France), 25

Dolto, Françoise, 171–72

Dupont-Bernard, Grace, 58, 107–8, 136

duration of cases/hearings: caseloads and, 71, 96–97; in France vs. Quebec, 40; limitation of expectations regarding interventions, 113; resources and, 71; socio-economic inequalities and duration of time with lawyers, 56–57; time with legal aid lawyers, 45; unreasonable delay in, 37; upper classes and, 50; women and duration of time with lawyers, 47

duration of cases/hearings (France), 26, 96–97; in case history, 28; and co-parenting, 174; judges' caseloads and, 38; legal representation and, 55; mutual consent divorce and, 53–54; social classes and, 55; socio-economic status and, 53–54; wait time for non-divorce family procedures, 53

duration of cases/hearings (Quebec), 26–27, 37; adversarial approach to proof and, 36; variation in, 28–29

earnings: family lawyers (France), 90; family lawyers (Quebec), 90; gender and, 92–93; judges (France), 64, 69; judges (Quebec), 66; of judges (Quebec), 66; women lawyers (Quebec), 94; of women lawyers in France vs. Quebec, 92–93. *See also* costs; fees

École nationale d'administration (France), 217

École nationale de la magistrature (National School of Magistrates) (France), 68, 80

economic inequality/inequalities. *See* lower classes; poverty; socio-economic inequalities

education levels: and common law partnerships, 254*n*58; and mediation, 52; secondary school democratization and, 248–49

employment: and attitude toward court procedures, 130–31; bread-winner model of, 260*n*53; gender and, 154; and joint physical custody, 163, 174; and parent relocation, 155; single mothers (France), 216; and visitation rights, 174; of women, 15–16

Eric v Lola, 11

European Convention on Human Rights, 8, 41

European Court of Human Rights, 8, 39–40, 246

expectations: contained vs. disruptive adjustments to, 127–28; disruptive adjustment to, 129; legal aid lawyers and limitation of, 117; of legal professionals regarding upper-class men, 141–42; limitation of, 111, 112–13, 115–17, 132; lower classes and, 112–13, 115–17; men's refusal of limitations on, 129; power relationships and, 242; professional power in limitation of, 111, 112, 115–16; professional power in production of, 109; social classes and "right," 241; socially constructed, 242; upper classes and, 112, 132–33; upper-class women's compliance with, 144. *See also* gendered expectations

experts. *See* professionals

FAFMRQ. *See* Fédération des associations de familles monoparentales et recomposées du Québec (FAFMRQ) (Federation of Associations of Single-Parent and Blended Families)

familialism, 16, 214, 217

family allowance (Quebec), 198, 209

family law: as "bourgeois law" in France, 214; and *Civil Codes*, 17; and democracy, 5; and emancipation of women, 243–44; federal/provincial jurisdiction over, 35–36; federal/provincial jurisdictions of, 251*n*11; French influence on Quebecois, 247; in law practice, vs. judges' specialization in, 86; married vs. unmarried couples in, 25; men practising, 92–93; politicization, and social change, 95; prestige of, 90; private conflict prevention/resolution processes in, 35; psychological/behavioural knowledge and, 9; in Quebec vs. France, 17–18, 64; and relationship to state, 5; size of firms, 90, 94; social construction as feminine, 68; status, 64; trial courts in, 25; women in, 64, 86–87, 90–92

family lawyers. *See* lawyers

family mediation. *See* mediation

family policy/policies: in France, 16, 196, 212–13; in Quebec, 210, 211

fathers: ability to pay, and amount of child support, 190; and child support, 177, 186–87, 218–19; with children from different partnerships, 129; custody, in France, 231; Dolto and, 171; episodic/elective child care, 152; incomes, 177(f); involvement with children, 167–68; involvement in co-parenting, 159; and joint custody, 159, 169–70; and labour market, 154; and physical custody, 153; poverty, in

France, 216; risks from absence of, 172; as symbolic figures, 172; visitation rights, 159, 160. *See also* lower-class fathers; middle-class fathers; upper-class fathers

fathers' groups: Bouchard as spokesman, 259n36; and child custody, 152–53; and child support, 211–12; feminists and, 175; and joint custody, 168; on judges favouring mothers, 175; and parental equality, 175; and representation of families, 195; and shared physical custody, 175

fathers/men: absence from court hearings, 128–29; avoidance of institutions, 130; disruptive adjustments, 128–29, 130, 131; distancing from co-parenting, 129; and judicial independence, 144; and legal aid eligibility, 46–47; and legal counsel, 46; as unrepresented, 46–47; and visitation rights, 129

Federal Action Committee on Access to Justice in Civil and Family Matters, 35

Federal-Provincial-Territorial Family Law Committee, 205

Fédération des associations de familles monoparentales et recomposées du Québec (FAFMRQ) (Federation of Associations of Single-Parent and Blended Families), 198, 199, 200–1, 202, 206, 214, 216

Fédération des maisons d'hébergement pour femmes (Federation of Women's Shelters) (Quebec), 156

Fédération syndicale des femmes chefs de famille (Federation of Women Heads of Household) (France), 213–14

fees: disadvantaged clients and, 129; flat, 115; lawyers (France), 38; lawyers (Quebec), 33; upper classes and, 137. *See also* costs; earnings

feminism/feminists: and class-based analyses, 11; and family violence, 175; and fathers' groups, 175; and inequalities, 11; and move away from litigious divorce, 34; as social movement vs. state feminism, 195

feminism/feminists (France): and child support, 229, 231–32; compared with Quebec, 213–14; and compensatory benefit (*prestation compensatoire*), 145; and legal professionals, 155; and single mothers, 214; and women's independence, 231–32. *See also* women's groups/movement (France)

feminism/feminists (Quebec): and child support, 198–99, 200; and child support guidelines, 206–7; compared with France, 213–14; and economic inequalities of divorce, 147; on economic transfers and women's autonomy, 147. *See also* Association féministe d'éducation et d'action sociale (AFEAS) (Feminist Association for Education and Social Action); women's groups/movement (Quebec)

Flores, Maria, 170, 203

Fontaine, Gisèle, 77, 147–48

Forest, Gabriel, 51, 76, 77, 179–80

Fragonard, Bertrand, 217, 218, 223, 225–26, 234

French Civil Code: on child support, 176; family law in, 17; on parental authority, 151

Front commun pour un véritable service de perception des pensions (United Movement for a Real Child Support Collection Service), 198

Garantie contre les impayés de pension alimentaire (GIPA) (Child Support Enforcement Guarantee) (France), 227, 228

gender: and career paths, 80, 87; class and, 55–56, 59; and competence in legal procedures, 130–31; and compliance, 127–31; and contrasts in judges' practices, 87; and discourse around family law, 87; and distribution of childcare, 243; divorce by consent and, 12; and earnings, 92–93; and institutional oversight regarding private life, 242; and legal representation, 55–56; liberalization of divorce and, 59; and mediation vs. litigation, 89; and misdemeanour punishment, 238; neutrality in *French Civil Code,* 151; in politicized family law practice, 95; and poverty, 177(f); and professional interactions, 109–10; professional power and, 111, 112; "redoing," 15; and requests for child physical custody, 153; social classes and, 112; and social constraints, 12; and socialization, 92; and specialization in law practice, 86; and state constraints, 239

gender equalities/inequalities: child support and, 189–90, 191, 220; in childcare labour in Quebec vs. France, 19; civil law liberalization and, 238–39; co-parenting and, 150–51; family law liberalization and, 248–49; judges and, 147–48; among lower classes, 44; minority groups and, 124; in professional/household labour, 145; in Quebec vs. France, 245; recognition of right to divorce and, 24–25; in Scandinavia, 208; separations and, 4–5; social groups and, 177(f); socio-economic inequalities

and, 241; women judges and, 145–46; women's emancipation and, 243–44

gendered division of labour: and child physical custody, 153–54; in child-rearing, 131; and gendered parenting, 243; household, 146

gendered expectations: co-parenting and, 151–52; legal professionals', 141, 165; psycho-social professionals and, 173

gendered parenting: gendered division of labour and, 243; legal professionals and ideology of, 152; lower classes and, 243; and parental deviance, 158(t), 159; and parental roles, 161, 191, 193; professionals and, 161, 243; social classes and, 152; among upper/middle classes, 165; women's mothering roles, 175–76

GIPA. *See* Garantie contre les impayés de pension alimentaire (GIPA) (Child Support Enforcement Guarantee) (France)

Giroud, Françoise, 214

Giscard d'Estaing, Valéry, 216

Gittelman, Marie-Line, 94, 105

governmentality, 6–7

Groupe d'entraide aux pères et de soutien à l'enfant (Society for Support and Mutual Aid for Fathers and Children), 211

Guinchard, Serge, 41, 221

Haut Conseil de la famille (High Council on Family Affairs) (France), 223, 230, 234, 261*n*71

hearings: closing arguments, 103; concluding remarks, 78–79; costs of, 104–5; divorces without, 24. *See also* courts

hearings (France): conciliation, 28; happenings outside of, 97–98;

judicial proactivity in, 38; lawyers' participation in, 27–28; Quebec compared to, 98; reduction in numbers of, 39; standardization of, 29

hearings (Quebec): adversarial system, 26, 33–34; child custody, 29; disagreement/non-agreement and, 26–27; France compared to, 98; lawyers' participation in, 28–29; preliminary, 27, 33, 101; variation in, 29–30

hierarchy/hierarchies. *See* social classes

Hollande, François, 223, 224, 227, 233

household labour: attitudes in France vs. Quebec toward, 147; gender and, 145, 146

immigrants: and ethno-psychiatry, 125; judges and, 126–27; lawyers and, 117–18; lawyers from minority groups and, 124–25; and length of procedures, 54; national background, and liberalization of divorce, 59

impartiality: and conciliation, 78; and court spatial organization, 74; distancing and, 82–83; judges (Canada), 74; judges (France), 68–69; judges (Quebec), 66–67, 82–83; paternalism and, 85

individual autonomy/responsibility: and child support, 207; emphasis on, 246; history of, 8–9; and inequalities, 7–8, 22; and privatization of divorce, 8–9; and restriction of public aid, 207; and social inequalities, 58–59; state self-limitation and, 6–7; targeting of, 6–7; and women working outside home, 144

inequality/inequalities: of access to lawyers/judges, 14; civil justice and, 23; feminism and, 11; increase in separations, and, 249; individual liberty and, 7–8; individual rights and,

22; institutional production of, 239–44; intervention mode differentiation, 23–24; judicial policies and, 5; moralization in counteracting, 249; race/racialization and, 12, 13; redistributive policies and, 239; socio-professional availability and, 23, 24; surveillance in counteracting, 249. *See also* gender equalities/inequalities; socio-economic inequalities

International Convention on the Rights of the Child. *See* United Nations Convention on the Rights of the Child

interventions/interventionism: best interests of the child and, 240, 242; courts and, 13; hybridization of public/private, 7; judges and, 13, 80–81, 83–87; moralization, 80; neo-liberalism and, 7; non-contested divorce and, 8; norms relating to, 246; psychological/behavioural knowledge and, 9; public administrative reforms and, 240; public policy rights and, 240; right to privacy vs., 8; segmentation of modes, 23; social background and, 84; women judges and, 80–81, 83; in written rulings, 86

Investing-in-Children Policy Paradigm, 211

"isolated" mothers (France). *See* single mothers (France)

joint custody: age of child and, 163, 171; best interests of the child and, 166; child support and, 222; defined, 170; fathers and, 169–70; fathers' groups and, 168; in France, 170–75, 222; in France vs. Quebec, 165, 170–71; household income and, 163; judges and, 166–67, 169; lawyers and, 169; legal professionals and, 166;

lower classes and, 163; mediation and, 167–68; middle class and, 142–43, 170; parental agreement and, 166; and parental alienation syndrome, 168; popularity of, 167; primary attachment figure and, 171; psychiatrists and, 170–75; psycho-social professionals and, 169; in Quebec, 165–66; upper classes and, 142–43. *See also* shared custody

joint legal custody: defined, 151; fathers and, 159; hearings, 160; non-Western families and, 162; and visitation rights, 159

joint physical custody: and child support in France, 229; child support guidelines (Quebec) and, 204–5; criteria for, in Quebec, 205; defined, 151; employment and, 163, 174; French law regarding, 166; as legal principle in France, 155; middle classes and, 162–64; mutual consent divorce and, 163; and parental relocation, 155; revenue and, 163; upper classes and, 162–64. *See also* child physical custody; shared physical custody

judges: as arbiters, 37, 70, 83; and child support, 185, 186–87, 189; civil vs. common law traditions and, 64, 66, 71; as conciliators, 70, 83; and conspicuous consumption, 141; and court decorum in Canada, 73–74; distancing from clients' private lives, 82–83, 129–30; as experts, 85–86; and family morality, 141; on family violence, 156; in France vs. Quebec, 63–64, 65(t), 68, 69, 79, 244; and immigrants, 126–27; impartiality/independence, 37, 74, 144; inequalities of access to, 14; interventionism, 83–87, 120; and joint custody, 166–

67, 169; and lower classes, 48; as managers, 70, 83; and middle classes, 132; moralization by, 80, 82, 120–22; and national vs. international norms, 246; need for, in Quebec vs. France, 24; and parental alienation syndrome, 168; and paternalism, 103–4; as priests, 84; and professional/institutional intervention, 13; provocativeness/loquaciousness, 82; and psycho-social evaluations, 173; relationship with lawyers in Quebec vs. France, 103–4; roles, 64; and self-representation, 114–15; and sexual orientation, 81; social backgrounds, 83, 189; styles of practice, 79–87, 87(t); and transnational circulation, 247; and upper classes, 132, 141, 240; and upper-class men's non-compliance, 142–44; and violence, 123–24; working conditions, 64; written rulings, 86. *See also* legal professions/professionals; women judges

judges (France): all cases brought before, 96; as arbiters, 71–73; caseloads, 38, 39, 97–98; and child support, 43, 212, 220, 221–23, 224, 231; civil servants compared, 64, 68, 69, 71–72; and compensatory benefit (*prestation compensatoire*), 144–46; as conciliators, 70–71; courtroom management, 39; discretionary power, 71, 73; divorce without, 24; dockets, 27; and duration of cases, 174; earnings, 64, 69; and ethno-psychiatry, 125; and family cases, vs. out-of-court alternatives, 41; fathers' groups on, 175; fewer intermediaries between parties and, 71–72; homologation of agreements, 43; impartiality/independence, 39, 68–69; "judge for all" principle, 59; *jugement collégial*,

141; and lower classes, 57; as managers, 73; merit-based promotion, 69; Ministère de la justice and, 40, 69; and mutual consent divorce, 27–28, 41; on partner violence, 157; political debate on role of, 39; power of, 68, 69; prestige, 64; proactivity in hearings, 38; recruitment, 68; social backgrounds, 68; and social services, 235; as social workers, 73; socialization of litigants, 72–73; specialization in more complex cases, 44; training, 68; and violence against children, 156–57; and visitation rights, 174; vulnerable people and, 42; women as, 68; working conditions, 73

judges (Quebec): as arbiters, 74–75; backgrounds, 255n1; caseloads, 39; characteristics, 67; and child custody, 50; and child support, 182–83; civil servants vs., 30; and conciliation, 75, 76–78; concluding remarks, 78–79; court modernization and, 41; discretionary decisions, 79; as facilitators in settlement conferences, 77–78; family law reforms and, 37; federal minister of justice appointment of, 66; and gendered economic inequalities, 147–48; and gendered roles in upper classes, 147; and household labour, 147; impartiality/independence, 66–67, 82–83; and lower classes, 48; lower classes, and access to, 59; as managers, 75–76; Ministère de la justice and, 40; and out-of-court alternatives, 41; and parental deviance, 48; paternalism, 19, 125; political aspect of appointments, 66; power of, 68; private lives, 67; professional backgrounds, 66; right of access to, 41; salaries, 66; shrinking jurisdiction of, 32; social

backgrounds/status, 19, 65–66, 68; special clerks vs., 30; specialization in more complex cases, 44; traditional functions, 41; upper classes and, 19, 50; women among, 66; working with other professionals, 67–68

justice: accessibility to, 19, 35, 61; moral principles vs. institutional emphasis in definition of, 34

labour market. *See* employment

Lacan, Jacques, 171

Lachance, Marc, 67, 69, 74, 143–44, 176, 183

Lagacé, Madeleine, 85–86, 136, 139–40, 141

Lamy, Stéphanie, 231, 232

Lavoie, Charles, 47, 180

Lavoie, Louise, 28–29, 38, 75, 114–15

lawyers, 139; demand in family law for services, 89; distancing by, 129; diversity/heterogeneity, 89; fees/costs, 49; in France vs. Quebec, 87–89, 140–41; gender/generational identity sharing, 138–39; and immigrants, 117–18; inequalities of access to, 14; institutional knowledge/role, 110; and joint custody, 169; and litigation vs. negotiation, 95–96; lower classes, and access to, 59; men practising family law, 92–93; and minority groups, 122–27; moralizing by, 118–22, 128; and national vs. international norms, 246; neutrality, 139–40; "Othering" by, 122–27; reasons for working on family cases, 89; and self-representation, 114–15; as specialists in family law, 89; teaching client role, 102–3; teams of associates/secretaries, 137–38; and transnational circulation, 247; types of law practised, 89; and upper classes, 49–50, 137,

138–41. *See also* legal professions/ professionals; women lawyers

lawyers (France): absence in court, 72; caseloads, 97–98; and child support cases, 56; costs, 44; in court proceedings, 38; and duration of trials, 55; earnings, 90; fees, 38; gender and, 55–56; lower classes and, 54–55; and mediation, 44; and mutual consent divorce, 44; participation in hearings, 27–28; and penal mediation, 116; prioritization of cases, 56; sharing by parties, 38, 44; and social class, 56

lawyers (Quebec): adversarial system and, 26; earnings, 90; and family law reforms, 36–37; family law reforms and, 37; fees/costs, 33; frequency of use, 31; and legal aid, 46–47; and mediation, 51–52; participation in hearings, 28–29; roles in court, 103; sharing by parties, 33

Lawyers in Society (Abel, Lewis), 63

Le Hot, Élizabeth, 223, 225–27, 229, 232

Le Meur, Anaïs, 121, 154, 174

legal aid: availability, 23; family lawyers and, 94; and family lawyers' earnings, 90; low-income people and, 23; and professional power, 117–18; surveillance and, 119; women lawyers, 253n39

legal aid (France), 28; eligibility for, 55; and mediation costs, 38

legal aid (Quebec): characteristics of lawyers, 45; and child support modifications, 211; duration of time with lawyers, 47; eligibility, 45–47, 50–51; freezing of, 209; immigrants and, 45; income threshold, 33; lower classes and, 45–48; and mediation, 33; private law firms and, 46–47; recipients, and rarity of trials, 47–48; women clients, 46

legal aid lawyers: and limitation of expectations, 117; moralizing by, 119–20; percentages of cases, 48; and self-representation, 115

legal profession/professionals: about, 105–6; and child support, 177, 187; commodification of, 240; in comparative vs. single-nation studies, 63; COVID-19 pandemic and, 60–61; expectations regarding upper classes, 141; and family violence, 157–58; French feminist movement and, 155; gendered expectations, 141, 165; and gendered parenting, 161; and gendered stereotypes of deviance, 159; and joint custody, 166; judges (Quebec) working with, 67–68; manipulation of symbols, 110–11; and political life/public action, 240; power over laypeople, 14; and public policy, 105–6, 240; and social classes, 180; social status vs. laypeople's, 14; and upper classes, 149; upper-class French men and, 55–56; upper-class women's compliance with expectations, 144; and upper-/middle-class parents, 164–65; in US, 32. *See also* judges; lawyers; professionals

Lenoir, Daniel, 228, 229, 230, 234

Lenoir, René, 216, 217

Lévesque, Brigitte, 154, 160, 162, 166

Lévesque, René, 199

LGBTQ people: *Civil Code of Quebec* and, 151

LGBTQ persons, 80–81, 94, 95

litigation: agreement vs., regarding child support, 47; costs, 32, 33, 51; dispute resolution vs., 34; feminism/ feminist move away from, 34; gender, and mediation vs., 89; lawyers and, vs. negotiation, 95–96; mediation vs., in Quebec, 31; out-of-court alternatives

vs., 104–5; role of, 104–5; socio-economic inequalities and costs of, 33
livre noir de la résidence alternée, Le (The Dark Side of Joint Custody), 170–71, 173
lower-class fathers/men: and child support, 185, 191, 193, 224, 229; involvement with children, 164; lack of compliance with norms, 149; self-representation, 115; visitation rights, 161
lower-class mothers/women: and child support, 46, 211; compliance with norms, 149; dependence on social services in France, 197; and sole custody, 46
lower classes: access to judges, 59; access to lawyers, 59; contained vs. disruptive adjustments to interactions, 127; and co-parenting, 161, 162; COVID-19 and, 3; difficulties in courts, 48; ethno-racial trait assignment to, 125; fatalistic attitudes toward, 121–22, 133; gender inequalities among, 44; and gendered division of child-rearing labour, 131; gendered division of parenting roles, 243; gendered social relations, vs. in upper classes, 135; horizontal redistribution among, 208; institutional oversight regarding private sphere, 242; judges and, 48; lawyers and relationship with, 138; and legal aid, 23; and legal aid (Quebec), 45–48; and length of procedures, 54; limitation of expectations, 112–13, 115–17; and mediation, 23; moralizing by lawyers, 118–22; neoliberalism and, 245; professional perceptions of divorce among, vs. upper classes, 133; and public services, 241; separations as impoverishing both parties in, 133;

and shared custody, 113; and sole custody, 113; state oversight, 10; surveillance of, 14, 48, 118–19; welfare state and, 10; women and bureaucratic proficiency, 136
lower classes (France): duration of court time, 59; employment bonus, 230; judges and, 57; and lawyers, 54–55; social workers and, 57–58

Macron, Emmanuel, 233
March for Bread and Roses, 201
marital status: and compensation for women in home, 148; in family law, 25; among social classes, 17; social classes (France) and, 53
Marois, Pauline, 199
mediation, 99–100; and amicable conflict resolution, 52; and child support, 105; and children, 34; costs, 32–33, 51–52; cultural capital and, 52; emergence of mediators, 7; family violence and, 156; influence of Quebec on France in, 247; and joint custody, 167–68; lawyers and, 51–52, 99–101; legalization, vs. psychosocial professionals, 100; litigation vs., 99–100; low-income people and, 23; middle classes and, 51; notaries and, 101; and out-of-court settlements, 100; private practices in, 60; public funding, 23; upper classes and, 49, 50; victims of violence and, 34–35; women and, 89. *See also* collaborative law
mediation (France), 99–100; costs, 38; lawyers/notaries and, 44; as mandatory, 43; numbers of mediators, 38; as percentage of cases, 38; Quebec system upheld in, 99, 235
mediation (Quebec): and agreement, 31; and child support guidelines,

204–5; frequency of use, 31; legal aid and, 33; litigation vs., 31; mediators as legal professionals, 31; notaries and, 31; psycho-social professionals and, 31, 34; public funding, 31; public involvement in process, 36; social classes and, 209; upheld in France, 99, 235

Meech Lake Accord, 205

men. *See* fathers/men

middle-class fathers/men: and childcare labour, 15; involvement with children, 163–65; and joint custody, 170; non-compliance with professionals' expectations regarding, 141–42

middle-class mothers/women: financial situation in Quebec vs. France, 245; and joint custody, 170

middle-class mothers/women (France): and compensatory benefit (*prestation compensatoire*), 145–46; working outside home, 144

middle classes: asymmetries with professionals, 131; and child support, 187–89, 193; and co-parenting, 162; COVID-19 and, 3; custody sharing, 142–43; defining, 251*n*8; gendered parenting among, 165; interventions and, 14–15; and joint physical custody, 162–64; judges (France) social background as, 68; and mediation, 51; vertical redistribution to, 208

middle classes (Quebec): divorce law liberation and, 58; flat-rate childcare and, 209; mediation and, 209; use of courts, vs. wealthier people, 50–51

Ministère de la justice (France): and child support, 184–85, 212, 219, 220–23, 229, 230; and demands of fathers, 231; and judges, 39, 40, 69; lawyers in, 67; and SOS Les Mamans, 231

Ministère de la justice (Quebec), 40; and child support, 184, 185, 188, 197, 202, 203, 204; and judges, 40, 67; special clerks, 30

Ministère de la sécurité du revenu (Ministry of Income Security) (Quebec), 203

Ministère des solidarités et de la santé (France), 217, 233

Ministère des solidarités et de la santé (Quebec), 203, 204

minority groups: and gender equality, 124; lawyers and, 122–27; lawyers from, 124–25; national background, and liberalization of divorce, 59; religious framing, 126–27; social norms and, 124

Mitterrand, François, 215

moralization: by judges, 80, 82; by lawyers, 118–22, 128; and lower classes, 118–22; mechanisms counteracting inequalities, and, 249; social classes, and professional, 149

Morneau, Denise, 90, 91, 92, 93, 99–100, 101

mothers/women: allocatory mechanisms for, in Quebec, 147; awarding of physical custody to, 152–53; and child support, 177; compensatory benefit (*prestation compensatoire*) in France, 144–46; contained adjustments, 127–28, 130, 131; day-to-day child care, 151–52; domestic/child-rearing labour, 153–54; exposure of private lives, 47; in family law, 64, 86–87; as first to seek legal counsel, 46; incomes, 177(f); initiation of legal proceedings, 46; as judges (France), 68; and labour market, 154; and legal aid (Quebec), 46; and legal counsel, 47; motherhood in choice of family law specialty, 95; and parental alienation syndrome, 168, 173; and poverty, 177(f); as primary attachment figures, 171; relocation of, 154–55; requesting child physical custody, 153; sexual orientation, 81; and sole custody, 159, 160, 161. *See also* lower-class mothers/women; middle-class mothers/women; upper-class mothers/women

mutual consent divorce: and class, 12, 54; cost, 98; and gender, 12; and joint physical custody, 163; judges and, 41; lawyers' costs, 44; popularity of, 53; rise in, 8; social classes and, 53

mutual consent divorce (France), 27–28, 252*n*6; and duration of cases, 53–54; judges and hearings, 27–28; as out-of-court procedure, 42; and sharing of lawyers, 38

Nadeau, Philippe, 84–85, 166–67

neoliberalism: and child support system (Quebec), 206, 211; and family solidarity vs. public redistribution, 203; and lower classes, 245; and public policy, 196; and Quebec welfare state, 196; and redistribution, 239; and state interventions, 7

non-divorce family procedures: rates of, 18; social classes and, 53; wait times for, 53, 54

non-legal professionals. *See* professionals

non-representation. *See* self-representation

notaries: and civil union dissolution, 253*n*29; and financial aspect of divorce, 101; and mediation, 31, 44, 101; representation of clients, 256*n*42

Organisation for Economic Co-operation and Development countries, 17, 68, 194

Othering: by lawyers, 122–27; private sphere behaviours and, 14

out-of-court alternatives: child support modifications in Quebec, 210; and cost reduction, 43–44; financing, 33; in France, 41, 42–43; judges and, 41; mutual consent divorce and, 42; professional power and, 109. *See also* alternative dispute resolution

Paletot, Étienne, 54, 82

Pan-Canadian Family Law Committee, 85

parental alienation syndrome (PAS), 168, 173

parental deviance, 48

parental roles: in France vs. Quebec, 174–75; gender and, 161, 191, 193; social classes and, 191, 193

Parti Québécois, 199–200, 202, 203, 205, 209–10, 261–62*n*4

Partnership of acquests, 47, 257–58*n*34

patriarchy: and poverty, 16; and violence, 16; welfare states and, 13

Pelletier, Monique, 171–72, 214

penal mediation, 116

phone meetings, 60–61

Pinard-Garon, Andrée, 74–75, 78–79, 85

Pineault, Séverine, 117, 119–20, 126–27, 178–79, 181

Pour les Québécoises: égalité et indépendance (For Quebecois Women: Equality and Independence) (Conseil du statut de la femme), 199

poverty: child, 194–95, 198, 202, 206; gender and, 177(f); mothers and, 177(f); patriarchy and, 16; single-parent households and, 177(f), 194–95, 245

poverty (France): ASF and, 218; divorced fathers and, 216; "isolated"/

single mothers and, 216, 217; separation and, 213, 215; single-parent households and, 220

poverty (Quebec): child support collection/enforcement and, 202; "Investing-in-Children Policy Paradigm" and, 211; single-parent households and, 198, 200, 201–2, 208

power relations: child support and, 223; child support (France) and, 234–35; child support direct collection and, 201; compromise and, 242; individualization of, 12–13; privatization of divorce and, 9; and socially constructed expectations, 242. *See also* professional power

private transfers: in Canada, 210; child support enforcement and, 208; in France, 212, 213, 216, 223, 234, 235, 237; and gender inequality, 216; middle-class women and, 208; public redistribution vs., 22, 194, 196, 212, 235, 244; in Quebec, 194, 196, 208, 210, 237, 244

Procureur de la République (Prosecutor of the Republic) (France), 213

professional power: asymmetries and, 109, 110, 111–12, 128; and consent, 109; and gender, 111, 112; and hierarchies of social groups, 148–49; legal aid and, 117–18; and limitation of expectations, 111, 112, 115–16; mastery of law and, 117; and out-of-court negotiation/settlement, 109; and production of expectations, 109; as relational with laypeople, 108–9; and social classes, 111–12; social norms and, 117; and spoken/unspoken language, 149; trust and, 110. *See also* power relations

professionals: access to, 59; and gendered parenting, 161, 243; inequal-

ities in access to, 44; judges (Quebec) working with, 67–68; and mediation, 31; outsourcing to, 24; and parental deviance, 48; and privatization of divorce, 9; public institutions vs., 9; and social classes, 10; social workers, 57–58; socio-economic status and, 57–58; upper classes and, 10, 50, 138, 240. *See also* legal profession/professionals; psychosocial professionals

Protecteur du Citoyen (Ombudsman) (Quebec), 34

psycho-social professionals: availability, and inequality, 23, 24; behaviourist approach, 169; and best interests of the child, 202; on child-rearing, 173; emergence of, 7; and gendered expectations, 173; increasingly prominent role, 240; and joint custody, 169, 170–75; and mediation (Quebec), 31, 34. *See also* professionals

public interventions. *See* interventions/interventionism

public policy/policies: comparative approaches by Quebec, 246–47; coparenting and, 150; critical analysis, 13; ethnography in studies regarding, 248; French influence on, 246–47; and hierarchy, 12; legal professionals and, 105–6, 240; managerialization of, 246; neoliberalism and, 196; in Quebec vs. France, 244; single-parent households as focus in France, 197; social class and, 10; and social relations structuring, 5; and social reproduction, 12; as state-centred in France vs. Quebec, 247; transnational similarity of, 245–46. *See also* family policy/policies; social policy/policies

public redistribution. *See* redistribution

Québec fou de ses enfants, Un (Quebec Treasures Its Children), 167–68, 201–2, 211
Québec Solidaire, 209–10
Quebec Women's Federation, 200

race/racialization: and co-parenting, 162; within couples, 125–26; and inequalities, 12, 13; lawyers and, 124–25; othering and, 123–24; professional interactions and, 110
redistribution: horizontal vs. vertical, 208; and inequalities, 239; neoliberalism and, 239; private transfers vs., 22, 194, 196, 212, 235, 244; in Scandinavia, 208; single-parent families and, 9, 22; weakening of, 242
relocation, 154–55
Revenu du Solidarité Active, 259n22
Robin, Claire, 90–92, 93, 107–8, 109, 127–28, 184
Rosenberg, Morris, 35
Roudy, Yvette, 145, 215, 218

salaries. *See* earnings
same-sex couples. *See* LBGTQ people
Savard, Albert, 78, 83, 114, 115
Schaaf, Aurélie, 227–28, 230–31
Schiappa, Marlène, 233
scrutiny. *See* surveillance
Secrétariat à la condition féminine (Women's Secretariat) (Quebec), 199
Secrétariat d'Etat aux droits des femmes (Ministry for Women's Rights) (France), 230
self-representation: and access to law, 114–15; in contested divorces, 33; judges and, 114–15; lawyers and, 114–15; legal aid lawyers and, 115; low-income men and, 115; men as, 46–47; and preliminary hearing

rolls (Quebec), 101; and procedural requirements, 114–15
separations: increase in, and inequalities, 249; liberalization of, 6; private ordering of, 8–9; rates of, 17–18, 246, 249
Service administratif de rajustement des pensions alimentaires pour enfants (Child Support Recalculation Service) (Quebec), 30, 210
Service d'aide à l'homologation (Homologation Assistance Service) (Quebec), 30, 210–11
settlement conferences, 77–78; and arbitration, 254n54; private mediation vs., 60; upper classes and, 50
shared custody, 78–79; child-rearing costs compared, 176; COVID-19 and, 4, 60, 61; lack of agreement regarding, 144; lower class and, 113; upper-class men and, 50. *See also* joint custody
shared physical custody: and child support, 190–91; co-parenting and, 243; fathers' groups and, 175; in Quebec vs. France, 245; social classes and, 243. *See also* child physical custody; joint physical custody
single mothers: and social policy, 16; and welfare in Quebec, 203–4, 206
single mothers (France): and ASF, 218, 225; benefits, 216–18; employment, 216; as "isolated mothers," 214; and poverty, 216, 217
single-parent families: COVID-19 and, 3–4; and flat rate childcare, 209; and poverty, 177(f), 194–95, 245; and redistribution, 9, 22; and social policy, 16
single-parent families (France): ASF and, 217–18; as focus of public policy, 197; poverty, 220; social welfare

system and, 224; tax system and, 224

single-parent families (Quebec): and child poverty, 198; income redistribution and, 196; numbers, 198; and poverty, 200, 201–2, 208; public aid for, 209. *See also* Fédération des associations de familles monoparentales et recomposées du Québec

social classes: and access to judicial elite, 132; child support among, 180; civil law liberalization and, 238–39; and client national background/gender, 118; and court decorum, 122; defining, 251*n*8; divorce by consent and, 12; and duration of case, 53–54; and ethno-psychiatry, 125; and flexibility in law, 241; gender and, 59, 112, 152; and institutional/professional oversight, 241–42; institutions and, 10; and interventionism, 84; of judges, 68, 83, 189; of judges in Quebec, 19, 65–66; legal professionals and, 180; liberalization of divorce and, 59; marital status among, 17; and mediation, 52; and parental roles, 191, 193; and professional moralization, 149; professional power and, 111–12, 148–49; professionals and, 10, 109–10; public policy and, 10, 12; and "right" expectations, 241; and shared physical custody, 243; and social constraints, 12; and state constraints, 239; and use of experts, 57–58. *See also* lower classes; middle classes; upper classes

social classes (France): and divorce, 238; and divorce rates, 52–53; and duration of trials, 55; gender and, 55–56; lawyers and, 56; marital status among, 53; and mutual con-

sent divorce, 53; and non-divorce family procedures, 53

social inequalities. *See* socio-economic inequalities

social policy/policies: co-parenting and, 150; and economic impact of separation, 194–95; neoliberalism in, 245; single-mother households and, 16. *See also* family policy/policies; public policy/policies

social policy/policies (France): means testing, 217; women as target of, 213

social policy/policies (Quebec): French influence on, 247; private transfers and, 210

social reproduction: child support and, 133; courts and, 12; family law and, 243–44; institutionalization and, 13; public policy and, 12

social status. *See* social classes

social workers, 57–58, 73

socio-economic inequalities, 44; in access to professionals, 44; common law partnerships and, 242–43; co-parenting and, 15; courts and, 11; divorce/separation and, 4; family law liberalization and, 248; in France, 54; gender inequalities and, 241; individual rights and, 58–59; in language skills, 114, 149; and lawyers' time spent with clients, 56–57; and length of procedures, 54; litigation costs and, 33; among men, in child support, 183; mutual consent divorce and, 54; non-divorce family cases and, 54; private ordering of separation, 239; and professional interactions outside courtroom, 56–57; in Quebec vs. France, 44, 244–45; recognition of right to divorce and, 24–25; separation and, 5; in upper-class marriages, 134–35; women's emancipation and, 243

socio-economic status (SES). *See* social classes

socio-professionals. *See* psycho-social professionals

sole custody: lower classes and, 113; mothers and, 159, 160, 161; and relocation of mothers, 154–55; and visitation rights, 159, 161, 172

Sommet de la Justice (Justice Summit) (Quebec), 34, 204

SOS Les Mamans (SOS for Moms) (France), 231

Sourice, Caroline, 96–97, 98, 99, 115–16, 137–38, 141

special clerks, 30

spousal support, 104–5

state interventions. *See* interventions/interventionism

status. *See* social classes

Stoléru, Lionel, 216

Supreme Court of Canada: on custody arrangement changes, 155; *Eric v Lola*, 11; on joint physical custody, 166; on prenuptial agreements and separations of unmarried couples, 11; on unreasonable delay, 37, 40

surveillance: and child support, 119, 183; of household spending for child support, 178–79; legal aid and, 119; of lower classes, 14, 118–19; mechanisms counteracting inequalities, and, 249; waning of, 150

Syndicat de la magistrature (France), 42, 68–69

Tabarès, Mathilde, 27–28, 29, 38, 54, 140, 141, 181

Terreau, Pierre, 56, 70–71, 74, 82, 83, 129–30, 160, 179, 188–89

Thélot, Claude, 226

transnational circulation, 245–48

Trépanier, Violette, 34

Trudeau, Pierre Elliott, 6

Union nationale des associations familiales (National Union of Family Associations) (France), 214

United Nations Convention on the Rights of the Child, 167–68, 201–2, 246

United States: judges' power in, 68; legal professionals' roles in, 32; marital status among social classes in, 17; parental alienation syndrome in, 168; research regarding co-parenting, 169; restriction of public aid, 207; women judges in, 66; workfare, 211

Universal Declaration of Human Rights, 135

unrepresented clients. *See* self-representation

upper-class fathers/men: and child support, 55, 183; and childcare labour, 15; and co-parenting, 193; involvement with children, 163–65; lawyers and, 55–56; non-compliance, 141–44; and shared custody, 50, 55

upper-class mothers/women: and compensatory benefit (*prestation compensatoire*), 145–46; compliance with legal professionals' expectations, 144; financial situation in Quebec vs. France, 245; working outside home, 144

upper classes: access to professionals, 10, 44; appeals, 134–35; asymmetries with professionals, 131; and child custody, 50; and child support, 187–89, 193; and conspicuous consumption, 141; and co-parenting, 162;

and courts, 50–51; cultural capital, and legal procedures, 135–36; custody sharing, 142–43; defined, 48–49, 251n8; and duration of trials, 50; financial stakes, 50; gendered parenting among, 165; gendered social relations in, vs. in lower classes, 135; immigrants, 125; institutional encounters, 48–50; institutional oversight regarding private sphere, 242; and joint physical custody, 162–64; judges and, 50, 66, 240; law practices specializing in, 132–33, 137; lawyers and, 49–50, 138–41; legal profession/professionals and, 15, 141, 149; lifestyle maintenance, 138; and lowering of expectations, 112, 132; and maintenance of lifestyle/social status, 133; marriage rates, 50; and mediation, 49, 50; and norm production, 10; preservation of privacy, 136; and private mediation, 60; and private professionals, 240; procedural capital, 136; professional perceptions of divorce among, vs. lower classes, 133; and professionals, 50; and raising of expectations, 132–33; and relativism of rules, 15; shared norms, 112; shared social experiences with professionals, 136–37; social capital, and legal procedures, 135–36; vertical redistribution to, 208; working parents among, 50

upper classes (France): child support rates, 212; and collaborative law, 58; divorce law liberation and, 58; judges and, 64

upper classes (Quebec): flat rate childcare and, 209; judges, and and gendered roles in, 147; judges and, 68; mediation and, 209

Urvoas, Jean-Jacques, 43

Vallaud-Belkacem, Najat, 226–27
Veil, Simone, 217
violence: and child custody, 127–28, 156; against children, 29; against children vs. partner, 156; and co-parenting, 155–57; courts (Quebec) and, 156; COVID-19 and, 60; female punishment for, 238; feminists and, 175; judges and, 123–24, 156–57; legal professionals and, 157–58; and mediation, 156; mediation, and victims of, 34–35; non-European couples and, 162; parental alienation syndrome and, 168; patriarchy and, 16; protection orders against, 157; responsibility assignment for, 156; separation and, 4–5; as structural vs. parental deviance, 157–58; toward children, 156–57; women's emancipation and, 243

visitation rights: best interests of the child and, 48; COVID-19 pandemic and, 61; defined, 151; employment and, 174; fathers and, 129, 159, 160; joint legal custody and, 159; judges and, 174; lower-class fathers and, 161; overnight stays, 117; sole custody and, 159, 161, 172

welfare state(s), 239; breadwinner model and, 260n53; fragility of, 249; and lower classes, 10; and patriarchy, 13; in Quebec, 196; structure, and child maintenance, 196; weakening of, 240

women. See mothers/women
women judges: family law specialization, 86–87; interventionist stance, 83; non-litigated divorce and, 105;

proportion compared to male, in Quebec, 66. *See also* judges

women judges (France): and divorcing women's domestic specialization costs, 145–46; and gender inequalities, 145–46; interventionist stance, 80–81; and professional women, 145

women lawyers: earnings in France, 92–93; earnings in Quebec, 93, 94; in France compared to Quebec, 95; in legal aid, 253n39; and mediation, 89; and motherhood, 95; non-litigated divorce and, 105; prestige, 95; public profiles, 95; specialization in family law, 90–92; and wealth of clientele, 95. *See also* lawyers

women's groups/movement (France), 196–97; and child support, 231–32; and child support guidelines, 223; and CNAF studies, 216; and mutual consent divorce as out-of-court procedure, 42. *See also* feminism/feminists (France)

women's groups/movement (Quebec): and child support collection, 202; and child support guidelines, 206; and Parti Québécois, 199–200; and women's policy agencies, 199, 200. *See also* feminism/feminists (Quebec)

women's rights: and child maintenance systems, 195; and child support system, 197; judicial system and, 24; right to divorce and, 4

Yellow Vest movement (France), 232–33